THE COMPLETE GUIDE TO PUBLIC EMPLOYMENT

Books and CD-ROM by Drs. Ron and Caryl Krannich

The Almanac of American Government Jobs and Careers
The Almanac of International Jobs and Careers
Best Jobs for the 1990s and Into the 21st Century
Change Your Job, Change Your Life
The Complete Guide to International Jobs and Careers
The Complete Guide to Public Employment
Discover the Best Jobs for You!
Dynamite Answers to Interview Questions
Dynamite Cover Letters
Dynamite Resumes
Dynamite Salary Negotiations
Dynamite Tele-Search
The Educator's Guide to Alternative Jobs and Careers
Find a Federal Job Fast!
From Army Green to Corporate Gray
From Navy Blue to Corporate Gray
High Impact Resumes and Letters
Interview for Success
Job Power Source (CD-ROM)
Job Search Letters That Get Results
Jobs and Careers With Nonprofit Organizations
Jobs for People Who Love Travel
Mayors and Managers
Moving Out of Education
Moving Out of Government
The New Network Your Way to Job and Career Success
The Politics of Family Planning Policy
Re-Careering in Turbulent Times
Shopping and Traveling in Exotic Asia
Shopping and Traveling in Exotic Hong Kong
Shopping and Traveling in Exotic India
Shopping and Traveling in Exotic Indonesia
Shopping and Traveling in Exotic Morocco
Shopping and Traveling in Exotic Singapore and Malaysia
Shopping and Traveling in Exotic Thailand
Shopping and Traveling the Exotic Philippines
Shopping in Exciting Australia and Papua New Guinea
Shopping in Exotic Places
Shopping the Exotic South Pacific

THE COMPLETE GUIDE TO PUBLIC EMPLOYMENT

Third Edition

Ronald L. Krannich, Ph.D.
Caryl Rae Krannich, Ph.D.

IMPACT PUBLICATIONS
Manassas Park, VA

THE COMPLETE GUIDE TO PUBLIC EMPLOYMENT

Third Edition

Library of Congress Cataloging-in-Publication Data

Krannich, Ronald L.
The complete guide to public employment / Ronald L. Krannich, Caryl Rae Krannich.—3rd ed.
p. cm.
Includes bibliography references and index
ISBN 0-942710-72-X (hard) : $34.95.—ISBN 0-942710-94-0 (paper) : $19.95
1. Civil service positions—United States. I. Krannich, Caryl Rae. II. Title.
JK716.K68 1994
353.001'03—dc20 94-13519
CIP

For information on distribution or quantity discount rates, Tel. 703/361-7300, Fax 703/335-9486, or write to Sales Department, IMPACT PUBLICATIONS, 9104-N Manassas Drive, Manassas Park, VA 22111. Distributed to the trade by National Book Network, 4720 Boston Way, Suite A, Lanham, MD 20706, Tel. 301/459-8696

CONTENTS

PART VI
TAKE EFFECTIVE ACTION

PREFACE

The 1990s offer many exciting opportunities for individuals interested in pursuing public sector careers. However, in recent years government has come under attack from many quarters for being wasteful, unproductive, unresponsive, and corrupt. Viewing government as a culprit rather than a catalyst for change, the critics tell public employees to do more and better with less and, at the same time, expect fewer career rewards in the form of salaries, benefits, and advancement opportunities. For many seasoned observers, the public service appears to be in crisis as fewer and fewer individuals choose careers in government. Politicians at all levels want to downsize governments while, at the same time, seek to "reinvent" government with demoralized public employees. Not surprising, they want their political cake and eat it too. Indeed, all does not appear well with public sector jobs and careers.

But appearances can be deceiving. There are other sides to the public employment equation which are encouraging for anyone seeking employment in the public sector. This is the subject of our book. For we find a very dynamic public sector offering numerous opportunities in spite of occasional cutbacks and low morale in government. As we stress throughout this book, the public sector is much more than government employees doing the business of governing. The public sector includes many nongovernmental institutions performing similar functions as government agencies. Many of these organizations chart their own public agendas with or without the involvement of government.

Numerous governmental and nongovernmental institutions are closely related to one another in terms of goals, functions, budgets, and personnel. When governments cutback, they often contract-out or devolve their functions to nongovernmental organizations which, in turn, increase their budgets, organizational infrastructures, and personnel. In fact, the trend in government is to increase budgets and expenditures but not increase in-house personnel. The implications of this trend are clear: limited career advancement within the government and a growing public sector outside government among contracting and consulting firms, nonprofit organizations, associations, foundations, research organizations, and political management groups.

We wrote this book because there is a need to bring together a comprehensive concept of the public sector related to specific "how-to" employment strategies and opportunities. Millions of individuals are primarily oriented to public sector employment. Many of these people want to have a positive impact on others and make a decent living at the same time. Yet, too often individuals seeking public sector employment are at the mercy of highly generalized and often inappropriate or inaccurate career advice based upon experiences with private sector organizations.

We have attempted to fill a major gap in the literature on job search approaches and the public sector as well as bring to life what is often viewed as a dull and boring subject. The book is designed for anyone who is interested in beginning a public service career or advancing their career among public sector organizations. In the process, we hope it helps generate renewed interest in public sector careers.

The third edition of this book again represents a synthesis of our collective training, research, and work experience in the public sector as well as in career planning. Much of the basic research for the book began in 1980 at the state and local levels as well as on Capitol Hill while we were both university professors in political science/public administration and speech communication. During the next six years we were involved in a great deal of consulting, contracting, and training work in the fields of career planning, procurement, public management, communication, and international development. When the first edition of this book appeared in 1986, it outlined a comprehensive concept of public employment as well as established a baseline for subsequent editions of the book.

The primary emphasis in this edition is on the critical "what" and "how" questions of public employment. Answers to "where" questions are best found by referring to the numerous directories, databases, and job listing services recommended throughout the book. As such, this book is more oriented toward the *process* of public employment than to providing listings of specific jobs along with names, addresses, and phone numbers of potential employers. In this sense the book again reflects our strong preference for first learning how the process operates *prior to* making contacts with specific employers. Only after knowing how the process operates and acquiring the necessary job search skills to be effective should you then begin marketing your skills to specific employers. If, for example, you just want to leap into this job market armed only with lists of "hot" names and addresses, you may be in for some big disappointments as you learn from trial and error that you need a lot more than just names, addresses, and a boiler-plated resume. This book is designed to minimize your trial and error experiences, make sense out of the chaotic world of public employment, and give you the necessary knowledge and skills so that you will know what to do once you have those promising names, addresses, and telephone numbers, and a powerful resume and application package. If read and followed in its entirety, the book should give you an "extra edge" over the less informed and well organized competition.

As with previous editions, this third edition is by no means complete. The subject is both enormous and complex, reflecting the number, size, diversity, and complexity of institutions found in American society. It requires a great deal of additional work on employment cultures of public institutions which we begin to outline as well as many others not included in our coverage. For example, when we examined Political Action Groups (PACs), we began unraveling a fascinating world of employment possibilities little understood by people inside or outside PACs. Consequently, we only introduce you to the basics of PACs and point you in the right direction for initiating a job search requiring your own research into how various PACs operate.

The same is true for contracting and consulting firms—important growth arenas for public employment. Little is known about the structure and culture of these organizations. We present basic information and "how-to" strategies relevant to these groups to get you oriented toward employment with these firms.

The book is designed to *link understanding to action*. For "how-to" advice not firmly rooted in data and analysis can be misleading, useless, and dangerous advice. At times we go to the top of the hill to preach the "how-tos" of success, but we always try to do so knowing the "how-tos" are based on an analysis of on-going realities and cases of success. In this sense we have attempted to be honest in our treatment of the subject.

We again dedicate this book to our readers who, in putting it into practice, should contribute to a better public sector as well as enrich their lives. You may not get financially rich following our advice, but if you successfully implement the information in this book, you will probably enjoy what you do and make a decent living at the same time.

Most important, you need not get locked into jobs which may turn sour or become deadend careers. The pages that follow chart some important career options and strategies within the public sector which should give you the freedom to make informed choices about your future —and make changes when necessary without fear of failure.

We wish you the very best and hope this book will give you that "extra edge" in today's job market. If the first half of the 1990s are any indication, the second half of the 1990s may well become one of the most interesting periods for public service careers. Join us as we take time to sail into this fascinating employment arena!

THE COMPLETE GUIDE TO PUBLIC EMPLOYMENT

1 DISCOVER AN EXCITING AND REWARDING EMPLOYMENT ARENA

We've heard all the stories and self-serving analyses. We've suffered the testimonials, shared the emotions, and absorbed the predictions—both positive and negative—from public servants, pessimists, and political pundits.

On the positive side, we're told there are great career opportunities available in the public sector. Being a public servant is very rewarding. Keen competition for government jobs results in hiring the best qualified candidates. Jobs in the public sector come with excellent health and retirement benefits. You can't beat the job security. A new public service will arise and blossom in the decade ahead. Let's "reinvent" government!

On the negative side, we're warned there are few jobs available in the public sector; agencies at the federal, state, and local levels are experiencing further cutbacks, downsizing, and reductions-in-force. Government work is bureaucratic and boring. Public servants are under-paid, under-worked, and under-appreciated. They often work for agencies known for waste, fraud, and abuse rather than for purpose, productivity, and performance. This is not a good time to seek public employment. Further cutbacks will occur in governments at all levels. Once you plateau your career in government, there's nothing you can do to get ahead except wait for retirement and maybe start a new career. Government employees lack the necessary skills and motivation to find rewarding jobs and careers outside government. There's a crisis in the public service. It's much better to go into business and pursue a private sector career.

The public sector is one of today's most over-rated, maligned, misunderstood, and myth-ridden employment arenas.

OUTSIDE IN, INSIDE OUT

It's funny what people believe, especially about government and the public sector. Americans have a long history of suspicion, mistrust, and criticism toward the public sector. After all, government consumes enormous resources, employs millions of people, and does a poor job of explaining what it really does for the individual other than deliver the mail, pick up garbage, police the streets, run the schools, and extract taxes—often at questionable levels of effectiveness and fairness.

Not surprising, most people stand where they sit, confirming what we've known all along—the public sector is one of today's most over-rated, maligned, misunderstood, and myth-ridden employment arenas.

Whether you stand on the outside looking in or sit on the inside looking out, chances are the public sector is not what you've come to believe. It's bigger than government; it's more private than its public presence would indicate; and it does much more than just consume public resources for the ostensible purpose of "governing". Viewed from both the inside and outside, the public sector performs an incredible range of functions—both visible and invisible—that generates millions of jobs.

Rather than being the big bad or troubled employer of the 1990s, the public sector offers some of the most exciting and rewarding jobs available today. In spite of bad press, this public employment arena is well and alive and functioning everywhere. Despite dire predictions to the contrary, the public sector is likely to thrive in the decade ahead.

You are well advised to take a fresh look at this much maligned complex of institutions and employers that make up the public sector. Please indulge us for a few hours. Put aside your stereotypes, suspicions, and wishful thinking as we take a new look at the realities of this fascinating employment arena. It's where you may find your next job, develop new professional relationships, and nurture a rewarding career and lifestyle. A job in the public sector may well become the most important work of your life! So let's begin by approaching it right.

KNOWLEDGE AND NONSENSE

Don't believe everything you hear from those inside or outside the public sector. The advertisers, optimists, promoters, and pessimists often miss the day-to-day realities of the public sector. Few understand its employment dynamics. Indeed, a great deal of nonsense is propagated about public careers by well-meaning individuals who do not understand government and the public sector, or by those who should know better. Baffled by complex structures and functions which appear illogical to well-organized, tidy, and apolitical minds—or being too close to their subject to put their situations in proper context—ignorance rather than information dominates a great deal of thinking about the public sector.

This book is about improving your public sector employment I.Q. by increasing your job search knowledge, skills, and effectiveness. Based on a comprehensive concept of the public sector, we outline how you can best find employment and advance your career within the public sector, despite all the stories to the contrary.

Please be forewarned that this is not your usual treatment of the subject. Some books, for example, outline how to find employment with federal, state, or local governments. Others specify job alternatives for individuals interested in international careers. Most primarily outline the formal rules and regulations, include sample application forms, and list names, addresses, and telephone numbers of government agencies. As you will quickly discover, this book also covers some of these subjects. But it includes much more from the perspective of those in the process of seeking jobs and careers in the public sector. Going far beyond the formal rules and regulations, this book is designed to provide you with an understanding of public sector dynamics relevant to both the formal and informal hiring processes of governmental and nongovernmental organizations pursuing public goals. As such, the following chapters should provide you with a solid understanding from which to make informed career decisions.

A DIFFERENT APPROACH

Similar to the first and second editions of this guide, this third edition is oriented to both understanding and action. Based on our experience in working with numerous individuals interested in making career changes, finding public employment, and becoming involved in public issues, we see a need for a different type of book which is both *educational and usable*. Focusing on structure, function, process, and performance, it is designed for both *understanding and action*. As such, our approach:

- Assesses present trends and projects these into the future for better understanding public employment issues and taking effective job search action.

- Combines a career alternatives perspective (*what jobs exist and where to find them*) with a job search skills perspective (*how to get a job*) directly related to a series of institutions (*governmental and nongovernmental*) defining the public sector.

- Explores government as an interrelated system of 86,743 units of federal, state, and local government. This system consists of executive, legislative, and judicial branches of government at all levels which generate over 18 million jobs with an average annual turnover of nearly 15 percent.

- Relates the governmental units to several nongovernmental public organizations which are critically important to the overall functioning of the public sector.

- Examines the public sector and the job search process from a perspective based upon research, cases of success, and future public sector trends as well as a solid understanding of how public institutions are structured and function.

- Links public jobs in one institutional complex with similar jobs in other institutional complexes, so individuals can better plan for career transitions among various public sector institutions as well as develop skills appropriate for private sector jobs.

We do much more than just present you with "the facts" and then let you draw your own conclusions. We frequently draw our own conclusions, some of which may be controversial; we make value judgments based on our experience, and assess and critique numerous aspects of this process. While we have yet to become passionate about this subject, we do feel strongly about what we know, what we observe, and how we advise our readers. Since this is basically a "how to" book, we must make judgments in the process of charting previously uncharted territory. In addition to describing and explaining, we predict and prescribe. To do otherwise would be to do you a disservice in not sharing our experience and judgments.

Throughout this book we have avoided the common practice of over-simplifying processes which are inherently complex and difficult to manage. To identify where the jobs are and how to land a suitable public sector job in specific institutions and organizations require a great deal of hard work. It first requires a realistic understanding of the public sector today and tomorrow. It further involves weeks of research, careful planning, and implementation through the use of telephones, letters, and meetings with individuals and organizations. Above all, it requires you to link your job search skills with a thorough knowledge of how specific institutions and organizations operate.

Therefore, it is necessary to adapt your job search skills to particular situations which may or may not operate according to the general advice you receive about finding a job. Indeed, much of the highly generalized career planning advice you receive from career counselors or popular job search books may be inappropriate for public sector employment.

TURN UNDERSTANDING INTO ACTION

Each of the following chapters is designed to provide you with the maximum basic information and advice on how to navigate your job search among public sector organizations. While we neither claim nor attempt definitive treatments of each subject, we lay the ground work in each chapter for what could easily be expanded into separate in-depth volumes on finding a job in a particular type of public sector organization.

Our basic organizing principle for each chapter stresses both *understanding and action.* We attempt to provide you with a solid framework for understanding how various institutions and processes operate and then offer specific advice on how to conduct an effective job search within each organizational complex. Wherever possible, we include useful addresses and telephone numbers for your further research. This contact information is your bridge to more in-depth information on each organization and process.

USE THE TELEPHONE

In many cases we include only a telephone number for an organization. We have done this for two reasons. First, many organizations move locations within a community, but they retain their original telephone number. Should an address change, the U.S. Postal Service only forwards mail for one year. On the other hand, should a telephone number change, you can always call Information for the new number.

Second, despite the inconvenience of many voice mail systems, we still urge you to use the telephone in your job search. Writing letters is important in some situations, but writing letters to receive basic information is often inefficient and ineffective. You will consistently get better information by using the telephone than by writing letters. Letter writing takes time, and frequently you do not get replies or the written information you receive is incomplete.

Use the telephone before you write a letter. In fact, one purpose of a telephone call is to get the name of an individual to whom you will address your letter. A long distance telephone call may cost you a few dollars, but it will pay for itself in the long run. Our experience has been consistently positive when telephoning for job information and advice with various public institutions both inside and outside government. Most people will give you a great deal of useful information over the telephone. Most important, they will tell you to whom you should address your written correspondence. It is also advisable to use the telephone to follow-up your written correspondence.

If you learn only one useful thing from this book, we hope it is our concept of the public sector.

BLURRING THE PUBLIC AND PRIVATE SECTORS

If you learn only one useful thing from this book, we hope it is our concept of a dynamic, interdependent public sector offering an incredible number of job and career alternatives. Our concept of the public sector should become increasingly useful for individuals seeking and pursuing public service careers. At least in the United States, the public sector is much larger than just federal, state, and local governmental units. Several private institutions work closely with government institutions in pursuing public goals.

Other private institutions, especially nonprofit organizations and foundations, have their own public agendas paralleling those of government agencies. For example, the American Association of Retired Persons (AARP), with its awesome membership of over 32 million people, lobbies Congress for legislation favorable to the health and welfare interests of its ostensibly retired members who are actually anyone over 50 years of age and who are willing to pay a nominal $8.00 a year membership fee. The National Association of Manufacturers (NAM), representing the interests of major manufacturers, pursues restrictive legislation on foreign imports. Martin Marietta, Northrop, TRW, and General Electric receive billions of dollars in defense contracts each year. Each year Development Associates Incorporated and Robert R. Nathan

Associates receive millions of dollars in USAID contracts to provide development assistance to Third World countries. Common Cause organizes citizen efforts to pressure government to enact more restrictive consumer and environmental legislation. Brookings Institution, American Enterprise Institute, Heritage Foundation, and the Urban Institute issue research reports designed to affect the liberal and conservative direction of public policy. All of these organizations stand at the *periphery of government* with talented workforces experienced in pursuing public sector goals. Altogether, these government and nongovernmental institutions employ nearly 25 million individuals—one of the largest employment segments (20 percent) in American society.

Most of the so-called "crisis in the public service" is directly related to how we view government jobs and careers. Unfortunately, many individuals who enter government only see public service careers as government careers. They further compartmentalize their careers by only working within a particular office of a single agency within one unit of government, many of which are too small to offer career advancement opportunities. Some government employees make career transitions from one office or agency to another. A few even move from one level of government to another—from county to city, city to state, or state to federal. Nonetheless, many of these government employees find their careers plateau at mid-age; advancement, promotion, and salary increments are very limited once one enters certain positions and ranks in government.

Some of the most attractive public sector jobs are found in what is ostensibly the private sector!

Other types of organizations provide job and career alternatives for government employees who either plateau their careers or wish to leave government service. While many individuals believe leaving government means going into profit-making businesses primarily oriented to sales, numerous organizations outside government perform functions similar to government. In fact, in many cases—especially consulting firms and nonprofit organizations funded by government agencies—similar and sometimes more attractive policy-relevant "public" functions are performed by private organizations. Only after government employees leave government and work for such organizations do they begin to see that much of the public work they had hoped to do in government is actually performed by these nongovernmental organizations. Ironically, they quickly discover that some of the most attractive public sector jobs are found in what is ostensibly the private sector!

PRIVATIZING AND CONTRACTING-OUT PUBLIC FUNCTIONS

Our concept of public sector employment generally follows important trends and transformations taking place within government over the past four decades. These trends will continue within the foreseeable future. Indeed, the Office of Management and Budget recently (1994) reported that the federal government alone spends over $105 billion a year just on service contracts. The costs of hiring consultants is probably 40 percent higher than hiring permanent civil servants to perform the same jobs. While hiring consultants may not be the most cost effective way of getting the work government done, it is the political thing to do given public resistance to expanding government employee payrolls. In fact, the political costs of shifting "government employment" to the private sector are low, because consultants are less visible to the public and government does not keep nor publicize statistics on this alternative work force.

While local governments are the primary direct-service units of government or "street-level governments", state and federal governments tend to provide indirect services. More and more public services, including important planning and management functions, are being contracted-out to consultants and nonprofit organizations. Other functions are being "privatized" by transferring them to the private sector. In fact, many government employees who wish to leave government are individuals who went into government with the expectation of becoming involved in providing services in a particular public policy area. Many of these people become dissatisfied with their work, because it involves routine administrative tasks for issuing and monitoring government contracts, grants, and cooperative agreements to consultants, contractors, and nonprofit organizations.

As governments at all levels increasingly privatize as well as contract-out public services, some of the most interesting and rewarding public service jobs will be found in the private sector rather than in government agencies. As we stress throughout this book, these *nongovernmental public service institutions* provide numerous job and career alternatives for individuals primarily oriented toward public service careers. One important trend should continue over the next decade: government budgets may increase, but government employment will remain relatively stable, either declining or growing very little. On the other hand, the nongovernmental public service sector should experience considerable employment growth during the next decade as it becomes the major benefactor of government budgetary increases. This sector will also benefit from the so-called new thinking of the "reinventing" government movement. This movement will most likely result in the accelerated transfer of personnel payments, from government to the private sector at all levels, via a greatly enlarged "consulting arena". More and more procurement officers and contract managers will need to be hired within government in order to manage and support the growing army of consultants and their high-overhead operations. The costs of government will increase accordingly.

START WITH POSITIVE MOTIVATIONS

While individuals seek public service careers for several reasons, money is not one of the driving motivations. Public service jobs provide adequate to low compensation. Unless one's fingers are in the public till, one does not get rich in the public service. Yet, many public sector jobs can provide very comfortable middle to upper-middle class lifestyles.

Many people go into the public service because they prefer the security, pay, benefits, or the nature of the work. Others enter the public service for negative reasons: do not like working in business which may require long hours, pressures to produce a profit, stress, and unpredictable security.

Whatever one's motivation, public service careers are becoming more like jobs in the private sector—longer hours, pressures to produce, stress, and less security. Therefore, it is best to enter public service careers for positive rather than negative reasons. You should have specific goals in mind which will lead to positive career experiences. If you seek public employment because you do not like other types of employment, you will most likely become unhappy in the public sector. Always start by examining your motivations and identifying what it is you want to do—not what you don't like to do. In the long run such positive motivation will serve you well as you navigate your career along the most productive lines within the public sector.

ORGANIZE FOR SUCCESS

The remainder of this book examines the major components involved in acquiring public employment and making career transitions among both governmental and nongovernmental public service organizations at the local, state, and federal levels. The book is divided into six parts consisting of 25 chapters. While you may want to read each chapter in sequence, feel free to go directly to those chapters of most interest to you. The chapter on nonprofit organizations, for example, is sufficiently self-contained to stand alone. However, you may want to put it in a larger context by reading the other chapters in Part V. If you already are familiar with general job search skills, such as identifying your skills, developing an objective, and writing resumes and letters, you may want to skip the chapters in Part II.

The four chapters in Part I, "Employment Realities and Strategies", provide a useful orientation toward the public sector. These chapters introduce the concept of "the public sector"; explore myths and realities; examine past, present, and future employment trends; and outline career alternatives and effective approaches to finding public sector jobs.

The four chapters in Part II, "Effective Job Search Skills and Strategies", present the basic job search skills for organizing and conducting an effective job search among most types of organizations. These skills involve getting organized, identifying skills, stating job objectives, writing resumes and letters, networking, communicating, conducting job interviews, and negotiating salaries. The chapters stress the importance of adapting these skills to specific public sector organizations.

The five chapters in Part III, "Approaching Government", provide an orientation for acquiring government employment. They examine the advantages and disadvantages of working in government, outline key structural aspects of government institutions and the hiring process, specify how to gather information on government opportunities, and identify both formal and informal job search strategies appropriately adapted to the government hiring process.

The four chapters in Part IV, "Moving Into Government", outline how to find employment in executive, legislative, and judicial institutions with governments at the local, state, and federal levels.

Six chapters in Part V, "Working on the Periphery", examine the key peripheral institutions defining the nongovernmental public sector: consulting firms, trade and professional associations, nonprofit organizations, foundations, research organizations, and political support groups. Each chapter outlines the structure of various hiring cultures and specifies effective job search strategies which must be adapted to each institution.

The concluding section and chapter pull together the previous chapters by focusing on the key to taking action—*implementation*. These chapters stress the importance of translating this book into an effective action plan which will result in rewarding public service careers.

Detailed *indexes and table of contents* are important for quickly accessing information. They should play extremely important roles in how-to books. Therefore, our table of contents is designed to elaborate in detail each chapter as well as sections within chapters. As such, the table of contents functions as a secondary index, but with one major difference: the index is organized by *subject* whereas the table of contents —as well as the whole book—is organized by *process*. If, for example, you are interested in learning more about interviews, look under "Interview" in the index as well as Chapter 9 in the table of contents. The index will point you to different sections of the book that deal with various subject aspects of the interview. Chapter 9 breaks down the interview according to each step in the interview process. If you refer to both the table of contents and the index when looking for information, you should be able to quickly find what you want.

GETTING STARTED

Chances are you chose this book because you want to learn more about getting into or advancing your career within the public sector. Attempting to uncover the mystery of public employment, you seek to understand what you need to know and do to be most effective in finding public employment today.

Before we venture further into this subject, we suggest you do two things immediately. First, begin orienting yourself to the public sector by addressing several practical questions about your future:

1. How well do I understand the:
   - structure, functions, and relationships of public sector institutions?
   - relative advantages and disadvantages of working in the public sector?
   - various job search strategies and techniques appropriate for different public sector institutions?
2. To what degree will my present understanding of government and job search strategies help me find public employment?
3. What background, qualifications, and skills are best for public employment?
4. Where do I find public sector jobs?
5. How long will it take me to get a job with government or other public sector institutions?
6. What job search skills do I need to become successful in the public sector job market?
7. How realistic am I about my capabilities to both find public employment and function well within a public environment?
8. Where do I go and what do I do next?

These questions have important personal implications for you. They require thoughtful and realistic answers to help you take effective action to acquire public employment and advance your public sector career.

The second thing you need to do is begin acquiring the necessary knowledge and skills to be effective in the public sector job market. Few people are as effective as they could be in this job market. Indeed, the realities of government and public employment are often at odds with individuals' perceptions. Lacking a clear understanding of the realities, many individuals:

- Avoid public employment altogether, or
- Use ineffective job search strategies which result in either (1) failing to find a job, or (2) finding a job inappropriate for their true capabilities and interests.

This should not happen to you. The following chapters have been carefully structured so you can acquire the necessary knowledge and skills to be most effective in the public sector job market. They are based upon years of experience and success in what is one of the most fascinating, challenging, and rewarding job arenas for individuals who understand and appreciate public sector work.

USE USEFUL RESOURCES

Each year millions of job hunters turn to career planning books for assistance. Normally they begin with a general book and next turn to resume and interview books. They may also find a few books, such as this one, that provide career information on specific employment fields.

If this book represents your first career planning book, you may want to supplement it with a few other key books. Many of these books are available in your local library and bookstore or they can be ordered directly from Impact Publications by completing the order form at the end of this book. Contact Impact Publications to receive a free copy of the most comprehensive, annotated career catalog available today—*"Jobs and Careers for the 1990s"*:

IMPACT PUBLICATIONS
ATTN: Careers Catalog
9104-N Manassas Drive
Manassas Park, VA 22111

They will send you a copy upon request.

PART I

EMPLOYMENT REALITIES AND STRATEGIES

What exactly is the public sector? How does it relate to the private sector? What are the major trends for the public sector in the decade ahead? Will government drawdowns, cutbacks, and reductions-in-force continue? Which agencies are likely to experience growth or decline? What types of jobs are available in the public sector? Which jobs are most appropriate for someone with my interests, skills, and qualifications? How many jobs are there? Where are the jobs? Will I need to move to Washington, DC? How do I go about finding a government job? What are some of the major alternatives to working for government? If I leave government, what could I do? How can I become most effective in acquiring public employment and advancing my career in the public sector? What myths might prevent me from being effective in this rather confusing job market?

Many job seekers want thoughtful answers to these and other public employment questions. Encountering numerous organizations and hiring systems, they seek advice on how to simplify the job finding process in today's public sector job market. While the answers to these questions are anything but simple, in the following chapters we outline a useful concept of public employment which should help clarify understanding of this process. Furthermore, this concept is the basis for developing the "how-to" job search strategies and tactics outlined in subsequent chapters of this book.

The four chapters in this section address these and other key orienting questions. They analyze the public sector in terms of its size, characteristics, changes, and future growth and decline. Taken together, the chapters prepare you for the two major prerequisites for effectiveness in today's public sector job market:

- **You must understand how the public sector operates as well as know the realities of public employment before committing your time and energy to this employment arena.** This requires going beyond the many myths that commonly misinform and mislead casual observers of the public sector.

- **You must use job search strategies appropriately designed for the public sector.** This requires developing and implementing a job search that is responsive to both the formal and informal employment arenas operating inside and outside government.

Each chapter in this section is designed to simplify the overall complexity of public employment by placing this arena within the larger context of important job trends, realities, networks, and job and career alternatives. Accordingly, this section focuses on better understanding:

- public employment trends
- common myths impeding job search effectiveness
- public sector networks and networking
- alternative job markets relating to public employment

Part I outlines a basic action orientation for developing an effective job search in today's public sector job market. The remaining sections and chapters will help you develop effective job search strategies for particular organizations both inside and outside government as well as at the federal, state, and local levels.

One word of caution is in order before you begin these initial chapters. It is one thing to *understand* realities and another to *apply* them to your particular situation. The trends we outline are based upon large amounts of data which hold true for society and organizations *as a whole*. They do not necessarily apply to you *as the individual*. Indeed, subsequent chapters are specifically designed to equip you with the necessary knowledge and skills to get what you want in spite of these and other general trends.

The bottom line is for you to set goals and be persistent—indeed tenacious—in following through with strategies to get what you want. Statistics and trends outlined in these chapters merely provide an important *context* within which you will develop your own effective public sector job search strategies.

2

PUBLIC TRENDS & TRANSFORMATIONS

*T*he public sector consists of a relatively stable and predictable set of organizations which affects the way government conducts business. Well integrated into the private sector, the public sector also is highly decentralized, fragmented, and chaotic. Understanding the structure and changing nature of this system is the first step to identifying present and future employment prospects with public sector organizations.

THE PUBLIC SECTOR

The public sector encompasses all organizations and institutions directly or indirectly related to the business of governing communities, states, and nations. It includes government organizations as well as peripheral groups primarily oriented toward and dependent upon government. Involving numerous types of institutions and organizations, the *primary peripheral organizations* consist of:

- **Trade and professional associations** involved in influencing public policy through legislative, executive, and judicial agencies.

- **Contracting and consulting firms** which primarily receive government contracts.

- **Nonprofit organizations** performing public service functions.

- **Foundations** providing resources to other peripheral groups.

- **Research organizations** engaged in public-related research.

- **Public support groups, lobbyists, and law firms** influencing both the formulation and implementation of public policy.

The following figure illustrates this comprehensive and interrelated concept of the public sector:

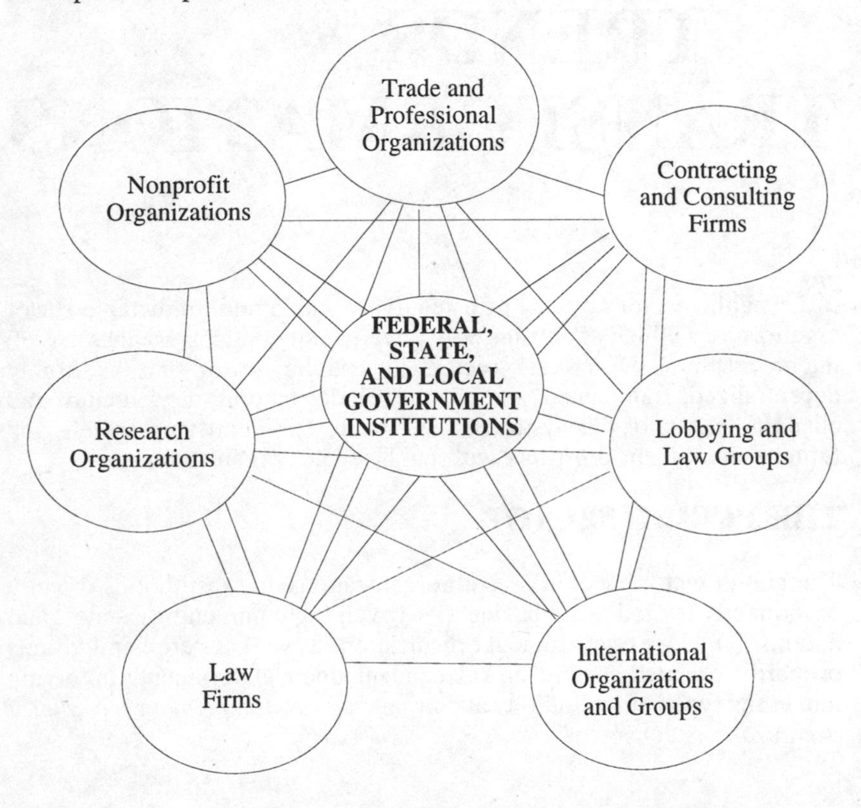

While this is not the usual definition of the public sector, it is very useful for our purposes. As you will see throughout this book, government is one of many institutions—albeit the most significant given its substantial monopoly of financial resources and scope of decision-making—involved in governing communities and influencing the specific direction and content of public policies. For job seekers, governments and their peripheral institutions comprise an *interrelated network* of public sector job and career opportunities. These institutions offer thousands of job vacancies each day. By familiarizing yourself with this network, as well as each institution within this network, you will be better able to identify job opportunities and advance your public sector career.

Governments and their peripheral institutions offer thousands of job vacancies each day.

THE GOVERNMENT COMPLEX

Government is the single largest employer in the United States. One in seven civilian employees, or nearly 18 million individuals, work for government organizations. Millions of other nongovernment jobs depend on providing services to government agencies. Of these, approximately eight million jobs in the private sector are paid through federal government contracts. In fact, the U.S. Department of Defense alone, which spends over $250 billion each year on contractors, is responsible for generating nearly 3.5 million jobs in private industry. Another 10 to 20 million private sector jobs are dependent upon contractual relationships with state and local governments, especially the more than 100,000 educational institutions and 7.5 million educators that define America's public educational complex.

The civilian government complex consists of numerous units of government and public employees distributed in a variety of functional areas as outlined in the charts on page 18. While loosely related to one another, each unit of government manages its own personnel and engages in different hiring practices.

Even within a single unit of government, several hiring systems will operate for different types of employees and different government units. For example, each agency in the federal government has its own personnel system, and many offices within agencies also operate their own systems which include separate hiring programs and practices. Within most municipalities, schools, police, and fire protection have their

GOVERNMENT UNITS AND EMPLOYEES, 1992

Level	Units	Employees
TOTAL	**86,743**	**18,554,000**
Federal	1	3,103,000
State	50	4,521,000
Local	86,692	10,930,000
■ Counties	3,043	2,196,000
■ School Districts	14,556	5,045,000
■ Townships/Towns	16,666	415,000
■ Municipalities	19,296	2,662,000
■ Special Districts	33,131	612,000

Source: U.S. Bureau of Census

GOVERNMENT PAYROLL BY FUNCTION, 1992
(in millions of dollars)

	Total	Federal[1]	State	Local
TOTAL	41,237	9,687	9,437	22,113
■ National defense[2]	3,294	3,294	(X)	(X)
■ Postal Service	2,359	2,359	(X)	(X)
■ Space research and technology	109	109	(X)	(X)
■ Education	15,724	41	3,551	12,132
■ Highways	1,238	18	613	607
■ Health & hospitals	4,048	876	1,584	1,587
■ Public welfare	982	34	464	485
■ Police protection	2,253	304	250	1,699
■ Fire protection				
■ Sanitation	771	(X)	(X)	771
& sewerage	518	(X)	7	510
■ Parks & recreation	489	66	69	353
■ Nature resources	1,150	732	349	70
■ Financial administration	1,119	400	343	376
■ Other government administration	646	95	126	424
■ Judicial & legal	952	172	338	442
■ Other	5,585	1,187	1,743	2,657

X = Not applicable [1] Includes employees outside US [2] Includes international relations
Source: U.S. Bureau of the Census

own personnel systems. Consequently, viewed as a "government job market", this system is highly decentralized and fragmented—both within and between governmental units. It continues to become even more decentralized and fragmented as the federal government engages in new decentralized reform efforts, and local governments, especially special districts which increased by 3,599 units since 1987, continue to proliferate.

The largest single category of government employees—and also the fastest growing—is educators (8.1 million), which comprises 52 percent of the government workforce at the state and local levels. Educational positions also have been primarily responsible for recent major growth and decline trends in public employment.

Federal government employment constitutes 18 percent of all public employment. Nearly 98 percent of all federal employees work for 110 executive agencies. Three agencies—Defense, Postal Service, and Veterans Affairs—employ nearly 7 of every 10 federal workers. Despite recent cutbacks in the Department of Defense personnel, this department still employs 3 out of every 10 federal workers. As the following table indicates, the six largest agencies employ 79.6 percent of all federal civilian employees.

LARGEST FEDERAL AGENCIES BY CIVILIAN EMPLOYEES, 1994

Agency	Employees	Percent
TOTAL FEDERAL EMPLOYMENT	**2,984,597**	**100.0**
▪ Legislative Branch	36,949	1.2
▪ Judicial Branch	27,945	.9
▪ Executive Branch	2,919,703	97.8
SIX LARGEST AGENCIES	**2,376,971**	**79.6**
▪ Department of Defense	898,154	30.0
▪ Postal Service	809,369	27.1
▪ Veterans Affairs	262,474	8.7
▪ Department of Treasury	162,058	5.4
▪ Department of Health and Human Services	129,374	4.3
▪ Department of Agriculture	115,542	3.8

Source: U.S. Office of Personnel Management, Office of Workforce Information, May 1994

Government employment does not stop with 18 million employees attached to executive branch bureaucracies. Another 500,000 individuals occupy elected and appointed legislative and judicial positions at the federal, state and local levels. The government complex also includes the District of Columbia and five territorial governments. Furthermore, 2.3

million individuals are employed in the armed forces. Overall, government employment is nearly 21 million.

The concentration of government employees varies by geographical area. For every 1,000 citizens, for example, there are 57.9 state and local employees, ranging from a high of 82 per 1,000 in Alaska to a low of 38 per 1,000 in Pennsylvania. California alone has nearly 1.5 million state and local employees whereas Vermont has fewer than 30,000. Federal government concentration averages 13 employees for every 1000 citizens.

The federal civilian workforce is widely distributed throughout the country as well as abroad. Nearly 88 percent of federal employees are located outside the Washington, DC Metro area. About 150,000 civilian employees work overseas, although only 83,000 are U.S. citizens. The State of California alone has nearly as many federal employees as the Washington Metro area—over 300,000. Since the federal government is divided into 10 administrative regions, the regional centers of New York, Philadelphia, Boston, Chicago, Atlanta, Kansas City, Dallas, Denver, San Francisco, and Seattle have a disproportionate concentration of federal workers, employing 36.9 percent of all federal civilian employees.

As the following chart indicates, federal employees work in all 50 states. Most of them work in major metropolitan areas or in smaller communities with military bases, research facilities, and Department of Energy installations. The largest percentage of civilian federal employees work for the Department of Defense and U.S. Postal Service.

CIVILIAN FEDERAL EMPLOYEES BY STATE, 1991[1]

State	Total Employees (1,000)	Percent Defense
TOTAL	**2,906**	**31.4**
Northeast	**481**	**26.3**
CT	24	20.7
MA	60	19.5
ME	124	26.6
NH	17	58.8
NJ	75	34.6
NY	152	11.8
PA	129	38.1
RI	10	41.8
VT	5	12.5
Midwest	**492**	**24.7**
IA	18	8.0
IL	104	19.4
IN	41	37.0
KS	25	27.3

MI	56	20.1
MM	32	9.0
MO	66	28.9
ND	8	25.8
NE	15	26.7
SD	9	15.3
WI	27	11.5
South	**1,254**	**33.9**
AL	57	44.5
AR	19	25.6
DC	212	8.1
DE	5	32.7
FL	112	29.4
GA	88	41.2
KY	35	35.4
LA	34	25.7
MD	133	31.0
MS	24	43.6
NC	46	33.0
OK	45	50.2
SC	32	59.0
TN	56	13.9
TX	177	33.9
WV	15	11.0
VA	161	66.2
West	**642**	**37.4**
AK	15	32.2
AZ	39	26.0
CA	315	39.5
CO	53	26.0
HI	25	75.6
ID	10	13.5
MT	11	11.6
NM	26	36.5
NV	11	18.9
OR	29	10.2
UT	36	57.9
WA	65	43.8
WY	6	17.0

[1] Excludes members and employees of Congress, Central Intelligence Agency, Defense Intelligence Agency, employees overseas, temporary census enumerators, seasonal and on-call employees, temporary Christmas help of the U.S. Postal Service, and National Security Agency)

Source: U .S. Office of Personnel Management and U.S. Bureau of the Census

While over 90 percent of government employees work for executive agencies, numerous job opportunities also are available in the bureaucracies of the legislative and judicial branches of government. For example, within the federal government the legislative branch employs just under 39,000 individuals; the judicial branch employs over 26,000. Although less visible to the public, agencies within these two branches of government have been growing rapidly in the past decade. Employment in the legislative branch, for example, has increased by 68.7 percent since 1965 (25,947). Employment in the judicial branch has more than quadrupled (474.5 percent) in the same period (from 5,904 to 28,000+)—the fastest growing branch of the federal government.

GROWTH, DECLINE, AND STABILITY

As illustrated in the following table, the number of units of government actually declined by 50 percent—from 155,116 to 78,269—during the period 1942-1972. Between 1972 and 1992 government units increased by nearly 11 percent, primarily driven by the continuing proliferation of small special districts.

EVOLUTION OF GOVERNMENT UNITS, 1942-1992

Government Level	1942	1952	1962	1972	1982	1992
TOTAL	**155,116**	**116,743**	**91,237**	**78,269**	**82,341**	**86,743**
U.S. Government	1	1	1	1	1	1
States	48	48	50	50	50	50
Local Govts.	155,067	116,694	91,186	78,218	82,290	86,692
Counties	3,050	3,049	3,043	3,044	3,041	3,043
Municipalities	16,220	16,778	18,000	18,517	19,076	19,296
Townships/Towns	18,919	17,202	17,142	16,991	16,734	16,666
School District	108,579	67,346	34,678	15,781	14,851	14,556
Special Districts	8,299	12,319	18,323	23,885	28,588	33,131

Source: U.S. Bureau of the Census

Despite the decline in the number of government units—primarily precipitated by the consolidation of thousands of school districts during the 1940s, 1950s, and 1960s—the number of government employees nearly tripled from 1950 to 1990. Following general population growth and labor participation trends, the long-term pattern for government employment is toward growth. However, the annual growth in government employment has been slower than the nation's annual population increases and employment increases in other sectors of the economy.

While government employment more than doubled during the past three decades, most of this growth took place at the state and local levels during the 1960s and 1970s. For the period 1950 to 1990, for example, state government employment increased by 243 percent and local government employment grew by 217 percent. The following table summarizes the growth in public employment from 1950 to 1990:

CHANGING GOVERNMENT EMPLOYMENT, 1950-1990

Level of Government	1950	1960	1970	1980	1990
TOTAL EMPLOYEES (1,000s)	**6,503**	**8,808**	**13,028**	**16,213**	**17,638**
■ Federal (civilian)	2,117	2,421	2,881	2,898	3,167
■ State and Local	4,285	6,387	10,147	13,315	14,671
(Percent of total)	66.9	72.5	77.9	82.1	83.2
■ State	1,057	1,527	2,755	3,753	4,231
■ Local	3,228	4,860	7,392	9,562	10,240
AVERAGE ANNUAL PERCENT CHANGE					
■ Employees (Total)	+.5	+3.5	+4.2	+1.5	+.8
■ Federal	-8.9	+.4	+2.2	+1.0	+.9
■ State	(NA)	(NA)	+6.3	+1.5	+1.3
■ Local	(NA)	(NA)	+4.4	+1.7	+.7

Source: U.S. Bureau of the Census

The most rapidly growing units of government have been special districts. Between 1970 and 1983, employment with special districts increased an average of 5 percent each year—a rate 2 to 10 times higher than all other forms of government combined. By 1987 the largest number of special district governments dealt with natural resources (6,360 units), fire protection (5,070 units), and housing and community development (3,464 units). While the number of township governments and school districts continued to decline, special districts continued to increase in number during the 1980s and 1990s:

CHANGING UNITS OF LOCAL GOVERNMENT, 1982-1987

Unit of Government	1982	1992	Percent Change
■ Counties	3,041	3,043	+.0006
■ School Districts	14,851	14,556	-.0198
■ Township/Towns	16,734	16,666	-.0040
■ Municipalities	19,076	19,296	+.0115
■ Special Districts	28,588	33,131	+.1589

Source: U.S. Bureau of the Census

Increases and decreases in the number of governmental units has had relatively little effect on public employment. Special districts, for example, are usually small and employ few officials. Overall, a 1 to 2 percent annual growth rate in government employment at all levels is more a reflection of the general population growth rate than increases in the number of governmental units. In fact, the growth in government employment is generally lower than the overall rate of population growth.

Most public employment increases during the past three decades responded to three general changes in society:

- Post-World War II population increases requiring extensive expansion of educational facilities, highways, and other local infrastructure and services.

- The increased demand for more community and social services in response to a generally more affluent and aging population.

- Revitalized and more liberal state legislatures and bureaucracies which played increased social advocacy roles.

Federal employment trends differed from state and local patterns. From 1950 to 1990, federal employment increased by only 49 percent, at an incremental annual rate of 0.5 to 1.5 percent. Most of this growth took place during the period 1950 to 1970. The period 1970 to 1981 actually witnessed a 1.0 percent decline in federal employment. Yet, the federal budget increased by over 1200 percent (from $40 billion to $526 billion) during the same period.

Why did federal employment fail to grow as dramatically as state and local bureaucracies, especially given major budgetary capabilities to do so? The answer to this question relates to two general trends off-setting the need to increase federal personnel in direct proportion to budgetary increases. First, much of the budgetary increase was in the form of transfer payments to states and localities: categorical and block grants and revenue sharing funds. From 1960 to 1981, federal aid to state and local governments increased 1200 percent, from $7.0 billion to $86 billion; by 1986 federal aid had increased another 31 percent to $113 billion. And by 1994 it had increased another 61 percent to $182 billion. In 1992 the majority (89 percent) of aid was targeted for health ($71 billion or 39 percent), welfare ($44 billion or 24 percent), education ($29 billion or 15 percent, and transportation ($21 billion or 11 percent).

One of the major impacts of federal aid was to stimulate the growth of state and local bureaucracies—especially in the areas of health, welfare, education, and transportation—rather than enlarge the federal bureaucracy. State and local bureaucracies had to increase their staffs to handle the influx of federal funds.

Second, private contractors and consultants played a greater role in providing federal government services. Contracting-out government services and employment increased significantly during the 1960s and 1970s as federal agencies shifted from providing direct services to obligating funds and managing contracts. Procurement became a major growth industry in the federal government. Contractors not only provided goods and services to agencies, many also supplied contract workers to staff agencies. In the most extreme case, over 80 percent of the employees in the Department of Energy are contract workers hired by private contractors to operate Department of Energy facilities. By the early 1980s a "hidden bureaucracy" of contracting and consulting firms was well entrenched in relation to the federal government. Washington, DC metropolitan area alone—where they are frequently referred to as "Beltway Bandits" and "Suburban Consultants"—has over 3,000 such firms doing business with the bureaucracy.

While many contracting and consulting firms specialize in defense contracting, others provide services to numerous agencies, ranging from project design to delivering specific services to agency clientele. Similar firms do business with state and local governments.

An overall employment pattern in government is evident: state and local governments tend to increase personnel in response to budgetary increases; federal budgetary increases tend to stimulate the growth of state and local bureaucracies as well as the increased involvement of contracting and consulting firms specializing in the delivery of public services.

CUTBACKS, PRIORITIES, AND CONTRACTORS

Since the early 1980s, the pattern of growth in state and local bureaucracies has been altered somewhat. Recessions combined with taxpayers' revolts resulted in public employment declining for the first time since the immediate post-World War II period.

Major declines in public employment began in 1980. The sharpest declines took place at the state and local levels. Between 1980 and 1981, employment in municipalities declined by 3.6 percent; counties by 2.4 percent; townships by 2.0 percent; and school districts by 1.1 percent. Only special districts registered an increase in employment—1.7 percent. Declines were evident in all functional areas except police protection. Education experienced the greatest cutbacks; highway departments registered the largest percentage decrease in employees. Indeed, by 1981 there were 245,000 fewer government employees, representing a 1.8 percent decline at the state and local levels.

Declines in public employment during the early 1980s were fairly predictable. Cutbacks were most urgently needed for many state and local bureaucracies in the Northeast and Midwest. Hit hard by recession, the public services in these areas had become bloated during the 1960s and

1970s due to the growth of liberal social services and public employee unions. Examples of such problems abound. New York City lived far beyond its means, faced repeated financial crises, and nearly defaulted. New York State government followed a similar pattern of excessive spending in the face of declining revenues. Ubiquitous patronage in the 1970s gave Boston an average of 44.4 public employees for every 1,000 inhabitants—76 percent above the national average!

Something had to give. In Massachusetts, for example—a state noted for liberal programs, strong public employee unions, and high taxes—taxpayers revolted with passage of the infamous Proposition 2½ ballot initiative; 40,000 jobs were eliminated from the public payroll shortly thereafter. New York City, despite strong opposition from public unions, managed to reduce its public employees from 283,000 in 1974 to 210,000 in 1982. The financially strapped cities of New York, Boston, Philadelphia, Providence, Newark, Cleveland, and Detroit began practicing a long-overdue version of "cutback management" as government jobs became increasingly insecure and unpredictable.

The federal bureaucracy also experienced personnel declines during the 1980s. Shortly after taking office, President Reagan did what new presidents only talk about—trim the federal bureaucracy. Reduction-in-force (RIF) procedures went into effect, frightening and demoralizing thousands of federal employees from Hawaii to Maine who began thinking the unthinkable—possible job loss and insecurity. During the 1980s there were several winners and losers as public policy priorities were reordered among agencies, as evidenced in the figures on page 27.

While cutbacks in most agencies resulted in temporarily downsizing the total number of full-time employees, they disguised increases in part-time employees and the increased use of contractors and consultants. An extreme case is the Department of Energy. By 1990 more than 85 percent of the employees in Department of Energy offices were private contractors rather than full-time federal employees! A recent (1994) GAO report concludes that these contractors cost the Department of Energy 40 to 55 percent more than permanent government employees, although other analysts might challenge these figures.

While full-time personnel declined in many agencies, budgets continued to increase and peripheral organizations participated more in the day-to-day operations of agencies. Furthermore, despite RIFs and other downsizing efforts, the federal bureaucracy actually grew by 237,000 jobs or a relatively incremental rate of 0.8 percent during the Reagan administration. Major employment increases took place in the Department of Defense during this period.

Certain "downsizing" patterns emerged during the Reagan years which continue today under the new "reinventing" government philosophy. While nearly 60,000 federal employees lost their jobs by 1984, the federal government continued to hire approximately 1,000 new employees each day. In most months it hires about 20,000 new workers, but in some

FEDERAL GOVERNMENT WINNERS AND LOSERS, 1980-1992

Executive agencies	Employment 1980	Employment 1992	Increase/ Decrease	Percent Change
THE WINNERS				
■ U.S. Postal Service	666,228	834,258	+168,030	+25.2
■ Defense	967,890	1,080,469	+112,579	+11.6
■ Treasury	131,713	155,492	+23,779	+18.1
■ Justice	57,041	80,611	+23,570	+41.3
■ Veterans Affairs	239,625	247,219	+7,594	+3.2
■ U.S. Courts	14,404	21,341	+6,923	+47.0
■ Federal Deposit Insurance Corp.	3,587	8,826	+5,239	+146.1
■ State	23,791	25,580	+1,789	+7.5
THE LOSERS				
■ Commerce	196,544	66,689	-129,855	-66.1
■ Health and Human Services	163,921	124,559	-39,362	-24.0
■ Tennessee Valley Authority	51,531	25,546	-25,985	-50.4
■ General Services Administration	38,620	20,154	-18,466	-47.8
■ Agriculture	144,124	127,478	-16,646	-11.5
■ Interior	88,924	78,166	-10,758	-12.1
■ Transportation	74,368	65,494	-8,874	-11.9
■ Labor	24,482	18,565	-5,917	-24.2
■ Energy	21,680	17,418	-4,262	-19.7
■ Housing and Urban Development	17,413	13,600	-3,813	-21.9
■ Education	7,167	4,737	-2,430	-33.9
■ Government Printing Office	6,949	5,058	-1,891	-27.2
■ Office of Personnel Management	8,564	6,972	-1,592	-18.6
■ U.S. International Development Agency	6,271	4,895	-1,376	-21.9
■ Interstate Commerce Commission	2,067	706	-1,361	-65.8
■ Small Business Administration	5,891	4,644	-1,247	-21.2
■ Federal Trade Commission	1,896	922	-974	-51.4

Source: U.S. Office of Personnel Management

months it hires as many as 50,000. Instead of substantially shrinking the federal bureaucracy, the Reagan administration actually slowed the rate of job growth by reordering personnel priorities among and within agencies as well as between grades of officials. It tinkered with a few politically vulnerable programs. For example, the Department of Health and Human Services (HHS) lost a disproportionate number of employees in weak service programs; HHS employees in GS-11 to GS-15 positions—classifications which grew dramatically during the 1970s—were more vulnerable to the personnel cuts than employees in lower grades. For many government employees, such reforms efforts appeared to be another shell game for public employment.

Cutbacks in most agencies disguised increases in part-time employees and the increased use of contractors and consultants.

By 1994 the Clinton administration was calling for further "streamlining" of the federal bureaucracy. Led by Vice President Gore, this ostensibly new reform movement was supposed to eliminate more than 272,000 jobs over a five-year period. Middle management, personnel, procurement, and administrative staffs would be especially hard hit by this latest round of cutbacks. The big losers would probably be the Office of Personnel Management and the Department of Defense. A trendy new reform philosophy—"reinventing government"—influenced these efforts. Efforts to eliminate unnecessary regulations, reorganize regional field operations, and downsize personnel took center stage in these reforms. A new round of hiring freezes, early retirements, buyouts, and reductions-in-force would most likely be initiated, repeating the perennial effort to make government both look and feel more efficient and effective.

While the end result of these reforms would probably be to further slow the incremental growth of federal employment, they might also increase procurement activities: agencies may need to hire more contractors and consultants to make up for new personnel shortfalls created by these latest reforms. Ironically, one of the major goals of these reforms was to downsize agency procurement offices—the very ones that were supposed to help prevent waste, fraud, and abuse in government!

Another trend emerged during this cutback era and continues today: government budgets continue to increase but at a slower rate than in previous decades. Some government employees will be cut from the public payroll, but fewer new employees will be hired in general. However, the "hidden government" of contracting and consulting firms will continue to do business as usual with government agencies. Many will increase their employees in direct proportion to declines in government employment. Except in defense, contracting and consulting should continue to be growth industries in the decade ahead.

Indeed, in 1994 public employee unions finally began to turn their attention to the hidden government of contractors and consultants in criticizing the Clinton administration's reinventing government initiatives. In its simplest form, the criticism went like this: why should contractors and consultants be exempt from reinventing government? Shouldn't they, too, be required to engage in cost-cutting efforts just like government agencies? Many public employees felt they were unfairly being singled out for reform efforts, which actually translated into reductions-in-force, when studies showed it was more cost-effective to hire full-time bureaucrats rather than consultants. Had contractors and consultants, who largely operate outside public view and political criticism, become sacred cows immune to government reform efforts? The answer seemed clear: of course. How else can you expect to run a complex government affected by over-zealous politicians and administrators who constantly seek the limelight by beating up on a politically weak bureaucracy? Ironically, contractors and consultants could provide continuity within government while government agencies went on their periodical "reform" journeys to look more efficient and effective.

As we move into the second half of 1990s with a restructured world order that witnesses a substantial decline in "Cold War" military hardware and personnel, major cutbacks are taking place within the Department of Defense (DOD) as well as amongst defense contractors—key beneficiaries of the reordered pro-military budgetary and personnel priorities during the 1980-1987 period. Depending on the extent of cutbacks, this new trend may have a devastating impact on defense contractors who got fat and happy during the post-World War II Cold War era. Indeed, in 1994 two of the nation's largest defense contractors symbolized the financial and employment realities of this new downsizing era. On March 7, 1994, Martin Marietta Corporation and Grumman Corporation—which in 1993 had combined revenues of $12.6 billion and employed 109,000 people—agreed to a $1.93 billion merger. Northrop Corporation muddied the waters by countering this offer and finally winning the bidding war on April 4, 1994 with a price tag of $2.17 billion. This merger would guarantee the continuing existence of Grumman Corporation, a well established and highly respected defense contractor specializing in military aircraft, defense electronics, computer software, reconnaissance, intelligence, and space, which faced a daunting future of trying to cope with its declining fortunes in the post-Cold War era. While Northrop won this major merger battle, Martin Marietta will most likely emerge as the world's largest defense electronics firm and retain its position as the nation's largest defense and aerospace contractor. The outcomes for other defense contractors—both prime contractors and subcontractors—also appeared certain: less business and fewer employees.

Similar mergers, buyouts, and downsizings were taking place in 1993 and 1994 within the defense industry as contractors scrambled to adjust to this new era of uncertain but substantially lower military spending. In 1993, for example, Martin Marietta acquired GE Aerospace from General Electric for $3 billion. In 1994 Martin Marietta announced the future acquisition of General Dynamics Corporation's rocket division for $208 million, and Loral Corporation finalized plans to acquire IBM's Federal Systems Division for $1.5 billion. As one Grumman executive summarized the realities of this new defense contracting era, "You acquire somebody, get acquired, or go out of business" (*Washington Post,* March 8, 1994). And Raytheon Corporation, a major defense contractor best known for producing the popular Patriot Missile, announced the closing of several plants and the impending layoff of 4,400 workers. Consequently, job and career opportunities with defense and aerospace contractors throughout the 1990s will most likely be unpredictable and insecure as "Cold War careers" either come to an end or are transformed into "post-Cold War careers". As many defense contracts negotiated in the late 1980s were scheduled to terminate in 1994 and 1995, defense contractors quickly moved to diversify their businesses. Many restructured their businesses away from producing military aircraft and other defense and aerospace related hardware and moved toward producing electronics and computers for the civilian market. Much of the remaining business within defense contracting shifted from manufacturing military hardware to producing defense electronics and engaging in research, development, and testing activities.

Whether such cutbacks result in substantially reducing the national deficit as well as reallocating resources to other government agencies and contractors is one of the most interesting questions facing the public sector in the 1990s—a sector not noted for making radical shifts in budgetary priorities. Our best guess follows our "Law for Downsized Public Spending": money will flow to those areas experiencing high political support and low resistance—to "Mom and Apple Pie" issues. We put our bets on reallocating resources to the high profile policy areas of health and public safety—the great government growth industries for the next decade. The health and criminal justice bureaucracies of federal, state, and local governments, as well as amongst peripheral institutions—contractors, consultants, nonprofit organizations, foundations, associations, research groups—should expand accordingly.

PREDICTING THE FUTURE

Given past patterns of growth, stability, and decline in public employment, what can we expect in the future? Certain trends are evident based on knowledge of future demographic changes, basic public service needs, and a significant restructuring of public policy priorities. We see several broad trends during the past few years that argue for some major, if not revolutionary, departures for the public sector in the decade ahead. We see twelve important changes for the public sector:

1. **A changing world order attendant with new regimes in Eastern Europe and the former Soviet republics, renewed economic rivalry between the U.S. and Asia, continuing poverty and political turmoil in Third and Fourth World countries, and the expansion of drug wars and terrorism in the Third World will result in new public policy initiatives and hiring emphases within the federal government as well as amongst relevant consultants, contractors, nonprofit organizations, and research groups.**

   These trends have by far the most revolutionary consequences for the public sector. The break-up of communist regimes in Eastern Europe, the restructuring of Soviet politics and economics, continuing political turmoil in the Middle East and Central America, and the changing roles of China, Japan and other major Asian economies could have far reaching consequences for the public sector in the United States. The major casualties will be the U.S. Department of Defense and its hundreds of contractors and consultants that made lucrative careers out of providing the hardware for managing the Cold War as well as the much criticized Central Intelligence Agency which seemed to lack intelligence for its failure to predict major international changes and for engaging in questionable, if not incompetent, covert operations. With the ending of the Cold War, the demilitarization of the Soviet Union in Eastern Europe, the collapse of the Warsaw Pact, and the reluctance of the Russia to militarily support revolutionary causes in Third and Fourth World countries, the rationale for continuing high levels of military spending will be seriously challenged by new thinking on budgetary priorities. This rationale will be replaced with major arguments for making significant cuts in the defense budget. These cutbacks could mean very bad times for major defense contractors, retrenchment for both military and civilian personnel in the Department of Defense, and a reallocation of resources to domestic and foreign aid programs. The 1990s may be the worst of times for U.S. military and intelligence agencies but perhaps the best of times for the State Department, Agency for International Development, and international-related agencies in the Departments of Commerce, Agriculture, Transportation, Treasury, and Health and Human Services.

However, given the volatility of such changes, as well as the incremental nature of the federal budgetary process, dramatic changes will be slow in coming. By 1997 Russia will re-emerge as a significant military force affecting international political developments. Ironically, Department of Defense adjustments to the changing world order will most likely lag by one to two years given constraints inherent in the annual budgetary process. Disappointing economic opportunities in Europe, continuing rivalry between the U.S. and Japan, the emergence of huge consumer economies in China, India, and Southeast Asia, and a stronger U.S. dollar abroad will result in refocusing attention on managing trade and monetary relationships in the dynamic economies of Asia and the Pacific Rim. Problems with poverty and political turmoil in Third and Fourth World countries will place greater emphasis on improving the U.S. presence abroad through the activities of the State Department, the Agency for International Development, and the Peace Corps. Continuing problems with drug wars and terrorism will mean increased employment within the Defense, State, and Justice departments. Indeed, the role of the military may be transformed during the 1990s to better deal with the problems of terrorism and drugs.

The 1990s may be the worst of times for U.S. military and intelligence agencies, but dramatic changes will be slow in coming.

2. A downsizing military results in 500,000 fewer employees, both civilian and military, within the Department of Defense by 1996 as well as greater competition for federal jobs.

Competition for federal jobs becomes keener than ever as many downsized Department of Defense employees seek jobs with other federal agencies. Large numbers of deactivated non-commissioned officers turn to the federal government for civilian employment. More and more retired officers, who normally avoid federal employment because of retirement pay restrictions, look to the federal government for employment; many of their traditional post-military job opportunities in the private sector with defense contractors disappear within the rapidly shrinking defense establishment. Individuals seeking federal jobs without veterans preference face increased difficulty competing in this new and highly competitive environment.

3. **The defense contracting game undergoes major transformations as prime contractors and subcontractors scramble for survival in the post-Cold War era of the new defense establishment.**

Defense contractors experience the most significant upheaval in the history of defense contracting as the Department of Defense downsizes, consolidates, and reorders its spending priorities. Several contractors go out of business while others consolidate and diversify in order to survive. Given the heavy concentration on defense manufacturing in California, employment in that state is disproportionately affected by these changes; thousands of defense workers loose their jobs and join the ranks of the structurally unemployed. By 1995 Martin Marietta Corporation emerges as the mega defense and aerospace contracting firm, the largest such firm in the world. Contracting priorities shift from manufacturing military hardware to producing defense electronics and providing research, development, and testing services for both the defense and aerospace establishments.

4. **Continuing public safety problems attendant with drug problems, unemployment, and poverty require increased government expenditures and hiring to contain public safety problems.**

Expect steady increases in employment within the criminal justice system—police, courts, and prisons as well as among peripheral organizations involved with criminal justice issues. The judiciary at all levels will continue to grow in response to public safety and criminal justice problems. Lawyers and paralegals can expect more and more job opportunities within this troubled criminal justice system. Prisons become a major growth industry throughout the 1990s. New and innovative approaches to incarceration, such as prisons operated by private contractors, will take center stage in public debates about government responses to community safety.

5. **Public health becomes the "hot" public policy issue for the later half of the 1990s. Health care financing and delivery requirements result in increased public expenditure on health care.**

Despite public debates to the contrary, federal, state, and local health care bureaucracies experience significant growth as do associations, nonprofit organizations, and consultants and contractors specializing in health care issues. A public health service, modeled after HMO's, expands in order to provide universal health coverage. Public employment opportunities abound for individuals with health care expertise.

6. **Aging and deteriorating public infrastructure will require increased expenditures on public works.**

   Roads, bridges, and water and sewerage systems in many parts of the United States are in a terrible state of disrepair. Expect a steady increase in employment among contractors with experience in building and maintaining roads, bridges, and water and sewerage systems at the state and local levels.

7. **Energy and environmental problems take center stage in public policy debates and capture a larger share of local, state, and federal budgets. Greater emphasis will focus on handling toxic waste dumps that endanger the well-being of communities.**

   Governments at all levels will attempt to solve energy and environmental problems by contracting-out both policy-making and implementation to private consultants and contractors. Communities near military bases will receive considerable attention since many of the adjacent bases are literally aging toxic waste dumps endangering community health. The U.S. Department of Energy will become the model of a highly "privatized" public agency; contractors and consultants largely run this agency from top to bottom. Expect employment opportunities for environmental specialists to increase accordingly both within government and amongst businesses, nonprofit organizations, and associations involved with these issues.

8. **The 1990s will witness greater employment mobility between the public and private sectors.**

   Given changes in the federal application and retirement systems and the portability of federal pension funds, more and more federal employees will move back and forth between the public and private sectors. As part of the federal government's continuing decentralization of personnel matters to agencies, the U.S. Office of Personnel Management ends the unpopular Standard Form 171 (SF 171) and thereby permits agencies to issue their own application forms as well as accept resumes. More individuals will apply for federal positions under this new application system which is also likely to create chaos in some agencies which are not equipped to handle resumes and other types of applications. Expect changes in the retirement system to help revitalize the public sector.

9. **Federal employees will experience layoffs or reductions-in-force as the government continues to downsize its personnel.**

While previous downsizing efforts within the federal bureaucracy was primarily accomplished through attrition brought about by hiring freezes and buyouts rather than layoffs, downsizing in the 1990s will likely result in numerous reductions-in-force. As competition for federal jobs increases and fewer federal employees voluntarily leave government in response to early retirement incentives or for jobs in the private sector, agencies will be forced to layoff employees in order to reach their new personnel targets.

10. **While public employment will most likely continue to increase in response to population increases, the actual rate of increase will be relatively small compared to previous decades of rapid expansion in government employment.**

Continuing declines and no-growth patterns for government employment will take place in many states and locales throughout the 1990s. On an average, government employment growth will probably fluctuate from 0 to 1.0 percent each year. This is about one-third the growth rate projected for all employment in the United States for the decade ahead and about one-half the annual population growth rate.

11. **Education will face continuing turbulence over the next decade due to a leveling of student enrollments in secondary and higher education and increasingly restrictive state and local government spending on education.**

According to U.S. Department of Labor projections, between 1978 and 1990 the demand for secondary school teachers declined by 20.8 percent; college and university faculty declined by 9.2 percent. On the other hand, beginning in 1985, more jobs became available in elementary education as the children of the post-World War II baby boom generation began entering schools in large numbers. Between 1978 and 1990 the demand for elementary teachers increased by nearly 25 percent. To a very large extent, the slow growth in public employment is due to changes in the structure of education and demographics. This is especially true in the case of state government employment where approximately 30 percent of all employees work in higher education institutions. As higher education continues through another decade of slow-growth and cutbacks, state employment growth can expect to slow. California, once a high spending growth state but now experiencing economic and population decline, will experience major cutbacks in education at all levels. Other states experiencing slow growth, such as Illinois, Michigan, New York, and Pennsylvania, will experience continuing cutbacks in education employment.

12. State and local government jobs will increase in some areas and decrease in others in response to continuing demographic shifts from the Northeast and Midwest into the South and West.

At the same time, several older cities and states in the Northeast and Midwest will experience further public service declines. The states of New York, Rhode Island, Massachusetts, Pennsylvania, Ohio, Michigan, and Illinois—as well as the cities of Boston, New York, Philadelphia, Chicago, Detroit, and St. Louis—are still adjusting to declining tax bases caused by population and industrial migration to the South and West. Governments of these states and cities will probably cutback further, because they are caught in a vicious circle: population, industries, and revenues decline at the same time costs increase for providing social services and physical infrastructure as well as for maintaining generous public employee pension plans. These cutbacks may have a more permanent impact on the bureaucracies than many patchwork measures initiated in the late 1970s and early 1980s.

The good news is in the South and mountain West and in areas where major universities are linked to high-tech industries. Population growth and industrial development will most likely continue in Florida, Texas, New Mexico, Arizona, Colorado, Utah, and Nevada. Massachusetts, an extremely resilient state, which rebounded in the mid-1980s by transforming its economy in line with its major emerging strength—high technology tied to an incredible educational complex near Boston, especially the booming Route 128 area—will go through further turmoil as it experiences downturns in its highly volatile high-tech industries. Illinois, Ohio, Michigan, and Indiana may undergo similar transformations and turmoil as they shed older smokestack industries in favor of high-tech industries linked to several major higher educational complexes. State and local bureaucracies in these areas will probably grow in response to increases in population, industry, and revenue. Education and public safety bureaucracies will be the major beneficiaries.

Most growth states and cities are developing around service industries. Since their relatively young, conservative, well educated, and affluent populations neither require nor demand extensive social services, governments in these states and cities will concentrate on developing basic infrastructure to accommodate continuing growth. As service industries undergo turbulent growth and decline, local government bureaucracies in these areas will be less affected because of their limited initial growth. States and cities experiencing little or no population and economic growth will most likely further shrink their bureaucracies as well as contract-out various services.

13. The federal government will probably continue to replace personnel at the present stable, incremental growth rate of approximately 1,000 new employees each day.

The Defense Department will decline in size due to changing military priorities. Cutbacks will be especially deep in the acquisitions and procurement areas. However, the Departments of Justice, State, and Veterans Affairs and the Environmental Protection Agency will continue to increase in size due to public policy priorities to expand in these areas. The Environmental Protection Agency will become a cabinet level Department of Environment. In so doing it will experience a 20 percent increase in personnel. The number of positions related to the procurement process will increase in all agencies except Defense due to an expanding government contracting role and continuing problems with the government procurement process. As the federal budget grows and government employment plateaus, non-military private contracting and consulting firms will probably expand their business with federal, state, and local government agencies.

14. A quiet revolution has been taking place in government during the recession of 1991-1994 as the quality of new employees has increased significantly. A new and highly competitive public service emerges in the late 1990s as a result of transformations in personnel taking place in the early 1990s.

Recessions tend to bring out the best of people, as least for government employment. The tight and restructured job market of the early 1990s saw more and more people leaving the private sector for government jobs. Indeed, for many people facing a recessionary job market, government employment seemed to be a relatively open, secure, and well paying alternative to the declining number of private sector jobs which also were increasingly becoming low paying jobs. The overall education, skill, and experience levels of these new government employees is high—much higher than many current employees who joined government five or ten years ago. Consequently, we can expect a much more competent public service in the future as well as greater conflicts between older and newer employers who exhibit marked differences in education and skill levels. Despite frustrated efforts at the federal level to reinvent government by tinkering with organizational structures and downsizing personnel, the real revolution in government has already taken place through the intake of a new generation of public employee. It has little to do with reinventing government—just hiring better quality personnel. This revolution will not be apparent for at least another seven years. Public service will once again be seen as an attractive employment arena for well educated and skilled individuals.

The total number of annual job vacancies in the public sector is probably closer to 8 million.

15. Public employment opportunities will be numerous regardless of overall growth and decline patterns in government employment.

After all, a group of 18 million government employees, with an annual turnover rate of 14 percent (due to resignations, retirements, deaths, and dismissals), automatically generates nearly 2,520,000 job vacancies each year. Added to this number are a similar number of vacancies occurring among the peripheral organizations doing business with government agencies—organizations which have even higher turnover rates than government. The total number of annual job vacancies in the public sector is probably closer to 8 million.

16. Government personnel procedures today are more apolitical and professional than ever before. They will continue to be so in the future.

Except for a few patronage-entrenched states and locales, gone are the good-ole-boy days when politicians dumped incompetents into government agencies and political connections could get you a job with little or no demonstrated skills or experience. Patronage systems have given way to merit systems based upon systematic recruitment, selection, and promotion procedures. Even counties—often considered the last havens of political patronage—have become increasingly urban and highly professional. While the ubiquitous "connection" is still important for getting a government job—indeed, essential for you to use—it tends to be professional in nature. The name of the game today is "professional networking" rather than using "political pull" —a significant shift in how the game is played.

The name of the game today is "professional networking" rather than using "political pull"—a significant shift in how the game is played.

17. Public sector jobs are increasingly technical and competitive.

Once largely a job market for generalists, the public sector today engages in highly technical activities requiring substantial educational and technical skills. Given the relatively good pay and security of government employment, not surprisingly many people want to work for government. Thus, you can expect to encounter competition from numerous candidates who possess relatively strong educational and technical backgrounds.

Knowing these trends, your task should be to identify how you can best link your skills and abilities to job vacancies in the public sector. Because of no-growth and limited-growth job situations in government, it is very important to plan your job search. The evidence is clear: numerous and exciting job opportunities are available, but only for those who prepare well for an increasingly competitive, professional, and technical public sector where careers tend to plateau within a short period of time.

3

OLD JOB MYTHS, NEW EMPLOYMENT REALITIES

"*W*here are the jobs, and how do I get one?" Underlying these two frequently asked questions are certain assumptions about the job market. While such questions may anticipate easy answers, the answers are much more complex when examining job opportunities amongst the multitude of institutions that define the public sector job market.

Let's begin answering these questions by first examining 27 myths that could impede your job search. These myths focus on important employment issues affecting both you and employers. This discussion should help you start your job search in the right direction.

MUDDLERS AND THEIR MYTHS

Most job seekers are unprepared and naive in approaching the job market; some might be best termed "job dumb". They muddle-through the job market with questionable perceptions of how it works. Combining facts, stereotypes, myths, and folklore—gained from a mixture of logic, experience, and advice from well-meaning friends and relatives—these perceptions lead job seekers down several unproductive paths. Such perceptions are often responsible for the self-fulfilling prophecy of the unsuccessful job seeker: "There are no jobs available for me".

OVERCOMING JOB MARKET MYTHS

Fifteen basic myths often prevent individuals from being effective in finding a job in today's employment market. You may recognize yourself in several of these myths:

MYTH 1: Anyone can find a job; all you need to know is how to find a job.

REALITY: This classic "form versus substance" myth is often associated with career counselors who were raised on popular career planning exhortations of the 1970s and 1980s that stressed the importance of having positive attitudes and self-esteem, setting goals, dressing for success, and using interpersonal strategies for finding jobs. While such approaches may work well in an industrial society with low unemployment, they constitute myths in a post-industrial, high-tech society which requires employees to demonstrate both *intelligence and concrete work skills* as well as a *willingness to relocate* to new communities offering greater job opportunities. For example, many of today's unemployed are highly skilled in the old technology of the industrial society, but they live and own homes in economically depressed communities. These people lack the necessary *skills and mobility* required for getting jobs in high-tech, growth communities. Knowing job search skills alone will not help these people. Indeed, such advice and knowledge may frustrate such highly motivated and immobile individuals who possess skills of the old technology.

MYTH 2: The best way to find a job is to respond to classified ads, use employment agencies, join electronic job search databases, and submit applications to personnel offices.

REALITY: Except for certain types of organizations, such as government, these formal application procedures are not the most effective ways of finding jobs. Such approaches assume the presence of an organized, coherent, and centralized job market—but no such thing exists. The job market is highly decentralized, fragmented, and chaotic. Classified ads, employment agencies, and personnel offices tend to list low paying yet highly competitive jobs or high paying highly skilled positions that are hard to fill. Most of the best jobs—high level, excellent pay, least competitive—are neither listed nor advertised; they are most likely found through word-of-mouth. Your most fruitful strategy will be to conduct research and informational interviews on what career counselors call the "hidden job market."

MYTH 3: **Few jobs are available for me in today's competitive job market.**

REALITY: This may be true if you lack marketable skills and insist on applying for jobs listed in newspapers, employment agencies, or personnel offices. Competition in the advertised job market usually is high, especially for jobs requiring few skills. Numerous jobs with little competition are available on the hidden job market. Jobs requiring advanced technical skills often go begging. Little competition may occur during periods of high unemployment, because many people quit job hunting after a few disappointing weeks of concentrating job search efforts on working the advertised job market.

MYTH 4: **I know how to find a job, but opportunities are not available for me.**

REALITY: Most people don't know the best way to find a job, or they lack marketable job skills. They continue to use ineffective job search methods, such as only responding to classified ads with resumes and cover letters. Opportunities are readily available for individuals who understand the structure and operation of the job market, have appropriate work-content skills, and use job search methods designed for the hidden job market. They must learn to develop an effective networking and informational interviewing campaign for uncovering promising job leads. And they must persist in prospecting for new job leads as well as learn to handle rejections.

MYTH 5: **Employers are in the driver's seat; they have the upper-hand with applicants.**

REALITY: Most often no one is in the driver's seat. Not knowing what they want, many employers make poor hiring decisions. They frequently let applicants define their hiring needs. If you can define employers' needs as your skills, you might end up in the driver's seat!

If you can define employers' needs as your skills, you might end up in the driver's seat!

MYTH 6: **Employers hire the best qualified candidates. Without a great deal of experience and numerous qualifications, I don't have a chance.**

REALITY: Employers hire people for all kinds of reasons. Most rank experience and qualifications third or fourth in their pecking order of hiring criteria. Employers seldom hire the best qualified candidate, because "qualifications" are difficult to define and measure. Employers normally seek people with the following characteristics: competent, intelligent, honest, enthusiastic, and likable. "Likability" tends to be an overall concern of employers—will you "fit in" and get along well with your superiors, co-workers, and clients? Employers want *value* for their money. Therefore, you must communicate to employers that you are such a person. You must overcome employers' objections to any lack of experience or qualifications. But never volunteer your weaknesses. The best qualified person is the one who knows how to get the job—convinces employers that he or she is the *most* desirable for the job.

MYTH 7: **It is best to go into a growing field where jobs are plentiful.**

REALITY: Be careful in following the masses to the "in" fields. First, many so-called growth fields can quickly become no-growth fields, such as aerospace engineering, nuclear energy, and defense contracting. Second, by the time you acquire the necessary skills, you may experience the "disappearing job" phenomenon: too many people did the same thing you did and consequently glut the job market. Third, since many people leave no-growth fields, new opportunities may arise for you. Fourth, if you go after a growth field, you will try to fit into a job rather than find a job fit for you. If you know what you do well and enjoy doing (Chapter 7), and what additional training you may need, you should look for a job or career conducive to your particular mix of skills, interests, and motivations. In the long-run you will be much happier and more productive finding a job fit for you.

If you go after a growth field, you will try to fit into a job rather than find a job fit for you.

MYTH 8: People over 40 have difficulty finding a good job; employers prefer hiring younger and less expensive workers.

REALITY: Yes, if they apply for youth jobs. Age should be an insignificant barrier to employment if you conduct a well organized job search and are prepared to handle this potential negative with employers. Age should be a positive and must be communicated as such. After all, employers want experience, maturity, and stability. People over 40 generally possess these qualities. As the population ages and birth rates decline, older individuals should have a much easier time changing jobs and careers.

MYTH 9: It's best to use an employment firm to find a job.

REALITY: It depends on the firm and the nature of employment you are seeking. Employment firms that specialize in your skill area may be well worth contacting. For example, many law firms use employment firms to hire paralegals rather than directly recruit such personnel themselves. Many employers now use temporary employment firms to recruit both temporary and full-time employees at several different levels, from clerical to professional. Indeed, many temporary employment firms have temp-to-perm programs that link qualified candidates to employers who are looking for full-time employees. But make sure you are working with a legitimate employment firm. Legitimate firms get paid by employers or they collect placement fees from applicants only *after* the applicant has accepted a position. Beware of firms that want up-front fees for promised job placement assistance.

MYTH 10: **I must be aggressive in order to find a job.**

REALITY: Aggressive people tend to be offensive and obnoxious people. Try being purposeful, persistent, and pleasant in all job search activities. Such behavior is well received by potential employers!

MYTH 11: **I should not change jobs and careers more than once or twice. Job-changers are discriminated against in hiring.**

REALITY: While this may have been generally true 30 years ago, it is no longer true today. America is a skills-based society: individuals market their skills to organizations in exchange for money and position. Furthermore, since most organizations are small businesses with limited advancement opportunities, careers quickly plateau for most people. For them, the only way up is to get out and into another organization. Therefore, the best way to advance careers in a society of small businesses is to change jobs frequently. Job-changing is okay as long as such changes demonstrate career advancement and one isn't changing jobs every few months. Most individuals entering the job market today will undergo several career and job changes regardless of their initial desire for a one-job, one-career life plan.

MYTH 12: **People get ahead by working hard and putting in long hours.**

REALITY: Success patterns differ. Many people who are honest, work hard, and put in long hours also get fired, have ulcers, and die young. Some people get ahead even though they are dishonest and lazy. Others simply have good luck or a helpful patron. Moderation in both work and play will probably get you just as far as the extremes. There are other ways, as outlined near the end of this chapter, to become successful in addition to hard work and long hours.

MYTH 13: **I should not try to use contacts or connections to get a job. I should apply through the front door like everyone else. If I'm the best qualified, I'll get the job.**

REALITY: While you may wish to stand in line for tickets, bank deposits, and loans—because you have no clout—standing in line for a job is dumb. Every employer has a front door as well as a back door. Try using the back door if you can. It works in many cases. Chapter 9 outlines in detail how you can develop your contacts, use connections, and enter *both* the front and back doors.

MYTH 14: **I need to get more education and training to qualify for today's jobs.**

REALITY: You may or may not need more education and training, depending on your present skill levels and the needs of employers. What many employers are looking for are individuals who are intelligent, communicate well, take initiative, and are trainable; they train their employees to respond to the needs of their organization. You first need to know what skills you already possess and if they appear appropriate for the types of jobs you are seeking.

MYTH 15: **Once I apply for a job, it's best to wait to hear from an employer.**

REALITY: Waiting is not a good job search strategy. If you want action on the part of the employer, you must first take action. The key to getting a job interview and offer is follow-up, follow-up, follow-up. You do this by making follow-up telephone calls as well as writing follow-up and thank you letters to employers.

GOVERNMENT MYTHS AND REALITIES

While the fifteen myths are relevant to the job market in general and should assist you in penetrating the public sector job market, another twelve myths are particularly relevant for government employment.

MYTH 15: Government agencies are not hiring.

REALITY: Government agencies always hire. They have an average turnover rate of 14 percent. If they did not hire, they would collapse. The fact they don't advertise widely is no reason to believe they are not hiring. Even during cutback periods, hiring takes place. You need to learn how to get information on job vacancies in government.

MYTH 16: Working for the federal government means moving to Washington, DC.

REALITY: Only 13 percent of the federal workforce is located in the Washington Metro area. The remaining 87 percent is spread throughout the country. Mainly centered around 10 regional cities, federal employees also work in small communities, remote areas, and abroad. In fact, you'll be lucky if you get to Washington!

MYTH 17: Competition for government jobs is so great—I don't have a chance.

REALITY: The same is probably true for jobs in the private sector. While government employment is competitive, your chances of getting a job are excellent if you have the right mix of knowledge, skills, and experience and know how to present yourself to agencies. Much of your competition is poorly organized for this job market. Assuming you have the necessary qualifications, the key to success is learning how to best make your application form, resume, and interview stand above the crowd.

MYTH 18: Government salaries are lower than those in the private sector.

REALITY: This may be true if you make $86,589 a year—the most a federal employee on the General Schedule can make. Comparable private sector positions may pay $100,000 or more a year. However, government salaries are very generous in the $20,000 to $50,000 annual salary ranges, especially for generalists and relatively unskilled individuals. Comparable positions in the private sector tend to pay less. Salary inequities are more a problem for individuals making at least $50,000 a year and whose careers have plateaued in the public sector. Despite periodic self-serving studies by government agencies and public employee unions on comparable pay, many government employees are overpaid compared to similar work performed in the private sector.

MYTH 19: **Government work is generally dull, boring, and full of red tape.**

REALITY: Work in general has dull and boring moments. Regardless of how exciting we attempt to make work, only a small percentage of the workforce is fortunate to have jobs they really love. Public organizations have by no means cornered the market on dull and boring jobs and red tape. Large organizations and governmental agencies have similar organizational maladies normally associated with bureaucracy. Like many jobs in the private sector, many government jobs also are exciting, challenging, and devoid of red tape. The quality of the job depends on where you are in the organizational hierarchy and what you are doing.

The real myth is that business and private industry are substantially more efficient and effective than government.

MYTH 20: **A great deal of incompetence and deadwood exists in government.**

REALITY: A great deal of incompetence and deadwood also exists in business and private industry. One major difference is that the private sector periodically cleans out its deadwood during recessions when the red ink requires cost-saving techniques. However, once recessions are over and businesses show profits, they again acquire and keep incompetence and deadwood. Government, on the other hand, operates according to a seniority system: the last hired are the first fired during downsizing periods. In other words, the "new blood" is the first to go. Such a system is structured to keep its deadwood on board. The real myth is that business and private industry are substantially more efficient and effective than government. Remember, over 500,000 businesses fail each year in the United States; many failures are due to mismanagement, incompetence, and deadwood. Government, on the other hand, is not allowed to fail, and thus it lacks a key imperative to clean its house. Moreover, with nearly 13 percent of the workforce unionized, many organizations are constrained in making the necessary personnel decisions to get rid of their incompetence and deadwood.

MYTH 21: Government tends to hire generalists and unskilled individuals.

REALITY: Government tends to hire all types of individuals. It more and more hires qualified specialists who can demonstrate proficiency in particular skill areas. Few government jobs are available for the unskilled.

MYTH 22: The best way to find a government job is to get a high score on an examination.

REALITY: High scores on tests of skills are important, but they do not guarantee you a job. In addition, many government jobs do not require examinations. Depending on which position you apply for, application forms and resumes, along with recommendations and interviews, may be the only screening requirements. You will need to develop informal relationships with individuals in agencies, present yourself well in writing and in person, and follow-through the application process with personal contacts. Chapters 11-19 outline how to best gain entrance into positions in general and government positions in particular.

MYTH 23: Political patronage and personal contacts are still important in getting a government job.

REALITY: Political patronage still exists, but it is by no means widespread. Professional selection procedures and merit systems are firmly entrenched in most governmental units. Who you know, however, can play an important and decisive role in the selection process. But the ubiquitous personal contact and the use of political pull have undergone a positive transformation: personal contacts tend to be professional contacts which help locate and screen qualified candidates. In this sense, personal contacts are important and functional for the employment process.

MYTH 24: **Once I work for government, I will have difficulty finding work in the private sector. Business doesn't want to hire former government employees.**

REALITY: Many government skills are directly transferable to business and industry. For example, firms doing business with government—especially contracting and consulting firms—readily hire former government employees. They need personnel who know the details of government. Indeed, a big revolving door exists between government and business. When you attempt to move from government to the private sector, your major problems will be in the areas of networking and communication. You must learn how to network outside government as well as present yourself in the language and style of business.

Many government skills are directly transferable to business and industry. Indeed, a big revolving door exists between government and business.

MYTH 26 **Government employees work eight-hour days, get generous benefits, and have great job security.**

REALITY: This is true in many cases but not so in other cases. Many government employees, especially in the Washington, DC Metro area, have reputations for hard work and workaholism. Some governments are not too generous with benefits. Job security is not what it used to be. Government bureaucracies are being held more accountable for productivity, which affects work hours, salaries, benefits, and security.

MYTH 27: **It's better to work for government than business—and vice versa.**

REALITY: Yes, most people tend to "stand where they sit"! "Being better" is a function of which side of the fence you are sitting on or where you think the grass is greener at any particular moment. Most jobs are not inherently exciting or rewarding. They are often what you make of them. Organizational charts and job descriptions merely give you a license to do a job. You and others will define the job, including its positives and negatives.

MAJOR REALITIES

The facts of public employment are often quite different from the dominant image and myths guiding job searches. At the very least, you should be aware of these realities when preparing your job search:

1. **The government hires almost every type of skilled worker.** For example, the federal government's workforce includes approximately 150,000 engineers and architects, 120,000 accountants and budget specialists, 120,000 doctors and health specialists, 87,000 scientists, 45,000 social scientists, and 2,700 veterinarians.

2. Regardless of government cutbacks, **public employment opportunities are numerous** and will remain so in the foreseeable future. Indeed, over 2.3 million vacancies occur in government each year. Millions of additional vacancies occur each year with the peripheral public sector organizations.

3. Although the government hiring process is more formalized than hiring in business, **an informal hiring system also operates in government**. This informal system works similarly to the informal system, or "hidden job market", in the private sector. Networking is the key to making the informal system work to one's advantage.

4. **A great deal of mystery and complexity seems to shroud the public sector hiring process**; it dissuades many highly qualified candidates from entering the public sector.

5. **It may take you longer to get a government job than a private sector job** because of more complex hiring procedures in government. On the other hand, some positions in government can be quickly filled—within a matter of minutes.

6. **Government jobs are similar to other jobs**—rewarding and unrewarding, with advantages and disadvantages. Don't expect

too much or too little from public sector jobs. Like jobs elsewhere, government jobs should be viewed as career opportunities.

7. **Government salaries in general compare favorably to private sector salaries**. With benefits included, many government salaries—especially federal—are more generous than comparable positions in the private sector.

8. **Government employees have more long-term job security than employees in business.** However, they pay a price for this security—limitations on salary and career mobility. The limitations reflect the fact that most government employees are not expected to be risk-takers, entrepreneurs, and producers. The system protects them from failure. However, this too, is changing in government as more and more agencies and personnel are being held accountable for producing measurable results.

9. **Successful candidates know how to best get a job they are qualified to perform.** You will have a high probability of entering the public service if you develop the necessary skills and practice effective job search strategies as outlined in subsequent chapters.

10. **The qualifications for government employees are becoming increasingly technical in nature** and require individuals who are well educated and have track records of performance. Like similar positions in the private sector, good jobs in government go do those who have high levels of education and training and who can demonstrate they are "doers".

You should now have a more realistic perspective from which to begin answering the questions we posed at the beginning of this chapter: "Where are the jobs, and how do I get one?" This chapter presented a basic orientation. Chapters 4 and 5 provide details on the important "where" of the public sector job market. Chapters 6, 7, 8, and 9 outline the critical "how". The remainder of the book links the "where" to the "how" in presenting strategies for taking effective action within the public sector job market.

4

YOUR OPPORTUNITY STRUCTURE FOR NETWORKING

The public sector encompasses a network of organizations and relationships centered around various governmental and public functions. From a public employment perspective, this network is an "opportunity structure" for potential job seekers. It is composed of numerous jobs relating to government and the public sector. Movement within this network takes place through a combination of personal contacts, formal application procedures, and placement services.

As you begin your job search in the public sector, you should primarily concentrate on developing networks within this opportunity structure. The process of developing and using networks in this manner is commonly referred to as "networking" your way to a job that is right for you. This chapter presents a framework for understanding the basic elements of these structures as well as specifies the necessary networking for being successful in finding a public sector job. Chapter 9 outlines detailed networking strategies for implementing your job search.

COMMUNITY NETWORKS AND LINKAGES

It is useful to view communities as made up of interacting social, economic, political, and governmental structures. Comprising a potential network of job opportunities, these structures also extend beyond single communities. Corporations, associations, and political, social, cultural, and educational affiliations link individuals and organizations to other communities as well as to the state, national, and international levels. Most communities have similar networks, even though the individuals, groups, and institutions may differ.

While communities differ in many respects, the institutional actors and their games are relatively predictable from one community to another. The Yellow Pages of your telephone book, for example, identify the major players in this game: banks, mortgage companies, advertising firms, car dealers, schools, churches, small businesses, industries, hospitals, law firms, governments, and civic and voluntary groups. Each player pursues its own interests. While internal power structures exist, no one player dominates the game all of the time. Numerous groups overlap with one another because of shared economic, political, and social interests. Banks, for example, must loan money to businesses and churches. Businesses, in turn, need educational institutions for personnel, expertise, and markets. And educational institutions need businesses and government to absorb their graduates. Dependent upon one another, the players tend to compete, cooperate, and co-op one another to ensure the successful continuation of the game. Overlapping memberships on school boards, medical boards, and boardrooms of banks and corporations give the appearance of a centralized power structure. But in reality power is diffused in what is essentially a decentralized and fragmented decision-making system.

These networks and opportunity structures also extend to other communities. During the past 50 years, local institutions have become integrated into a larger economic, social, cultural, and political system by means of corporations, associations, and affiliations. For example, today's small mom-and-pop business is most likely affiliated with a relevant professional association headquartered in Washington, DC, New York City, or Chicago. Professional associations provide a variety of support services to members: lobbying, resource and information centers, training, consulting, newsletters, journals, and insurance. The day of the large firm owned by a local family has largely passed in favor of corporations headquartered outside the community.

The organizations linked within and beyond communities comprise your opportunity structure for penetrating both the advertised and hidden job markets. You will need to identify both the organizations and the linkages by conducting research with individuals who occupy positions within the networks.

PERIPHERAL INSTITUTIONS

The basic public sector network consists of federal, state, and local government institutions interacting with a variety of peripheral institutions. While many of the peripheral institutions actively influence the content and/or implementation of government policies, government agencies also actively influence the activities of other peripheral institutions to achieve certain public policy goals. The figure on page 16 of Chapter 2 outlines the basic elements and relationships of the public sector network. This network consists of six distinct groups of interrelated nongovernmental organizations focused on public sector issues.

Trade and professional associations are good examples of major peripheral institutions involved in influencing public policy. Representing dues-paying members, these organizations either pursue a monetary interest or promote the advancement of knowledge. Many associations have permanent staffs—mainly located in state capitals, Washington, DC, New York City, and Chicago—which lobby both legislatures and executive agencies on a full-time basis. The largest association is the American Association of Retired Persons with 32 million members and a staff of 1,200 individuals located in Washington, DC. Hundreds of large associations have annual budgets of more than $5 million, employ staffs of 50 or more individuals, and maintain Political Action Committees (PACs) to help fund the election or re-election campaigns of their favorite presidential and congressional candidates. In addition to providing specific services to their members, trade associations lobby legislators to influence the content of public policy. They lobby agencies to alter the implementation of legislation and agency directives. Furthermore, many of these organizations retain lawyers who influence the interpretation of public policies in the courts. These organizations are possible targets for your job search. Approximately 100,000 associations operate at the state level. Over 2,300 associations are located in and around Washington, DC—twice the number of a decade ago.

Other groups also influence public policy. Many are single issue ad hoc groups lacking permanent organizations and staffs. Several associations are very small and thus rely on *professional association management firms* to conduct their affairs. The largest and oldest such firm is the Washington-based Smith, Bucklin and Associates. Established nearly 35 years ago, it currently provides services in the areas of government relations, trade show management and promotion, generic market development, public relations, statistical surveys and reporting, financial management, membership development, and travel and transportation to more than 100 small associations. While small associations offer few job opportunities relating to the public sector, the association management firms are an increasing source of public job opportunities.

A second grouping of peripheral institutions relevant to your job search are **contracting and consulting firms**. They constitute one of the most dynamic growth sectors relating to government. Thousands of these organizations specialize in various government functions and activities, from producing complex weapons systems to managing day-care centers. While many of these firms are small—with staffs of five to ten individuals—others are extremely large with staffs of over 10,000. Martin Marietta Corporation, the nation's largest defense contractor, has over 90,000 employees. These are the specialists and technocrats whose career paths involve circulating in and out of government (the "revolving door") as well as among firms doing government business. Most of these firms are located in the Washington, DC—Virginia—Maryland Metropolitan area, New York, and Chicago.

Firms diversified in several government activities tend to be more stable and capable of weathering periodic downturns in economic and budgetary cycles.

Contracting and consulting firms fall into two categories according to their size and degree of diversification. First, several firms are solely specialized in government business. Some firms specialize in a single area—construction, energy systems, procurement, mass transit, defense systems, planning, or management training. Others are diversified into several related areas, such as defense systems, energy systems, and procurement. Bechtel Corporation, for example, has over 33,000 employees in the United States and abroad. It provides government and management consulting, procurement, engineering, and construction services in such diverse fields as nuclear power, mining, irrigation, mass transit, petrochemicals, conservation, food, land management, and airport development. With nearly 100 percent of their business tied to government, these organizations tend to be vulnerable to the shifting budgetary priorities of government. Indeed, many firms specializing in a single government area went bankrupt during the recessions of the 1970s, 1980s, and 1990s. Several firms specializing in defense systems in the 1990s are following suit as government enters a period of major cutbacks in military expenditures. However, firms diversified in several government activities tend to be more stable and capable of weathering periodic downturns in economic and budgetary cycles.

A second set of contracting and consulting firms consists of organizations doing business in both the public and private sectors. Coopers and

Lybrand, a British-based multinational, for example, has offices in 97 countries and employs 30,000. They specialize in over 50 technical areas relevant to finance and management. Other examples include large corporations which maintain government contracting divisions. Major auto, aircraft, shipbuilding, and high tech industries—such as Chrysler, Boeing, IBM, and Texas Instruments—have such divisions. Many of these firms do a great amount of work with the U.S. Department of Defense. Straddling both public and private sectors, their public divisions perform two important international organizational functions: (1) acquire public funds for research and development activities important for future corporate development, and (2) serve as a buffer against private market fluctuations.

Texas Instruments is a case in point. During the early 1980s Texas Instruments laid off nearly 10,000 employees due to declining private market shares precipitated by its failures in the digital watch and microcomputer markets. However, its defense contracting division actually increased in both budget and personnel during this same period. This division generates important research and development activities to help Texas Instruments develop new products for the private sector market. Important research and development activities—normally scaled down during recessions—can continue given a safety net of federal contracts. It will be interesting to see how Texas Instruments adjusts to a new period of major cutbacks in military expenditures attendant with the restructuring of public budgetary priorities in the 1990s.

A third major group of peripheral institutions are **nonprofit organizations**. While all associations and foundations as well as many consulting firms have nonprofit tax status, they are not nonprofit organizations in terms of their public orientations. Most groups we consider to be nonprofit organizations are organizations specifically structured to pursue a particular social, political, or economic course. They receive the bulk of their funding from some combination of government grants and contracts, private foundation grants, and public donations. In contrast to associations and consulting firms which influence both the formation and implementation of public policy, government agencies often use nonprofit organizations to pursue public goals within the scope of their missions. By providing funds for various categories of programs, government becomes a major interest group of what are ostensibly private, nonprofit organizations.

Thousands of nonprofit organizations are found at the local, state, national, and international levels. At the local level, many nonprofits, such as the Salvation Army, YWCA, and the Red Cross, are known as community service organizations. Many of these and other local nonprofits are branches of national and state organizations. International nonprofits, such as CARE and Catholic Relief Services, have annual budgets of more the $250 million and staffs of more than 175 full-time employees.

A fourth category of peripheral institutions are **foundations**. These are primarily philanthropic organizations which provide funding for nonprofit organizations. However, some foundations, especially those operating in the international arena, provide services similar to nonprofit organizations. At the local level, community foundations and the United Way are most active. At the national and international levels, some of the larger foundations include the Lily Endowment, Rockefeller Foundation, and the Johnson Foundation.

Our fifth major category of peripheral public service institutions are **research organizations**. Many operate similarly to consulting firms, nonprofit organizations, and universities. Their basic goal is to generate new knowledge for improving the public policy process. Examples of such groups include the Rand Corporation, Stanford Research Institute (SRI), Hoover Institute, American Enterprise Institute, Brookings Institution, and the Urban Institute.

Our final category of peripheral institutions consists of several **political support, influence, and management groups**. Political Action Committees, political parties, professional lobbyists, lawyers, and political consultants are in the business of financing and winning election campaigns as well as influencing the shape of public policy. Several of these organizations are closely linked to trade associations and key personnel on Capitol Hill and in the White House.

KEY RELATIONSHIPS

Each of the six peripheral networks has its own hiring culture and formal and informal employment assistance networks. For example, many nonprofit organizations operating in the international arena belong to InterAction, a Washington, DC-based professional association promoting the work of its members. It publishes a weekly newsletter, *Monday Developments*, which lists vacancies with member organizations. Access, a New York City-based group promoting nonprofit organizations, publishes a monthly newspaper for job hunters—*Community Jobs*. Many associations belong to the American Society of Association Executives which operates its own placement service for member organizations. Two weekly association newspapers—*Association Trends* and *United States Association Executive*—regularly include job vacancy announcements as well as available candidates in its job market sections.

Most individuals will work for a particular type of peripheral organization and advance within the hierarchy of organizations which make up the particular group of organizations. Their career tends to focus on the public sector network—government, associations, consulting firms, nonprofit organizations, foundations, and research organizations.

Other individuals make career transitions from government to associations and from these to consulting firms, or from nonprofits to associations and consulting firms. Many employees of associations and consulting firms at one time worked for government. Indeed, one essential qualification for many positions is previous government experience. At the same time, many government employees previously worked for these organizations. A "revolving door" phenomenon—the movement of personnel from government agencies to peripheral public service organizations and back—is evident at all levels of government. While this phenomenon is especially visible between members of legislative institutions (committee and staff members) and businesses (particularly associations, lobbying groups, and law firms), it is less visible, but extremely prevalent, between executive agencies and consulting and contracting firms.

As you prepare for a public career or plan to advance within the public sector, you need to become more aware of both the employment networks within each institutional complex as well as networks for making transitions from one type of public organization to another. Your ability to make job moves within and between public institutions will provide you with the greatest degree of career mobility possible in the public sector.

PREVALENCE OF NETWORKS

The prevalence of these networks and the extent of public employment opportunities is mainly a function of the size and location of government institutions. Rural county governments, for example, deal with few peripheral organizations. Small municipalities are involved with local law firms and companies providing basic infrastructural engineering and construction services, such as streets, sewers, water, and public buildings. Faculty from local colleges or universities may offer limited, ad hoc consulting services in the areas of social welfare and management systems. Local governments also lobby state legislatures and executive agencies. One permanent staff member—on a part-time basis—often performs this function by shuttling back and forth to the state capital. The mayor or city manager may lobby on important issues.

At the state level, larger municipalities tend to have a permanent staff presence as well as use professional associations, lobbyists, and law firms. In addition, several consulting and contracting firms specialize in municipal contracts. Many of these firms are based in state capitals and in Washington, DC rather than in local communities. Cities such as New York, Chicago, and Los Angeles have their own local revolving doors. As cities increasingly privatize municipal services—such as mass transit, sanitation, and water—more opportunities should develop for consulting firms at the local level.

Opportunity networks are increasingly evident at the state level. Law firms and representatives of professional associations and interest groups lobby state legislatures and agencies. Consulting and contracting firms vie for business with state agencies. Many firms operate only within a particular state. Multi-state firms, such as Bechtel, have branch offices at the state level to generate business with state and local governments.

AT THE CENTER

Washington, DC has a well defined network of opportunity structures. This network provides thousands of alternative job opportunities for enterprising individuals willing to work in the nation's capital. Trade and professional associations alone employ nearly 100,000 individuals in the Washington Metropolitan area.

The ubiquitous "personal contact" provides access to influential people who can be helpful in making job and career moves.

Job-changing from Congress to agencies to associations to consulting and contracting firms is a time-honored practice in Washington. The ubiquitous "personal contact" provides access to influential people who can be helpful in making job and career moves within and among various organizations dependent upon government business. For example, the following political and administrative institutions function as "alternative opportunity structures": congressional staffs, congressional committees, congressional subcommittees, congressional bureaucracy, executive staff, departments, independent executive agencies, and independent regulatory agencies. Each of these institutions generates thousands of job opportunities and recruits on the basis of different personnel practices. Outside, but linked to the federal government are the five types of peripheral groups as outlined on page 16 of Chapter 2. A disproportionate number of these groups are headquartered in the Washington Metropolitan area. These groups provide employment and career advancement opportunities for individuals in the public sector job market.

For years Washington insiders have learned how to use these networks to advance their careers. A frequent career pattern is to work in a federal agency for three or four years. During that time you make important contacts on Capitol Hill with congressional staffs and committees as well as with contractors and associations. Since you have specialized knowledge on the inner workings of government, you have important skills to offer other groups. And if you change jobs frequently, you may be able to advance your career quickly. Indeed, in contrast to job-changers in many other communities, the job-changer in Washington, DC is often seen as someone "in demand" rather than someone with an unstable employment pattern!

The job-changer in Washington, DC is often seen as someone "in demand" rather than someone with an unstable employment pattern!

NETWORKING

Using specific strategies and techniques designed for acquiring information and contacts through people to move within these structures is also known as "networking". You must network to be effective in the public sector job market. Effective networking strategies and techniques are outlined in Chapter 9. Specific networking methods for various types of public sector institutions are examined in chapters of Parts IV, V, and VI on dealing with government and the periphery.

Throughout the remainder of this book we examine two types of networks and networking phenomena—one you create and another already created for your use. The first is **interpersonal networks**. This involves the use of prospecting techniques to generate informational interviews which result in useful job information, advice, and referrals to other informed individuals who generate additional information, advice, and referrals within an ever expanding job search network. Similar to establishing new clients in sales, you take the initiative to develop these networks in hopes they will eventually result in sales. In the job search, "sales" are job interviews and job offers.

The second type of network and networking involves **formal job services networks**. This consists of established groups and organizations specifically designed to provide employment assistance to job seekers. These networks provide all types of assistance, from informal job clubs to job listings, placement services, and electronic job search databases. Dealing with these networks involves locating the services and fully using the most useful components of the services. Government agencies, as well as each of the six peripheral groups, have established various types of these networks. Some are better organized and more useful than others. Indeed, the effectiveness of some services—especially those found among associations—provides a refreshing look at an employment phenomenon unknown to many career counselors and job seekers.

5

JOB AND CAREER ALTERNATIVES

*N*umerous job alternatives are available for individuals who understand the size, structure, requirements, and trends of today's job market. Altogether, the American workforce consists of approximately 125 million jobs. According to the *Dictionary of Occupational Titles*, published by the U.S. Department of Labor, these jobs fall into nearly 14,000 categories. With approximately one-third of all jobs relating to the public sector, public employment alternatives are nearly as numerous as those in the private sector.

JOB GROWTH AND TRANSFORMATION

During the past three decades, an incredible number of new jobs were created in both the public and private sectors. This period of major demographic and economic change transformed the basic nature of the job market. Between 1955 and 1980, for instance, the number of jobs increased from 68.7 million to 105.6 million—an average annual increase of 1.5 million new jobs. During the 1970s, jobs increased by over 2 million each year. Between 1980 and 1985, 2.2 to 2.7 million jobs were created each year for an annual growth rate of 1.6 to 2.4 percent.

Job growth during the 1990s is expected to slow but remain steady at about 1.5 million new jobs each year, reflecting the coming demographic changes in society. By the year 2000 the labor force should consist of nearly 140 million workers—up 15 percent from 1990.

The remarkable growth in jobs during the past decade took place despite recurring recessions and cutbacks in public employment. Both the economy and workforce underwent major transformations which have important implications for the future job market. Among these changes were shifts from:

- Blue collar to white collar occupations.
- Manufacturing occupations to service occupations.
- Primarily male workforce to an more balanced male-female workforce.
- Old technology to new technology in the workplace.
- Single job and career pattern to a multi-job and career pattern.
- Narrow specialization to flexible specialization requiring continuous retraining.
- A smokestack economy to a service and high-tech economy.
- Old manufacturing centers in the Northeast and Midwest to new manufacturing, service, and high-tech centers in the South and West.

While the 1980s witnessed a fundamental restructuring of the economy and job market, job trends for the 1990s appear to be in the following directions:

1. **Shortage of competent workers,** with basic literacy and learning skills, creates serious problems in developing an economy with an adequate work force for the jobs of the 90s.

2. **Boom and bust economic cycles will continue through the 1990s** as the economy experiences a combination of good times and bad times which, in turn, create a great deal of uncertainty for planning individual careers and lifestyles.

3. **Millions of jobs will be created and eliminated** through the 1990s. New jobs will be created at the rate of 1 to 2 million each year, with some boom years resulting in the creation of 3 million new jobs. At the same time, nearly 1 million new jobs will be eliminated each year. In the midst of these changes nearly 20 million Americans will experience some form of unemployment each year; between 6 and 12 million Americans will be unemployed each day.

4. **The rapidly expanding service sector will create the largest number of new jobs.** These will be disproportionately found at the two extreme ends of the job market—high paying jobs requiring high-level skills and low paying jobs requiring few specialized skills.

5. **Structural unemployment will accelerate** due to a combination of business failures in the boom-bust economy and continuing productivity improvements in both the manufacturing and service sectors as new technology and improved decision-making and management systems are introduced to the workplace.

6. **Thousands of stagnant communities will generate few job and career opportunities.** "Rust belt" and "welfare-subsidy" communities, and those lacking a diversified service economy, will provide few job opportunities in the decade ahead.

7. **Public policy failures** to resolve education, training, and unemployment problems as well as initiate effective job generation, relocation, and job search approaches for promoting a more employable society will continue throughout the 1990s.

8. **A renewed and strong U.S. manufacturing sector** will create few new jobs; service industries will be responsible for most job growth throughout the 1990s.

9. **Unemployment remains high,** fluctuating between a low of 5 percent and a high of 12 percent.

10. **Government efforts to stimulate employment** continue to be concentrated at the periphery of the job market.

11. **The U.S. deficit declines** and trade becomes more balanced as the U.S. regains a more competitive international trade and debt position due to improved productivity of U.S. manufacturing industries and the devaluation of the U.S. dollar.

12. **A series of domestic and international crises**—shocks and "unique events", some that already occurred in the 1980s—emerge in the 1990s to create new boom and bust cycles contributing to high rates of unemployment.

13. **A major shortage of skilled craftspeople** will create numerous production and service problems throughout the 1990s.

14. **Fewer young people will be available for entry-level positions** during the 1990s as baby-boomers reach middle age and as the birth-rate continues at a near zero-population growth rate.

15. **More job and career choices will be available for the elderly.**

16. **More blacks and Hispanics will enter the job market** due to their disproportionately high birth rates and immigration.

17. **Women will continue to enter the labor market,** accounting for over 60 percent female participation during the 1990s.

18. **More immigrants will enter the U.S.**—both legally and illegally—to meet labor shortages at all levels.

19. **Part-time and temporary employment opportunities will increase.**

20. **White-collar employment will continue to expand** in the fast growing service sector.

21. **The need for a smarter work force** with specific technical skills will continue to impact on the traditional American educational system with a demand for greater job market relevance in educational curriculum.

22. **Union membership will continue to decline** as more blue-collar manufacturing jobs disappear and interest in unions wanes among both blue and white-collar employees.

23. **The population will continue to move into suburban and semi-rural communities** as the new high-tech industries and services move in this direction.

24. **The population, along with wealth and economic activity, will continue to shift into the West, Southwest, and Florida.** This will be at the expense of the Northeast and Pacific regions.

25. **The number of small businesses will continue to increase** as new opportunities for entrepreneurs arise in response to the high-tech and service revolutions and as more individuals find new opportunities to experiment with re-careering.

26. **Major job growth will take place among small companies** and millions of new start-up businesses as large companies continue to cutback personnel and operations.

27. **Opportunities for career advancement will be increasingly limited within more organizations.**

28. **Job satisfaction will become a major problem** as many organizations will experience difficulty in retaining highly qualified personnel.

29. **Many employers will resort to new and unorthodox hiring practices** and improved working conditions in order to recruit and retain critical personnel.

30. **Job-hopping will increase** as more and more individuals learn about the importance of changing jobs and careers for career advancement.

PUBLIC SECTOR JOBS

The composition of government employment also has undergone major transformation since 1950. Similar to changes in the private sector workplace, government employs more white collar and female workers than ever before. The jobs require greater specialization, and new technologies are rapidly being introduced into the workplace.

The increase in government employment, especially at the state and local levels, has been more dramatic than in the private sector—361 percent increase for state governments and 289 percent increase for local government versus 90 percent increase in the overall job market. Since 1950, federal government employment increased by only 36 percent. While a disproportionate amount of the state and local government increase was in education—responding to the post-World War II baby boom children entering public schools—increases were across-the-board in every government occupational category. Government simply grew and grew.

Ironically, the number of governmental units dramatically declined during this same period of major growth in public employment. In the early 1950s, for example, the American governmental system consisted of nearly 150,000 units of government. Today, the same system consists of more than 86,000 governmental units. Most of the decline was due to a major reform movement in the immediate post-World War II period to consolidate school and special districts. While the consolidation eliminated nearly half of the American government system, it retained, in a much expanded form, one of the key dynamics of this system—executive bureaucracies which continuously increased their personnel.

These transformations as well as recent changes in government policies toward deficit spending, decentralization, and privatization of government functions has generated several trends for the public sector job market. Among these are:

1. **Slow and declining growth in state and local governments:** Growth in state and local government employment will continue to slow at the rate of the 1980s. This decline will be most evident in the case of secondary and higher education—the areas with the highest concentration of state and local employees.

2. **Stability and incremental growth in federal employment:** Federal employment will remain relatively stable over the next decade. Continuing efforts to control budgetary deficits will ensure recurring freezes on hiring new personnel and the creation of few new positions and programs. On the other hand, some agencies will experience major personnel increases while others will experience personnel cuts, depending on shifting policy priorities. For example, the Department of Defense is likely to undergo a 10-15 percent cut in personnel while the Department of Justice and the Federal Deposit Insurance Corporation will probably increase personnel by 15-20 percent.

3. **Declines in defense-related employment:** The impact of major military and economic changes in Eastern Europe and the former Soviet Union will create new opportunities to restructure federal budgetary priorities. Both civilian and military employment within the Department of Defense is likely to decline by 10-15 percent, or by nearly 400,000 employees, over the next decade; defense contractors are likely to experience a 30 percent decline in government business over the same period. Most defense contractors employing a disproportionate number of high-tech personnel responsible for developing sophisticated military hardware systems are especially in for a decade of hard times. Cutbacks in military spending and employment are more likely to be applied toward lowering the federal budgetary deficit than reallocated toward social and environmental programs.

4. **Continuing growth of associations and movement of headquarter operations to Washington, DC:** As the trade sector rapidly expands over the next decade, associations will become larger, provide more services to their members, and increase their lobbying and public relations activities. More associations will move their headquarters to the Washington Metro area where they will constitute a rapidly expanding labor market of association specialists. Coupled with the continuing growth in contracting activities and a rapidly growing private sector, the Washington Metro area will remain one of the country's five hottest job markets throughout the 1990s.

The Washington Metro area will remain one of the country's five hottest job markets throughout the 1990s.

5. **Consulting and contracting businesses will expand considerably at all levels:** While government employment at all levels will remain relatively stable, government budgets will continue to increase in most areas except military spending. Much of the increase will go for purchasing public services from consulting and contracting firms. Excepting the Department of Defense, where nearly 30,000 acquisitions positions will be eliminated, procurement elsewhere in government will become an even bigger business during the 1990s.

6. **Nonprofit organizations and nongovernmental organizations (NGOs) will increase the scope of their activities:** Both government and private foundations will further expand their funding of nonprofit organizations and NGOs to achieve public goals largely relinquished by government agencies. Government agencies will further move to privatize public functions through these organizations.

7. **Research organizations will play a more important role in government:** Government agencies will increasingly purchase information gathering and analysis from private research organizations rather than increase their own specialized in-house information gathering, processing, and analytical capabilities.

8. **Professional lobbying organizations, association management firms, and law firms representing businesses and associations will continue to expand:** As associations expand in number and size, they will require the specialized legal, management, and political services of groups organized to provide such services.

9. **International opportunities will increase for experienced professionals:** While international job and career opportunities have been limited during the past decade, they should begin increasing in the 1990s due to political and economic changes in Eastern Europe and the former Soviet Union, the continuing political turmoil in the Middle East and Central America, new economic structures in Western Europe, and the astronomical growth of Asian economies. While few new opportunities will be available within the federal government, most will be found among contracting and consulting firms funded by government to provide various forms of economic assistance.

10. **More and more government employees will seek public service careers outside government:** As government continues to redefine its "public" role and provide a more portable pension system and as government employees experience limited career growth, plateau their careers, receive fewer retirement benefits, increasingly play routine contracting and procurement roles, and become more aware of public service careers outside government, they will seek to make successful career transitions to nongovernmental public organizations.

The overall trend for the public sector over the next decade will be slow growth in government institutions, especially executive bureaucracies. Government spending will continue to increase, but the number of government personnel and direct services performed by government agencies will remain stable, with a few cases of major increases and declines in personnel. Major growth, however, will take place among most peripheral institutions. Rather than witness a shrinking public sector, over the next decade we should see steady growth among nongovernmental institutions involved with public policy issues. In so doing, the role of government will increasingly shift toward that of a contractor directing public funds into organizations which have the capabilities to provide public services efficiently and effectively. Government agencies will become more like interest groups as they attempt to influence the direction and activities of these nongovernmental public institutions. Government jobs will increasingly emphasize the importance of managing these nongovernmental organizations.

GOVERNMENT INSTITUTIONS AND MULTIPLE BUREAUCRACIES

Consisting of 86,743 units of government and over 18 million public employees and despite cutbacks and no-growth trends, today's governmental system yields numerous job opportunities in thousands of job categories. Except for many manufacturing and sales occupations, most job categories found in the private sector also have counterparts in government. Since government produces both goods and services, numerous occupational skills can be transferred from the private sector into government, and vice versa.

The major opportunities for government jobs are primarily found within four units of government: federal, state, municipal, and county. Townships, school districts, and special districts yield a sizeable number of jobs, but they tend to have limited job alternatives, salaries, and advancement opportunities. Taken together, this is a highly fragmented system of government where no one is really in control.

Federal employment opportunities remain relatively constant. The federal government hires about 1,000 individuals each day. This mainly represents replacement of existing personnel who have an average annual turnover rate of 14 percent. The federal government hires individuals in thousands of job categories. After all, it engages in a broad spectrum of activities, ranging from managing large self-contained communities, such as military bases and the Pentagon, to the more mundane and stereotypical aspects of government. Work of federal employees includes:

- Issuing social security checks, welfare payments, and intergovernmental funds.
- Regulating private industry.
- Managing public lands and water resources.
- Extending aid to cities and states.
- Conducting research.
- Providing health care.
- Publishing books and documents.
- Stimulating entrepreneurship and business investment.
- Dispensing grants and loans.
- Regulating trade.
- Protecting minorities.
- Printing and managing money.
- Developing communication and security systems.
- Delivering mail.
- Policing individuals and organizations.
- Exploring outer space, the oceans, and polar regions.
- Gathering and analyzing demographic, economic, and social data.
- Maintaining public buildings, monuments, and cemeteries.

- Assisting the international community.
- Incarcerating criminals.
- Providing support services for all of its activities.
- Collecting artifacts and memorabilia.
- Housing public employees.
- Gathering intelligence on potential enemies.

Such a variety of activities means there are many types of government jobs available, including those for: janitors, drivers, groundskeepers, undertakers, typists, secretaries, plumbers, mechanics, typesetters, printers, teachers, scientists, researchers, policy analysts, grants specialists, case workers, lawyers, program officers, artists, movie directors, and clergymen. The list goes on and on.

State employment opportunities also run the gamut with education being the largest single category of state employment. State governments require a large variety of employees to manage increasingly complex organizational activities. Indeed, during the past two decades, state governments have asserted stronger governance roles with new and expanded functions. State governments tend to perform more indirect regulatory and administrative services than do local governments, especially in the areas of inspecting, licensing, and collecting revenue. Major direct services provided by state governments tend to be in the areas of higher education, welfare, mental health, highway maintenance and safety, and parks and recreation. Most of these state services have federal government counterparts.

Municipal employment opportunities are tied to specific city services. While city governments are supposed to have a single bureaucracy, in practice three bureaucracies tend to operate simultaneously, each in response to a particular set of local functions and constituents. The first bureaucracy relates to education. Even when education is placed under city government—rather than in special districts (45 of 50 states)—educators tend to be managed by a separate bureaucracy. This bureaucracy has its own rules and regulations as well as separate personnel and wage systems. In some communities the education bureaucracy may constitute 30 to 40 percent of all public employees.

The second bureaucracy relates to public safety, especially police and fire. They, too, constitute a bureaucracy within a bureaucracy, structured similarly to a military organization with separate rules and regulations and personnel and wage systems. In addition, this group tends to be more highly organized and militant than other municipal employees.

The final bureaucracy includes the diverse group of remaining city employees. Relatively unorganized and specialized in particular functions, this bureaucracy has numerous subgroups which tend to be relatively autonomous. In many communities, the parks and recreation department has experienced significant growth during the past two decades.

Overall, city governments tend to be *internally decentralized and fragmented*, posing particular challenges to job seekers who often assume most job action is centralized around the personnel department. Similar situations prevail in the cases of state and federal governments where the hiring process is largely decentralized within individual agencies.

Depending on the specific state and community, school districts, townships, and a variety of special districts may function within and around urban areas. In some cases—especially in the Northeast and Midwest—the number and variety of these local government organizations overlap and conflict in a truly mind-boggling manner. Illinois, for example, has about twice as many local jurisdictions per capita than most states—the epitome of a government jungle! Organized chaos is the fundamental characteristic of government in these areas. In spite of major and successful efforts to consolidate these units in the 1950s, an incredible number of overlapping jurisdictions, inefficiency of operations, and just pure chaos remains. Such a local government structure gives the American governmental system the image of being an essentially decentralized, fragmented, and chaotic system—an image it justly deserves.

For the job seeker, these local units of government offer numerous job opportunities and challenges. However, on the whole, they do not offer great opportunities. Because of their small size, the economies of scale do not permit them to offer generous salaries, benefits, and advancement opportunities. Managerially, they lack sufficient resources and thus are often frustrating units of government. Governmental units with substantial functions encompassing a population of at least 200,000 are most likely to yield significant job opportunities. Municipalities and counties—not special districts, townships, and school districts—tend to meet this criteria.

County governments are perhaps the most overlooked units of local government. This is unfortunate, because in many cases they offer good job opportunities with adequate salaries, benefits, and advancement opportunities. Gone are the days when most counties were essentially rural and dominated by political machines. Today, the majority of counties are urban and are increasingly staffed by professionals. Indeed, recent trends in local government are to transfer more and more municipal services to the urban county level. In metropolitan areas, it makes both economic and political sense to transfer such major municipal services as police, fire, mass transit, sanitation, and education to the county level. Where politically feasible, urban county governments should grow considerably over the next two decades as a new reform movement further consolidates local governments. The growth in urban county governments will most likely be at the expense of city bureaucracies.

Take, for example, the county in which we live. In Prince William County (Virginia) the number of county government employees doubled from 1980 to 1990—reflecting a doubling of the county population during this same period. Within the next decade employment with Prince

William county government should nearly triple as the county continues to experience unprecedented population growth.

Examples of consolidated urban governments includes Los Angeles County, Miami-Dade County, and Fairfax County adjacent to Washington, DC. In the Washington Metro area alone several urban county governments in Maryland and Virginia have undergone phenomenal growth in population, revenue, and public services in the period 1960 to 1986. Montgomery (Maryland) County's budget went from $54 million to $967.6 million; Prince George's (Maryland) County's budget increased from $21.9 million to $605 million; and Fairfax (Virginia) County's budget grew from $21.1 million to $783.8 million during this 26 year period. These counties provide models for other urban counties as well as for what many observers believe is the coming consolidation movement at the local level.

PERIPHERAL GROUPS

The periphery consists of numerous institutions and organizations which regularly interact with government as well as pursue public goals. It includes both profit and nonprofit organizations as well as voluntary groups. The total number of job opportunities with these organizations is difficult to accurately estimate. A conservative figure is at least another 18 million positions are found among peripheral organizations in the public sector.

The Washington, DC Metro public sector network is a good example. Although many people still believe government employs a majority of the workforce in and around Washington, beginning in 1983 government ranked second to private business. More than 50 percent of the job opportunities in the Washington Metro area are found in the nongovernmental "service" sector—contracting and consulting firms; law and public relations firms; professional and trade associations; nonprofit organizations; foundations; and research organizations. This sector should continue to grow in direct proportion to the growth in the federal budget.

At the state and local levels, similar growth has taken place in this nongovernmental service sector. Lacking specific data on the size and shape of the sector, our best guess is that it continues to grow in spite of state and local government cutbacks. Moreover, we expect the periphery to expand as state and local governments shift more functions to private sector organizations. Expect public employment to level off at the state and local levels, even though budgets will continue to increase. Following the pattern at the federal level, state and local governments will probably intensify the contracting-out of public services. In addition, local governments will privatize more of their basic service functions.

While peripheral organizations at the state and local levels include associations, consulting firms, foundations, and lobbying groups, numerous nonprofit organizations are also prevalent. The United Way and

Red Cross, for example, are large organizations in terms of both budget and personnel. Operating mainly in municipalities, they offer job opportunities for enterprising public sector job seekers. Hundreds of other nonprofit community service organizations also generate employment alternatives.

INTERNATIONAL ARENA

Identifying as well as structuring a job search aimed at the international public sector is often difficult to do. The international arena is extremely fragmented, and information is difficult to access. Nonetheless, numerous and exciting job opportunities exist in this arena.

The international public sector consists of many international-oriented state and local government agencies, federal agencies, regulatory and development organizations, research and consulting firms, nonprofit organizations, international organizations, and an assortment of organizations difficult to classify. A majority of these organizations provide development assistance to Third and Fourth World countries. Others focus on strengthening economic, political, and military relations among both developed and developing countries. Many are oriented toward U.S. foreign policy interests.

Both state agencies and local governments are involved in international affairs. States with international trade and tourism interests, such as California, Illinois, New York, and Florida, will have positions relevant to developing international relations. Many of these positions will be directly attached to the Governor's office or found in trade sections of commerce departments. Some large cities also have positions in their economic development departments for promoting foreign investment and tourism. Employees in these positions are expected to develop public relations approaches and establish contacts with potential clients both in the U.S. and abroad. Realizing both the reality and importance of foreign investment in the U.S., an increasing number of cities are beginning to establish international relations requiring qualified international personnel. In many large cities, World Affairs Councils—comprised of local officials, business leaders, and educators—join together in promoting local interest in international issues.

The federal government is a major employer of international specialists. In addition to the Department of State and the Department of Defense, every department and numerous agencies have either direct or counterpart international interests requiring full-time international specialists and related support personnel. Trade negotiators, commercial officers, Foreign Service Officers, cultural affairs officers, foreign intelligence officers, agronomists, economists, policy analysts, engineers, doctors, teachers, and librarians are only a few of the many international jobs available. Within the Executive Office of the President, the Council of Economic Advisors, National Security Council, Office of Management and Budget, Office of Science and Technology, and Office of the U.S. Trade Representative have major international interests and thus employ international specialists.

Within the Executive Departments, over 100 agencies have international interests and employ international specialists. Independent and quasi-governmental agencies also have international interests and employees as do the lesser known federal commissions, committees, and advisory groups.

Within the legislative branch of the federal government, the House and Senate committee and personal staffs as well as the legislative bureaucracy, primarily consisting of the Congressional Budget Office, General Accounting Office, and the Library of Congress, provide international employment opportunities.

Related to U.S. government involvement in international affairs are numerous international consulting and research firms based in the United States and abroad. The consulting firms generally provide services to government in the areas of research, management, engineering, and basic public services. The majority of these firms work in developing countries. Several research organizations also do international work directly related to the interests of the U.S. government.

The United Nations is the primary non-American international organization providing employment opportunities for Americans. The United Nations is divided into six UN organs, 12 specialized agencies, and numerous related organizations. Regional international organizations, such as the North Atlantic Treaty Organization (NATO) and the Organization of American States (OAS), also provide job opportunities for enterprising job seekers. However, regional "Cold War" defense organizations such as NATO may experience major cutbacks in the near future—or perhaps NATO may be completely dissolved within the decade if it doesn't soon find a new mission for itself.

Several nonprofit organizations, foundations, and educational and communication groups function in the international arena. They, too, offer interesting job and career opportunities for those who have the requisite skills and know-how to locate job opportunities.

Job and career opportunities in the international arena are discussed at length in our three separate volumes on this subject: *The Complete Guide to International Jobs and Careers: Your Passport to a World of Exciting and Exotic Employment*, *The Almanac of International Jobs and Careers: A Guide to Over 1001 Employers*, and *Jobs for People Who Love Travel: Opportunities at Home and Abroad*. These three books are available through Impact Publications along with several other international job books such as *Guide to Careers in World Affairs, Jobs Worldwide, Jobs in Russia and the Newly Independent States,* and *The New Relocating Spouse's Guide to Employment.*

PART II

EFFECTIVE JOB SEARCH SKILLS AND STRATEGIES

Knowing *where* the jobs are is important to your job search. But knowing *how to find a job* is even more important. Before you acquire names, addresses, and phone numbers of potential public employers, you should possess the necessary job search skills and strategies for gathering and using job information effectively.

In this section we outline the most important skills and strategies for conducting an effective job search. These are general skills and strategies appropriate for most public and private sector employment situations. In later sections of the book we outline additional skills and strategies most appropriate for particular public sector environments.

The skills and strategies discussed in this section are directly transferable to most public sector situations. They constitute the *foundation skills and strategies* from which you must custom-design effective approaches for different public sector jobs and careers.

However, one important word of caution is in order before you plunge into this skills section and become a true-believer in such concepts as functional skills, combination resumes, referral letters, prospecting, networking, and informational interviewing. Government agencies, associations, consulting firms, foundations, and research organizations each have their own hiring cultures, consisting of both formal and informal personnel practices. Even within each group, individual organizations will differ in how they recruit, evaluate, and select individuals. Some organizations will have highly formalized application and testing procedures. Others maintain computerized talent banks or belong to electronic job search services which they regularly use for recruiting new personnel. Many work strictly on an informal, word-of-mouth basis. Others have developed important formal and informal networking mechanisms. And still others frequently use professional recruiting services to identify and select job candidates.

There is no one best approach which can be used universally for all organizations and employment situations.

The federal government is a good case in point. At present most applicants for federal government positions must complete the Standard Form 171 (SF 171). However, after December 31, 1994 the U.S. Office of Personnel Management will no longer require applicants to complete the SF 171. After that date agencies will be permitted to develop their own application forms as well as accept resumes. New computer and telecommunication-based electronic application systems, such as the experimental Microcomputer Assisted Rating Schedule (MARS) and Telephone Application Processing (TAP), could eliminate the need for paper applications.

These major application changes reflect the federal government's continuing effort to decentralize hiring to the agency level as well as "re-invent" the government's employment procedures. In the future federal applications will more closely resemble those found in the private sector. Applicants will need to know how to write resumes appropriate for federal positions as well as use a language appropriate for the electronic scanning of their application—major departures in federal hiring practices. Thus, most of the information found in the next four chapters on job search skills will become even more relevant than ever for finding jobs with federal agencies in the future.

If you fail to adapt the generic skills and strategies outlined in the next four chapters to specific public employment situations, you will encounter difficulties with your job search. Based upon your research activities, you must adapt, adapt, adapt, adapt. In the end, you will learn there is no one best approach which can be used universally for all organizations and employment situations.

6

PREPARE TO TAKE ACTION

Preparation for a job search involves a combination of knowledge, skills, and abilities relevant to both the job market and particular jobs. To be successful, you must understand where you are going, how you will get there, and the prerequisites for successfully achieving your goals.

DEVELOP YOUR JOB SEARCH COMPETENCIES

Knowing *where* the jobs are is important to your job search. But knowing *how to find a job* is even more important. Before you acquire names, addresses, and phone numbers of potential employers, you should possess the necessary job search knowledge and skills for gathering and using job information effectively.

Answers to many of your job related questions are found by examining your present level of job search knowledge and skills. Successful job seekers, for example, use a great deal of information as well as specific skills and strategies for getting the jobs they want.

Let's begin by testing for the level of job search information, skills, and strategies you currently possess as well as those you need to develop and improve. You can easily identify your level of job search competence by completing the following exercise:

YOUR JOB SEARCH COMPETENCIES

INSTRUCTIONS: Respond to each statement by circling which number at the right best represents your situation.

SCALE:
1 = strongly agree
2 = agree
3 = maybe, not certain
4 = disagree
5 = strongly disagree

1. I know what motivates me to excel at work. 1 2 3 4 5
2. I can identify my strongest abilities and skills. 1 2 3 4 5
3. I have seven major achievements that clarify a pattern of interests and abilities that are relevant to my job and career. 1 2 3 4 5
4. I know what I both like and dislike in work. 1 2 3 4 5
5. I know what I want to do during the next 10 years. 1 2 3 4 5
6. I have a well-defined career objective that focuses my job search on particular organizations and employers. 1 2 3 4 5
7. I know what skills I can offer employers in different occupations. 1 2 3 4 5
8. I know what skills employers most seek in candidates. 1 2 3 4 5
9. I can clearly explain to employers what I do well and enjoy doing. 1 2 3 4 5
10. I can specify why employers should hire me. 1 2 3 4 5
11. I can gain support of family and friends for making a job or career change. 1 2 3 4 5
12. I can find 10 to 20 hours a week to conduct a part-time job search. 1 2 3 4 5
13. I have the financial ability to sustain a three-month job search. 1 2 3 4 5

14. I can conduct library and interview research on different occupations, employers, organizations, and communities. 1 2 3 4 5

15. I can write different types of effective resumes and job search/thank you letters. 1 2 3 4 5

16. I can produce and distribute resumes and letters to the right people. 1 2 3 4 5

17. I can list my major accomplishments in action terms. 1 2 3 4 5

18. I can identify and target employees I want to interview. 1 2 3 4 5

19. I can develop a job referral network. 1 2 3 4 5

20. I can persuade others to join in forming a job search support group. 1 2 3 4 5

21. I can prospect for job leads. 1 2 3 4 5

22. I can use the telephone to develop prospects and get referrals and interviews. 1 2 3 4 5

23. I can plan and implement an effective direct-mail job search campaign. 1 2 3 4 5

24. I can generate one job interview for every 10 job search contacts I make. 1 2 3 4 5

25. I can follow-up on job interviews. 1 2 3 4 5

26. I can negotiate a salary 10-20% above what an employer initially offers. 1 2 3 4 5

27. I can persuade an employer to renegotiate my salary after six months on the job. 1 2 3 4 5

28. I can create a position for myself in an organization. 1 2 3 4 5

TOTAL ____________

You can calculate your overall job search competencies by adding the numbers you circled for a composite score. If your total is more than 75 points, you need to work on developing your job search skills. How you scored each item will indicate to what degree you need to work on improving specific job search skills. If your score is under 50 points, you appear well on your well to job search success. Therefore, you may wish to skip this and the next two chapters; go directly to the chapters on public sector employment. The remainder of this section will focus on developing your job search competencies. After completing this section, you should be well prepared to conduct your own job search in both the public and private sectors.

ACQUIRE MORE EDUCATION AND TRAINING

Do I have the necessary skills and experience employers require as prerequisites to be considered for a position? Do I need to go back to school for a degree, diploma, or certificate? These questions are frequently asked by individuals entering the job market or those making a job or career change. The questions are especially important when approaching public sector jobs. For example, many international positions require professional degrees. Federal government jobs tend to emphasize formal education credentials. And many specialized education programs are now offered for managing trade and professional associations.

It is difficult to provide simple answers to these questions. However, you should first know what it is you want to do. It is always best to find employment that is conducive to your particular mix of interests, skills, and abilities rather than try to locate jobs which may utilize your weaknesses. Second, you must conduct research to identify what skills training is really required for particular positions. Notice, we say *skills training*—not education. Although related, there is an important difference between skills training and education. Many employers are looking for specific skills rather than educational credentials. Unfortunately, most educational institutions are still oriented toward transferring disciplines and subject matters to students rather than teaching specific skills relevant to the world of work. If you fail to keep these two points in mind, you may waste a great deal of time and money on unnecessary training or seek jobs you are unqualified to perform.

So how should you proceed? Do the necessary self-assessment and data gathering required to answer these questions. Begin by asking yourself a key question for orienting your job search: "What do I really want to do?" Follow the exercises in Chapter 7 to conduct a self-assessment and set goals. Once you have a clear idea of your job and career goals, you will be prepared to target your job search toward particular organizations, positions, and individuals.

Assuming you know what you want to do, your next step is to gather information to determine whether you possess the necessary skills to qualify for the job. Obviously, if you are a high school graduate wishing to become a medical doctor, engineer, lawyer, or accountant, you will need several years of highly specialized training for certification in these fields. However, if you want to become an FBI agent, just what educational background, experience, and demonstrated skills do you need? Where do you find this information?

You can begin answering these questions by consulting several publications identified in Chapter 7 for conducting a job search. Next, talk to individuals who have a working knowledge of the particular job or career you desire. Contact people in similar positions to what you are seeking. While many educators can be helpful, they should rank as a secondary information source. Few educators are objective sources for information about education and training requirements for particular jobs. Remember, most educators are relatively isolated from day-to-day job market realities. Furthermore, educators are in the business of keeping themselves employed by recruiting more students into existing programs and by developing new degree and certification programs. They literally "stand where they sit" by promoting more formal education, degrees, and certification—whether or not such training and documentation is really necessary and relevant to the world of work.

If you read materials and talk to informed individuals and employers, you will quickly learn what you need to do to be successful in your job search. If you learn you must return to school for a formal degree or certificate, your information sources will identify the most appropriate type of training you should acquire as well as recommend where best to receive the training. In many cases you will find you do not need additional training to qualify for a position. Since many employers prefer conducting their own in-house training, they primarily look for individuals who are motivated, enthusiastic, trainable, and likable.

The U.S. Department of Labor identifies nine structured training programs individuals should familiarize themselves with prior to making educational and training choices. Most of these sources emphasize practical hands-on training in specific occupational fields. Private trade schools, for example, are flourishing at a time when university enrollments are stagnant and declining—an indication of the shift to practical skills training in education. Each alternative has various advantages and disadvantages, and costs differ considerably.

1. **Public vocational education:** Public vocational education is provided through secondary, postsecondary, and adult vocational and technical programs. The emphasis in many secondary schools is to give high school students vocational training in addition to the regular academic program. Postsecondary vocational education is provided for individuals who have left high school but who are not seeking a baccalaureate degree. Adult vocational and technical programs emphasize retraining or upgrading the skills of individuals in the labor force. The traditional agricultural, trade, and industrial emphasis of vocational education has been vastly expanded to include

training in distribution, health, home economics, office, and technical occupations. Most programs train individuals for specific occupations, which are outlined in the *Occupational Outlook Handbook*. Each year over 20 million people enroll in public vocational education programs.

2. **Noncollegiate postsecondary vocational education:** Nearly 2 million people enroll in over 6,500 noncollegiate postsecondary schools with occupational programs each year. Most of these schools specialize in one of eight vocational areas: cosmetology/barber, business/commercial, trade, hospital, vocational/technical, allied health, arts/design, and technical. They offer programs in seven major areas: agribusiness, marketing and distribution, health, home economics, technical, business and office, and trade and industrial. Over 75 percent of these schools are privately owned institutions. And over 70 percent of the privately owned schools are either cosmetology/barber schools or business and commercial schools. Over 75 percent of the independent nonprofit schools are hospital schools. Over 1 million people complete occupational programs in noncollegiate postsecondary schools each year.

3. **Employer training:** Employers spend over $200 billion a year on in-house training and education programs. These programs usually involve training new employees, improving employee performance, or preparing employees for new jobs. Skilled and semi-skilled workers are trained through apprenticeship programs, learning-by-doing, and structured on-the-job instruction. Structured classroom training is increasingly offered to skilled workers by in-house trainers, professional associations, private firms, or colleges and universities. Tuition-aid programs are used by firms lacking in-house training capabilities.

4. **Apprenticeship programs:** Apprenticeship programs normally range from one to six years, depending on the particular trade and organization. These programs are used most extensively in the trade occupations, especially in construction and metalworking. They involve planned on-the-job training in conjunction with classroom instruction and supervision. Over 500,000 individuals are involved in apprenticeship programs each year. These numbers are likely to increase in the coming decade as America faces an acute shortage of skilled trade workers. Expect apprenticeship programs to expand accordingly.

5. **Federal employment and training programs:** Federal employment and training programs largely function through

state and local governments. The major federal program is the Job Training Partnership Act (JTPA) program. Working through Private Industry Councils (PICs), the JTPA program is designed to train the economically disadvantaged as well as displaced workers who need assistance with skills training, job search, and job relocation. JTPA also operates two youth programs—The Job Corps and the Summer Youth Employment Program. Other major federal programs include two administered through the Employment and Training Administration: The Trade Adjustment Act program to assist workers displaced by foreign competition, and the Work Incentive (WIN) program for employable recipients of Aid to Families with Dependent Children, migrant and seasonal farm workers, Native Americans, and workers 55 and over. New training programs initiated by the Clinton administration in 1994 should consolidate some federal programs as well as create new ones for displaced workers affected by economic restructuring.

6. **Armed Forces Training:** The Armed Forces provide training in numerous occupational skills that may or may not be directly transferred to civilian occupations. Thousands of military recruits complete training programs in several transferable areas each year, such as computer repair, medical care, food service, metalworking, communications, and administration. Occupations unique to the military, such as infantry and guncrew, are less transferable to civilian occupations.

7. **Home study (correspondence) schools:** Home study or correspondence schools provide a variety of training options. Most programs concentrate on acquiring a single skill; others may even offer a BA, MA, or Ph.D. by mail! Some programs are of questionable quality while others may be revolutionizing the education and training landscape of America. For many people, this is a convenient, inexpensive, and effective way to acquire new skills. Over 5 million people enroll in home study courses each year. Colleges and universities are quickly moving into the home study business by offering numerous televised courses for academic credit. The Public Broadcast System (PBS) offers several home study courses through its Adult Learning Service: computer literacy and applications, basic skills and personal enrichment, sales and customer service, effective communication skills, and management skills.

8. **Community and junior colleges:** Community and junior colleges in recent years have broadened their missions from primarily preparing individuals for university degree programs

to preparing them with skills appropriate for the job market. Accordingly, more of their programs emphasize vocational and occupational curriculums, such as data processing or dental hygiene, which are typically two-year programs resulting in an associate degree. Community and junior colleges will probably continue to expand their program offerings as they further adjust to the employment needs of communities. Nearly 5 million students enroll in community and junior college programs each year.

9. **Colleges and universities:** Colleges and universities continue to provide the traditional four-year and graduate degree programs in various subject fields. While many of the fields are occupational-specific and require some form of certification—such as engineering, law, medicine, and business—many other fields are not. The exact relationship of the degree program to the job market varies with different disciplines. As noted earlier, in recent years, graduates of many programs have had difficulty finding employment in their chosen fields. This is particularly true for students who only have a generalist background in the liberal arts. During the past decade many colleges and universities have adjusted to declining enrollments by offering several nontraditional occupational-related courses and programs. Continuing education, special skills training courses, short courses, evening course offerings, "telecourses," and workshops and seminars on job-related matters have become popular with nontraditional, older students who seek specific skills training rather than degrees. At the same time, traditional academic programs are placing greater emphasis on internships and cooperative education programs in order to give students work experience related to their academic programs.

Additional training programs may be sponsored by local governments, professional associations, women's centers, YWCA's, and religious and civic groups. As training and retraining become more acceptable to the general public, we can expect different forms and types of training programs to be sponsored by various groups.

We also can expect a revolution in the training field, closely related to high-tech developments. Televised education and training courses should continue to increase in number and scope. Computer-based training, similar in some respects to traditional home study programs, will become more prevalent as computer software and interactive video training packages are developed in response to the new technology and the rising demand for skills training.

Individuals in tomorrow's education training markets will become examples of Toffler's "prosumer society": in a decentralized information market, individuals will choose what training they most desire as well as control when and where they will receive it. With the development of interactive video and computer training programs, individuals will manage the training process in a more efficient and effective manner than with the more centralized, time consuming, and expensive use of traditional student-teacher classroom instruction. This type of training may eventually make many of the previously discussed categories of education and training obsolete.

BECOME AN INFORMED CONSUMER

Several resources can help you decide which training path is more appropriate for you. If you use the popular *Discover II* computerized career planning system, for example, you will find it includes a section that matches education and training programs with career interests. A few other computer software programs also match career interests with education and training programs. Contact your local secondary school, community college, or library for information on these programs.

You should begin your search for useful education and training information by consulting several useful publications. The major sources will be found in the reference section of libraries as well as in guidance offices and career planning centers of schools, colleges, universities, and specialized employment assistance centers. Most of these organizations maintain catalogues, directories, and files listing educational and training opportunities.

Two useful sources for information on education and training programs are *Peterson's Guides* and *Barron's Educational Series* which publish several excellent directories. Most of the directories are updated annually and include basic information on choosing programs and institutions best suited to your interests. Among the many titles offered by Peterson's and Barron's are:

- *Guide to Four-Year Colleges*
- *Guide to Two-Year Colleges*
- *The College Money Handbook*
- *Guides to Graduate Study:*
  —Graduate and Professional Programs
  —Humanities and Social Sciences
  —Biological Agricultural and Health Sciences
  —Physical Sciences and Mathematics
  —Engineering and Applied Sciences
- *Regional Guides to Colleges*
  —Middle Atlantic
  —Midwest
  —New England
  —New York

—*Southeast*
—*Southwest*
—*West*

- *Job Opportunities in Engineering and Technology*
- *Job Opportunities in Health Care*
- *Job Opportunities Business*
- *Job Opportunities in Environment*
- *Guide to Medical and Dental Schools*
- *How to Prepare for the SAT*
- *Competitive Colleges*
- *Colleges With Programs for Learning-Disabled Students*
- *National College Databank*
- *Handbook for College Admissions*
- *Guide to College Admissions*
- *Corporate Tuition Aid Programs*

Most major libraries have copies of these publications in their reference section. If you cannot find them in your local library, check with your local bookstore or contact the publishers directly: Peterson's Guides, P.O. Box 2123, Princeton, NJ 08543-2123, Tel. 609/924/5338; and Barron's Educational Series, 250 Wireless Blvd., Hauppauge, NY 11788, Tel. 516/434-3311.

If you decide you need to acquire a specific skill, consult various professional or trade associations; many can provide you with a list of reputable institutions providing skills training in particular fields. The names, addresses, and telephone numbers of all major associations are listed in the *Encyclopedia of Associations* (Gale Publishers) and *National Trade and Professional Associations* (Columbia Books), two extremely useful directories found in the reference section of most libraries.

The U.S. Department of Labor's *Occupational Outlook Handbook* also lists useful names and addresses relating to employment training in specific fields. Consult the *"Leads To More Information"* section in the latest edition of this biannual directory. This book is also available in most libraries or can be purchased from Impact Publications by completing the order form at the end of this book.

For information on **private trade and technical schools**, be sure to get a copy of the *Handbook of Accredited Private Trade and Technical Schools* which is distributed by the Career College Association: 750 1st St., NE., Washington, DC 20002, Tel. 202/659-2460.

For information on **apprenticeship programs**, get a copy of *The National Apprenticeship Program and Apprenticeship Information* through the Bureau of Apprenticeships and Training (BAT), U.S. Department of Labor, 200 Constitution Ave., NW, Washington, DC 20210, Tel. 202/535-0545. BAT offices are also found in each state. To find if there is a BAT office near you, consult the White or Blue Pages of your telephone directory under *"United States Government—*

Department of Labor." Your local library and public employment service office should also have information on apprenticeship programs.

If you are interested in **home study and correspondence courses**, contact the National Home Study Council (NHSC) for information on home study programs. NHSC distributes copies of a useful publication entitled *Directory of Accredited Home Study Programs*. For information on this and other NHSC publications, contact: National Home Study Council, 1601 18th St., NW, Washington, DC 20009, Tel. 202/234-5100.

You also need to determine the quality and suitability of these education and training programs. Many programs have reputations for fraud, abuse, and incompetence—primarily take your time and money in exchange for broken promises. After all, this is a business transaction—your money in exchange for their services. As an informed consumer, you must demand quality performance for your money. Therefore, when contacting a particular institution, ask to speak to former students and graduates. Write to the Council on Postsecondary Accreditation (One Dupont Circle, Suite 760, Washington, DC 20036) to inquire about the school's credentials. Focus your attention on the *results* or *outcomes* the institution achieves. Instead of asking workload questions—how many faculty have Master's or Ph.D. degrees, or how many students are enrolled—ask these performance or outcome questions:

- What are last year's graduates doing today?
- Where do they work and for whom?
- How much do they earn?
- How many were placed in jobs through this institution?

Institutions that can answer these questions focus on *performance*. Beware of those that can't answer these questions, for they may not be doing an adequate job to meet your needs.

Most colleges and universities will provide assistance to adult learners. Contact student services, continuing education, academic advising, adult services, or women's offices at your local community college, college, or university. Be sure to talk to present and former students about the *expectations and results* of the programs for them. Always remember that educators are first in the business of keeping themselves employed and, second, in the business of delivering educational services. And today, more than ever, educational institutions need students to keep their programs alive. Don't necessarily expect professional educators to be objective about your future vis-a-vis their interests, skills, and programs. At the very least, you must do a critical evaluation of their programs and services.

If you need further assistance, contact a local branch of the National Center for Educational Brokering. While there is no national clearinghouse to help you match your goals with appropriate educational programs, NCEB can assist you nonetheless. NCEB counselors will help you identify your goals and career alternatives. For information on the center nearest you, contact the National Center for Educational Brokering, 329 9th St., San Francisco, CA 94103, Tel. 415/626-2378.

Other useful sources of information on education and training programs are your telephone book and employers. Look under "Schools" in the Yellow Pages of your telephone directory. Call the schools and ask them to send you literature and application forms and discuss the relevance of their programs to the job market. You should also talk to employers and individuals who have work experience in the field that interests you. Ask them how best to acquire the necessary skills for particular occupations. Most important, thoroughly research education and training alternatives before you invest any money, time, or effort.

Beware of education and training myths. Additional education and training is not always the answer for entry or advancement within the job market. Remember, education is a big $300 billion a year business. Exhibiting a great deal of inertia, few educational institutions are prepared to describe their performance in relation to today's job market. At best, educational institutions are most adept at keeping their businesses well and alive through the marketing of degree programs to relatively uninformed, accepting, and compliant consumers.

Contrary to what educators may tell you, additional education and training may not be necessary for entering or advancing within today's job market. But it is a good investment for the job markets of tomorrow. To determine if you need additional education and training, you should first learn what it is you do well and enjoy doing (through self-assessment) and then identify what it is you need to do to get what you want (through research). Education and training may be only one of several things you need to do. You may, for example, determine that you need to change your behavior by setting goals, becoming more focused on achieving results, and improving your dress and appearance. Or you may need to develop effective job search skills as well as relocate to a new community. After all, employers spend more than $200 billion each year on employee training and retraining—much of which is spent because of the failure of traditional educational institutions.

You may learn it is best to find an apprenticeship program or get into a particular organization that provides excellent training for its employees. Such training will be both up-to-date and relevant to the job market. Most of the best run corporations rely on their own in-house training rather than on institutions outside the corporation. When making hiring decisions, such organizations are more concerned with your overall level of intelligence as reflected in your ability to learn, acquire new skills, and grow within the organization than with the specific work-content skills you initially bring to the job. Even government is providing more and more training for its employees, although it still places a great deal of emphasis on formal educational credentials for entry into the government service.

SEEK PROFESSIONAL ASSISTANCE WHEN NECESSARY

While some people can successfully conduct a job search based on the advice of books such as this, many others also need the assistance of various professional groups that offer specific career planning and job search services. These groups offer everything from testing and assessment services to offering contacts with potential employers, including job vacancy information and temporary employment services. Some do one-on-one career counseling while others sponsor one to three-day workshops or six to twelve-week courses on the various steps in the career planning process. You should know something about these services before you invest your time and money beyond this and other career planning and job search books.

SELECT USEFUL OPTIONS

You have two options in organizing your job search. First, you can follow the principles and advice outlined in this and many other self-directed books. Just read the chapters and then put them into practice by following the step-by-step instructions. Second, you may wish to seek professional help to either supplement or replace this book. Indeed, many people will read parts of this book—perhaps all of it—and do nothing. Unwilling to take initiative, lacking sufficient time or motivation, or failing to follow-through, many people will eventually seek professional help to organize and implement their job search. They will pay good money to get someone else to tell them to follow the advice found in this book. Some people need this type of expensive motivation and organization.

At the same time, we recognize the value of professional assistance. Especially with the critical assessment and objective setting steps (Chapters 7), some individuals may need more assistance than our advice and exercises provide. You may, for example, want to take a battery of tests to better understand your interests and values in relation to alternative jobs and careers. And still others, due to a combination of job loss, failed relationships, or depression, may need therapy best provided by a trained psychologist or psychiatrist rather than career testing and information services provided by career counselors. If any of these situations pertain to you, by all means seek professional help.

You also should beware of pitfalls in seeking professional advice. While many services are excellent, other services are useless and fraudulent. Remember, career planning and job assistance are big businesses involving millions of dollars each year. Many people enter these businesses without expertise. Professional certification in these areas is extremely weak to non-existent in some states. Indeed, many so-called "professionals" get into the business because they are unemployed. In other words, they major in their own problem! Others are frauds and hucksters who prey on vulnerable and naive people who feel they need a "specialist" or "expert" to get them a job. They will take your money in exchange for promises. You will find several services promising to assist you in finding all types of jobs. You should know something about these professional services before you venture beyond this book.

If you are interested in exploring the services of job specialists, begin by looking in the Yellow Pages of your telephone directory under these headings: Management Consultants, Employment, Resumes, Career Planning, and Social Services. Several career planning and employment services are available, ranging from highly generalized to very specific services. Most services claim they can help you. If you read this book, you will be in a better position to seek out specific services as well as ask the right questions for screening the services. You may even discover you know more about finding a job than many of the so-called professionals!

At least twelve different career planning and employment services are available to assist you with your job search. Each has certain advantages and disadvantages. Approach them with caution. Never sign a contract before you read the fine print, get a second opinion, and talk to former clients about the *results* they achieved through the service. With these words of caution in mind, let's take a look at some of these services.

1. **Public employment services:** Public employment services usually consist of a state agency which provides employment assistance as well as dispenses unemployment compensation benefits. Employment assistance largely consists of job listings and counseling services. However, counseling services often screen individuals for employers who list with the public employment agency. If you are looking for an entry-level job in the $15,000 to $25,000 range, contact this service. Most employers do not list with this service, especially for positions paying more than $35,000 a year. Although the main purpose of these offices is to dispense unemployment benefits, these offices also offer useful employment services, including self-assessment and job search workshops as well as job banks that match skills and experience with available job vacancies. Many of these offices are linked to America's Job Bank, an electronic database which includes job listings throughout the U.S. and abroad. Many jobs listed with state employment offices are for veterans.

2. **Private employment agencies:** Private employment agencies work for money, either from applicants or employers. Approximately 8,000 such agencies operate nationwide. Many are highly specialized in technical, scientific, and financial fields.

The majority of these firms serve the interests of employers since employers—not applicants—represent repeat business. While employers normally pay the placement fee, many agencies charge applicants 10 to 15 percent of their first year salary. These firms have one major advantage: job leads which you may have difficulty uncovering elsewhere. Especially for highly specialized fields, a good firm can be extremely helpful. The major disadvantages are that they can be costly and the quality of the firms varies. Be careful in how you deal with them. Make sure you understand the fee structure and what they will do for you before you sign anything.

3. **Temporary employment firms:** During the past decade temporary employment firms have come of age as more and more turn to them for recruitment assistance. They offer a variety of employment services to both applicants and employers who are either looking for temporary work and workers or who want to better screen applicants and employers. Many of these firms recruit individuals for a wide range of positions and skill levels as well as full-time employment. If you are interested in "testing the job waters," you may want to contact these firms for information on their services. Employers—not job seekers—pay for these services.

4. **College/university placement offices:** College and university placement offices provide in-house career planning services for graduating students. While some give assistance to alumni, don't expect too much help if you have already graduated. Many of these offices are understaffed or provide only rudimentary services, such as maintaining a career planning library, coordinating on-campus interviews for graduating seniors, and conducting workshops on how to write resumes and interview. Others provide a full range of well supported services including testing and one-on-one counseling. Indeed, many community colleges offer such services to members of the community on a walk-in basis. You can use their libraries and computerized career assessment programs, take personality and interest inventories, or attend special workshops or full-semester career planning courses which will take you through each step of the career planning and job search processes. You are well advised to enroll in such a course since it should help you assess your motivated abilities and skills and assist you in implementing a successful job search plan. Check with your local campus to see what services you might use.

5. **Private career and job search firms:** Private career and job search firms help individuals acquire job search skills. They do not find you a job. In other words, they teach you much—maybe more but possibly less—of what is outlined in this book. Expect to pay anywhere from $1,500 to $10,000 for this service. If you need a structured environment for conducting your job search, contract with one of these firms. One of the oldest and most popular firms is Haldane Associates. Many of their pioneering career planning and job search methods are incorporated in this book. You will find branches of this nationwide firm in many major cities.

6. **Executive search firms and headhunters:** Executive search firms work for employers in finding employees to fill critical positions in the $60,000 plus salary range. They also are called "headhunters," "management consultants," and "executive recruiters." These firms play an important role in linking high level technical and managerial talent to organizations. Don't expect to contract for these services. Executive recruiters work for employers—not applicants. If a friend or relative is in this business or you have relevant skills of interest to these firms, let them know you are available—and ask for their advice. On the other hand, you may want to contact firms that specialize in recruiting individuals with your skill specialty. Several books identify how you can best approach "headhunters" on your own: *How to Select and Use an Executive Search Firm* (A. R. Taylor); *How to Answer a Headhunter's Call* (Robert H. Perry); *The Headhunter Strategy* (Kenneth J. Cole); *The Directory of Executive Recruiters* (Consultants News); and *How to Get a Headhunter to Call* (Howard S. Freedman).

7. **Marketing services:** Marketing services represent an interesting combination of job search and executive search activities. They can cost $2,500 or more, and they work with individuals anticipating a starting salary of at least $75,000 but preferably over $100,000. These firms try to minimize the time and risk of applying for jobs. A typical operation begins with a client paying a $150 fee for developing psychological, skills, and interests profiles. Next, a marketing plan is outlined and a contract signed for specific services. Using word processing equipment, the firm normally develops a slick "professional" resume and mails it along with a cover letter, to hundreds—maybe thousands—of firms. Clients are then briefed and sent to interview with interested employers. While you can save money and achieve the same results on your own, these firms do have one major advantage. They save you *time* by doing most of the

work for you. Again, approach these services with caution and with the knowledge that you can probably do just as well—if not better—on your own by following the step-by-step advice of this and other job search books.

8. **Women's Centers and special career services:** Women's Centers and special career services have been established to respond to the employment needs of special groups. Women's Centers are particularly active in sponsoring career planning workshops and job information networks. These centers tend to be geared toward elementary job search activities, because their clientele largely consists of homemakers who are entering or re-entering the work force with little knowledge of the job market. Special career services arise at times for different categories of employees. For example, unemployed aerospace engineers, teachers, veterans, air traffic controllers, and government employees have formed special groups for developing job search skills and sharing job leads.

9. **Testing and assessment centers:** Testing and assessment centers provide assistance for identifying vocational skills, interests, and objectives. Usually staffed by trained professionals, these centers administer several types of tests and charge from $300 to $800 per person. You may wish to use some of these services if you feel our activities in Chapters 7, 8, and 9 generate insufficient information on your skills and interests to formulate your job objective. If you use such services, make sure you are given one or both of the two most popular and reliable tests: *Myers-Briggs Type Indicator* and the *Strong-Campbell Interest Inventory*. You should find both tests helpful in better understanding your interests and decision-making styles. However, try our exercises before you hire a psychologist or visit a testing center. If you first complete these exercises, you will be in a better position to know exactly what you need from such centers. In many cases the career office at your local community college or women's center can administer these tests at minimum cost.

10. **Job fairs or career conferences:** Job fairs or career conferences are organized by employment agencies to link applicants to employers. Usually consisting of one to two-day meetings in a hotel, employers meet with applicants as a group and on a one-to-one basis. Employers give presentations on their companies, applicants circulate resumes, and employers interview candidates. Many such conferences are organized to attract hard-to-recruit groups, such as engineers, computer programmers, and clerical

and service workers. While private companies typically organize job fairs, the federal government increasingly uses job fairs for quickly recruiting many specialized personnel. These are excellent sources for job leads and information—if you get invited to the meeting or they are open to the public. Employers pay for this service—not applicants.

11. **Professional associations:** Professional associations often provide placement assistance. This usually consists of listing job vacancies and organizing a job information exchange at annual conferences. These meetings are good sources for making job contacts in different geographic locations within a particular professional field. But don't expect too much. Talking to people (networking) at professional conferences may yield better results than reading job listings and interviewing at conference placement centers.

12. **Electronic databases:** Several companies now offer computerized job search services to individuals who enroll in their organizations. The usual procedure is to pay a yearly enrollment fee accompanied with a copy of your resume. Your resume is then converted into an electronic resume which is entered into a database. When employers contact the organization to search for qualified candidates, your resume may be included in the search. Such databases are a quick and easy way of searching for a job—your resume literally works 24-hours a day. How successful individuals are in finding a job via these databases is still uncertain. The major companies offering these services include Job Bank USA, kiNexis, and Connexion. Yearly membership fees range from $30 to $79. For more information on these services, see Peter Weddle's *Electronic Resumes for the New Job Market*, (Impact Publications, 1995) Joyce Lain Kennedy's and Daryl Laramore's two new books, *Electronic Job Search Revolution* and *Electronic Resume Revolution* (Wiley & Sons, 1994).

Other types of career planning and employment services are growing and specializing in particular occupational fields. You may wish to use these services as a supplement to this book. Whatever you do, proceed with caution, know exactly what you are getting into, and choose the best. Remember, there is no such thing as a free lunch, and you often get less than what you pay for. At the same time, the most expensive services are not necessarily the best. Indeed, the free and inexpensive career planning services offered by many community colleges—libraries, computerized career assessment programs, testing, and workshops—are often superior to alternative services which can be expensive.

After reading this book, you should be able to make intelligent decisions about what, when, where, and with what results you can use professional assistance. Shop around, compare services and costs, ask questions, talk to former clients, and read the fine print with your lawyer before giving an employment expert a job using your hard earned money!

BE SUCCESSFUL

Success is determined by more than just a good plan getting implemented. We know success is not determined primarily by intelligence, time management, or luck. Based upon experience, theory, research, common sense, and acceptance of some self-transformation principles, we believe you will achieve job search success by following many of the following 20 principles:

1. **You should work hard at finding a job:** Make this a daily endeavor and involve your family.

2. **You should not be discouraged with set-backs:** You are playing the odds, so expect disappointments and handle them in stride. You will get many "no's" before finding the one "yes" which is right for you.

3. **You should be patient and persevere:** Expect three to six months of hard work before you connect with the job that's right for you.

4. **You should be honest with yourself and others:** Honesty is always the best policy. But don't be naive and stupid by confessing your negatives and shortcomings to others.

5. **You should develop a positive attitude toward yourself:** Nobody wants to employ guilt-ridden people with inferiority complexes. Focus on your positive characteristics.

6. **You should associate with positive and successful people:** Finding a job largely depends on how well you relate to others. Avoid associating with negative and depressing people who complain and have a "you-can't-do-it" attitude. Run with winners who have a positive "can-do" outlook on life.

7. **You should set goals:** You should have a clear idea of what you want and where you are going. Without these, you will present a confusing and indecisive image to others. Clear goals help direct your job search into productive channels. Moreover, setting high goals will help make you work hard in getting what you want.

8. **You should plan:** Convert your goals into action steps that are organized as short, intermediate, and long-range plans.

9. **You should get organized:** Translate your plans into activities, targets, names, addresses, and telephone numbers. Develop a good filing system, and use a large calendar to set time targets, record appointments, and compile useful information.

10. **You should be a good communicator:** Take stock of your oral, written, and nonverbal communication skills. How well do you communicate? Since most aspects of your job search involve communicating with others, and communication skills are one of the most sought-after skills, always present yourself well both verbally and nonverbally.

11. **You should be energetic and enthusiastic:** Employers are attracted to positive people. They don't like negative and depressing people who toil at their work. Generate enthusiasm both verbally and nonverbally. Check on your telephone voice—it may be more unenthusiastic than your voice in face-to-face situations.

12. **You should ask questions:** Your best information comes from asking questions. Learn to develop intelligent questions that are non-aggressive, polite, and interesting to others. But don't ask too many questions and thereby become a bore.

13. **You should be a good listener:** Being a good listener is often more important than being a good questioner or talker. Learn to improve your face-to-face listening behavior (nonverbal cues) as well as remember and use information gained from others. Make others feel they enjoyed talking with you—they feel you actually *listen* to what they say.

14. **You should be polite, courteous, and thoughtful:** Treat gatekeepers, especially receptionists and secretaries, like human beings. Avoid being aggressive or too assertive. Try to be polite, courteous, and gracious. Your social graces are being observed. Remember to send thank you letters—a very thoughtful thing to do in a job search. Even if rejected, thank employers for the "opportunity" given to you. After all, they may later have additional opportunities, and they will remember you.

15. **You should be tactful:** Watch what you say to others about other people and your background. Don't be a gossip, backstabber, or confessor.

16. **You should maintain a professional stance:** Be neat in what you do and wear, and speak with the confidence, authority, and maturity of a professional.

17. **You should demonstrate your intelligence and competence:** Present yourself as someone who gets things done and achieves results—a *producer.* Employers generally seek people who are bright, hard working, responsible, communicate well, have positive personalities, maintain good interpersonal relations, are likable, observe dress and social codes, take initiative, are talented, possess expertise in particular areas, use good judgment, are cooperative, trustworthy, and loyal, generate confidence and credibility, and are conventional. In other words, they like people who score in the "excellent" to "outstanding" categories of the annual performance evaluation.

18. **You should not overdo your job search:** Don't engage in overkill and bore everyone with your "job search" stories. Achieve balance in everything you do. Occasionally take a few days off to do nothing related to your job search. Develop a system of incentives and rewards—such as two non-job search days a week, if you accomplish targets A, B, C, and D.

19. **You should be open-minded and keep an eye open for "luck":** Too much planning can blind you to unexpected and fruitful opportunities. You should welcome serendipity. Learn to re-evaluate your goals and strategies. Seize new opportunities if they appear appropriate.

20. **You should evaluate your progress and adjust:** Take two hours once every two weeks and evaluate what you are doing and accomplishing. If necessary, tinker with your plans and reorganize your activities and priorities. Don't become too routinized and thereby kill creativity and innovation.

These principles should provide you with an initial orientation for starting your job search. As you become more experienced, you will develop your own set of operating principles that should work for you in particular employment situations.

TAKE TIME TO SAIL

Let's assume you have the necessary skills to open the doors to employers for the job you want. Your next step is to organize and effective job search appropriate for the public sector. Organization, however, does not mean a detailed plan, blueprint, or road map for taking action. If you strictly adhere to such a plan, you will most likely be disappointed with the outcomes. Instead, your job search should approximate the art of sailing—you know where you want to go and the general direction for getting there. But the specific path, as well as the time for reaching your destination, will be determined by your environment, situation, and skills. Like the sailor dependent upon his sailing skills and environmental conditions, you tack back and forth, progressing within what is considered to be an acceptable time period for successful completion of the task.

While we recommend planning your job search, we hope you will avoid the excesses of too much planning. The plan should not become the *end*—it should be a flexible *means* for achieving your stated job and career goals. Planning makes sense, because it requires you to set goals and develop strategies for achieving the goals. However, too much planning can blind you to unexpected occurrences and opportunities, or that wonderful experience called *serendipity.*

We outline on page 101 a hypothetical plan for conducting an effective job search. This plan incorporates seven distinct but interrelated job search activities over a six month period. If you phase in the first four job search steps during the initial three to four weeks, and continue the final four steps in subsequent weeks and months, you should begin receiving job offers within two to three months after initiating your job search. Interviews and job offers can come at any time—often unexpectedly—during your job search. An average time is three months, but it can occur within a week or take as long as five months. If you plan, prepare, and persist at the job search, the pay-off will be interviews and offers.

While three months may seem a long time, especially if you need to work immediately, you can shorten your job search time by increasing the frequency of each job search activity. If you are job hunting on a full-time basis, you may be able to cut your job search time in half. But don't expect to get a professional level job quickly. It requires time, hard work, and persistence.

This hypothetical time frame is generally applicable to most nongovernment public and private sector jobs. The time frame for government jobs, however, may be similar. Many government jobs only require a three to six week waiting period between initial application and final selection and notification. The federal government, for example, has streamlined its hiring procedures for many hard-to-fill positions—especially clerical and high-tech jobs. In some cases it only takes two to three days between the initial application and final hiring decision. Other government units may take several weeks to make a hiring decision given their lengthy bureaucratic selection procedures.

ORGANIZATION OF JOB SEARCH ACTIVITIES

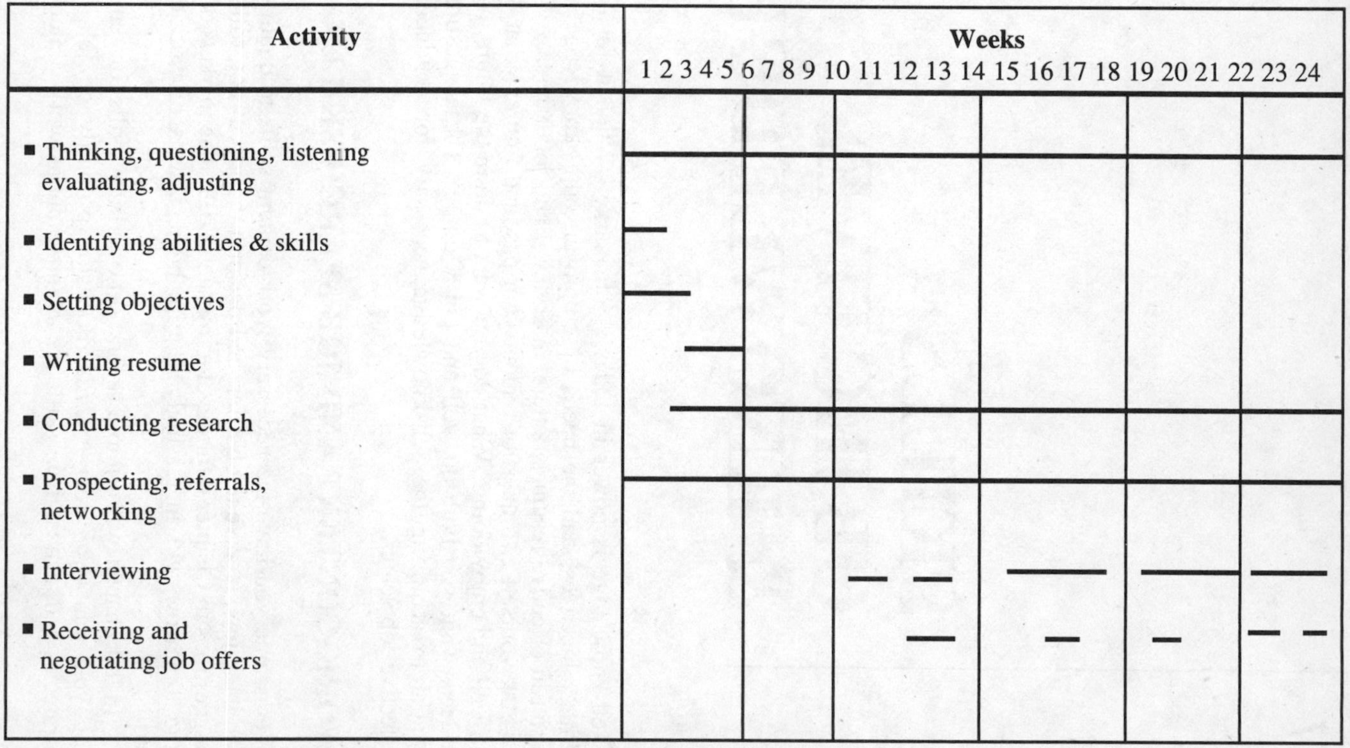

Activity	Weeks 1 2 3 4 5 6 7 8 9 10 11 12 13 14 15 16 17 18 19 20 21 22 23 24
■ Thinking, questioning, listening evaluating, adjusting	
■ Identifying abilities & skills	
■ Setting objectives	
■ Writing resume	
■ Conducting research	
■ Prospecting, referrals, networking	
■ Interviewing	
■ Receiving and negotiating job offers	

7

SKILLS, OBJECTIVES & KNOWLEDGE

Self-knowledge is power in today's job market. When it focuses on skills, objectives, and the needs of employers, this knowledge should result in effective resumes, letters, interviews, and job offers.

Ask yourself two questions about your past and future: What do you do well and enjoy doing? What do you want to do in the future that best reflects what you both do well and enjoy doing? These questions are central to acquiring the self-knowledge necessary for conducting an effective job search.

WORK-CONTENT AND JOB SEARCH SKILLS

We assume you have the necessary work-content skills to qualify for a job interview, receive a job offer, and perform the job. If not, follow our suggestions in Chapter 6 for developing such skills. The markets of today and tomorrow will increasingly require higher levels of work-content skills.

In this chapter we turn to a second set of critical skills for getting the job you want—*job search skills*. Focusing primarily on job finding strategies and tactics, these skills are as important as work-content skills for getting a job interview and receiving a job offer. They also help advance your career once you are on the job. In this sense, they are *basic job market survival skills* you must acquire and practice on a continuous basis. In Chapter 6 you identified the degree to which you possessed several of these skills by completing an exercise for identifying your job search competencies. Here we examine several important job search skills necessary for finding a job.

One word of caution before we proceed further. The soft job search skills outlined in this and subsequent chapters do not substitute for concrete work-content skills. Form and presentation should never be confused with or replace substance. You must be able to perform the job you are being hired to do; deliver what you say you can deliver. The bottom line is that you probably won't fool enough people to get the job. However, should you fool enough and get the job, you won't keep it long.

Form and presentation should never be confused with or replace substance. You must be able to perform the job you are being hired to do.

For it doesn't take long before an employer learns he or she has made a mistake by hiring someone who misrepresented credentials and qualifications—they simply don't deliver with quality performance.

JOB SEARCH SKILLS AND STEPS

Several job search skills help you prepare for face-to-face meetings with potential employers. They stress how you must (1) organize yourself, and (2) communicate your value to employers. These skills also are important *sequential steps* required for planning and implementing an effective job search. These skills and steps include:

- Identifying your strengths
- Stating your job objective
- Conducting job research
- Writing resumes and job search letters
- Dressing appropriately to meet people who have input into the hiring process
- Prospecting, networking, and informational interviewing

- Interviewing for the job
- Negotiating salary

The figure on page 105 illustrates the relationship of these steps to one another in the overall job search. Each step has a well defined set of rules —based upon employers' expectations and job searchers' successful experiences—you should learn and practice.

In this chapter we examine the first three job search steps—identifying strengths, stating objectives, and conducting job research. These steps focus on becoming better acquainted with yourself and your environment. They must be completed *prior to* the three image management steps in Chapter 8—writing resumes and letters and dressing appropriately—and the three action steps in Chapter 9—networking, interviewing, and negotiating salary.

The job search skills and steps examined in this and subsequent chapters are generally valid for acquiring both public and private sector employment. However, additional job search activities are required when seeking employment with the government and international agencies. For example, many government agencies have their own application forms which must be completed according to specific instructions. We will address unique job search skill requirements and activities for particular public sector organizations in the appropriate chapters of Parts III, IV, V, and VI. This chapter and Chapters 8 and 9 outline the *foundation skills* for conducting an effective job search regardless of the particular setting or circumstances.

COMMUNICATE YOUR STRENGTHS

What do you do well and enjoy doing? Why should I hire you? What will you give me in exchange for this position, salary, and benefits? Although they may not directly ask you these questions, employers nonetheless want answers to these questions. It is to your advantage to prepare thoughtful answers to these basic questions *before* you communicate your qualifications to employers.

Put yourself in the shoes of the employer. He or she has a problem— how to select someone who will be a winner for the organization. Winners are not born every day. They have a unique set of skills and abilities employers readily seek but have difficulty both defining and finding. Contrary to popular myth, employers often do not know what type of individual they should hire or what the requirements for a particular position should be. Furthermore, most employers make less than perfect hiring decisions. Many fear they will spend a great deal of time and money selecting a candidate, yet still make the wrong hiring decision. Only after a few months of on-the-job experience with the new employee will the employer begin to confirm or reject initial hiring anxieties.

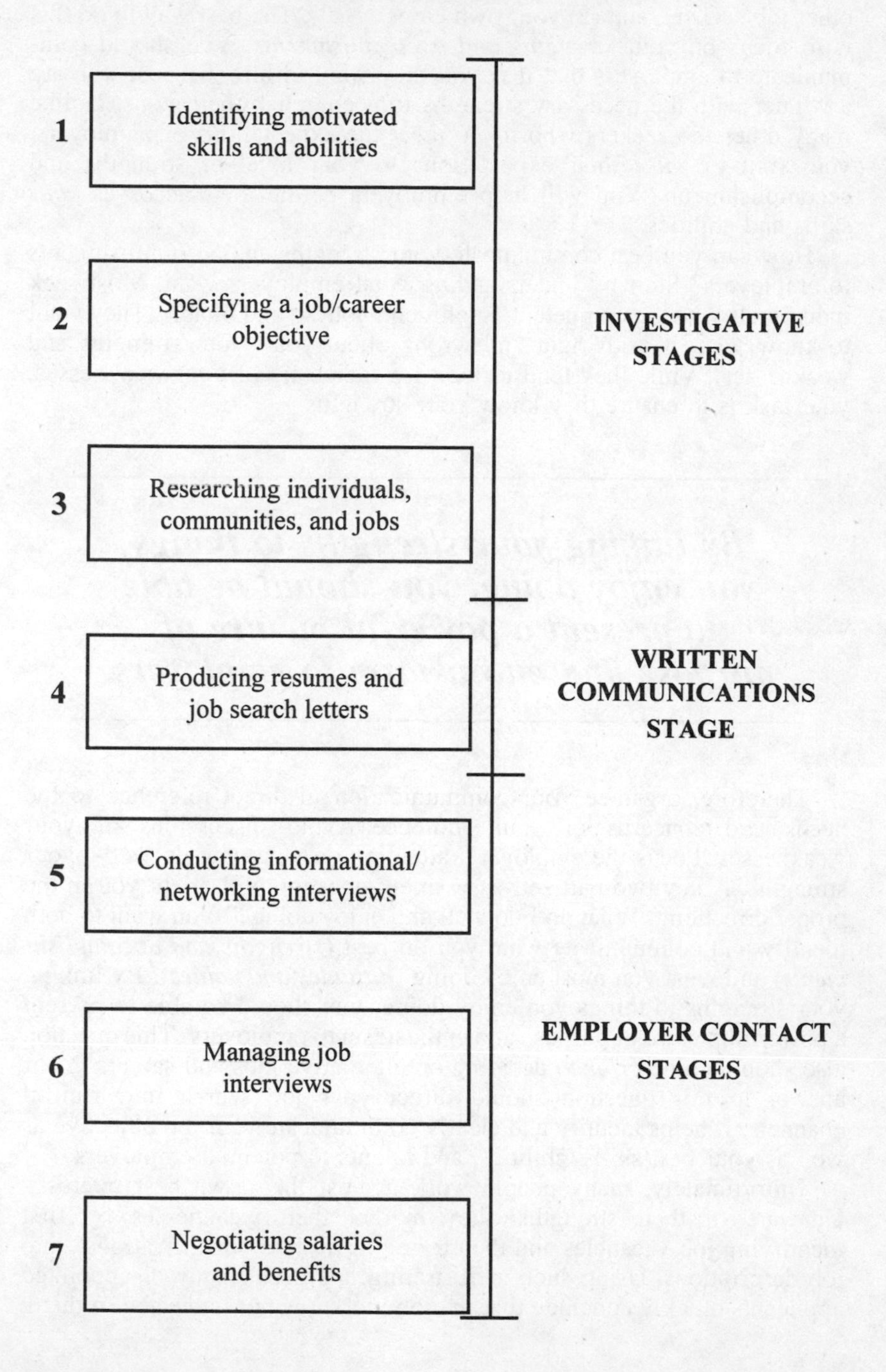
JOB SEARCH STEPS
1
Identifying motivated skills and abilities
2
Specifying a job/career objective
3
Researching individuals, communities, and jobs
INVESTIGATIVE STAGES
4
Producing resumes and job search letters
WRITTEN COMMUNICATIONS STAGE
5
Conducting informational/ networking interviews
6
Managing job interviews
7
Negotiating salaries and benefits
EMPLOYER CONTACT STAGES

Knowing this, you should try to lower employers' hiring anxieties as well as position yourself well within the job market in relation to (1) other job seekers, and (2) your own career goals. The best way to do this is to focus on your *strengths and accomplishments*. You should communicate to employers that it is you they want to hire, because you are a winner with the necessary strengths to accomplish their goals. Unlike many other job seekers who try to *meet* the expectations of employers, you want to *raise* their expectations to your level of strengths and accomplishments. You will help employers define their needs as *your* skills and abilities.

How can you best communicate your strengths and accomplishments to employers? Start by understanding what employers want. Most seek individuals who are competent, intelligent, honest, and likable. They want to know what is both right and wrong about you—your strengths and weaknesses. While they tend to look for indicators of your weaknesses, your task is to ensure they know your strengths.

By linking your strengths to things you enjoy doing, you should be able to present a powerful picture of purpose and enthusiasm to employers.

Therefore, organize your communication in direct reference to the needs and concerns of your audience. Avoid discussions of your weaknesses. Focus the employer's attention on what you do well—your strengths. A key two-part self-assessment question will orient you in the proper direction: "What do I do well and enjoy doing?" You want to both identify and communicate what you do best (*strengths and accomplishments*) and what you most enjoy doing (*attitudes and values*). By linking your strengths to things you enjoy doing, you should be able to present a powerful picture of purpose and enthusiasm to employers. This question also should come *prior to* deciding on alternative jobs and careers. Your answer to this question should direct your job search into fruitful channels. It helps identify and clearly communicate your job objective as well as your best skills, abilities, and talents to potential employers.

Unfortunately, many people work against their own best interests. Unaware of their strengths, they market their weaknesses by first identifying job vacancies and then trying to fit their "qualifications" into job descriptions. Using such a frustrating approach, many disappointed applicants quickly conclude that the job market is not interested in them.

Some attempt to acquire new work-content skills in hopes of finding a job in a "growing" field, even though they do not enjoy using such skills.

Two types of skills relate to your strengths and accomplishments. *Work-content skills* tend to be technical and job-specific in nature. Proficiency in typing, programming computers, operating a crane, or welding are work-content skills. They require formal training, are associated with specific trades or professions, are used only in certain job and career settings, and use a separate skills vocabulary, jargon, and subject matter for specifying technical qualifications for individuals entering and advancing in an occupation. While these hard skills do not transfer well from one occupation to another, they are critical for entering certain occupations.

A second skills category is called *functional or transferable skills*. These skills are associated with numerous job settings, are acquired through experience rather than formal training, and can be communicated through a general skills vocabulary. While most people have only a few work-content skills, they possess numerous—perhaps as many as 300—transferable skills. These skills enable job seekers to change jobs and careers without acquiring additional specialized education and training. These skills can be classified into two general transferable skill categories—organizational/interpersonal skills and personality/work-style traits:

Organizational and Interpersonal Skills

___ communicating
___ problem solving
___ analyzing/assessing
___ planning
___ decision-making
___ innovating
___ thinking logically
___ evaluating
___ identifying problems
___ synthesizing
___ forecasting
___ tolerating ambiguity
___ motivating
___ leading
___ selling
___ performing
___ reviewing
___ attaining
___ team building
___ updating
___ coaching
___ trouble shooting
___ implementing
___ self-understanding
___ understanding
___ setting goals
___ conceptualizing
___ generalizing
___ managing time
___ creating
___ judging
___ controlling
___ organizing
___ persuading
___ encouraging
___ improving
___ designing
___ consulting
___ teaching
___ cultivating
___ advising
___ training

___ supervising
___ estimating
___ negotiating
___ administering
___ interpreting
___ achieving
___ reporting
___ managing

Personality and Work-Style Traits

___ diligent
___ patient
___ innovative
___ persistent
___ tactful
___ loyal
___ successful
___ versatile
___ enthusiastic
___ out-going
___ expressive
___ adaptable
___ democratic
___ resourceful
___ determining
___ creative
___ open
___ objective
___ warm
___ orderly
___ tolerant
___ frank
___ cooperative
___ dynamic
___ self-starter
___ precise
___ sophisticated
___ effective
___ honest
___ reliable
___ perceptive
___ assertive
___ sensitive
___ astute
___ risk taker
___ easy going
___ calm
___ flexible
___ competent
___ punctual
___ receptive
___ diplomatic
___ self-confident
___ tenacious
___ discrete
___ talented
___ empathic
___ tidy
___ candid
___ adventuresome
___ firm
___ sincere
___ initiator
___ competent
___ diplomatic
___ efficient

Use the following exercises to identify both your work-content and transferable skills. These self-assessment techniques stress your positives or strengths rather than identify your negatives or weaknesses. They should generate a rich vocabulary for communicating your "qualifications" to employers. Each exercise requires different investments of your time and effort as well as varying degrees of assistance from other people. We recommend using the most complete and extensive activity—the Motivated Skills Exercise—to gain a thorough understanding of your strengths.

These exercises, however, should be used with caution. There is nothing magical or particularly profound about them. Most are based upon a *deterministic theory of behavior*—understanding your past patterns of behavior are good predictors of your future behavior. Not a bad theory for most individuals, but it is rather simplistic and disheartening for individuals who wish to, and can, break out of past patterns as they embark on a new future. Furthermore, most exercises are historical devices. They provide you with a clear picture of your past, which may or may not be particularly useful for charting your future. Nonetheless, these exercises do help individuals (1) organize data on themselves, (2) target their job search around clear objectives and skills, and (3) generate a rich vocabulary of skills and accomplishments for communicating strengths to potential employers.

If you feel these exercises are inadequate for your needs, by all means seek professional assistance from a testing or assessment center staffed by a licensed psychologist, as outlined in Chapter 6. These centers do in-depth testing which goes further than our self-directed, historical motivated skill exercises.

Checklist Method

This is the simplest method for identifying your strengths. Review the two lists of transferable skills outlined on pages 107-108. Place a "1" in front of the skills that *strongly* characterize you; assign a "2" to those skills that describe you to a *large extent*; put a "3" before those that describe you to *some extent.* After completing this exercise, review the lists and rank order the 10 characteristics that best describe you on each list.

Skills Map

Richard N. Bolles has produced two well-known exercises for identifying transferable skills based upon John Holland's typology of work environments. In his book, *The Three Boxes of Life*, hc develops a checklist of 100 transferable skills. They are organized into 12 categories or types of skills: using hands, body, words, senses, numbers, intuition, analytical thinking, creativity, helpfulness, artistic abilities, leadership, and follow-through.

Bolles' second exercise, *"The Quick Job Hunting Map"*, expands upon this first one. The *"Map"* is a checklist of 222 skills. This exercise requires you to identify seven of your most satisfying accomplishments, achievements, jobs, or roles. After writing a page about each experience, you relate each to the checklist of 222 skills. The *"Map"* should give you a comprehensive picture of what skills you (1) use most frequently, and (2) enjoy using in satisfying and successful settings. While this exercise may take six hours to complete, it yields an enormous amount of data on past strengths. Furthermore, the *"Map"* generates a rich skills vocabulary for communicating your strengths to others. The *"Map"* is found in the appendix of Bolles' *What Color Is Your Parachute?* or it can be purchased separately in beginning, advanced, or "new" versions from Ten Speed Press. Order information on these assessment instruments also is included in the resource section of this book.

Autobiography of Accomplishments

Write a lengthy essay about your life accomplishments. This could range from 20 to 100 pages. After completing the essay, go through it page by page to identify what you most enjoyed doing (working with different kinds of information, people, and things) and what skills you used most frequently as well as enjoyed using. Finally, identify those skills you wish to continue using. After analyzing and synthesizing this data, you should have a relatively clear picture of your strongest skills.

Motivated Skills Exercise

The Motivated Skills Exercise is one of the most complex and time consuming self-assessment exercises. However, it yields some of the best data on skills, and it is especially useful for those who feel they need a more thorough analysis of their skills. Developed by Haldane Associates, this particular exercise is variously referred to as "Success Factor Analysis" or "System to Identify Motivated Skills". While you can use this technique on your own, it is best to work with someone else. Be prepared to devote from six to eight hours to this exercise. It is divided into five steps. The steps follow the basic pattern of generating raw data, identifying patterns, analyzing the data through reduction techniques, and synthesizing the patterns into a transferable skills vocabulary. You need strong analytical skills to complete this exercise on your own. The five steps are as follows:

STEP 1: Take 15 to 20 sheets of paper and at the top of each sheet write one achievement. Your *achievements* are those things you enjoyed doing and felt a sense of accomplishment in doing. These include childhood experiences as well as educational, military, recreational, home, or work-related achievements. For example, at the top of the paper you might state:

> "I learned to play the guitar and joined a rock group while in high school."
>
> "I received an 'A' in physics from the toughest teacher in school."

"I reorganized the files of our office which improved the efficiency of operations."

"I competed in the marathon and finished in the upper third."

"I organized a committee to investigate reducing the number of customer complaints."

"I sang a solo in our church choir."

STEP 2: Select from among your achievements the seven most important ones and prioritize them. Identify the factors that explain your success in each achievement. Examples of these success factors might include various aspects of managing, communicating, creating, analyzing, designing, supervising, coordinating, and problem solving. On each page detail your achievements—how you got involved, what you did, how you did it, and what the outcome was.

STEP 3: Further detail the "what" and "how" of your achievements by having your spouse or a friend interview you over a 60-minute period. Have them ask you to elaborate on each of your achievements and note the terminology you use to elaborate on your skills and abilities. Record your answers for each achievement on separate pieces of paper.

STEP 4: Combine the self-generated and interview data on your achievements into a single master list of success factors. Group the factors into related categories beginning with the most important factor. For example, if "supervising" is your strongest achievement, "decision-making" and "delegating" may be related to this factor. Therefore, the factors would cluster as follows:

supervising decision-making delegating	selling promoting demonstrating
creating designing initiating	decision-making managing strategizing

STEP 5: Synthesize the clusters into new combinations for projecting your past skills into the future. For example, the clusters "supervising—decision-making—delegating" and "creating—designing—initiating" may combine into a new skill category called "creative management". This is the key step in this exercise, because it begins to relate your past strengths to your future goals. It functions as a **bridge** between your skills and your objective.

Try to find a job "fit for you" rather than try to "fit into a job" you think looks interesting.

SPECIFY YOUR OBJECTIVE

When you identify your strengths, you also create the necessary data base and vocabulary for developing your job objective. Using this vocabulary, you should be able to communicate to employers that you are a talented and purposeful individual who achieves *results*.

If you fail to do the preliminary self-assessment work necessary for developing a clear objective, you will probably wander aimlessly in the job market looking for interesting jobs you might fit into. Your goal, instead, should be to find a job or career that is compatible with your interests, motivations, skills, and talents. In other words, try to find a job fit for you rather than try to fit into a job you think looks interesting.

Job hunters with clearly stated objectives have several advantages over those who do not. Their job search is much easier and enjoyable, because they approach it with confidence and optimism. They gain greater control over the job market, because they structure the job market around their goals. They communicate a reassuring sense of purpose and self-confidence to employers who worry about hiring individuals who don't know what they want. They write well designed resumes and letters that help employers make clear choices. For employers lacking basic hiring criteria, such applicants help them better define their "needs" as the applicant's job objective.

Therefore, if you want to achieve the best results, you must have an objective *before* conducting your job search. With a clear objective, you can target your job search at specific high pay-offs in the job market. A clear objective will help you organize your job search into a coherent and manageable whole.

Objectives can be stated in many different forms. Most people think of an objective as a statement of what they would *like to do*. However, such an objective is self-centered. Employers, on the other hand, want to know what *you will do for them*. The best job objective, therefore, is an employer-centered one: state *what it is you can and will do for employers*.

Some people know precisely what they want to do and can state their objective in employer-centered terms. Others find identifying and stating a job objective to be the most difficult and frustrating aspect of the whole job search process. If you are not one of the lucky ones, here are some approaches you can use to help formulate a clear and effective objective.

A clear objective will help you organize your job search into a coherent and manageable whole.

Develop Your Database

Several practical self-directed exercises can alleviate the frustrating aspects of this task. The exercises require you to generate and analyze data about yourself. Begin thinking of your objective as being composed of several ingredients relating to your work values, skills, and knowledge of work environments. Five activities or steps will help you generate a complete set of data for stating your objective.

The first step is to *identify your work and career values* by completing several exercises:

1. List 10 things you would like to achieve before you die. Alternatively, write your obituary for the year 2010 stressing highlights or achievements of your career and life.

2. Think of 10 answers to this questions: "If I had $1,000,000 I would..."

3. List 10 things you prefer and enjoy doing. Prioritize each item.

4. Identify 10 working conditions which you view as negative. Prioritize each condition.

5. List 10 working conditions which you view as positive. Prioritize each item.

6. Check as many of the following work values you feel are desirable in your employment:

__ contribute to society	__ be creative
__ have contact with people	__ supervise others
__ work alone	__ work with details
__ work with a team	__ gain recognition
__ compete with others	__ acquire security
__ make lots of money	__ make decisions
__ work under pressure	__ help others
__ use power and authority	__ solve problems
__ acquire new knowledge	__ take risks
__ be a recognized expert	__ work at own pace

7. Write an essay on your ideal job. Include a weekly calendar of daily activities divided into one hour segments. Specify your duties, responsibilities, authority, salary, working conditions, and opportunities.

The second step is to *gather information on how others see you and your goals*. Ask your spouse or two or three close friends to frankly critique both your strengths and weaknesses. You want them to respond to these questions:

- What are my strengths and weaknesses?
- How can they be improved?
- What working conditions do I enjoy?
- What are my career goals?

The third step is to examine the data you generated in the previous section of this chapter on your strengths. Include it with the information you just generated yourself and received from your spouse and friends. *Rank order which skills you most and least prefer to use in your job or career.*

The fourth step is optional, depending on whether you feel you need more information on your work values, interests, and skills. *Take one or two psychological, aptitude, or vocational tests*. Your options include:

- *Strong-Campbell Interest Inventory*
- *Myers-Briggs Type Indicators*
- *Career Assessment Inventory*
- *The Self-Directed Search*
- *Temperament and Values Inventory*
- *Sixteen Personality Factor Questionnaire*
- *Edwards Personal Preference Schedule*
- *The Occupational View Deck*

- *Self-Description Inventory*
- *Kuder Occupational Interest Survey*

Information from these tests should reinforce and validate the information you gathered from the self-assessment exercises. See a career counselor or a licensed psychologist for identifying and administering the proper tests.

The fifth step is to *test the information concerning your objective against reality and the future* by asking yourself these questions:

- Is my objective realistic?
- Can it be achieved within the next year, 5 years, or 10 years?
- Who needs my skills?
- What factors might help/hinder me in achieving my objective?

You will further clarify your objective as you expose yourself to more job market information while conducting library research and talking to people about your skills, different jobs, and career opportunities. Procedures for gathering such information are outlined in this and Chapter 9.

State Skills As Outcomes

You now should be prepared to develop a one sentence statement of your job objective. Begin by stating your objective at a general level. Next, restate it at a more specific level on your resume.

We recommend developing a **functional job objective**. Recommended by Germann and Arnold in *Bernard Haldane Associations Job and Career Building*, this type of objective combines *skills* and *outcomes*. At a general level it would appear in the following skills-outcomes form:

> "I would like a job where I can use my ability to (a primary skill) which will result in (an outcome)."

If, for example, you wish to write grant and research proposals, you might state the general objective in these terms:

> "I would like a job where my technical research and writing experience will result in new and expanded programs."

The same objective should be re-written at a more specific level for your resume:

> "A management consulting position where strong grantsmanship, research, and writing abilities will be used for expanding human resource development operations."

Including both skills and outcomes, this objective is *targeted* toward particular employers.

As you develop your objective statement, keep in mind that employers want to know how you will achieve *their* goals. Always remember to develop a work-related objective responsive to the needs of your audience. Above all, tell employers what you have to offer—strengths, skills, competencies—and what you will do for them. Emphasize that you are a *doer* who produces concrete results.

While you have certain self-centered goals you wish to achieve for yourself, employers are less interested in what they can do for you. As many employees quickly learn, they are expendable commodities. Most employers feel no need to love them, take care of them, and become sensitive to their personal and professional needs. Employment is a business transaction—their money for your talent. "You're fired!" expresses the fact that employers did not get *value* for their money. Communicate your value loud and clear from the very beginning of your job search.

CONDUCT JOB RESEARCH

You should continuously conduct research on the job market. Research will provide you with a strong knowledge base from which to plan and implement your job search. It will give you critical information for writing your resumes and letters, networking, interviewing, and negotiating salaries.

Research, the process of uncovering information, is central to every step in your job search. It should be a continuous process aimed at developing two general areas of information. First, you must understand the structure and operation of the job markets—both the advertised and hidden job markets. Second, you must acquire specialized knowledge on the key elements in the job markets—individuals and organizations. You gather this information by conducting research in libraries, by mail and telephone, and through face-to-face conversations. This research begins the first day of your job search and continues until the final day and beyond.

Advertised Versus Hidden Job Markets

Your research should be directed initially toward understanding the structure of the job market. The so-called job market actually consists of two structurally different arenas for locating job opportunities. Both are characterized by a high degree of decentralization. Neither should be underestimated nor overestimated.

The **advertised job market** consists of job vacancy announcements and listings found in newspapers, professional and trade journals, newsletters, employment agencies, and personnel offices. Most people focus on this market because it is relatively easy to locate, and because they believe it accurately reflects available job vacancies at any given moment. In reality, however, the advertised job market may include no more than 40 percent of actual job openings. Furthermore, this market tends to represent positions at the extreme ends of the job spectrum—low paid unskilled or high paid highly skilled jobs. The majority of positions lying between these two extremes are not well represented in the listings. And many of the advertised jobs are either nonexistent or are filled prior to being advertised. However, a larger percentage of public employment jobs will appear on the advertised job market because many employers are required to list job vacancies in professional publications, newspapers, and electronic databases. We estimate that nearly 70 percent of all public employment vacancies are advertised. For an excellent and comprehensive examination of the advertised job market relevant to federal, state, and local government as well as nonprofit organizations, see Daniel Lauber's two books: *The Government Job Finder* and *The Nonprofit's Job Finder* (Planning/Communications, 1994).

You should spend an adequate amount of time looking for employment on the advertised job market. Monitor this market, but don't assume it represents the entire spectrum of job opportunities. Your job search time and money may be better spent elsewhere—on the hidden job market.

However, as you will quickly discover in Lauber's two books, there are exceptions to the general rule of minimizing your job search time in the advertised job market. Each occupational specialty has its own internal recruitment and job finding structure. Some occupations are represented more by professional listing and recruitment services than others. For example, many professional urban government positions, such as city manager and city planner, have their own professional associations with highly developed job listing and recruitment services. Indeed, as we move into the high-tech society, greater efforts will be made to increase the efficiency of employment communication by centralizing job listings and recruitment services for particular occupational specialties. These services will be designed to reduce the *lag time* between when a job becomes vacant and is filled. Electronic databases and computerized job banks are increasingly being used by employers to locate qualified candidates, and vice versa. Depending on your job objective and relevant career field, you should investigate such services to determine if, indeed, they are useful for your job search.

The **hidden job market** should be an important arena for your job search. Lacking a formal structure, this job market may encompass as many as 60 percent of all job openings at any given moment, but probably no more than 30 percent in the case of public employment. Many employers turn to the advertised job market *after* they fail to recruit candidates on the hidden job markets. The lag time between when a position becomes vacant, is listed, and then filled is a critical period for your attention and *intervention*. Your goal should be to locate high quality job vacancies on the hidden job market *before* they become listed on the advertised job market.

Your research efforts will be the key to penetrating the hidden job market. Consider, for example, the hiring problems of employers by putting yourself in their place. Start this scenario by supposing one of your employees suddenly gives you two weeks notice, or you terminate someone. Now you have a problem—you must hire a new employee. It takes time and is a risky business you would prefer to avoid. After hours of reading resumes and interviewing, you still will be hiring an unknown who might create new problems for you. Like many other employers, you want to *minimize your time and risks*. You can do this by calling your friends and acquaintances and letting them know you are looking for someone; you would appreciate it if they could refer some good candidates to you. Based on these contacts, you should receive referrals. At the same time, you want to hedge your bets or fulfill affirmative action and equal opportunity requirements by listing the job vacancy in the newspaper or with your personnel office. While 300 people respond by mail to your classified ad, you also get referrals from the trusted individuals in your network. In the end, you conduct ten telephone interviews and three face-to-face interviews. You hire the *best* candidate—the one your former classmate recommended to you on the first day you informed her of your need to fill the vacancy. You are satisfied with your excellent choice; you are relatively certain this new employee will be a good addition to your organization.

This scenario is played out regularly in many organizations—both public and private. It demonstrates the importance of getting into the hidden job market and devoting most of your time and energy there. If you let people know you are looking for employment, chances are they will keep you in mind and refer you to others who may have an unexpected vacancy. Your research will help you enter and maneuver within this job market of interpersonal networks and highly personalized information exchanges. Chapter 9 outlines how to do this with maximum impact.

Work the Library

Libraries are filled with useful job and career information. Reference and documents rooms of libraries have some of the best career resources—books, directories, trade journals, newspapers, computer software, CD-ROM, videos, and online services. Career planning offices at colleges and universities have a wealth of job and career information in their specialized libraries—a wider selection than most general libraries.

Your goal should be to acquire as much written information as possible on individuals and organizations relating to your job objective. Normally this means examining directories, books, magazines, and reports. These publications will provide general surveys of occupational fields, information on particular individuals and organizations, as well as names, addresses, and telephone numbers of key individuals within organizations. At this stage you need to understand the organizations and collect many names, addresses, and telephone numbers for initiating your writing and telephoning activities.

You should start your research by examining several of the following resources normally found in the reference sections of libraries relevant to public employment:

Directories of Reference Materials

- *Ayer Directory of Publications*
- *Applied Science and Technology*
- *Business Periodicals Index*
- *Directory of Directories*
- *Guide to American Directories*
- *Readers' Guide to Periodical Literature*
- *Standard Periodical Directory*
- *Ulrich's International Periodicals Directory*
- *Working Press of the Nation*

Career and Job Alternatives

- *Ad Search*
- *Advance Job Listings*
- *Affirmative Action Register*
- *The College Placement Annual*
- *Dictionary of Occupational Titles*
- *Encyclopedia of Careers and Vocational Guidance* (4 vols.)
- *Guide to Occupational Exploration*
- *Occupational Outlook Handbook*
- *Occupational Outlook Quarterly*
- *Work Related Abstracts*

Government

- *American Almanac of Politics*
- *The Book of the States*
- *Congress Business Daily*
- *Congressional Directory*
- *Congressional Record*
- *Congressional Staff Directory*
- *Congressional Yellow Book*
- *Directory of Federal Executives*
- *Federal Register*

- *Federal Yellow Book*
- *Municipal Yearbook*
- *National Directory of State Agencies*
- *National Organizations of State*
- *Government Officials*
- *State Administrative Officials Classified By Function*
- *State Elected Officials and the Legislatures*
- *State Legislative Leadership, Committees, and Staff*
- *Taylor's Encyclopedia of Government Officials*
- *United States Government Manual*
- *Washington Information Directory*

Peripheral Public Institutions

- *The Consultants and Consulting Organizations Directory*
- *Encyclopedia of Associations* (4 vols.)
- *The Foundation Directory*
- *National Trade and Professional Associations of the U.S.*
- *Research Center Directory*
- *Washington* (yearly)
- *Washington Representatives*
- *Who's Who in Consulting*

International

- *Encyclopedia of Associations: International Organizations*
- *Europa Year Book*
- *Yearbook of International Organizations*
- *Yearbook of the United Nations*

Other Resources

- Trade journals (the *Directory of Libraries and Subject Collections: A Guide to Special Book Collections in Libraries* compiles information on specialized business, government, and association libraries).
- Publications of Chambers of Commerce; state manufacturing associations; federal, state, and local government agencies.
- Telephone books—especially the Yellow Pages (if not in library, contact your local telephone company which may have a telephone book collection).
- Trade books on how to get a job.

As you accumulate names and addresses from your library research, write or call individuals and organizations for further information. Many organizations will give you copies of their annual reports and related literature. Government agencies publish reports and newsletters which are worth examining. Your library may have additional job-related resources on opportunities in the local community.

Talk to People

Beware of becoming *too* preoccupied with library research. This research may give you a false sense of making progress with your job search. Stop when you feel you have enough information to begin other types of research or start other job search activities. Two weeks or 40 hours in the library should get you off to a good start. If you are examining a highly specialized field where there are few names and addresses, you may achieve a high degree of redundancy within 10 hours.

Informal, word-of-mouth communication is still the most effective channel of job search information.

Your most productive research activity will be talking to people. Informal, word-of-mouth communication is still the most effective channel of job search information. In contrast to reading books, people have more current, and probably more accurate, information. In addition, most people are flattered to be asked for advice. They freely give it and will be happy to assist you with referrals to others. Don't hide the fact you are looking for a job, but don't ask for a job. Ask people about:

- Occupational fields
- Job requirements and training
- Interpersonal environments
- Performance expectations
- Their problems
- Salaries
- Advancement opportunities
- Future growth potential of the organization
- How best to acquire more information and contacts in a particular field
- How you can improve your resume

Techniques for conducting this type of research—referred to as networking and informational interviews—are outlined in Chapter 9.

You may be surprised how willing friends, acquaintances, and strangers give useful job information. But before you talk to people, do your library research so you are better able to ask thoughtful questions.

Knowledge is power. Research will help increase your power in the job market. You should always collect new information, revise previous conceptions, and adjust your job search efforts to new realities uncovered through your research. As you do this, your research will affect your original objective and resume as well as guide you in accomplishing the other job search steps. Your power to give some structure and coherence to the hidden job market in your area of interest should increase accordingly.

8

RESUMES, LETTERS, AND YOUR IMAGE

At every stage in the job search you must communicate a positive image to potential employers. The initial impression you make on an employer through applications, resumes, letters, telephone calls, or informational interviews will determine whether the employer is interested in interviewing you and offering you a position.

Developing and managing effective job search communication should play a central role in everything you do related to finding employment. This communication takes many verbal and nonverbal forms. Your first communication with employers will most likely be by letter or in a face-to-face meeting. Job search letters often include your calling card—the resume. These documents are essentially nonverbal forms of communication.

Face-to-face meetings involve both verbal and nonverbal communication. However, the nonverbal aspect is especially important for the informational and job interviews (Chapter 9). Employers place a great deal of emphasis on how you look. Whether you like it or not, appearance, both of your written communications and of you, yourself, play a key role in determining the outcomes of your job search.

In this chapter we examine three important nonverbal communication activities during the job search: resumes, letters, and dress. How you develop, target, and manage this communication will largely determine how far you progress through the interpersonal job search processes in Chapter 9.

At every stage in the job search you must communicate a positive image to potential employers.

WRITING RESUMES

Resumes are important tools for communicating your purpose and capabilities to employers. While many jobs only require a completed application form, you should always prepare a resume for influencing the hiring process. Application forms do not substitute for resumes.

Many myths surround resumes and letters. Some people still believe a resume should summarize one's history. Others believe it will get them a job. And still others believe they should be mailed in response to classified ads. The reality is this: A resume advertises your qualifications to prospective employers. It is your calling card for getting interviews.

Ineffective Resumes

Most people write ineffective resumes. Misunderstanding the purpose of resumes, they make numerous mistakes commonly associated with weak resumes and poor advertising copy. Their resumes often lack an objective, include unrelated categories of information, are too long, and appear unattractive. Other common pitfalls identified by employers include:

- Poor layout
- Misspellings and punctuation errors
- Poor grammar
- Unclear purpose
- Too much jargon
- Include irrelevant data

- Too long or too short
- Poorly typed and reproduced
- Unexplained time gaps
- Too boastful
- Deceptive or dishonest
- Difficult to understand or interpret

A resume advertises your qualifications to prospective employers. It is your calling card for getting interviews.

Your resume, instead, should incorporate the characteristics of strong and effective resumes:

- Clearly communicate your purpose and competencies in relation to employers' needs.
- Be concise and easy to read.
- Motivate the reader to read it in-depth.
- Tell employers that you are a responsible and purposeful individual—a doer who can solve their problems.

Keep in mind that most employers are busy people who normally glance at a resume for only 20 to 30 seconds. Your resume, therefore, must sufficiently catch their attention to pass the 20 to 30 second evaluation test. When writing your resume, ask yourself the same question asked by employers: "Why should I read this or contact this person for an interview?" Your answer should result in an attractive, interesting, unique, and skills-based resume.

Types of Resumes

You have four types of resumes to choose from: chronological, functional, combination, or resume letter. Each format has various advantages and disadvantages, depending on your background and purpose. For example, someone first entering the job market or making a major career change should use a functional resume. On the other hand, a person who wants to target a particular job may choose to use a resume letter. Examples of these different types of resumes are included at the end of this chapter. You should refer to these examples as you read the following section. Further assistance in developing each section of your resume is found in Krannich's and Banis' comprehensive resume development book, *High Impact Resumes and Letters*.

Employers are busy people who normally only glance at a resume for 20 or 30 seconds.

The **chronological resume** is the standard resume used by most applicants. It comes in two forms: traditional and improved. The **traditional chronological resume** is also known as the "obituary resume", because it both "kills" your chances of getting a job and is a good source for writing your obituary. Summarizing your work history, this resume lists dates and names first and duties and responsibilities second; it includes extraneous information such as height, weight, age, marital status, sex, and hobbies. While relatively easy to write, this is the most ineffective resume you can produce. Its purpose at best is to inform people of what you have done in the past as well as where, when, and with whom. It tells employers little or nothing about what you want to do, can do, and will do for them. This is the ultimate self-centered resume.

The **improved chronological resume** communicates directly to employers your purpose, past achievements, and probable future performance. You should use this type of resume when you have extensive experience directly related to a position you seek. This resume should include a work objective which reflects both your work experience and professional goals. The work experience section should include the names and addresses of former employers followed by a brief description of your accomplishments, skills, and responsibilities; inclusive employment dates should appear at the end. Do not begin with dates; they are the least significant element in the descriptions. Be sure to stress your *accomplishments* and *skills* rather than your formal duties and responsibilities. You want to inform your audience that you are a productive and responsible person who gets things done—a doer.

If you are changing careers or have an unstable employment history, avoid using a chronological resume. It communicates the wrong messages—you lack direct work experience, you are an unstable worker, or you have not advanced in your career. If you have such a career pattern, consider writing a functional or combination resume.

Functional resumes should be used by individuals making a significant career change, first entering the workforce, or re-entering the job market after a lengthy absence. This resume should stress your accomplishments and transferable skills regardless of previous work settings and job titles. This could include accomplishments as a housewife or house husband, volunteer worker, or Sunday school teacher. Names of employers and dates of employment should not appear on this resume.

Functional resumes have certain weaknesses. While they are important bridges for the inexperienced and for those making a career change, some employers dislike these resumes. Since many employers still look for names, dates, and direct job experience, this resume does not meet their expectations. You should use a functional resume only if your past work experience does not strengthen your objective when making a major career change.

Combination resumes are a compromise between chronological and functional resumes. Having more advantages than disadvantages, this resume may be exactly what you need if you are making a career change with related experience from one career to another.

Combination resumes have the potential to both *meet* and *raise* the expectations of employers. You should stress your accomplishments and skills as well as include your work history. Your work history should appear as a separate section immediately following your presentation of accomplishments and skills in the "Areas of Effectiveness" or "Experience" section. It is not necessary to include dates unless they enhance your resume. This is the perfect resume for someone wishing to change to a job in a related career field.

Resume letters are substitutes for resumes. Appearing as a job inquiry or application letter, resume letters highlight various sections of your resume, such as work history, experience, areas of effectiveness, objective, or education, in relation to employers' needs. These letters are used when you prefer not sending your more general resume. Resume letters have one major weakness: they give employers insufficient information and thus may prematurely eliminate you from consideration.

Structuring Your Resume

After choosing an appropriate resume format, you should generate the necessary information for structuring each category of your resume. You developed much of this information when you identified your strengths and specified your objective in Chapter 6. To complete your database for the resume, include the following information on separate sheets of paper:

CONTACT INFORMATION: name, address, telephone number.

WORK OBJECTIVE: refer to your data in Chapter 7 on writing an objective.

EDUCATION:	degrees, schools, dates, highlights, special training.
WORK EXPERIENCE:	paid, unpaid, civilian, military, and part-time employment. Include job titles, employers, locations, dates, skills, accomplishments, duties, and responsibilities. Use the functional language developed in Chapter 7.
OTHER EXPERIENCE:	volunteer, civic, and professional memberships. Include your contributions, demonstrated skills, offices held, names, and dates.
SPECIAL SKILLS OR LICENSES/ CERTIFICATES:	foreign languages, teaching, paramedical, etc. relevant to your objective.
MISCELLANEOUS INFORMATION:	references, expected salary, willingness to relocate and travel, availability dates.

Producing Drafts

Once you generate the basic data for constructing your resume, your next task is to reduce this data into draft resumes. If, for example, you write a combination resume, the internal organization of the resume should be as follows:

- Contact information
- Work objective
- Qualifications or functional experience
- Work history or employment
- Education

Be careful about including any other type of information on your resume. Other information most often is extraneous or negative information. You should only include information designed to strengthen your objective.

While your first draft may run more than two pages, try to get everything into one or two pages for the final draft. Most employers lose interest after reading the first page. If you produce a two-page resume, one of the best formats is to attach a single supplemental page to a self-contained one-page resume.

Your final draft should conform to the following rules for creating an excellent resume:

RESUME "DON'TS"

- **Don't** use abbreviations except for your middle name.
- **Don't** make the resume cramped and crowded; it should be pleasing to the eyes.
- **Don't** make statements you can't document.
- **Don't** use the passive voice.
- **Don't** change tense of verbs.
- **Don't** use lengthy sentences and descriptions.
- **Don't** refer to yourself as "I".
- **Don't** include negative information.
- **Don't** include extraneous information.

RESUME "DOS"

- **Do** use action verbs and the active voice.
- **Do** be direct, succinct, and expressive with your language.
- **Do** appear neat, well organized, and professional.
- **Do** use ample spacing and highlights (all caps, underlining, bulleting) for different emphases.
- **Do** maintain an eye pleasing balance. Try centering your contact information at the top, keeping information categories on the left in all caps, and describing the categories in the center and on the right.
- **Do** check carefully your spelling, grammar, and punctuation.
- **Do** clearly communicate your purpose and value to employers.
- **Do** communicate your strongest points first.

Evaluating

You should subject your resume drafts to two types of evaluations. An **internal evaluation** consists of reviewing our lists of "dos" and "don'ts" to make sure your resume conforms to these rules. An **external evaluation** should be conducted by circulating your resume to three or more individuals whom you believe will give you frank, objective, and useful feedback. Avoid people who tend to flatter you. The best evaluator would be someone in a hiring position similar to one you will encounter in the actual interview. Ask these people to critique your draft resume and suggest improvements in both form and content. This will be your most important evaluation. After all, the only evaluation that counts is the one that helps get you an interview. Asking someone to critique your resume is one way to spread the word that you are job hunting. As we will see in Chapter 9, this is one method for getting invited to an interview!

Final Production

Your final resume can be typed or typeset. If you type it, be sure it looks professional. Use an electric typewriter with a carbon ribbon. Varying the typing elements and styles can produce an attractive copy. Do not use a portable typewriter with a nylon ribbon since it does not produce professional copy. Many typists will do your resume on the proper machine for about $5 to $10.

If you have it word processed, be sure the final copy is printed on a letter quality printer using a carbon ribbon or on a laser printer. Dot matrix and near letter quality printers make your resume look mass produced.

Alternatively, you can have a printer typeset your resume. This may cost anywhere from $20 to $50. The final product should look first-class. However, it may look *too* professional or *too* slick; some employers may think you had someone else write the resume for you.

Whichever method you use, be sure to proofread the final copy. Many people spend good money on production only to later find typing errors.

When reproducing the resume, you must consider the quality and color of paper as well as the number of copies you need. By all means use good quality paper. You should use watermarked 20-pound or heavier bond paper. Costing 3 to 7 cents per sheet, this paper can be purchased through stationery stores and printers. It is important not to cut corners at this point by purchasing cheap paper or using copy machine paper. You may save $5 on 100 copies, but you also will communicate an unprofessional image to employers.

Use one of the following paper colors: white, off-white, light tan, light gray, or light blue. Avoid blue, yellow, green, pink, orange, red, or any other bright colors. Conservative, light-muted colors are the best. Any of these colors can be complemented with black ink. In the case of light gray—our first choice—a navy blue ink looks good. Dark brown ink is especially attractive on light tan paper.

Your choices of paper quality and color say something about your personality and professional style. They communicate nonverbally your potential strengths and weaknesses. Employers will use these as indicators for screening you in or out of an interview. At the same time, these choices may make your resume stand out from the crowd of standard black-on-white resumes.

You have two choices in reproducing your resume: a copy machine or an offset process. Many of the newer copy machines give good reproductions on the quality paper you need—nearly the same quality as the offset process. You should be able to make such copies for 10-20 cents per page. The offset process produces the best quality because it uses a printing plate. It also is relatively inexpensive—5 to 10 cents per copy with a minimum run of 100 copies. The cost per copy decreases with large runs of 300, 500, or 1000. In the end, you should be able to have your resume typed and 100 copies reproduced on high quality colored bond paper for less than $25. If you have it typeset, the same number of copies may cost you $50.

Whatever your choices, do not try to cut costs when it comes to producing your resume. It simply is not worth it. Remember, your resume is your calling card—it should represent your best professional image. Put your best foot forward at this stage. Go in style; spend a few dollars on producing a first-class resume.

Your resume is your calling card—it should represent your best professional image.

JOB SEARCH LETTERS

Resumes sent through the mail are normally accompanied by a cover letter. After interviewing for information or a position, you should send a thank-you letter. Other occasions will arise when it is both proper and necessary for you to write different types of job search letters. Examples of these letters, which follow this discussion, are presented at the end of this chapter.

Your letter writing should follow the principles of good resume and business writing. Job hunting letters are like resumes—they advertise you for interviews. Like good advertisements, these letters should follow four basic principles for effectiveness:

1. Catch the reader's attention.
2. Persuade the reader of your benefits or value.
3. Convince the reader with evidence.
4. Move the reader to acquire the product.

Basic Preparation Rules

Before you begin writing a job search letter, ask yourself several questions to clarify the content of your letter:

- What is the **purpose** of the letter?
- What are the **needs** of my audience?
- What **benefits** will my audience gain from me?
- What is a good opening sentence or paragraph for grabbing the

attention of my audience?
- How can I maintain the **interests** of my audience?
- How can I best end the letter so that the audience will be **persuaded** to contact me?
- If a resume is enclosed, how can my letter best **advertise the resume**?
- Have I spent enough **time** revising and proofreading the letter?
- Does the letter represent my **best professional effort**?

Since your letters are a form of business communication, they should conform to the rules of good business correspondence:

- Plan and organize what you will say by outlining the content of your letter.
- Know your purpose and plan the elements of your letter accordingly.
- Communicate your message in a logical and sequential manner.
- State your purpose immediately in the first sentence and paragraph; main ideas always go first.
- End your letter by stating what your reader can expect next from you.
- Use short paragraphs and sentences; avoid overly complex sentences.
- Punctuate properly and use correct grammar and spelling.
- Use simple and straight forward language; avoid jargon.
- Communicate your message as directly and briefly as possible.

The rules stress how to both *organize and communicate* your message with impact. At the same time, you should always have a specific purpose in mind as well as know the needs of your audience.

Types of Letters

Cover letters provide cover for your resume. You should avoid overwhelming a one-page resume with a two-page letter or repeating the contents of the resume in the letter. A short and succinct one-page letter which highlights one or two points in your resume is sufficient. Three paragraphs will suffice. The first paragraph should state your interests and purposes for writing. The second paragraph should highlight your possible value to the employer. The third paragraph should state that you will call the individual at a particular time to schedule an interview.

However, do not expect great results from cover letters. Many professional job search firms use word processing equipment and mailing lists to flood the job market with resumes and cover letters. As a result, employers are increasingly suspicious of the authenticity of such letters.

Approach letters are designed to develop job contacts, leads, or information as well as to organize networks and get interviews—the subjects of Chapter 9. Your primary purposes should be to get employers to engage in the 5R's of informational interviewing:

- **Reveal** useful information and advice.
- **Refer** you to others.
- **Read** your resume.
- **Revise** your resume.
- **Remember** you for future reference.

These letters help you gain access to the hidden job market.

Approach letters can be sent out *en masse* to uncover job leads, or they can target particular individuals or organizations. It is best to target these letters since they have maximum impact when personalized in reference to particular positions.

The structure of approach letters is similar to other letters. The first paragraph states your purpose. In so doing, you may want to use a personal statement for openers, such as "Mary Tillis recommended that I write to you..." or "I am familiar with your..." State your purpose, but do not suggest that you are asking for a job—only career advice or information. In your final paragraph, request a meeting and indicate you will call to schedule such a meeting at a mutually convenient time.

Thank-you letters may well become your most effective job search letters. They especially communicate your thoughtfulness. These letters come in different forms and are written for various occasions. The most common thank-you letter is written after receiving assistance, such as job search information or a critique of your resume. Other occasions include:

- **Immediately following an interview:** Thank the interviewer for the opportunity to interview for the position. Repeat your interest in the position.

- **Receive a job offer:** Thank the employer for his or her faith in you and express your appreciation.

- **Rejected for a job:** Thank the employer for giving you the "opportunity" to interview for the job. Ask to be remembered for future reference.

- **Terminate employment:** Thank the employer for the experience and ask to be remembered for future reference.
- **Begin a new job:** Thank the employer for giving you this new opportunity and express your confidence in producing the value he or she is expecting from you.

Examples of each type of letter are presented at the end of this chapter.

Being remembered by employers is the closest thing to being invited to an interview and offered a job.

Several of these thank-you letters are unusual, but they all have the same goal in mind—to be remembered by potential employers in a positive light. In a job search, being remembered by employers is the closest thing to being invited to an interview and offered a job.

DISTRIBUTION AND MANAGEMENT

The only good resumes are the ones that get read, remembered, referred, and result in a job interview. Therefore, after completing your resume and job search letters, you must decide what to do with them. Are you planning to only respond to classified ads and vacancy announcements? What other creative distribution methods might you use, such as sending it to friends, relatives, and former employers? What is the best way to proceed?

Responding to Classified Ads

Except for government agencies, most of your writing activities should focus on the hidden job market. At the same time, you should respond to job listings in newspapers, magazines, and personnel offices. While this is largely a numbers game, you can increase your odds by the way you respond to the listings.

You should be selective in your responses. Since you know what you want to do, you will be looking for only certain types of positions. Once you identify them, your response entails little expenditure of time and effort—an envelope, letter, stamp, resume, and maybe 20 minutes of your time. You have little to lose. While you have the potential to gain by sending a letter and resume in response to an ad, remember the odds are usually against you.

The only good resumes are the ones that get read, remembered, referred, and result in a job interview.

It is difficult to interpret job listings. Some employers place blind ads with P.O. Box numbers in order to collect resumes for future reference. Others wish to avoid aggressive applicants who telephone or "drop-in" for interviews. Many employers work through professional recruiters who place these ads. While you may try to second guess the rationale behind such ads, respond to them as you would to ads with an employer's name, address, or telephone number. Assume there is a real job behind the ad.

Most ads request a copy of your resume. You should respond with a cover letter and resume as soon as you see the ad. Depending on how much information about the position is revealed in the ad, your letter should be tailored to emphasize your qualifications vis-a-vis the ad. Examine the ad carefully. Underline any words or phrases which relate to your qualifications. In your cover letter you should use similar terminology in emphasizing your qualifications. Keep the letter brief and to the point.

If the ad asks you to state your salary history or salary requirements, state "negotiable" or "open". Alternatively, you can include a figure by stating a salary range 20 percent above your present salary base. For example, if you are making $30,000 a year, you can state this as "in the $30,000 to $36,000 range". Use your own judgment in addressing the salary question. There is no hard and fast rule on stating a figure or range. A figure helps the employer screen-out individuals with too high a salary expectation. We prefer keeping salary considerations to the end of the interview—after you have demonstrated your value.

You may be able to increase your odds by sending a second copy of your letter and resume two or three weeks after your initial response. Most applicants normally reply to an ad during the seven day period immediately after it appears in print. Since employers often are swamped with responses, your letter and resume may get lost in the crowd. If you send a second copy of your application two or three weeks later, the employer will have more time to give you special attention. By then, he or she also will have a better basis on which to compare you to the others.

Keep in mind that your cover letter and resume may be screened among 400 other resumes and letters. Thus, you want your cover letter to be eye catching and easy to read. Keep it brief and concise and highlight your qualifications as stated in the employer's ad. Don't spend a great deal of time responding to an ad or waiting anxiously at your mailbox or telephone for a reply. Keep moving on to other job search activities. For a good book on this subject, see Kenton Elderkin's *How to Get Interviews From Classified Job Ads* (Impact Publications, 1993).

Self-Initiated Methods

Your letters and resumes can be distributed and managed in various ways. Many people shotgun hundreds of cover letters and resumes to prospective employers. This is a form of gambling where the odds are against you. For every 100 people you contact in this manner, expect one or two who might be interested in you. After all, successful direct-mail experts at best expect only a 2 percent return on their mass mailings!

If you choose to use the shotgun methods, you can increase your odds by using the *telephone*. Call the prospective employer within a week after he or she receives your letter. This technique will probably increase your effectiveness rate from 1 to 5 percent. For more information on the use of the telephone for follow-up, see one of our other books, *Dynamite Tele-Search* (Impact Publications, 1995).

However, many people are shotgunning their resumes today. As more resumes and letters descend on employers with the increased use of word processing equipment, the effectiveness rates may be even lower. This also can be an expensive marketing method.

Your best distribution strategy will be your own modification of the following procedure:

- Selectively identify whom you are interested in working for.
- Send an approach letter.
- Follow up with a telephone call seeking an appointment for an interview.

In more than 50 percent of the cases, you will get an interview. It is best not to include a copy of your resume with the approach letter. Keep your resume for the end of the interview. Chapter 9 outlines the procedures for conducting this informational interview.

Recordkeeping

Once you begin distributing letters and resumes, you also will need to keep good records for managing your job search writing campaign. Purchase file folders for your correspondence and notes. Be sure to make copies of all letters you write since you may need to refer to them over the telephone or before interviews. Record your activities with each employer—letters, resumes, telephone calls, interviews—on a 4 x 6 card and file it according to the name of the organization or individual. These files will help you quickly access information and enable you to evaluate your job search progress.

Always remember the purpose of resumes and letters—*advertise you for interviews*. They do not get jobs. Since most employers know nothing about you, *you must effectively communicate your value in writing prior to the critical interview*. While you should not overestimate the importance of this written communication, neither should you underestimate it.

PROJECT A PROFESSIONAL IMAGE

Let's assume you present a positive image in your written and telephone communication. Based on these impressions, someone agrees to meet with you for an informational interview or invites you to a job interview. At this stage, you must convey a positive image in the way you look as well as the way you behave both verbally and nonverbally. Your appearance becomes a powerful indicator of your value to individuals who do not know you.

Appearance is the first thing you communicate to others.

Appearance is the first thing you communicate to others. Before you have a chance to speak, others notice how you dress and accordingly draw certain conclusions about your personality and competence. Indeed, research shows that appearance makes the greatest difference when an evaluator has little information about the other person. This is precisely the situation you find yourself in at the start of the interview.

Many people object to having their capabilities evaluated on the basis of their appearance and manner of dress. "But that is not fair," they argue. "People should be hired on the basis of their ability to do the job—not on how they look." But debating the lack of merit or complaining about the unfairness of such behavior does not alter reality. Like it or not, people do make initial judgments about others based on their appearance. Since you cannot alter this fact and bemoaning it will get you nowhere, it is best to learn to use it to your advantage. If you learn to effectively manage your image, you can convey marvelous messages regarding your authority, credibility, and competence.

Some estimates indicate that as much as 65 percent of the hiring decision may be based on the nonverbal aspects of the interview! Employers sometimes refer to this phenomenon with such terms as "chemistry", "body warmth", or that "gut feeling" the individual is right for the job. This correlates with findings of communication studies that approximately 65 percent of a message is communicated nonverbally. The remaining 35 percent is communicated verbally.

As much as 65 percent of the hiring decision may be based on nonverbal aspects of the interview!

Rules of the Game

Knowing how to dress appropriately for the interview requires knowing important rules of the game. Like it or not, employers play by these rules. Once you know the rules, you at least can make a conscious choice whether or not you want to play. If you decide to play, you will stand a better chance of winning by using the often unwritten rules to your advantage.

Much has been written on how to dress professionally, especially since John Molloy first wrote his books on dress for success in the 1970s. While this approach has been criticized for promoting a "cookie cutter" or "carbon copy" image, it is still valid for most interview situations. The degree to which employers adhere to these rules, however, will depend on particular individuals and situations. Your job is to know when, where, and to what extent the rules apply to you. When in doubt, follow our general advice on looking professional.

Knowing and playing by the rules does not imply incompetent people get jobs simply by dressing the part. Rather, it implies that qualified and competent job applicants can gain an extra edge over a field of other qualified, competent individuals by dressing to convey positive professional images.

Winning the Game

Much advice has been written about how to dress for success—some of it excellent. However, there is a major flaw in most of the advice you encounter. Researchers on the subject have looked at how people in positions of power view certain colors for professional attire. Few have gone beyond this to note that colors do different things on different people. Various shades or clarities of a color or combinations of contrast between light and dark colors when worn together may be unenhancing to some individuals and actually diminish that person's "power look".

For example, the combination of a white shirt or blouse paired with a navy suit—one of the success and power looks promoted by many—will be enhancing both to the appearance and the image of power on some individuals, but will be unenhancing and actually over-power the appearance of others. Or suppose you take the advice that a medium to charcoal gray suit is a good color in the professional world. It is, but the advice to wear medium to charcoal gray only recognizes differences of light to dark. In that medium to charcoal range we could pick scores of shades of gray from very blue grays to taupe grays. The wrong gray shade on individuals can make them look unattractive, unhealthy, and even older than their age. Who wants to hire someone who appears to be in poor health?

If we combine the results of research done by John Molloy on how colors relate to one's power look and that done by JoAnne Nicholson and Judy Lewis-Crum as explained in their book *Color Wonderful* (New York: Bantam) on how colors relate to us as unique individuals, we can achieve a win-win situation. You can retain your individuality and look your most enhanced while, at the same time, achieving a look of success, power, and competence.

Your Winning Appearance

The key to effective dressing is to know how to relate the clothing you put on your body to your own natural coloring. Let's pose a few questions to start you thinking about color in what may be some new ways. Ask yourself these questions:

- Can you wear black and white together and look good, or does that much contrast wear you?
- Can you wear navy and white together and retain your "power look" or does that much contrast actually diminish your look of power and authority?
- Can you wear a pure white or is a slightly cream toned white more flattering?
- Do you look better in clear or toned down shades of colors?

The answers to these questions vary with each individual's natural coloring. So it's important to know the appropriate answer for you.

Into which category does your coloring fit? Let's find out where you belong in terms of color type:

- **Contrast coloring:** If you are a contrast color type, you have a definite dark-light appearance. You have very dark brown or black hair and light to medium ivory or olive toned skin. Black men and women in this category will have clear light to dark skin tones and dark hair.
- **Light-bright coloring:** If you are of this color type, you have golden tones in your skin and golden tones in your blond or light to medium brown hair. Most of you had blond or light brown hair as children. Black men and women in this category will have clear golden skin in their face and dark hair.
- **Muted coloring:** If you are a muted color type, you have a definite brown-on-brown or red-on-brown appearance. Your skin tone is an ivory-beige, brown-beige, or golden-beige tone—that is, you have a beige skin with a golden-brown cast. Your hair could be red or light to dark brown with camel, bronze, or red highlights. Black men and women in this category will have golden or brown skin tones and dark hair.
- **Gentle coloring:** If you are of this color type, you have a soft, gentle looking appearance. Your skin tone is a light ivory or pink-beige tone and your hair is ash blond or ash brown. You probably had blond or ash brown hair as a child. Black men and women in this category will have pink tones in their skin and dark hair.

There are also some individuals who may be a combination of two color types. If your skin tone falls in one category and your hair color in another, you are a combination color type.

These color types will be referred to in the next two sections when guidelines are given for effectively combining shirts, suits, and ties for men, and skirted suits, blouses, and accessories for women to both enhance and maximize each individual's professional look.

However, if you are not certain which hair or skin tone is yours and are hence undecided as to which color type category you belong to, you may wish to contact Color 1 Associates at 1/800-523-8496 (2211 Washington Circle, NW, Washington, DC 20037).

Color 1 can provide you with an individualized color chart that allows you to wear every color in the spectrum, but in your best *shade* and *clarity* as well as written material telling you how to combine your colors for the best amounts of contrast for your natural coloring (color type).

The color chart is an excellent one-time investment considering the costs of buying the wrong colored suit, shirt, or blouse. It will more than pay for itself if it contributes to an effective interview as you wear your suit in your best shade and put your clothing together to work with, rather than against, your natural coloring. It can help you convey positive images during those crucial initial minutes of the interview—as well as over a lifetime.

Male Images of Success

Ken Karpinski and John Molloy have conducted extensive research on how men can dress most effectively. Aimed at individuals already working in professional positions who want to communicate a success image, their advice is just as relevant for someone interviewing for a public or private sector job.

Except for some blue collar jobs, basic attire for men interviewing for a position is a suit. Let's look at appropriate suits in terms of color, fabric, and style. The suit color can make a difference in creating an image of authority and competence. In general, blue, gray, camel, or beige are proper colors for men's suits. Usually the darker the shade, the greater amount of authority it conveys to the wearer. Given your situation (*the interview*) and your audience (*the interviewer*), you should aim at conveying enough authority to command attention and a positive regard, but not so much as to threaten the interviewer. Hence, the medium to charcoal gray or navy blue would be good suit colors. Black, a basic funeral attire, can threaten the interviewer by conveying too much authority.

When selecting your gray, navy, camel, or beige suit, choose a shade that is enhancing to you. Should you wear a blue-gray, a taupe-gray, or a shade in-between? Do you look better in a somewhat bright navy or a more toned-down navy; a blue navy or a black navy; a navy with a purple or a yellow base to it?

In general, most people will look better in somewhat blue grays than in grays that are closer to the taupe side of the spectrum. Most people will be enhanced by a navy that is not too bright or contain so much black that it is difficult to distinguish whether the color is navy or black. When selecting a beige or a camel, select a tone that complements your skin color. If your skin has pink tones, avoid beiges and camels that contain gold hues and select pink based beiges/camels that enhance your skin color. Similarly, those of you who have gold/olive tones to your skin should avoid the pink based camel and beiges.

Should your camels or beiges be pink-toned, ivory-toned or golden-toned? If you are unsure, get the name of the Color 1 Associate nearest you and schedule an appointment. If you are going to spend a lot of money on a suit—and if you buy a good, well-made suit you are going to spend a lot of money—buy a suit that will work for you.

Your suit(s) should be made of a natural fiber. A good blend of a natural fiber with some synthetic is acceptable as long as it has the "look" of the natural fiber. The very best suit fabrics are wool, wool blends, or fabrics that look like them. Even for the warmer summer months, men can find summer weight wool suits that are comfortable and look marvelous. They are your best buy. For really hot climates, linen, or a fabric that looks like linen tests well. Normally a linen will have to be blended with another fiber, often a synthetic, in order to retain a pressed, neat look. The major disadvantage of pure linen is that it wrinkles.

The style of your suit should be classic. It should be well-tailored and well-styled. Avoid suits that appear "trendy" unless you are applying for a job in a field such as arts or perhaps advertising. A conservative suit that has a timeless classic styling and also looks up-to-date will serve you best not only for the interview, but it will give you several years wear once you land the job. Select a shirt color that is lighter than the color of your suit.

We recommend two key books for men—Ken Karpinski's *Red Socks Don't Work: Messages From the Real World About Men's Clothing* (Impact Publications) and John Molloy's *New Dress for Success* (Warner Books). These books go into great detail on shirts, ties, and practically everything you might wear or carry with you. We recommend these books over others because they are based on research rather than personal opinion and promotional fads.

However, be careful with Molloy's book. You must take his advice one step beyond where he takes you: keep in mind your color type. If you have contrast or light-bright coloring, you will look great wearing your shade of white in a shirt with your navy blue shade in a suit. But if you have muted or gentle coloring, *this is too much contrast for you.* For muted or gentle coloring, the combination of navy and white will visually overpower you and you will not look your most enhanced.

If you are a muted or gentle color type, the look that gives you the greatest power look and yet does not overpower you will be a suit in your most flattering shade of gray worn with a shirt in your shade of white. You can expect your white to be less of a "pure" white (more creamy) than the white a contrast or a light-bright would wear. When you wear a navy suit, pair it with a blue shirt rather than a white one. This combines your colors in a level of contrast effective for your coloring.

Female Images of Success

Few men would consider wearing anything other than a suit to a job interview-especially an interview for a managerial or professional position. Women are often less certain what is appropriate. As a result of research conducted by John Molloy and others, the verdict is now in. A skirted suit is the definite choice for the interview. This attire allows a woman to best convey images of professionalism, authority, and competence. Wearing a skirted suit can initially help a woman overcome negative stereotypes that some men still hold toward women in managerial and other professional positions.

Let's survey appropriate suits in terms of color, fabric, and style. As in the case of men's suits, the color of your suit can help create an image of authority and competence. The suit colors that make the strongest positive statements for you are *your shade* of gray in a medium to charcoal depth or *your shade* of blue in a medium to navy depth of color. Other neutral shades, such as beige, test well as does camel. Avoid black, which can convey so much authority many interviewers find it threatening. Also, avoid solid brown. British looking tweeds and small plaids or herringbone designs in brown are acceptable, but a solid dark brown suit does not score well with most interviewers.

When selecting your gray, navy, camel, or any other colored suit, follow the same rules we outlined for men: choose a shade that is enhancing to you. If you are uncertain which shades are best for you, contact a Color 1 Associate for advice.

Similar to men's suits, your suit should be made of a natural fiber or have the "look" of a natural fiber. The very best winter-weight suit fabrics are wool or wool blends. For the warmer climates or the summer months, women will find few, if any, summer weight wool suits made for them. Hence linen, blended with a synthetic so it will not look as if it needs constant pressing, is your first choice. Other fabrics, such as polyester blended with rayon, in clothing of good quality often has the definite look of linen but without the hassles of caring for real linen. But the key word here is *quality*. A cheap polyester/rayon fabric will look just that.

When deciding on your professional wardrobe, always buy clothes to last and buy quality.

Your suit style should be classic. Following similar rules as for men, women's suits should be well-tailored, well-styled, and avoid a "trendy" look unless appropriate for certain occupations. A conservative, classic suit will last for years and is an excellent investment. Indeed, you can afford to buy good quality clothing if you know you will get a lot of use from the item. When deciding on your professional wardrobe, always buy clothes to last and buy quality.

Quality also means buying silk blouses if you can afford them. Keep in mind not only the price of the blouse itself, but the cleaning bill. There are many polyester blouse fabrics that have the look and feel of silk. Silk or a polyester that has the look and feel of silk are the fabrics for blouses to go with your wool suits. Cotton blouses should generally not be paired with a wool suit. Choose your blouses in your most flattering shades and clarity of color. For more information on up-to-date dress and business images for women, consult JoAnna Nicholson's new book, *110 Mistakes Working Women Make and How to Avoid Them: Dressing Smart in the '90s* (Impact Publications).

Remember to keep in mind your color type. Contrast or light-bright coloring types can look great wearing their shade of white in a blouse with their navy blue shade in a suit. Muted and gentle color types will find this to be too much contrast and thus overpower their natural coloring. Such a color combination actually diminishes their power look.

If you are a muted or gentle color type, why not try your coral red shade blouse with your navy suit or wear your shade of white with your gray shade suit. Once you are aware of your color type and how to best enhance it while retaining visual authority, you will find many new and flattering combinations.

Give your outfit a more "finished and polished" look by accessorizing it effectively. Collect silk scarves and necklaces of semiprecious stones in your suit colors. Wear scarves and necklaces with your suits and blouses in such a way that they repeat the color of the suit. For example, a woman wearing a navy suit and a red silk blouse could accent the look by wearing a necklace of navy sodalite beads or a silk scarf that has navy as a predominate color.

Wear shoes as dark or darker than your skirt.

The most appropriate shoe to wear with a business suit is a classic pump with a closed heel and toe and little or no decoration. Not only does this shoe stand by itself as creating the most professional look, it also teams best with a business suit and is flattering at the same time. A sling-back shoe (heel open with a strap across the heel) can be worn with a suit, but will slightly diminish the wearer's visual power. Avoid shoes with a sandal look. They can be beautiful shoes, but save them for evening wear. Sandals do not have the visual weight to balance a suit. In general, wear shoes as dark or darker than your skirt. If not, you may draw the other person's eyes to your feet when, instead, you want them to focus on your face and on what you are saying.

You may choose to carry a purse *or* an attache case, but not both at the same time. It is difficult not to look clumsy trying to handle both a purse and an attache case, and it is likely to diminish your power look as well. One way to carry both is to keep a slim purse with essentials such as lipstick, mirror, and money inside the attache case. If you need to go out to lunch, or any place where you choose not to carry the attache case, just pull out your purse and you're off.

Buy Quality Apparel

Aside from information on what articles of apparel to wear, a word on the quality of what you purchase is in order. Buy the best you can afford. If you are not gainfully employed, this may seem like impractical advice. But it still remains the most practical advice. Two really good suits with a variety of shirts or blouses will look better from the first day you own them than four suits of inferior quality—and will out last them as well. To buy quality rather than quantity is a good habit to form.

Stretch your money by shopping sales or good discount outlets if you wish. But remember, it isn't a bargain if it isn't right for you. A suit that never quite fits or isn't exactly your best shade is not a bargain no matter how many times it has been marked down.

In addition to buying natural fibers in clothing whenever possible, invest in real leather for shoes, attache case, and handbag—if you carry one. Leather conveys a professional look and will out last the cheap looking imitations you might buy.

Traditional Chronological Resume

RESUME

Sarah Taylor
2720 Euclid Drive
Philadelphia, Pennsylvania 19110

Weight: 125 lbs.
Height: 5'7"
Born: August 3, 1960
Health: Good
Marital Status: Married with two children

EDUCATION

1983-1984: M.A., Public Administration, Temple University, Philadelphia, Pennsylvania.
1978-1982: B.A., Political Science, State University of New York, Plattsburg.
1973-1977: High School Diploma, Furniss High School, Philadelphia, Pennsylvania.

WORK EXPERIENCE

9/2/87 to present: Planning Analyst, Department of Planning, City of Philadelphia. Responsible for housing plans. Terminated due to major cuts in municipal planning budget.
2/4/84 to 6/4/87: Research Associate, Coalition for Community Service Agencies, Philadelphia, Pennsylvania. Responsible for developing reports. Resigned to seek a government job.
4/2/81 to 11/21/83: Waitress, The Do Drop Inn, Philadelphia, Pennsylvania. Part-time while attending college.
6/5/78 to 11/14/80: Clerk Typist, Office of Admissions, State University of New York, Plattsburg. Part-time while attending college.

PROFESSIONAL AFFILIATIONS

American Society for Public Administration
American Planning Association
Daughters of the American Revolution
National Rifle Association

HOBBIES

I like to paint, garden, and jog.

REFERENCES

David Stoffer, Chief, Department of Planning, City of Philadelphia, Pennsylvania 19130, (315)721-6131.
Dr. Alice White, Professor, Department of Public Administration, Temple University, Philadelphia, Pennsylvania 19118 (215)719-3100.

Improved Chronological Resume

SARAH TAYLOR
2720 Euclid Drive
Philadelphia, Pennsylvania 19110 215/721-1982

OBJECTIVE: A research and public relations position with an association, where strong communication, research, and analytical skills will be used for furthering the goals of the association.

EXPERIENCE: Planning Analyst, City of Philadelphia, Pennsylvania. Developed community-wide plans for public housing and conducted research in response to requests for zoning variances. Regularly met with community groups to identify housing needs, communicate city's policies, and advise on policies and procedures. Wrote policy papers and reports on city planning issues. Worked closely with citizen groups, landlords, contractors, and lawyers representing interests of various local groups. Developed a new information system for responding quickly to requests for planning information. 1987-present

Research Associate, Coalition for Community Service Agencies, Philadelphia, Pennsylvania. Conducted research, analyzed data, wrote reports, and lobbied government agencies at both the local and state levels on various aspects of community service organizations. Research involved interviewing government officials and representatives of community service groups. Several reports were responsible for providing greater public assistance to strengthen community service organizations at the local level. Reports cited by supervisor as "outstanding contributions to making community service organizations a central issue on the local government agenda". 1984-1987

EDUCATION: M.A., Public Administration, Temple University, Philadelphia, Pennsylvania, 1984.

B.A., Political Science, State University of New York, Plattsburg, New York 1982.

REFERENCES: Available upon request.

Combination Resume

SARAH TAYLOR
2720 Euclid Drive
Philadelphia, Pennsylvania 19110 215/721-1982

OBJECTIVE A research and public relations position with an association, where strong communication, research, and analytical skills will be used for furthering the goals of the association.

AREAS OF EFFECTIVENESS

RESEARCH Conducted 22 research projects on various aspects of planning and community service groups. Developed research design, conducted field interviews, and analyzed data. Research resulted in several reports which were responsible for changing local government policies. Consistently cited by supervisors as making "outstanding" contributions to both understanding and action.

PUBLIC RELATIONS Developed press releases, issued reports, and met regularly with community groups, government officials, contractors, and the press. Devised an innovative information system to respond quickly to requests for information.

COMMUNICATION Authored numerous position papers and major reports on public policy issues for government agencies and community groups. Frequent speaker before community organizations. Conducted several briefings for supervisors, city council members, and the press.

WORK HISTORY Planning Analyst, City of Philadelphia, Pennsylvania, 1987-93.

Research Associate, Coalition for Community Service Agencies, Philadelphia, Pennsylvania, 1984-1987.

EDUCATION M.A., Public Administration, Temple University, Philadelphia, Pennsylvania, 1984.

B.A., Political Science, State University of New York, Plattsburg, New York 1975.

PERSONAL Enjoy developing innovative approaches to public issues which involve research, writing, and frequent contact with government officials and community groups.

Combination Resume—continued

SUPPLEMENTAL INFORMATION **SARAH TAYLOR**

CONTINUING EDUCATION AND TRAINING

- Completed 15 graduate level hours of research and communication courses directly related to the public service.
- Recently attended several workshops on strengthening research, communication, and community relations skills:

  "Survey Research Methods in Local Government," International City Manager Association, June 4-6, 1993

  "Briefing Techniques," American Management Associations, May 8, 1991

  "Public Speaking," Greater Philadelphia Chamber of Commerce, February 20-21, 1990

  "Effective Report Writing for Public Employees," November 12-13, 1989

  "Planning as a Community Process," American Planning Association, March 21-25, 1988

MAJOR RESEARCH CONDUCTED AND REPORTS AUTHORED

"Making Community Service Organizations Work More Effectively," Coalition for Community Service Agencies, 1992.

"Serving the Community: A Practical Manual for Working With Government and Other Community Organizations," Coalition for Community Service Agencies, 1990.

"Planning Our Housing Future: A Comprehensive Approach to Balanced Growth," City of Philadelphia, 1988.

"City Planning Research: A Manual for Conducting Survey Research in the City of Philadelphia," City of Philadelphia, 1987.

PROFESSIONAL AFFILIATIONS

American Society for Public Administration
American Society of Association Executives
Toastmasters International

EDUCATIONAL HIGHLIGHTS

Working toward Ph.D. in Public Policy with concentration on policy formation and community management.

Earned 4.0/4.0 grade point average in graduate studies.

Functional Resume

SARAH TAYLOR
2720 Euclid Drive
Philadelphia, Pennsylvania 19110 215/721-1982

OBJECTIVE: A research and public relations position with an association, where strong communication, research, and analytical skills will be used for furthering the goals of the association.

EDUCATION: M.A., Public Administration, Temple University, Philadelphia, Pennsylvania, 1988.

B.A., Political Science, State University of New York, Plattsburg, New York, 1985.

MAJOR STRENGTHS:

Research

Conducted 22 research projects on various aspects of planning and community service groups. Developed research design, conducted field interviews, and analyzed data. Research resulted in several reports which were responsible for changing local government policies. Consistently cited by supervisors as making "outstanding" contributions to both understanding and action.

Public Relations

Developed press releases, issued reports, and met regularly with community groups, government officials, contractors, and the press. Devised an innovative information system to respond quickly to requests for information.

Communication

Authored numerous position papers and major reports on public policy issues for government agencies and community groups. Frequent speaker before community organizations. Conducted several briefings for supervisors, city council members, and the press.

PERSONAL: Enjoy developing innovative approaches to public issues which involve research, writing, and frequent contact with government officials and community groups.

Resume Letter

2720 Euclid Drive
Philadelphia, PA 19110
April 17, _____

James Weston, Assistant Director
American Association of
Community Service Organizations
7210 Connecticut Avenue, Suite 223
Washington, DC 20036

Dear Mr. Weston:

AACSO is one of the most important groups providing assistance to community organizations. I know, because I have worked with these groups for several years at both the local and state levels.

My work has been very exciting, but I would now like to contribute to the work of the national association. My experience includes:

Research: Conducted 22 research projects on local planning and community service groups. Research resulted in several reports which significantly altered local government policies.

Public relations: Developed press releases, issued reports, and met regularly with community groups, government officials, contractors, and the press. Devised an innovative information system to respond to quickly requests for information.

Communication: Authored numerous position papers and major reports on public policy issues for agencies and community groups. Frequent speaker before community organizations. Conducted several briefings for supervisors, city council members, and the press.

In addition, I am completing my Ph.D. in Public Policy with emphasis on policy formation and community management.

I would like to meet with you to discuss how my experience and skills relate to the work of AACSO. Since I will be in Washington, DC next month, I would appreciate an opportunity to meet with you at that time. I will call your office on Thursday morning, April 24, to see if we might be able to arrange a mutually convenient time to meet. I especially want to share with you some of the innovative research and public relations work I have done with community service organizations.

I look forward to meeting with you.

Sincerely,

Sarah Taylor

Cover Letter

2720 Euclid Drive
Philadelphia, PA 19110
April 15, ____

James Weston, Assistant Director
American Association of
Community Service Organizations
7210 Connecticut Avenue, Suite 223
Washington, DC 20036

Dear Mr. Weston:

I enclose my resume in response to your announcement in The Washington Post for a Community Research Analyst.

I am especially interested in this position for several reasons. First, I have six years of thoroughly enjoyable experience in working closely with community service organizations at the local and state levels. Second, I have conducted several practical studies of community service organizations which have resulted in strengthening their roles at the local level. Finally, my research work has placed me at the center of the policy process where I have worked effectively with government officials and other community groups.

I would appreciate an opportunity to meet with you to discuss how my experience might best relate to your needs. My combined research and community relations approach may be of special interest to you since it has resulted in some innovative approaches to community action. I will call your office on Tuesday morning April 22, to see if your schedule would permit such a meeting.

I look forward to learning more about your research needs and sharing some of my experiences with you.

Sincerely,

Sarah Taylor

Approach Letter: Referral

2720 Euclid Drive
Philadelphia, PA 19110
April 8, _____

James Weston, Assistant Director
American Association of
Community Service Organizations
7210 Connecticut Avenue, Suite 223
Washington, DC 20036

Dear Mr. Weston:

Alice White suggested that I contact you about my interest in community service organizations. She enthusiastically mentioned you as one of the best people to talk to about careers in this public service field.

I am leaving local government after three years of progressively responsible experience in community planning where I worked extensively with community service organizations. But before I decide to seek a career in this field as well as relocate, I believe I would benefit greatly from your experience and insights into this field. Your advice would be very helpful at this stage in my career.

I will be in Washington during the seek of April 21-25. Would it be possible for us to meet briefly to discuss my career plans? I have several concerns you might be most helpful in clarifying. I will call your office on Thursday morning, April 15, to see if your schedule would permit such a meeting.

Sincerely,

Sarah Taylor

Approach Letter: Cold Turkey

2720 Euclid Drive
Philadelphia, PA 19110
March 23, _____

James Weston, Assistant Director
American Association of
Community Service Organizations
7210 Connecticut Avenue, Suite 223
Washington, DC 20036

Dear Mr. Weston:

I have been most impressed by your work with community service organizations in Philadelphia. Indeed, the recent article appearing in Association Trends on your promotion to assistant director of AACSO stressed what I learned a long time ago here in Philadelphia—you have an exceptional talent to get the local organization to work together in pursuing the national agenda of AACSO. Congratulations on a well deserved promotion!

Your public service career with community service organizations is one I hope to emulate. After six enjoyable years of working with these organizations at the local and state levels, I am convinced I want to pursue a long-term career in this field and especially from a much broader national perspective. My research and public relations work with these groups may also be of interest to you.

Would it be possible for us to meet briefly to discuss my career interests in this field? I believe your advice would be most valuable in helping me better define my future with community service organizations.

I will be in Washington, DC during the week of April 21-25. Perhaps your schedule would permit a meeting during that week. I will call your office on Tuesday morning, April 8, to see if such a meeting would be possible.

I look forward to meeting you and learning from your experience.

Sincerely,

Sarah Taylor

Thank-You Letter:
Post-Informational Interview

2720 Euclid Drive
Philadelphia, PA 19110
March 23, ____

James Weston, Assistant Director
American Association of
Community Service Organizations
7210 Connecticut Avenue, Suite 223
Washington, DC 20036

Dear Mr. Weston:

Our meeting yesterday was truly informative and extremely useful in helping me clarify various concerns regarding careers with community service organizations. Your experience and knowledge of this field is most impressive.

I want to thank you again for taking the time from your busy schedule to meet with me. Your suggestions for strengthening my resume were very helpful. I am now revising the resume in light of your thoughtful advice. I will sent you a copy of the revised resume next week.

Following your advice, I will contact Marilyn Plante tomorrow to see if she might have or know of any opportunities for someone with my interests and qualifications. I will give her your regards.

I hope to have a chance to meet with you again sometime.

Sincerely,

Sarah Taylor

Thank-You Letter: Post-Job Interview

2720 Euclid Drive
Philadelphia, PA 19110
March 23, ____

James Weston, Assistant Director
American Association of
Community Service Organizations
7210 Connecticut Avenue, Suite 223
Washington, DC 20036

Dear Mr. Weston:

I want to thank you again for the opportunity to interview for the Community Research Analyst position. You and your staff were most helpful in clarifying many questions about this position and AACSO.

Our meeting further convinced me that this position is ideally suited for my interests, skills, and experience. My prior research and public relations work with community service agencies at the local and state levels has prepared me well for this position. I am committed to giving AACSO my very best effort.

I look forward to meeting with you again to further discuss my candidacy.

Sincerely,

Sarah Taylor

Thank-You Letter: Job Rejection

2720 Euclid Drive
Philadelphia, PA 19110
March 23, ____

James Weston, Assistant Director
American Association of
Community Service Organizations
7210 Connecticut Avenue, Suite 223
Washington, DC 20036

Dear Mr. Weston:

I want to thank you again for considering me for the Community Research Analyst position. Although I am disappointed with the outcome, I appreciated the opportunity and learned a great deal about AACSO. I am especially pleased with the highly professional manner in which you and your staff conducted the interview.

Please keep me in mind for future vacancies. I have a strong interest in AACSO which wil certainly continue in the future. I believe I could contribute a great deal to AACSO. I am sure I would work well with you and your staff.

Best wishes.

Sincerely,

Sarah Taylor

Thank-You Letter: Job Offer Acceptance

2720 Euclid Drive
Philadelphia, PA 19110
March 23, ____

James Weston, Assistant Director
American Association of
Community Service Organizations
7210 Connecticut Avenue, Suite 223
Washington, DC 20036

Dear Mr. Weston:

I am pleased to accept your offer and look forward to joining AACSO later this month.

The Community Research Analyst position is ideally suited to my interests, skills, and experience. I will give you and AACSO my very best effort.

I understand I will begin work on May 14. Please contact me if I need to complete any paperwork prior to this starting date.

Thank you again for your consideration and confidence.

Sincerely,

Sarah Taylor

9 TAKE POSITIVE ACTION

*T*he job search skills discussed thus far prepare you for the most critical stages of the job search: networking, interviewing, and negotiating terms of employment. These are the face-to-face implementation stages of the job search. Specific skills and strategies are associated with success in these stages. This chapter outlines practical methods for developing the necessary interpersonal skills and for implementing the face-to-face strategies.

PROSPECTING, NETWORKING, AND INFORMATIONAL INTERVIEWS

What do you do after you complete your resume? Most people send cover letters and resumes in response to job listings; they then wait to be called for a job interview. Viewing the job search as basically a direct-mail operation, many are disappointed in discovering the realities of direct-mail—a five percent response rate is considered outstanding!

Successful job seekers break out of this relatively passive job search role by orienting themselves toward face-to-face action. Being proactive, they develop interpersonal strategies in which the resume plays a supportive rather than a central role in the job search. They first present themselves to employers; the resume appears only at the end of a face-to-face conversation.

Throughout the job search you will acquire useful names and addresses as well as meet people who will assist you in contacting potential employers. In both the public and private sector job markets, such information and contacts become key building blocks for generating job interviews and offers.

Since the best and most numerous jobs are found on the hidden job market, you must use methods appropriate for this job market. Indeed, research and experience clearly show the most effective means of communication are face-to-face and word-of-mouth. The informal, interpersonal system of communication is the central nervous system of the hidden job market. Your goal should be to penetrate this job market with proven methods for success. Appropriate methods for making important job contacts are *prospecting and networking*. Appropriate methods for getting these contacts to provide you with useful job information are *informational and referral interviews*.

Communicating Qualifications

Taken together, these interpersonal methods help you *communicate your qualifications to employers*. Although many job seekers may be reluctant to use this informal communication system, they greatly limit their potential for success if they do not. Swamped with 400 to 500 resumes for a single position, many employers prefer this informal system. In addition, many employers are uncertain what type of individual they should hire. By using this informal system, you help employers identify their needs, limit their alternatives, and thus make decisions and save money.

Most employers also want more information on candidates to supplement the "paper qualifications" represented in application forms, resumes, and letters. Studies show that employers in general seek candidates who have these skills: communication, problem solving, analytical, assessment, and planning. Surprising to many job seekers, technical expertise ranks third or fourth on employers' lists of most desired skills. These findings support a frequent observation made by employers: the major problems with employees relate to communication, problem solving, and analysis; individuals get fired because of political and interpersonal conflicts rather than technical incompetence.

Employers generally seek individuals they *like* both personally and professionally. Therefore, communicating your qualifications to employers entails more than just informing them of your technical competence. You must communicate that you have the requisite personal *and* professional skills for performing the job. Informal prospecting, networking, and informational interviewing activities are the best methods for communicating your "qualifications" to employers.

Employers generally seek individuals they like both personally and professionally.

Developing Networks

Networking is the process of purposefully developing relations with others. Networking in the job search involves connecting and interacting with other individuals who can be helpful to you. Your network consists of you interacting with these other individuals. The more you develop, maintain, and expand your networks, the more successful should be your job search.

Your network is your interpersonal environment. While you know and interact with hundreds of people, on a day-to-day basis you probably encounter no more than 20 people. You frequently contact these people in face-to-face situations. Some people are more *important* to you than others. You *like* some more than others. And some will be more *helpful* to you in your job search than others. Your basic network may encompass the following individuals and groups: friends, acquaintances, immediate family, distant relatives, professional colleagues, spouse, supervisor, fellow workers, close friends and colleagues, and local businessmen and professionals, such as your banker, lawyer, doctor, minister, and insurance agent. You should contact many of these individuals for advice relating to your job search.

You need to *identify everyone in your network* who might help you with your job search. You first need to expand your basic network to include individuals you know and have interacted with over the past 10 or more years. Make a list of at least 200 people you know. Include friends and relatives from your Christmas card list, past and present neighbors, former classmates, politicians, business persons, previous employers, professional associates, ministers, insurance agents, lawyers, bankers, doctors, dentists, accountants, and social acquaintances.

After identifying your extended network, you should try to *link your network to others' networks*. Individuals in these other networks also have job information and contacts. Ask people in your basic network for referrals to individuals in their networks. This approach should greatly enlarge your basic job search network.

What do you do if individuals in your immediate and extended network cannot provide you with certain job information and contacts? While it is much easier and more effective to meet new people through personal contacts, on occasion you may need to *approach strangers without prior contacts*. In this situation, try the "cold turkey" approach. Write a letter to someone you feel may be useful to your job search. Research this individual so you are acquainted with their background and accomplishments. In the letter, refer to their accomplishments, mention your need for job information, and specify a date and time you will call to schedule a meeting. An example of such a "cold turkey approach letter" is included on page 154. Another approach is to introduce yourself to someone by telephone and request a meeting and/or job information. While you may experience rejections in using these approaches, you also will experience successes. And those successes should lead to further expansion of your job search network.

The job search is a highly ego-involved activity often characterized by numerous rejections accompanied by a few acceptances.

Prospecting for Success

The key to successful networking is an active and routine *prospecting campaign*. Salespersons in insurance, real estate, Amway, Shaklee, and other direct-sales businesses understand the importance and principles of prospecting; indeed, many have turned the art of prospecting into a science! The basic operating principle is *probability*: the number of sales you make is a direct function of the amount of effort you put into developing new contacts and following-through. Expect no more than a 10 percent acceptance rate: for every 10 people you meet, 9 will reject you and 1 will accept you. Therefore, the more people you contact, the more acceptances you will receive. If you want to be successful, you must collect many more "nos" than "yeses". In a 10 percent probability situation, you need to contact 100 people for 10 successes.

These prospecting principles are extremely useful for your job search. Like sales situations, the job search is a highly ego-involved activity often characterized by numerous rejections accompanied by a few acceptances. While no one wants to be rejected, few people are willing and able to handle more than a few rejections. They take a "no" as a sign of personal failure—and quit prematurely. If they persisted longer, they would achieve success after a few more "nos". Furthermore, if their prospecting activities were focused on gathering information rather than making sales, they would considerably minimize the number of rejections. Therefore, this is what you should do:

- Prospect for job leads.
- Accept rejections as part of the game.
- Link prospecting to informational interviewing.
- Keep prospecting for more information and "yeses" which will eventually translate into job interviews and offers.

A good prospecting pace as you start your search is to make two new contacts each day. Start by contacting people in your immediate network. Let them know you are conducting a job search, but emphasize that you are only doing research. Ask for a few moments of their time to discuss your information needs. You are only seeking *information and advice* at this time—not a job.

It should take you about 20 minutes to make a contact by letter or telephone. If you make two contacts each day, by the end of the first week you will have 10 new contacts for a total investment of less than seven hours. By the second week you may want to increase your prospecting pace to four new contacts each day or 20 each week. The more contacts you make, the more useful information, advice, and job leads you will receive. If your job search bogs down, you probably need to increase your prospecting activities.

Expect each contact to refer you to two or three others who will also refer you to others. Consequently, your contacts should multiply considerably within only a few weeks.

Handling and Minimizing Rejections

These prospecting and networking methods are effective. While they are responsible for building, maintaining, and expanding multi-million dollar businesses, they work extremely well for job hunters. But they only work if you are patient and persist. *The key to networking success is to focus on gathering information while also learning to handle rejections*. Learn from rejections, forget them, and go on to more productive networking activities. The major reason direct-sales people fail is because they don't persist. The reason they don't persist is because they either can't take, or get tired of taking, rejections.

Rejections are no fun, especially in such an ego-involved activity as a job search. But you will encounter rejections as you travel on the road toward job search success. This road is strewn with individuals who quit prematurely because they were rejected four or five times. Don't be one of them!

Our prospecting and networking techniques differ from sales approaches in one major respect: we have special techniques for minimizing the number of rejections. If handled properly, at least 50 percent—maybe as many as 90 percent—of your prospects will turn into "yeses" rather than "nos". The reason for this unusually high acceptance rate is how you introduce and handle yourself before your prospects. Many insurance agents and direct distributors expect a 90 percent rejection rate, because they are trying to sell specific products potential clients may or may not need. Most people don't like to be put on the spot —especially when it is in their own home or office—to make a decision to buy a product.

Selling With Sincerity

The principles of selling yourself in the job market are similar. People don't want to be put on the spot. They feel uncomfortable if they think you expect them to give you a job. Thus, you should never introduce yourself to a prospect by asking them for a job or a job lead. You should do just the opposite: relieve their anxiety by mentioning that you are not looking for a job from them—only job information and advice. You must be honest and sincere in communicating these intentions to your contact. The biggest turn-off for individuals targeted for informational interviews is insincere job seekers who try to use this as a mechanism to get a job.

Your approach to prospects must be subtle, honest, and professional. You are seeking *information, advice, and referrals* relating to several subjects: job opportunities, your job search approach, your resume, and others who may have similar information, advice, and referrals. Most people gladly volunteer such information. They generally like to talk about themselves, their careers, and others. They like to give advice. This approach flatters individuals by placing them in the role of the expert-advisor. Who doesn't want to be recognized as an expert-advisor, especially on such a critical topic as one's employment?

This approach should yield a great deal of information, advice, and referrals from your prospects. One other important outcome should result from using this approach: people will *remember* you as the person who made them feel at ease and who received their valuable advice. If they hear of job opportunities for someone with your qualifications, chances are they will contact you with the information. After contacting 100 prospects, you will have created 100 sets of eyes and ears to help you in your job search!

The guiding principle behind prospecting, networking, and informational interviews is this: the best way to get a job is to ask for job information, advice, and referrals; never ask for a job. Remember, as we outlined in Chapter 8 (page 133), you want your prospects to engage in the 5-R's of informational interviewing: reveal, refer, read, revise, and remember. If you follow this principle, you should join the ranks of thousands of successful job seekers who paid a great deal of money learning it from highly-paid professionals.

The best way to get a job is to ask for job information, advice, and referrals; never ask for a job.

Approaching Key People

Whom should you contact within an organization for an informational interview? Contact people who are busy, who have the power to hire, and who are knowledgeable about the organization. The least likely candidate will be someone in the personnel department. Most often the heads of operating units are the most busy, powerful, and knowledgeable individuals in the organization. However, getting access to such individuals may be difficult. Some people at the top may appear to be informed and powerful, but they may lack information on the day-to-day personnel changes or their influence is limited in the hiring process. It is difficult to give one best answer to this question.

Therefore, we recommend contacting a variety of people. Aim for the busy, powerful, and informed, but be prepared to settle for less: Secretaries, receptionists, and the person you want to meet may refer you to others. From a practical standpoint, you may have to take whomever you can schedule an appointment with. Sometimes people who are not busy can be helpful. Talk to a secretary or receptionist sometime about their boss or working in the organization. You may be surprised with what you learn!

The best way to initiate a contact with a prospective employer is to *send an approach letter*. An example of such a letter appears on page 153. Begin this letter with a personal statement, such as: "James Chance suggested that I contact you..." Briefly state your purpose—seek information and advice-and mention you will call at a specific time to schedule a meeting. Do not enclose a resume with this letter. Remember, your purposes are to get information, advice, referrals, and remembered. While this is not a formal interview, it may well lead to one.

Most people will meet with you, assuming you are sincere in your approach. If the person tries to put you off when you telephone for an appointment, clearly state your purpose and emphasize that you are not looking for a job with this person—only information and advice. If the person insists on putting you off, make the best of the situation: write a nice thank-you letter in which you again state your intended purpose; mention your disappointment in not being able to learn from the person's experience; and ask to be remembered for future reference. You may enclose your resume with this letter.

While you are ostensibly seeking information and advice, treat this meeting as an important preliminary interview. You need to communicate your qualifications—that you are competent, intelligent, honest, and likable. These are the same qualities you should communicate in a formal job interview. Hence, follow the same advice given for conducting a formal interview and dressing appropriately for a face-to-face meeting (Chapter 7).

Structuring the Informational Interview

An informational interview will be relatively unstructured compared to a formal interview. Since you want the interviewer to advise you, you reverse roles by asking questions which should give you useful information. You, in effect, become the interviewer. You should structure this interview with a particular sequence of questions. Most questions should be open-ended, requiring the individual to give specific answers based upon his or her experience.

The structure and dialogue for the informational interview might go something like this. You plan to take no more than 45 minutes for this interview. The first three to five minutes will be devoted to small talk—the weather, traffic, the office, mutual acquaintances, or an interesting or humorous observation. Since these are the most critical moments in the interview, be especially careful how you communicate nonverbally. Begin your interview by stating your appreciation for the individual's time:

> "I want to thank you again for scheduling this meeting with me. I know you're busy. I appreciate the special arrangements you made to see me on a subject which is very important to my future."

Your next comment should be a statement reiterating your purpose as stated in your letter:

> "As you know, I am exploring job and career alternatives. I know what I do well and what I want to do. Before I commit myself to a new job, I need to know more about various career options. I thought you would be able to provide me with some insights into career opportunities, job requirements, and possible problems or promising directions in the field of ______________."

This statement normally will get a positive reaction from the individual who may want to know more about what it is you want to do. Be sure to clearly communicate your job objective. If you can't, you may communicate that you are lost, indecisive, or uncertain about yourself. The person may feel you are wasting his or her time.

Your next line of questioning should focus on "how" and "what" questions centering on (1) specific jobs and (2) the job search process. Begin by asking about various aspects of specific jobs:

- Duties and responsibilities.
- Knowledge, skills, and abilities required.
- Work environment relating to fellow employees, work flows, deadlines, stress, initiative.
- Advantages and disadvantages.
- Advancement opportunities and outlook.
- Salary ranges.

Your informer will probably take a great deal of time talking about his or her experience in each area. Be a good listener, but make sure you move along with the questions.

Your next line of questioning should focus on your job search activities. You need as much information as possible on how to:

- Acquire the necessary skills.
- Best find a job in this field.
- Overcome any objections employers may have to your background.
- Uncover job vacancies which may be advertised.
- Develop job leads.
- Approach prospective employers.

Your final line of questioning should focus on your resume. Do not show you resume until you focus on this last set of questions. The purpose of these questions is to: (1) get the individual to read you resume in-depth, (2) acquire useful advice on how to strengthen it, (3) refer you to prospective employers, and (4) be remembered. With the resume in front of you and your interviewee, ask the following questions:

- Is this an appropriate type of resume for the jobs I have outlined?
- If an employer received this resume in the mail, how do you think he or she would react to it?
- What do you see as possible weaknesses or areas that need to be improved?
- What should I do with this resume? Shotgun it to hundreds of employers with a cover letter? Use resume letters instead?

- What about the length, paper quality and color, layout, and typing? Are they appropriate?
- How might I best improve the form and content of the resume?

You should receive useful advice on how to strengthen both the content and use of your resume. Most important, these questions force the individual to *read* your resume which, in turn, may be *remembered* for future reference.

Your last question is especially important in this interview. You want to be both *remembered* and *referred*. Some variation of the following question should help:

> "I really appreciate all this advice. It is very helpful and it should improve my job search considerably. Could I ask you one more favor? Do you know two or three other people who could help me with my job search? I want to conduct as much research as possible, and their advice might be helpful also."

Before you leave, mention one more important item:

> "During the next few months, should you hear of any job opportunities for someone with my interests and qualifications, I would appreciate being kept in mind. And please feel free to pass my name on to others."

Send a nice thank-you letter within 48 hours of completing this informational interview. Following the example in Appendix B, express your genuine gratitude for the individual's time and advice. Reiterate your interests, and ask to be remembered and referred to others.

Follow-up on any useful advice you receive, particularly referrals. Approach referrals in the same manner you approached the person who gave you the referral. Write a letter requesting a meeting. Begin the letter by mentioning:

> "Mr./Ms. __________suggested that I contact you concerning my research on careers in _________."

If you continue prospecting, networking, and conducting informational interviews, soon you will be busy conducting interviews and receiving job offers. While 100 informational interviews over a two-month period should lead to several formal job interviews and offers, the pay-offs are uncertain because job vacancies are unpredictable. We know cases where the first referral turned into a formal interview and job offer. More typical cases require constant prospecting, networking, and informational interviewing activities. The telephone call or letter inviting you to a job interview can come at any time. While the timing may be unpredictable, your persistent job search activities will be largely responsible for the final outcome.

Telephoning for Job Leads

Telephone communication should play an important role in prospecting, networking, and informational interviews. However, controversy centers around how and when to use the telephone for generating job leads and scheduling interviews. Some people recommend writing a letter and waiting for a written or telephone reply. Others suggest writing a letter and following it with a telephone call. Still others argue you should use the telephone exclusively rather than write letters.

How you use the telephone will indicate what type of job search you are conducting. Exclusive reliance on the telephone is a technique used by highly formalized job clubs which operate phone banks for generating job leads. Using the Yellow Pages as the guide to employers, a job club member may call as many as 50 employers a day to schedule job interviews. A rather aggressive yet typical telephone dialogue goes something like this:

> "Hello, my name is Jim Morgan. I would like to speak to the head of the training department. By the way, what is the name of the training director?"
>
> "You want to talk to Ms. Stevens. Her number is 723-8191 or I can connect you directly."
>
> "Hello, Ms. Stevens. My name is Jim Morgan. I have several years of training experience as both a trainer and developer of training materials. I'd like to meet with you to discuss possible openings in your department for someone with my qualifications. Would it be possible to see you on Friday at 2pm?"

Not surprising, this telephone approach generates many "nos". If you have a hard time handling rejections, this telephone approach will help you confront your anxieties. The principle behind this approach is *probability*: for every 25 telephone "nos" you receive, you will probably get one or two "yeses". Success is just 25 telephone calls away! If you start calling prospective employers at 9am and finish your 25 calls by 12 noon, you should generate at least one or two interviews. That's not bad for three hours of job search work. It beats a direct-mail approach.

The telephone is more efficient than writing letters. However, its effectiveness is questionable. When you use the telephone in this manner, you are basically asking for a job. You are asking the employer: "Do you have a job for me?" There is nothing subtle or particularly professional about this approach. It is effective in uncovering particular types of job leads for particular types of individuals. If you need a job—any job—in a hurry, this is one of the most efficient ways of finding employment. However, if you are more concerned with finding a job that is right for you—a job you do well and enjoy doing, one that is fit for you—this telephone approach is inappropriate.

You must use your own judgment in determining when and how to use the telephone in your job search. There are appropriate times and methods for using the telephone, and these should relate to your job search goals and needs. We prefer the more conventional approach of writing a letter requesting an informational interview and following it up with a telephone call. While you take the initiative in scheduling an appointment, you do not put the individual on the spot by asking for a job. You are only seeking information and advice. This low-keyed approach results in numerous acceptances and has a higher probability of paying off with interviews than the aggressive telephone request. You should be trying to uncover jobs that are right for you rather than any job that happens to pop up from a telephoning blitz.

Using Job Clubs and Support Groups

The techniques we outlined thus far are designed for individuals conducting a self-directed job search. Job clubs and support groups are two important alternatives to these techniques.

Job clubs are designed to provide a group structure and support system to individuals seeking employment. These groups consist of about twelve individuals who are led by a trained counselor and supported with telephones, copying machines, and a resource center.

Highly formalized job clubs, such as the 40-Plus Club, organize job search activities for both the advertised and hidden job markets. As outlined by Azrin and Besalel in their book *Job Club Counselor's Manual*, job club activities include:

- Signing commitment agreements to achieve specific job search goals and targets.
- Contacting friends, relatives, and acquaintances for job leads.
- Completing activity forms.
- Using telephones, typewriters, photocopy machines, postage, and other equipment and supplies.
- Meeting with fellow participants to discuss job search progress.
- Telephoning to uncover job leads.
- Researching newspapers, telephone books, and directories.
- Developing research, telephone, interview, and social skills.
- Writing letters and resumes.
- Responding to want ads.
- Completing employment applications.

In other words, the job club formalizes many of the prospecting, networking, and informational interviewing activities within a group context and interjects the role of the telephone as the key communication device for developing and expanding networks.

Job clubs place excessive reliance on using the telephone for uncovering job leads. Members call prospective employers and ask about job openings. The Yellow Pages become the job hunting bible. During a two-week period, a job club member might spend most of his or her mornings telephoning for job leads and scheduling interviews. Afternoons are normally devoted to job interviewing.

We do not recommend joining such job clubs for obvious reasons. Most job club methods are designed for the hardcore unemployed or for individuals who need a job—any job—quickly. Individuals try to fit into available vacancies; their objectives and skills are of secondary concern. We recommend conducting your own job search or forming a support group which adapts some job club methods to our central concept of finding a job fit for you—one appropriate to your objective and in line with your particular mix of skills, abilities, and interests.

Support groups are a useful alternative to job clubs. They have one major advantage: they may cut your job search time in half. Forming or joining one of these groups can help direct as well as enhance your individual job search activities.

Your support group should consist of three or more individuals who are job hunting. Try to schedule regular meetings with specific purposes in mind. While the group may be highly social, especially if it involves close friends, it also should be *task-oriented*. Meet at least once a week and include your spouse. At each meeting set *performance goals* for the week. For example, your goal can be to make 20 new contacts and conduct five informational interviews. The contacts can be made by telephone, letter, or in person. Share your experiences and job information with each other. *Critique* each other's progress, make suggestions for improving the job search, and develop new strategies together. By doing this, you will be gaining valuable information and feedback which is normally difficult to gain on one's own. This group should provide important psychological supports to help you through your job search. After all, job hunting can be a lonely, frustrating, and exasperating experience. By sharing your experiences with others, you will find you are not alone. You will quickly learn that rejections are part of the game. The group will encourage you, and you will feel good about helping others achieve their goals. Try building small incentives into the group, such as the individual who receives the most job interviews for the month must be treated to dinner by other members of the group.

INTERVIEWING FOR THE JOB

Formal job interviews are required by nearly 95 percent of all organizations. The job interview is the single most important step to getting a job offer. How well you handle this interview is more important than your previous work experience, recommendations, and educational record.

The job interview also is the most stressful job search experience. Your application, resume, and letters may get you to the interview, but you must perform well in person in order to get a job offer. Knowing the stakes are high, most people face interviews with dry throats and sweaty palms; it is a time of great stress. You will be on stage, and you are expected to put on a good performance.

How do you prepare for the interview? First, you need to understand the nature and purpose of the interview. Second, you must prepare to respond to the interview situation and the interviewer. Make sure whoever assists you in preparing for the interview evaluates your performance. Practice the whole interviewing scenario, beginning with entering the door to leaving at that end. You should sharpen your nonverbal communication skills and be prepared to give positive answers to questions as well as ask intelligent questions. The more you practice, the better prepared you will be for the real job interview.

Communication

An interview is a two-way communication exchange between an interviewer and interviewee. It involves both verbal and nonverbal communication. While we tend to concentrate on the content of what we say, research shows that approximately 65 percent of all communication is nonverbal. Furthermore, we tend to give more credibility to nonverbal than to verbal messages. Regardless of what you say, how you dress, sit, stand, use your hands, move your head and eyes, and listen communicate both positive and negative messages.

Job interviews can occur in many different settings and under various circumstances. You will write job interview letters, schedule interviews by telephone, be interviewed over the phone, and encounter one-on-one as well as panel, group, and series interviews. Each situation requires a different set of communication behaviors. For example, while telephone communication is efficient, it may be ineffective for interview purposes. Only certain types of information can be effectively communicated over the telephone because this medium limits nonverbal behavior. Honesty, intelligence, and likability—three of the most important values you want to communicate to employers—are primarily communicated nonverbally. Therefore, be very careful of telephone interviews—whether giving or receiving them.

Job interviews have different purposes and can be negative in many ways. From your perspective, the purpose of an initial job interview is to get a second interview, and the purpose of the second interview is to get a job offer. However, for many employers, the purpose of the interview is a process of narrowing the field and eliminating applicants from further interviews and the eventual job offer. The interviewer wants to know why he or she should *not* hire you. The interviewer tries to do this by identifying your weaknesses. These differing purposes often create an adversarial relationship and contribute to the overall interviewing stress experienced by both the applicant and the interviewer.

Since the interviewer wants to identify your weaknesses, you must counter by *communicating your strengths* to lessen the interviewer's fears of hiring you. Recognizing that you are an unknown quantity to the employer, you must *raise* the interviewer's expectations of you.

Answering Questions

Hopefully your prospecting, networking, informational interviewing, and resume and letter writing activities result in several invitations to interview for jobs appropriate to your objective. Once you receive an invitation to interview, you should do a great deal of work in preparation for your meeting. You should prepare for the interview as if it were a $500,000 prize. After all, you may earn that much or more with the employer over the next 10 years.

You should prepare for the interview as if it were a $500,000 prize.

The invitation to interview will most likely come by telephone. In some cases, a preliminary interview will be conducted by telephone. The employer may want to shorten the list of eligible candidates from 10 to 3. By calling each individual, the employer can quickly eliminate marginal candidates as well as up-date the job status of each individual. When you get such a telephone call, you have no time to prepare. You may be dripping wet as you step from the shower or you may have a splitting headache as you pick up the phone. Telephone interviews always seem to occur at bad times. Whatever your situation, put your best foot forward based upon your thorough preparation for an interview. You may want to keep a list of questions near the telephone just in case you receive such a telephone call.

Telephone interviews often result in a face-to-face interview at the employer's office. Once you confirm an interview time and place, you should do as much research on the organization and employer as possible as well as learn to lessen your anxiety and stress levels by practicing the interview situation. *Preparation and practice* are the keys to doing your best.

During the interview, you want to impress upon the interviewer your knowledge of the organization by asking intelligent questions and giving intelligent answers. Your library and networking research should yield useful information on the organization and employer. Be sure you know something about the organization. Interviewers are normally impressed by interviewees who demonstrate knowledge and interest in their organization.

You should practice the actual interview by mentally addressing several questions most interviewers ask. Most of these questions will relate to your educational background, work experience, career goals, personality, and related concerns. The most frequently asked questions include:

Education

- Describe your educational background.
- Why did you attend _______ University (College or School)?
- Why did you major in _______?
- What was your grade point average?
- What subjects did you enjoy the most? The least? Why?
- What leadership positions did you hold?
- How did you finance your education?
- If you started all over, what would you change about your education?
- Why were your grades so low? So high?
- Did you do the best you could in school? If not, why not?

Work Experience

- What were your major achievements in each of your past jobs?
- Why did you change jobs before?
- What is your typical workday like?
- What functions do you enjoy doing the most?
- What did you like about your boss? Dislike?
- Which job did you enjoy the most? Why? Which job did you enjoy the least? Why?
- Have you ever been fired? Why?

Career Goals

- Why do you want to join our organization?
- Why do you think you are qualified for this position?
- Why are you looking for another job?

- Why do you want to make a career change?
- What ideally would you like to do?
- Why should we hire you?
- How would you improve our operations?
- What do you want to be doing five years from now?
- How much do you want to be making five years from now?
- What are your short-range and long-range career goals?
- If you could choose your job and organization, where would you go?
- What other types of jobs or companies are you considering?
- When will you be ready to begin work?
- How do you feel about relocating, traveling, working overtime, and spending weekends in the office?
- What attracted you to our organization?

Personality and Other Concerns

- Tell me about yourself.
- What are your major weaknesses? Your major strengths?
- What causes you to lose your temper?
- What do you do in your spare time? Any hobbies?
- What types of books do you read?
- What role does your family play in your career?
- How well do you work under pressure? In meeting deadlines?
- Tell me about your management philosophy.
- How much initiative do you take?
- What types of people do you prefer working with?
- How ___________(creative, analytical, tactful, etc.) are you?
- If you could change your life, what would you do differently?

Your answers to each question should be positive and emphasize your *strengths*. Remember, the interviewer wants to know about your *weaknesses*. For example, if you are asked "What are your weaknesses?", you can turn this potential negative question into a positive by answering something like this:

> "I sometimes get so involved with my work that I neglect my family as well as forget to complete work around the house. My problem is that I'm somewhat of a workaholic."

What employer could hold this negative against you? You have taken a negative and raised the expectations of the employer by basically saying you are a hard and persistent worker; the organization will get more for its money than expected.

Other questions are illegal, but some employers ask them nonetheless. Consider how you would respond to questions interviewers should not be asking:

- Are you married, divorced, separated, or single?
- How old are you?
- Do you go to church regularly?
- Do you have many debts?
- Do you own or rent your home?
- What social and political organizations do you belong to?
- What does your spouse think about your career?
- Are you living with anyone?
- Are you practicing birth control?
- Were you ever arrested?
- How much insurance do you have?
- How much do you weigh?
- How tall are you?

Don't get upset and say "That's an illegal question...I refuse to answer it!" While you may be perfectly right in saying so, this response lacks tact, which may be what the employer is looking for. For example, if you are divorced and the interviewer asks about your divorce, you might respond with "Does a divorce have a direct bearing on the responsibilities of this position?" It is improbable that employers ask such questions just to see how you answer or react under stress. Most do so out of ignorance of the law.

Asking Questions

Interviewers expect candidates to ask intelligent questions concerning the organization and the nature of the work. Moreover, you need information and should indicate your interest in the employer by asking questions. Consider asking some of these questions if they haven't been answered early in the interview:

- Tell me about the duties and responsibilities of this job.
- How does this position relate to other positions within this organization?
- How long has this position been in the organization?
- What would be the ideal type of person for this position?
- Skills? Personality? Working style? Background?
- Can you tell me about the people who have been in this position before? Backgrounds? Promotions? Terminations?
- Who would I be working with in this position?
- Tell me something about these people? Strengths? Weaknesses?
- Performance expectations?

- What am I expected to accomplish during the first year?
- How will I be evaluated?
- Are promotions and raises tied to performance criteria?
- Tell me how this operates?
- What is the normal salary range for such a position?
- Based on your experience, what type of problems would someone new in this position likely encounter?
- I'm interested in your career with this organization.
- When did you start? What are your plans for the future?
- I would like to know how people get promoted and advance in this organization?
- What is particularly unique about working in this organization?
- Can you explain the various benefits employees receive?
- What does the future look like for this organization?

You may want to write these questions on a 3 x 5 card and take them with you to the interview. While it is best to memorize these questions, you may want to refer to your list when the interviewer asks you if you have any questions. You might do this by saying: "Yes, I jotted down a few questions which I want to make sure I ask you before leaving." Then pull out your card and refer to the questions.

Nonverbal Communication

The interview is an image management activity. Interviewers normally make a positive or negative decision based upon the impression you make during the first four or five minutes of the interview. The major factors influencing this decision are your nonverbal cues communicated at the very beginning of the interview. Therefore, what you wear, how you look, the way you shake hands, how you smell, whether you are interested and enthusiastic, where and how you sit, and how you initiate the small talk are extremely important to the interviewer's decision. These factors may be more important than your answers to the interview questions. Your answers will tend to either reinforce or alter the initial impression.

While it may seem unfair for employers to make such snap decisions, it happens nonetheless. Accept it as an important reality of the job search, and learn to adjust your behavior to your best advantage. Remember, those first five minutes may be the most critical moments in your job search and for your future job or career. Put your best foot forward with the most positive image you can generate.

Be sure you dress appropriately for the interview, as we suggested in Chapter 7. Other nonverbal behaviors to sensitize yourself to are how you sit, stand, and listen. You may want to think through or practice each step of the interview, from arriving to leaving. Be sure you arrive at the interview on time—ten minutes early is best. When you enter the office area, remove your coat. On meeting the interviewer, extend your hand; women should do the same, particularly when interviewing with a male. Next, sit when and where the interviewer indicates; don't rush to a seat as if you are in a hurry to get started and finished.

Be particularly sensitive to *your listening behavior*. While the interviewer expects more than single "yes" and "no" answers to questions, the interviewer also needs nonverbal feedback in order to take you seriously. Indicate your attention and interest by maintaining frequent eye contact, nodding, smiling, and interjecting verbal responses. Listening is an active process, and effective listeners make others feel good about their communication.

Closing the Interview

Be prepared to end the interview. Many people don't know when or how to close interviews. They go on and on until someone breaks an uneasy moment of silence with an indication that it is time to go.

Interviewers normally will initiate the close by standing, shaking hands, and thanking you for coming to the interview. Don't end by saying "Goodbye and thank you". As this stage, you should summarize the interview in terms of your interests, strengths, and goals. Briefly restate your qualifications and continuing interest in working with the employer. At this point it is proper to ask the interviewer about selection plans: "When do you anticipate making your final decision?" Follow this question with your final one: "May I call you next week to inquire about my status?" By taking the initiative in this manner, the employer will be prompted to clarify your status soon, and you will have an opportunity to talk to her further.

Many interviewers will ask you for a list of references. Be sure to prepare such a list prior to the interview. Include the names, addresses, and phone numbers of four individuals who will give you positive professional and personal recommendations and whom you have alerted they may receive recommendation requests.

Telephone Interviews

Few people are effective telephone communicators. Several channels of nonverbal communication, such as eye contact, facial expression, and gestures, are absent in telephone conversations. People who may be dynamic in face-to-face situations may be dull and boring over the telephone. Since critical communication relating to the interview will take place over the telephone, pay particular attention to how you handle your telephone communication.

Two potential telephone interview situations may arise at any time. First, you may request an interview by calling an employer. Second, the employer may call you and conduct a screening interview over the phone. While the rules for both types of telephone conversations vary, certain principles should be followed.

When you telephone to request an interview, always know the name of the person you wish to contact. If you don't know the person's name, you can easily get the name by making two phone calls: one to the receptionist or secretary and another to the person you want to speak to. When calling the receptionist or secretary, just ask for the name of the person you wish to contact: "Who is the head of the ________ office?" Your second call should be directly to the person you wish to contact.

Most often your telephone calls will go through a secretary. The easiest way to avoid being screened out is to sound like you know the person or he or she is expecting your call. Do not ask: "May I speak with Mr. Casey?" This question often results in being screened out; a secretary next asks who you are and the nature of your business. Instead, try a more direct and authoritative statement for openers: "This is Mary Allen calling for David Casey." A surprising number of secretaries will put you directly through without asking you a series of screening questions.

Should the secretary want more information about the nature of your call, say you wish to make an appointment to see the person about some business. If the secretary persists in trying to identify what exactly you want, say it's "personal business". If this line of questioning fails to get you through, try to call at odd times, such as a half hour before the office opens and a half hour after it closes. Many managers arrive early and leave late—times when no one else is around to answer the telephone.

Telephone introductions are easier if you are following-up on a letter you sent earlier. You might begin by saying,

> "Hello, this is Mary Allen. I'm calling in regards to the letter I sent you last week. I mentioned I would call you today to see if we could meet briefly. You may recall my interests and experience in training and development. I would like to meet with you briefly to discuss..."

However, if this is a "cold turkey" request-for-interview call, you may have difficulty scheduling an interview. Many employers will not invite you to a job interview based on this aggressive approach. Be straightforward, assertive, and hope for the best. Try to avoid the "give-me-a-job" mentality often associated with such calls. Use an appropriate opening statement similar to those below to ease the aggressiveness of this call:

> "I heard about the innovative work you are doing in technical training..."

> "I've always wanted to learn more about opportunities with your organization. Would it be possible for us to get together briefly to discuss your training needs?"

"I was told you might know someone who would be interested in my background: 10 years of increasingly responsible training and development experience..."

It is best to write down these opening statements and refer to them in your conversation. Avoid a lengthy phone conversation. You do not want to turn this into a job interview. Your goal is to schedule a face-to-face interview. If the individual asks you interview-type questions, stress your strengths and specify an interview time.

Keep in mind that your telephone voice will be a slightly higher pitch than your normal voice. Knowing this, you should lower your pitch and speak in a moderate volume and rate. By varying volume, rate, and pitch for emphasis, you will sound relatively enthusiastic and interesting over the phone.

The second type of telephone encounter, as we noted earlier, is the unexpected call from the employer who is attempting to eliminate several finalists by conducting a telephone screening interview. If you receive such a call, be prepared for questions probing both your strengths and weaknesses. Although this may be a stressful situation for you, try to sound as enthusiastic, interested, and positive as possible. Stress your strengths and try to arrange a formal interview. Keep your list of questions near the telephone so you also can interview the employer. In closing this interview, try to arrange an interview:

"I would appreciate an opportunity to meet with you to further discuss how my skills might best meet your needs. Would it possible for us to meet briefly sometime in the next few days?"

Many interviewers will probe salary questions with you over the phone. They want to know if you are within a realistic range for further consideration. While it is always best to keep this question to the end of the final interview, be prepared to answer it over the telephone. Based on your research, you should already know the salary range for similar positions. You should either respond with "I'm open to discussions on this question", or state your range which also includes part of the employer's range, if known, as common ground for negotiations. Use this question as the basis for requesting an interview. Mention that you need more information on the position. Out of fairness to the employer, he or she needs to know more about you and your value. A job interview would be most appropriate at this time.

You can prepare for these telephone conversations. Role play them with a friend. Tape-record various conversation scenarios, but do not look at each other during these conversations. Have someone else critique the tape and discuss how you might improve your telephone answers and questions.

Dealing With Objections

Interviewers must have a healthy skepticism of job candidates. Few are naive. They expect people to exaggerate their competencies and overstate what they will do for the employer. They sometimes encounter dishonest applicants, and many people they hire fail to meet their expectations. Being realists who have made poor hiring decisions before, they want to know why they should *not* hire you. Although they may not always ask you these questions, be assured they think about such questions when asking you more indirect ones:

- Why should I hire you?
- What do you really want?
- What can you really do for me?
- What are your weaknesses?
- What problems will I have with you?
- How long will you last here?

Underlying these questions are specific employers' objections to hiring you:

- You're not as good as you say you are; you probably hyped your resume or lied about yourself.
- You talk too much; you'll constantly babble, waste everyone's time, and try our patience.
- All you want is a job and security.
- You have weaknesses like the rest of us. Is it alcohol, sex, drugs, finances, shiftlessness, petty politics?
- You'll probably want my job in another five months.
- You won't stay long with us.

Employers raise such suspicions and objections because it is difficult to trust strangers in the employment game and they may have been "burned" before. Indeed, there is an alarming rise in the number of individuals lying on their resumes or falsifying their credentials.

How can you best handle employers' objections? You must first recognize their biases and stereotypes and then *raise* their expectations. You do this by stressing your strengths and avoiding your weaknesses. You must be impeccably honest in doing so. Take, for example, the question "Why are you leaving your present job?" If you have been fired and you are depressed, you might blurt out all your problems:

> "I had a great job, but my crazy boss began cutting back on personnel because of budgetary problems. I got the axe along with three others."

You might be admired for your frankness, but this answer is too negative; it reveals the wrong motivations for seeking a job. Essentially you are saying you are unemployed and bitter because you were fired. A better answer would be:

> "My position was abolished because of budget reductions. However, I see this as a new opportunity for me to use the skills I acquired during the past 10 years to improve profits. Having worked regularly with people in your field, I'm now anxious to use my experience to contribute to a growing organization."

Let's try another question reflecting objections to hiring you. The interviewer asks:

> "Your background bothers me somewhat. You've been with this organization for 10 years. You know, its different working in our organization. Why should I hire you?"

One positive way to respond to this probing question is to clearly communicate your understanding of the objection and then give evidence that you have resolved this issue in a positive manner:

> "I understand your hesitation in hiring someone with my background. I would too, if I were you. Yes, many people don't do well in different occupational settings. But I don't believe I have that problem. I'm used to working with people. I work until the job gets done, which often means long hours and on weekends. I'm very concerned with achieving results. But most important, I've done a great deal of thinking about my goals. I've researched your organization as well as many others. From what I have learned, this is exactly what I want to do, and your organization is the one I'm most interested in joining. I know I will do a good job as I have always done in the past."

Always try to avoid confessing weaknesses, negatives, or lack of experience. You want to communicate your strengths and positives loud and clear to the interviewer. Be honest, but not stupid!

Follow-Up

Once you have been interviewed, be sure to follow through to get nearer to the job offer. One of the best follow-up methods is the thank-you letter. An example is included on page 155. After talking to the employer over the telephone or in a face-to-face interview, send a thank-you letter. This letter should be typed on good quality bond paper. In this letter express your gratitude for the opportunity to interview. Re-state your interest in the position and highlight any particularly noteworthy points made in your conversation or anything you wish to further clarify. Close the letter by mentioning that you will call in a few days to inquire about the employer's decision. When you do this, the employer should remember you as a thoughtful person.

If you call and the employer has not yet made a decision, follow through with another phone call in a few days. Send any additional information to the employer which may enhance your application. You might also want to ask one of your references to call the employer to further recommend you for the position. However, don't engage in overkill by making a pest of yourself. You want to tactfully communicate two things to the employer at this point: (1) you are interested in the job, and (2) you will do a good job.

Many applicants are paid much less than they are worth.

SALARY NEGOTIATIONS

Salary is one of the most important yet least understood considerations in the job search. Many individuals do well in handling all interview questions except the salary question. They are either too shy to talk about money—nice people don't talk about salaries—or they believe you must take what you are offered because salary is predetermined by employers. In some cases—especially government—salaries are specified for each position and thus are non-negotiable. But even in government, what is specified is often a salary *range*. Lacking experience in negotiating salaries, public employees generally do not know the first step to dealing with money questions. As a result, many applicants are paid much less than they are worth. Over the years, they will lose thousands of dollars by having failed to properly negotiate their salaries.

Government salaries are normally listed with specific position descriptions. Since most salaries outside government are negotiable and even within government negotiation is possible within a limited range, the salary question may arise at any time. Employers like to raise the question as soon as possible in order to screen candidates in or out. You, on the other hand, want to deal with the salary question toward the end—after you learn more about the job and demonstrate your value to the employer. Your goal should be to get a job interview and job offer as well as negotiate as high a salary as possible.

Strategies

A standard salary negotiation scenario is for the employer to raise this question: "What are your salary requirements?" When faced with this question, you should turn it around by asking the employer: "What is the normal range in your organization for a position such as this as well as for someone with my qualifications?" The employer will either try again to get you to state a figure by restating the original question or reveal the actual range. Expect a frank answer most of the time. If the employer indicates a range, the rest of the salary negotiation is relatively simple.

Having done your homework on salaries and knowing what you are worth and what the employer is willing to pay, you are now ready to do some friendly but earnest haggling. If, for example, the employer says his range for the position is $35,000 to $40,000, you might respond by saying "$40,000 is within my range". If his range is much more or less than you anticipated, avoid being emotional or overly positive or negative. Disregard the bottom figure and concentrate on working from the top by putting his highest figure into the bottom of your range. For example, if he says "$35,000 to $40,000", you should move the top figure into your $40,000 to $45,000 range. By doing this, you create common ground from which to negotiate or you neutralize the salary issue until later negotiations.

However, if the employer does not state a range or states only a single figure, such as $35,000, rely on your salary research or multiply this figure by 25 percent to arrive at a figure for negotiation. Thus, the $34,000 figure now becomes your $43,500 expectation. Respond by saying, "I'm thinking more in terms of $43,500". A $8,500 difference should give you room for negotiation. If you state $47,000, you may appear unreasonable, unless you can support this figure based upon your salary research on comparable positions. But your previous salary research should result in stating a reasonable salary range which can be documented for similar positions in this or other organizations.

Employers may praise their "benefits" package prior to talking about a cash figure. Be wary of such benefits. Most are standard and thus come with the job regardless of the salary figure you negotiate. Unless you can create some special benefits, such as an extra two weeks of vacation each year, you should focus your attention primarily on the base salary figure.

Raising the Base

The salary figure you negotiate will influence subsequent salaries with this and other organizations. In fact, many employers figure your present worth based on your salary history; they simply add 10 to 15 percent to what you made in your last job to arrive at your new salary. If you were a $20,000 a year teacher, such a procedure will discriminate against you and your talents. Since as a teacher you were working at a depressed salary, you may have difficulty justifying a major salary increase in the eyes of most employers. In this case, you need to change the rules of game. Disregard your salary history and, instead, focus on both your worth and the value of the position to the employer—not on what the employer can get you for. On the other hand, if you are coming from a $50,000 a year job to a $40,000 one, you must convince the employer that you will be happy with a salary decrease—if, indeed, you can live with it. Many employers will not expect you to remain long if you take such a salary cut; thus, they may be reluctant to offer you a position.

Renegotiations

You should make sure your future salary reflects your value. One approach to doing this is to reach an agreement to renegotiate your salary at a later date, perhaps in another six to eight months. Use this technique especially when you feel the final salary offer is less than what you are worth, but you want to accept the job. Employers often will agree to this provision since they have nothing to lose and much to gain if you are as productive as you tell them.

However, be prepared to renegotiate in both directions—up and down. If the employer does not want to give you the salary figure you want, you can create good will by proposing to negotiate the higher salary figure down after six months, if your performance does not meet the employer's expectations. On the other hand, you may accept his lower figure with the provision that the two of you will negotiate your salary up after six months, if you exceed the employer's expectations. It is preferable to start out high and negotiate down rather than start low and negotiate up.

Renegotiation provisions stress one very important point: you want to be paid on the basis of your performance. You demonstrate your professionalism, self-confidence, and competence by negotiating in this manner. More important, you ensure that the question of your monetary value will not be closed in the future. As you negotiate the present, you also negotiate your future with this as well as other employers.

Acceptance

You should accept an offer only after reaching a salary agreement. If you jump at an offer, you may appear needy. Take time to consider your options. Remember, you are committing your time and effort in exchange for money and status. Is this the job you really want? Take some time to think about the offer before giving the employer a definite answer. But don't play hard-to-get and thereby create ill-will with your new employer. How you interview and negotiate your salary will influence how well you get along with your employer on the job.

While considering the offer, ask yourself several of the same questions you asked at the beginning of your job search:

- What do I want to be doing five years from now?
- How will this job affect my personal life?
- Do I want to travel?
- Do I know enough about the employer and the future of this organization?
- Are there other jobs I'm considering which would better meet my goals?

Accepting a job is serious business. If you make a mistake, you could be locked into a very unhappy situation for a long time.

If you receive one job offer while considering another, you will be able to compare relative advantages and disadvantages. You also will have some external leverage for negotiating salary and benefits. While you should not play games, let the employer know you have alternative job offers. This communicates that you are in demand, others also know your value, and the employer's price is not the only one in town. Use this leverage to negotiate your salary, benefits, and job responsibilities.

If you get a job offer but you are considering other employers, let the others know you have a job offer. Telephone them to inquire about your status as well as inform them of the job offer. Sometimes this will prompt employers to make a hiring decision sooner than anticipated. In addition, you will be informing them that you are in demand; they should seriously consider you before you get away!

Some job seekers play a bluffing game by telling employers they have alternative job offers even though they don't. Some candidates do this and get away with it. We don't recommend this approach. Not only is it dishonest, it will work to your disadvantage if the employer learns that you were lying. But more important, you should be selling yourself on the basis of your strengths rather than your cleverness and greed. If you can't sell yourself by being honest, don't expect to get along well on the job. When you compromise your integrity, you demean your value to others and yourself.

Your job search is not over with the job offer and acceptance. One final word of advice. Be thoughtful by sending your new employer a nice thank-you letter. As outlined on page 158, this is one of the most effective letters to write for getting your new job off on the right foot. The employer will remember you as a thoughtful individual whom he looks forward to working with.

The whole point of our job search methods is to clearly communicate to employers that you are competent and worthy of being paid top dollar. If you follow our advice, you should do very well with employers in interviews and in negotiating your salary as well as working on the job.

PART III

APPROACHING GOVERNMENT

Whether you plan to work for a federal agency or a county office, you need to know how to best approach individual governmental units. You can apply most of the job search strategies and techniques outlined in Part II to the public sector, but you must make certain adjustments in the case of government. Given the decentralized, fragmented, and chaotic nature of government, hiring procedures follow a similar structure. However, they differ between and within levels and units of government. Knowing how to get a job in Boston City Hall, for example, provides little guidance when applying for a job with Cook County, the State of Wisconsin, or the federal government.

The chapters in this section provide a general orientation toward the government hiring process. Part IV examines uniquenesses of governmental institutions as well as provides details on how to find a job within each level of government—federal, state, and local—including formal application processes and informal networking activities.

The five chapters in this section outline how you can best prepare for approaching government agencies in general. The first rule is to *know yourself.* Why do you want to work for government? How realistic are your expectations in light of both government employment realities and your motivational pattern?

The second rule is to *know your audience*. What do you know about the particular government agency you wish to work for? Who are they? What do they do, where, how, and with what effects? How do they hire? What job search strategies and techniques are most appropriate for particular agencies?

The final rule is to custom-design your job search in response to what you learned from rules one and two.

In the end, there is no substitute for acquiring both self-knowledge and knowledge of your audience and then linking this knowledge to an appropriate action plan designed for particular government agencies. If you do this, you should have no problem successfully navigating your job search through the chaos of government.

10

REALITIES AND ALTERNATIVES

All jobs have their positives and negatives, advantages and disadvantages, pros and cons. Your decision to seek government employment should be partly based on a realistic assessment of the positives and negatives in relation to your skills and motivational patterns. If not, you may be in for a real surprise once you land the job. This chapter is designed to minimize surprises and place wishful thinking in a realistic perspective by carefully assessing where you may be going over the next few years.

JOB AND CAREER REALITIES

What's it like working for government? How does it differ from work in the private sector? Is it true what they say about government jobs? These questions are difficult to answer given the diversity of over 86,000 governmental units and 18 million positions in the United States. Such diversity makes it especially difficult to generalize across all units and agencies of government. For example, since many county and municipal governments are small, they have similar advantages and disadvantages as small organizations: few high-level opportunities, slow advancement, limited mobility, low pay, and numerous responsibilities.

On the other hand, the federal government is a large organization with many employment advantages and disadvantages generally associated with large organizations: bureaucracy, red tape, loss of identity, mobility, career advancement, specialization, and good pay and benefits. While it is easy to stereotype government, stereotypes are not good predictors of a specific situation.

MAJOR ADVANTAGES

Many people seek government employment because they are motivated by various perceived advantages. Among these are:

- **Salaries:** Government salaries are relatively good compared to comparable positions in the private sector. This is especially true in the case of many federal employees and for lower level, unskilled employees and generalists who are often overpaid for their level of skills and effort. However, as we will see shortly, this advantage becomes a disadvantage in many skilled areas and for individuals in high-level managerial positions. Salaries in these cases are not as competitive. But, in general, government salaries are good to excellent for comparable positions and labor value in the private sector.

- **Benefits:** Government benefits are good to excellent. The federal government, for example, still has one of the most generous pension plans available anywhere. Many state and local governments provide excellent pension plans, tuition assistance, medical insurance, and paid vacation and sick leave.

- **Work hours and lifestyle:** Government employees basically work an 8-hour day and a 40-hour week. Their evenings and weekends are normally free for other pursuits. Such a work situation enables most government employees to separate their personal from their professional lives. Their work need not be their life. In fact, many people seek government employment precisely because they are tired of working stressful 50 and 70 hour weeks, seven days a week, in the private sector.

- **Working conditions:** Since government is not profit driven, the work is relatively stressless. While there are deadlines to meet and individual employees sometimes encounter incompetent superiors, government work involves a great deal of ongoing routines. Indeed, higher educators are noted for occupying one of the least stressful occupations of all!

- **Job satisfaction:** Many public employees are relatively satisfied with their jobs. They find the work rewarding in both monetary and personal terms. There are far more employees willing to make government a career than there are those who want to leave government for jobs in the private sector. Especially at the local level, many public employees enjoy the direct contact they have with the public in providing needed services. This intangible "opportunity to serve the public" is rewarding for many people.

- **Security:** Government jobs are some of the most secure jobs found anywhere. Few government employees lose their jobs due to budgetary cutbacks, elimination of their offices or jobs, or incompetence. Even in the worst of economic times, government employees will adapt to potential job loss by finding more secure government positions. To be fired in government is unusual, unless one is obviously incompetent, rebellious, or corrupt.

- **Advancement and promotions:** Many public employees function within merit personnel and equal opportunity systems which assure relative fairness in promotions and advancement. Well defined grievance procedures protect government employees from whimsical and capricious bosses. Especially in large government agencies, the promotion hierarchy tends to be well defined and open to individuals who perform well.

- **Future career investment:** Government jobs are a good investment for jobs and careers in the private sector with organizations on the periphery of government. Indeed, government experience is a prerequisite for many such jobs and careers. If you go into government with the idea of gaining valuable experience and skills for a future career in the private sector, your government experience will most likely be a very rewarding one. However, if you enter government with the idea of making this a life-long career, you may be in for some disappointments and frustrations in your later years as you receive fewer and fewer rewards in government service.

DISTINCT DISADVANTAGES

Public employment also has several disadvantages which discourage individuals from seeking government employment as well as motivate others to leave government service for private sector employment. Many of these disadvantages are directly related to the advantages:

- **Salaries:** While government salaries in general are good to excellent, in certain cases they are not. Many skilled workers in high-demand occupations are underpaid when compared to their counterparts in the private sector. This is especially true in the case of medical, engineering, and computer personnel. High-level managers normally cannot exceed arbitrary salary ceilings set by legislatures. Therefore, these individuals may experience few financial rewards for performing well in their jobs.

- **Limited career mobility:** Especially in small governmental units, the advancement hierarchy may be limited. In larger governmental units it may be difficult to move to other government positions because of a narrow skill specialty which is programmed for a particular office within an agency.

- **Bureaucracy:** Government work in many agencies and units lacks challenges, involves a great deal of red tape, does not encourage initiative and creativity, and may involve working with deadwood. While these are characteristics of many large organizations, they may be more pronounced in government because government lacks clearly defined and measurable goals to achieve and measure performance. In addition, government employees are not expected to be creative risk-takers.

- **Politics, decision-making, and implementation:** Government is by nature political. But many people have a low tolerance for politics and thus find such environments frustrating and stressful. Good ideas often become compromised to the political interests of representatives, interest groups, and fellow bureaucrats. Decisions are seldom clear cut, decisive, and controllable. Implementation is inherently difficult given the political interests of parties involved who also affect the outcomes of implementation. Such a political environment frequently conflicts with individuals' professional values which stress finding and implementing the "one best solution" without interference from outside forces.

- **Limited extra income opportunities:** Government employees have few opportunities to make additional income either on or off the job. Except in the case of faculty in higher education, who are often permitted and encouraged to both "daylight" and "moonlight", most public employees are expressly prohibited from engaging in such extracurricular income generating activities. Government employees must learn to live within their salaried incomes.

- **Few perks:** Government employees receive few on-the-job perks normally associated with large organizations—car, expense accounts, and memberships. At best, government jobs come with a basic office—built by the lowest bidder and often windowless—equipped with a desk, chair, telephone, computer or typewriter, secretarial assistance, and access to a copy machine.

- **Status and public attitudes:** Most public employees are not held in high esteem, because they are not seen as "doers" who accomplish things of monetary value nor do they produce measurable results. Many individuals have negative attitudes toward public servants. They often view them as living off the public dole and being overpaid and under-worked.

- **Sense of powerlessness:** Much of government work is frustrating. Employees often find difficulty in deriving on-the-job satisfaction which is normally attendant with the nature of the work itself. A great deal of work gets processed, but concrete accomplishments are difficult to identify and little satisfaction is derived. In large agencies employees may feel like a cog in the wheel. They view their work as somewhat meaningless since it does not appear to accomplish anything of importance.

- **Plateaued careers:** Many public employees find their career plateaus quickly in government due to a combination of limited career mobility, short advancement hierarchies, and arbitrary salary ceilings. A great many public employees in the age range of 38 to 45 suffer from what Marilyn Moats Kennedy identifies as the Killer Bs: Blockage, Boredom, and Burnout. They feel they have advanced as far as they can possibly go; many have lost interest in their work. They have job security and they are paid well, but they dislike their jobs because their government careers have essentially stalled in terms of promotions, salary increments, responsibilities, and rewards for performance. These are the career distressed who do not look forward to another 20 years in their present jobs and careers.

WEIGHING THE ALTERNATIVES

Many observers may tell you the advantages of government service outweigh the disadvantages and vice versa. Others will tell you government work is challenging and exciting—the best possible career to enter. Don't believe everything you hear. Few people are lucky enough to have challenging and exciting jobs they love. Most jobs are a mixture of advantages and disadvantages, high points and low points. Try as we can to make work more challenging, exciting, and enjoyable, many jobs will remain dull and stressful. There simply is no objective way of determining the best alternatives for you. You do the best you can in terms of self-assessment, research, and planning. Then you acquire work experience which may or may not fulfill your career aspirations.

In many respects, government work is very similar to work in other small or large organizations. If you work for a small private firm, you are less likely to use your specialized skills on a full-time basis. You must learn to be adaptive, do things you may not particularly enjoy or be skilled in doing, but these are things you must do in order to get the work done. Chances are you operate in a situation that is understaffed, stressful, and not conducive to innovation. You are always trying to get the basics done. For individuals who like to practice only their specialty skills, such work environments are inherently frustrating and unstable. They tend to bring out one's weaknesses rather than enhance one's strengths. On the other hand, such organizations tend to be less bureaucratic and more adaptive, creative, and responsive to their environment than many large organizations. Small organizations are preferred by individuals who enjoy the challenges which come with developing and doing different things, making and implementing decisions quickly, receiving immediate feedback on performance, and being a "big fish" in a small pond. Indeed, many people thrive in such small and responsive organizations.

Large bureaucracies are found in both the public and private sectors. In this particular type of organization individuals tend to be conservative; they are more oriented toward maintaining existing patterns than with innovation, creativity, and risk-taking; and they play the games necessary to survive and advance within the hierarchy. Many individuals—especially entrepreneurial types—are ill-suited for such work environments. They would enjoy and prosper more in settings which permitted them greater freedom and control over their work. In fact, entrepreneurial types who are oriented toward the public sector are probably better off working for a well staffed small government organization or joining small and adaptive nongovernmental organizations which work with government.

Unfortunately, thousands of public employees are unhappy with their jobs precisely because their skills and motivational patterns are not conducive to the various work environments found in government. While at one time their jobs may have been exciting and challenging, their jobs today have changed, or they themselves have changed. As individuals acquire experience and their values, goals, and work situations change, many find themselves in different types of careers than they had previously enjoyed or anticipated for the future. These individuals might be happier in different jobs and careers if they were willing and able to make a career transition from government to the private sector. But good salaries, benefits, and security convince them to stick it out rather than change to jobs and careers which would be more appropriate for their particular mix of skills and motivations.

You can avoid becoming one of these career plateaued or displaced public employees if you do the proper self-assessment, gather information on alternative jobs and careers with different types of public organizations, and realistically assess whether or not a particular public sector job is best for you. In the end, only you can determine what will fulfill your needs.

COMPARABLE WORTH AND THE LIFE-LONG GOVERNMENT CAREER

Debates have gone on for years concerning whether public employees are overpaid or underpaid. Understandably, if you are a public employee, you may feel you are underpaid. After all, you know other people who make more money than you—and you feel you are just as hard a worker. On the other hand, if you work in the private sector, you may feel public employees are overpaid. What do they produce given their generous salaries, benefits, and work environments? The stereotyped government employee may be the postal employee most citizens encounter on a regular basis. Needless to say, the old adage that most people "stand where they sit" operates when evaluating the relative worth of most peoples' work. Not surprising, most people think they work harder than others, and they are worth much more than they are paid at present.

Many governmental units regularly study comparable salaries in the private sector in order to bring government salaries in line with the competition. In addition, several studies have been commissioned to review data concerning the question of federal salaries. For example, the president's Advisory Committee on Federal Pay reported in November of 1980 that salaries of federal white-collar workers were 1 to 2 percentage points behind similar positions in the private sector. At the higher levels the salary gaps were considerable: salaries of top executives were on an average seven percent behind comparable positions in the private sector; in some cases the lag was as much as 46 percent. Yet, government statistics showed the average federal white-collar worker earned $5,000 more than the private sector counterpart. However, skill requirements were higher for the federal employee. Other studies have shown that federal employees receive better pay and benefits than their private industry counterparts. The most recent study of comparable pay (1993) again stresses the widening gap between government and private sector salaries, with government employees at a distinct disadvantage.

Given the inconclusive and contradictory conclusions of the various studies, it is difficult to conclude one way or the other how government salaries compare with private industry salaries. We can say with certainty how salaries for many technical positions, such as engineers and computer programmers, compare to one another in government and the private sector. We can also easily compare many entry-level secretarial and staff support positions. However, many other positions, especially higher level managerial positions, are difficult to compare because they lack comparable performance criteria.

Indeed, the problem with most comparable pay studies and debates is in establishing the criteria for comparability of positions. Studies often end up comparing apples to oranges when instead they are dealing with lemons. Many public employees possess specialized skills on the inner workings of government which are not directly transferable to the private sector. While these individuals may be white-collar workers earning $50,000 a year as a welfare analyst or grants specialist, in reality they would have difficulty finding a comparable level job in the private sector. Indeed, one of the best indicators of comparable worth is what public employees actually do once they leave government for positions in the private sector. No studies have used actual career transitions as the basis for determining comparable worth. In the meantime, many government employees are convinced they are underpaid in comparison to their private sector counterparts.

Our experience with public employees tends to support the overpaid theory with major exceptions in the cases of technical personnel who are often underpaid. Even though many government officials feel they are underpaid, and some studies support this belief, most appear overpaid when they go job hunting in the private sector. When they begin marketing their public sector skills in private industry, many more individuals must take salary cuts than receive salary increases. Only after job hunting in the private sector do many public employees change their views about being underpaid. However, this situation will vary with different types of positions. For example, teachers are generally underpaid, and they can find employment in the private sector which pays better—but normally they must change their field of work. The same is true for many public safety positions. Individuals in these occupations must change careers in order to substantially increase their salaries in the private sector.

One major problem relates to the salaries of experienced managers and executives in government. Government salaries plateau at the upper levels because legislatures put pay caps on the top level positions. Consequently, a 50-year old official who reaches the top salary level is most likely to stay at that level the rest of their career regardless of their performance. While making $87,000 a year in government, this individual might be able to make $250,000 or more a year in the private sector in a comparable position entailing a similar level of responsibility.

Indeed, one of the major problems with salaries in government is the career orientation of many employees. Many years ago young individuals entered government service for a few years of "public service" and then left for long-term careers in the private sector. They knew when to both get in and get out of government. This orientation has changed considerably during the past four decades. Today, many individuals enter government service with the idea of making it a life-long career. Only after 10 to 20 years in government service do they realize that government salaries are not designed for individuals with life-long career aspirations within government. They don't know when to get out. Regardless of all the comparable pay studies and the periodical laments of legislators and public employees about the "crisis of the public service", legislators simply will not advance the caps on government salaries much in the coming years. The public still sees public employees earning $100,000 a year a bit excessive when it comes out of their tax dollars.

Salaries are not designed for individuals with life-long career aspirations in government.

A little more sacrifice and less preoccupation with making their government job a financially well rewarded career is probably in order. Consequently, when you reach the top in government, it's perhaps time to consider changing careers since you will never receive a salary comparable to what you feel you are truly worth. And helping open the ranks of government to newer and younger blood is probably not a bad idea after all. In other words, you need to know when to get out of government. Staying around too long can be detrimental to your career and your life!

In fact, you may do both yourself and government a favor by leaving government service after ten to fifteen years. Your government experience will most likely be rewarded in the private sector with a long-term career involving substantial financial rewards. And this is precisely what the thousands of "revolving door" players in government every year learn as they leave government positions for comparable "public sector" jobs with private organizations on the periphery of government—trade and professional associations, contractors and consultants, and nonprofit organizations. Their government experience was a necessary investment in a long-term and financially rewarding career in the private sector.

11

INFORMAL STRUCTURES AND HIRING PRACTICES

*H*ow will you approach a job market that is embedded within a highly decentralized, fragmented, and chaotic governmental system, one characterized by a high degree of overlapping functions and redundant structures? It's a confusing system for many individuals who expect to encounter a well defined, rational system of governance.

If this were a simple and rational structure, the American governmental system would be centralized with well defined points of decision-making and entry for jobs. One would expect to respond to job announcements or submit applications to a central personnel office which, in turn, would make hiring decisions. Indeed, most governments project an image of rational hiring by maintaining the appearance of a unified and centralized recruitment and selection process.

If you are to be most effective in this job market, you must first understand how governments are internally structured to hire individuals to fill positions. Once you understand this structure, as well as the attendant recruitment processes, you will be well on the road to developing a realistic and effective job search among government agencies. You will be better able to adapt many of the job search techniques outlined in Part II to the unique settings of government.

APPROACH A DECENTRALIZED STRUCTURE

America's passion for decentralized political and governmental structures is offset by its commitment to achieving greater efficiency and effectiveness in government or periodic attempts to "reinvent" government. To be efficient and effective yet decentralized and fragmented at the same time is one of the great dilemmas of American government. In trying to have their cake and eat it, American governments are adept at presenting pictures of rational organizations responding efficiently and effectively to public needs. This image of performance may or may not have a direct relationship to the day-to-day realities of government.

To be efficient and effective yet decentralized and fragmented at the same time is one of the great dilemmas of American government.

Underlying the facade of organizational efficiency and effectiveness are numerous organizational jungles and management nightmares. Not only do government units overlap with one another and duplicate functions, internally they often are loosely structured with a great deal of autonomy given to individual departments and offices. The extreme case of such highly decentralized organizations is state universities which are basically confederations of competing factions, i.e., departments and programs, held together by a common budget, organizational name, and college catalog. Each department functions as a relatively autonomous organizational entity which hires its own faculty, sets its own performance standards, and decides its own fate. Loyalty and identity to one's larger profession often takes precedent over commitment to the immediate institution, including an individual's department!

Other government institutions may not be as extremely decentralized as universities, but they are decentralized nonetheless. City governments, for example, tend to be affiliated with large state and national professional associations. Large groupings of employees may belong to public unions. Similar to universities, they are largely held together by a common budget, name, and public relations brochure. Several of the departments will be geographically separated from the others—with their own buildings and grounds—and largely function as governments within governments. For example, the education and public safety bureaucracies most likely will function separate from one another as well as from the city government bureaucracy in general. In fact, city managers and mayors in both small and large communities often experience difficulty in controlling these departments because of their highly decentralized nature.

State and federal governments function along similar decentralized lines. Each agency and department maintains its own personnel offices and recruitment practices. While state civil service commissions and the U. S. Office of Personnel Management develop personnel recruitment and performance standards and provide training and limited recruitment services for individual agencies and offices, most hiring takes place within particular agencies. And even within agencies, hiring tends to be decentralized to the actual operational units which have the hiring needs.

KNOW THE FORMAL AND INFORMAL HIRING SYSTEMS

Formal organizational charts outline the basic skeleton of organizations. They indicate how organizations, under the best of circumstances, should operate according to formal authority and responsibilities. These charts are good starting points for understanding the basic structure of government. These are not, however, to be taken too seriously as indicators of how government actually functions. For within all organizations, informal structures and processes operate in spite of the formal organizational chart. Indeed, most individuals within organizations neither understand nor are interested in the formal organizational chart. Many would be hard pressed to either locate or explain the chart! Rather, they behave according to the administrative and social processes and precedents which they are most familiar with and which are identified as "the organization" within their minds.

Identifying and explaining the formal organizational chart is the easy part of conducting a job search with government. Most government offices will have a government operations manual, annual report, or telephone directory outlining the formal structure and functions of government. Within the federal government, the *U.S. Government Manual*, *Federal Yellow Book*, *Congressional Yellow Book*, *Federal Directory*, *Congressional Directory*, *Washington Information Directory*, and telephone directories of departments and agencies published by the U.S. Government Printing Office adequately outline such information.

The informal structure, on the other hand, is the most important for identifying on-going realities but also the most difficult to identify and understand. It requires research on who does what, where, when, and with what effects. It involves using investigative skills to uncover the on-going realities of organizations. The results of such investigation often uncover the negative side of organizations—the deadwood, the powerful and powerless, the perversions, the power struggles, and personnel injustices—as well as positive opportunities for you. Such investigations strip away the pictures of performance portrayed in the public relations brochures and plant one's feet firmly on the ground by reaffirming what most observers of formal and informal organizations have learned over the years: organizations are organizations are organizations; they differ considerably in terms of their structures, functions, goals, and outcomes. Some are exciting places in which to work, while others are simply dreadful. Most are difficult to change in the short-run.

Unfortunately, most job seekers develop job search strategies and expectations aimed at the formal organization and the picture of performance projected for public consumption. Few ever delve into the inner workings of government to uncover the informal structure that really determines how things get done and by whom. Such information is usually acquired while on the job—after one has made a commitment to the organization. In many cases, the informal structure may be at considerable variance with what initially appeared to be the organizational reality. We strongly urge you to try to avoid any on-the-job surprises by learning as much as possible about the inner workings of the organization prior to accepting a particular job.

You need to identify and use the informal structure to your advantage prior to joining an organization. Part of your research should focus on understanding this structure. While most government organizations will have a similar formal structure, their informal structures may be considerably different. You will not know this until you do some intelligence work on an organization.

The following generalizations are valid for most government organizations. They will help you conduct your own investigation of government agencies in an intelligent manner:

- **Most government personnel offices do not perform important hiring functions.** Their primary function is to communicate vacancies of operational units, process applications and inquiries, conduct testing, initially screen applications to pass on to the operating unit, and generally engage in routine personnel functions such as maintaining personnel files, putting employees on the payroll, and conducting limited training. They do some hiring, but normally for low level positions with which operational units would rather not be bothered.

- **Most major hiring decisions are made at the operational levels.** Identifying vacancies, recruiting candidates, screening, and selection—are primarily made by operational units. Managers and supervisors within an office are the key decision-makers. They are the first to identify personnel needs, worry about whom to hire, and select the best individual to meet their needs. While they will share some of the hiring functions with personnel offices—normally administrative overhead and regulatory functions (issuing vacancy announcements, conducting testing and screening, ensuring equal opportunity)—they maintain a certain degree of hiring autonomy to ensure that the formal procedures will give them what they want. Appealing to higher level authorities or using political pull to force hiring decisions on these lower levels will be strongly resisted. Such actions threaten the very autonomy of operating units.

- **Lengthy application procedures may or may not be necessary.** Many government jobs can be filled immediately without undergoing a lengthy recruitment and selection process. For example, it is not unusual for congressional staff aids to walk into a congressman's office and be hired on the spot! Many federal agencies participate in job fairs where they hire many applicants on the spot. However, most positions will involve a waiting period precisely because the personnel office must follow a formal procedure, even though the operating unit may have already decided on a candidate prior to initiating the formal selection procedures.

- **In spite of claims to the contrary, many government jobs are "wired" for particular individuals.** Vacancy announcements and equal opportunity procedures may make the hiring process look open, competitive, and legitimate, but operating units continue to engage in the notorious practice of "wiring" positions. This involves the informal pre-selection of candidates. Individuals are informally recruited for a position and then the qualifications are written around the individual so that in the end he or she will be the best qualified candidate from the pool of qualified applicants. As many as 70 percent of high level government vacancies may be partly wired, or at least less than fully open and competitive. A simple fact of life operates among those who do the wiring and hiring: they seek stability, predictability, and control over the hiring process. By all means, they wish to avoid the surprise of hiring an unknown quantity who may or may not work out for a position. For it is better to know and like your future employee ahead of time than to engage in a recruitment crap-shoot sponsored by a personnel office that doesn't really understand your needs.

After all, people in personnel don't have to live with the new employee! Wiring is not an illegal practice since the formal hiring process does take place according to the rules and regulations, and the final selection takes place within this system. But unethical? Perhaps. Unfair? Certainly. Illegal? Of course not. This is "business as usual" for hiring in government. While most hiring authorities deny such practices, they take place in most units of government to some degree. Don't be surprised if you uncover such notorious practices. Better still, maybe you can become the subject of a wiring campaign!

A simple fact of life operates among those who do the wiring and hiring: they seek stability, predictability, and control over the hiring process.

TAKE EFFECTIVE ACTION

Given these guidelines to the informal hiring process in government, we suggest you do the following:

- **Do not be deceived by appearances.** Many people exaggerate their abilities, usefulness, and performance. Use your eyes and intuition as well as your ears when researching government organizations. Your goal should be to learn as much as possible about the informal organization. You want to know: How do things get done around here? Who makes the decisions? What kind of work environment is this? Do people enjoy their work? Who is on the "ins" and "outs"? While difficult questions to answer as an outsider, progress toward answering them will reveal a great deal of useful information for organizing your job search targeted on particular agencies.

- **Contact the personnel office and properly observe the formal application procedures**, but do not have high expectations or spend a great deal of time trying to get a job through this source. Personnel offices should be treated as a necessary step, but not the only one. If you let your job search stop at this office, your chances of getting a job will be minimal. To be most effective, you must go deeper into the organization.

- **Conduct research amongst those people who are most involved in making the hiring decisions**—usually the managers and supervisors in the operating units. If they have a vacancy and they like you, they may even promote you by wiring a position around your experience and qualifications, or at least make sure your application is forwarded to them from the personnel office.

- **Decide how you want to play this job search game.** Some people love to network, drop names, do investigative research, and talk about themselves. They have no qualms about being the subject of wiring, and they believe in the ethics and efficacy of "pulling their own strings". This works and is acceptable behavior for them. On the other hand, this approach may not be for you. Many people do get good jobs without networking, wiring, or pulling strings. But don't be naive about what's going on around you. Be aware that many of your competitors are practicing these job search techniques for getting the job they want. Thus, you may be at a disadvantage. Your odds of getting a job may not be as good as they could be, but you have to live with yourself, and some things may not come naturally, are personally objectionable, or make one feel uncomfortable. That is your choice. Our job is to outline alternative choices and suggest different probabilities for success, regardless of your particular preferences on how you should best relate to this job market.

12

KNOW THE HIRING PROCESS

The hiring process varies for each of the more than 86,000 units of government. Each has its own formal and informal systems for recruiting, screening, and selecting candidates. As we noted in Chapter 11, expect the structure of hiring to follow the general structure of government—decentralized, fragmented, and chaotic—both between and within governmental units.

LINK FORMAL AND INFORMAL PROCESSES

Most governmental units will follow several similar *formal steps* in the hiring process. These are specified in civil service regulations, personnel manuals, and merit criteria. They include:

1. Announce vacancies
2. Accept applications
3. Administer examinations
4. Review credentials
5. Select group of qualified finalists
6. Conduct interviews
7. Offer job to one candidate
8. Place new employee on payroll

The informal hiring process works only if it is closely tied to the formal process.

At the same time, an *informal hiring process* may supplement or reinforce the formal process. This informal process will:

- Communicate hiring needs through networks of friends and colleagues.

- Conduct conversations, discussions, or informational interviews with prospective candidates.

- Pre-select one or two interesting candidates.

- Coach candidates on how to best complete the formal application in order to become the best qualified and/or develop the position description and selection criteria around the qualifications of a particular individual, i.e., "wire" the position.

- Select the pre-selected candidate.

These two processes, in effect, are linked together. Hence, the informal hiring process works only if it is closely tied to the formal process. Given elaborate rules and regulations required by government agencies to ensure equity, fairness, and objectivity in identifying and selecting the best qualified individuals, candidates must enter through the front door and complete the necessary steps to become formally eligible. At the same time, the informal back door operates similarly to most non-governmental hiring practices. It enables individuals to use the job search skills outlined in Chapter 6-9: network, conduct informational interviews with hiring personnel, and circulate resumes. In fact, many managers and supervisors appreciate meeting individuals who use such self-marketing techniques, because it gives them important information and ideas for specifying their own personnel needs and requirements.

The effective job candidate learns to link the formal and informal hiring processes, as illustrated on the following page. While involving separate skills and strategies, the two processes come together at the eligibility and interview stages.

Therefore, when seeking government employment, you must develop an additional set of job search skills aimed at the formal hiring process. This involves being able to locate information on vacancy announcements, complete applications, take the necessary tests, and handle the formal selection interviews.

LOCATE VACANCY ANNOUNCEMENTS

Government agencies normally issue three types of announcements relating to jobs and hiring. *Vacancy or position announcements* outline the availability of specific position vacancies and specify the proper application procedures, including examination requirements and deadlines for submission of all required documents. *Open announcements*—most frequently used for positions with high turnover rates—permit applications to be submitted and considered at any time. *Examination announcements* state that a particular entrance exam will be given on specific dates and that individuals must apply to sit for the exam.

Government agencies regularly announce vacancies through personnel offices. The personnel office, in turn, may decide to distribute the announcement to numerous sources or restrict distribution to certain locations and publications. For example, at the state and local levels many high-level professional and technical positions are routinely listed in regional and nationwide professional newsletters, journals, and job banks. Among these information sources are:

- *Affirmative Action Register APWA Reporter* (American Public Works Association)
- *The City-County Recruiter* (Clearinghouse for Government Personnel)
- *ICMA Newsletter* (International City Manager Association)
- *The Job Finder: A Checklist of Openings for Administrative and Governmental Research Employment*
- *JobMart* (American Planning Association)

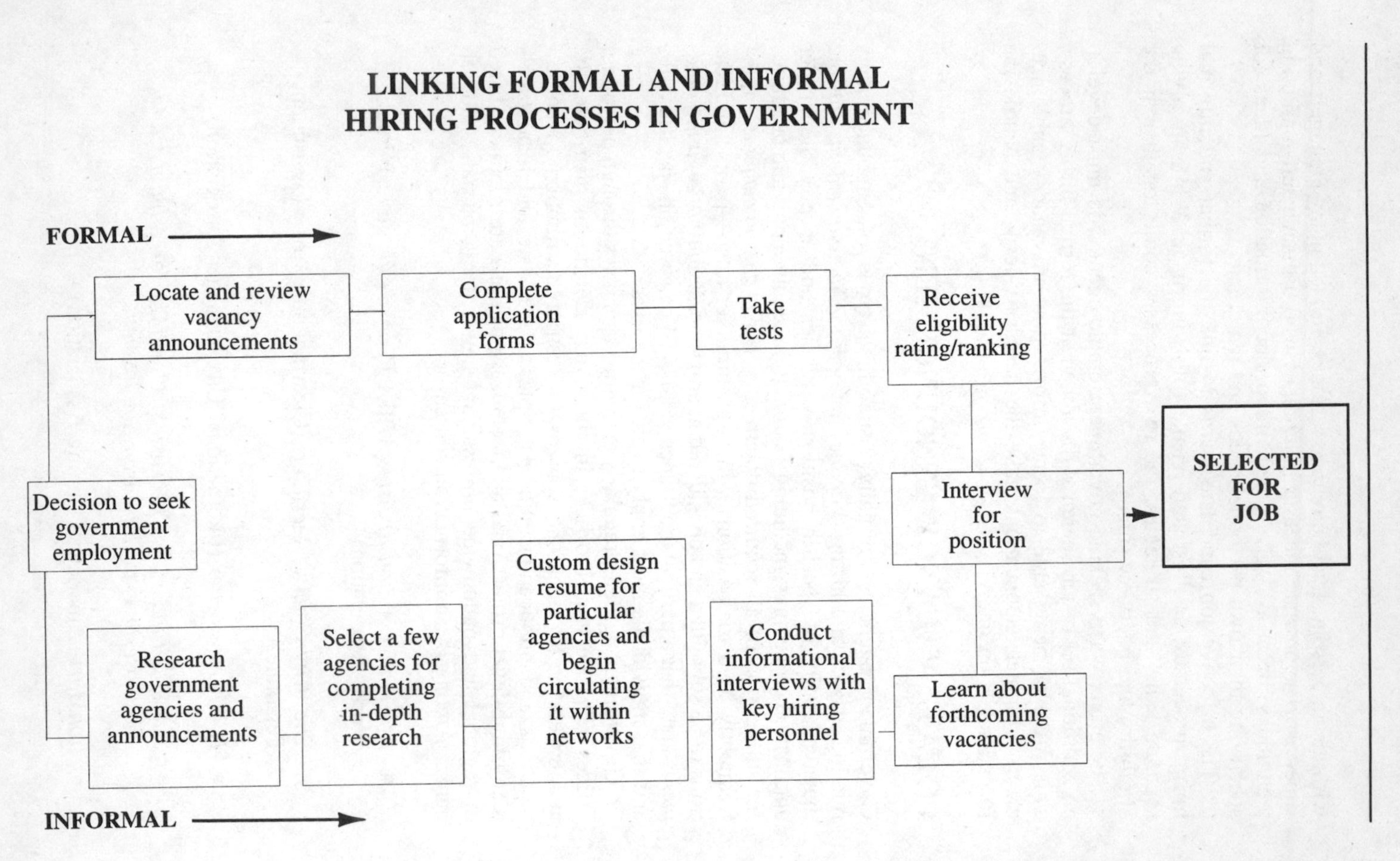
LINKING FORMAL AND INFORMAL
HIRING PROCESSES IN GOVERNMENT
FORMAL
Locate and review vacancy announcements
Complete application forms
Take tests
Receive eligibility rating/ranking
Decision to seek government employment
Interview for position
SELECTED FOR JOB
Research government agencies and announcements
Select a few agencies for completing in-depth research
Custom design resume for particular agencies and begin circulating it within networks
Conduct informational interviews with key hiring personnel
Learn about forthcoming vacancies
INFORMAL

- *Jobs Available: A Listing of Employment Opportunities in the Public Sector*

- *Mountain Plains States' Job Bank NAHRO Monitor* (National Association of Housing Redevelopment Officials)

- *New England Administrative, Professional, Technical Job Bank*

- *Public Administration Times* (American Society for Public Administration)

- *The State Recruiter* (Clearinghouse for Government Personnel)

Most positions found in government are associated with some professional organization which provides job information and referral services. For a comprehensive and detailed listing of job information sources in government, see Daniel Lauber, *The Government Job Finder.* This book can be ordered directly from Impact Publications by completing the order information at the end of this book.

At the federal level, the 1,000 plus vacancies occurring each day are announced through a variety of sources. No single federal government office compiles a listing. The most comprehensive listings of job vacancies are compiled biweekly by two private firms:

- Federal Research Service: *Federal Career Opportunities*

- Breakthrough Publications: *Federal Jobs Digest*

For more information on these firms and their publications, refer to our discussion in Chapter 17.

Most vacancy announcements in government will have limited distribution. The extent of distribution is unpredictable because individual agencies and hiring officials decide on how and where to disseminate such information. Distribution may take the form of a one-page announcement posted on a personnel office or cafeteria bulletin board. Wider distribution might include listing a vacancy in the local newspaper. Except for hard to fill high-level and technical positions requiring specific experience and skills, most government offices have little incentive to widely broadcast their vacancy announcements. Most will do the minimum advertising required to fulfill affirmative action and merit system requirements.

Since there is no single source you can consult to give you a comprehensive listing of alternative vacancy announcements at any particular time, your strategy for gathering information may include several alternative approaches:

- Survey specific professional journals and newsletters for job listings.
- Subscribe to a particular job listing or job bank service.
- Telephone or write to particular agencies for vacancy announcements (these come in a variety of names—Personnel Office, Civil Service Commission, Merit System, Career Services, Department of Labor, Employment, or Manpower).
- Visit government job information centers, personnel offices, libraries, and cafeterias to ask questions and survey bulletin boards.
- Contact the hiring agency directly for vacancy information.
- Register with the State Employment Office in order to get access to their job information bank.

The most effective strategy will be to focus your job search on a particular government agency. For example, after conducting a great deal of research, you may decide you really would like to work for the United States Information Agency (USIA). However, this is a big agency performing numerous functions, with thousands of employees.

The most effective strategy will be to focus your job search on a particular government agency.

The question is: "Where do you want to work doing what within USIA?" You must be specific. The personnel office as well as the private job listing services will include several USIA announcements. But during your research, you should identify a particular office within USIA within which you want to find employment. Take, for example, the Office of Private Sector Programs within the Bureau of Educational and Cultural Affairs. Focusing on this office, you should consult the *Federal Yellow Book*, the *Directory of Federal Executives*, or the *USIA Telephone Directory* for names and phone numbers of key people you should contact for information about vacancies. In this case, try both the Office of Personnel (within USIA this is located in the Bureau of Management and is divided into domestic and foreign service personnel divisions—

two separate personnel systems functioning within USIA) and the program unit—the Office of Private Sector Programs. After a few phone calls to these offices, you should have specific names and phone numbers for monitoring vacancy announcements. Most people will refer you to the proper individual and office. If you persist and ask the right questions, you will get the information you need. But it will take a few phone calls.

The general rule, then, is to focus on specific positions within specific offices of specific agencies and government units. Always move your information gathering activities to the lowest level in the organizational hierarchy at which hiring decisions are made. In other words, you must use a decentralized job search strategy to be effective in decentralized governmental systems. Job listings and job banks do just the opposite: they centralize the job information function by coordinating the chaos of job announcements. If you come at this from a shotgun approach, i.e., "Where are all the jobs I might fit into?", you may wander aimlessly, sinking before you swim, in the incredible morass of government agencies and offices.

Knowledge of specifics is power in this job finding game. It is best to start with the assumption that vacancy announcements with government offices are available only to those who are interested and willing to expend the time and energy to find them. It requires a great deal of initiative and perseverance on your part. The initiative will involve frequent use of the telephone, research by mail and in libraries, and your physical presence in offices. While you will find the telephone to be the most efficient approach, your physical presence will be the most effective approach. Job listings and job banks, although easy to access, are less effective sources of information. By the time you locate a job vacancy through these sources, chances are it has already been filled through the informal system or it will generate a great deal of competition. You must learn to "read" vacancy announcements to determine if they are wired for someone. This reading skill can only be acquired through experience in the informal system.

COMPLETE APPLICATION FORMS

Most government organizations require applications from job seekers. You must complete a standard application form when applying for a particular position or for a class of positions. This will range from a simple two to four-page biodata form to more complex forms used by agencies in the federal government. You must carefully complete this application form since it is one major determinant of whether you will be selected as a finalist and scheduled for an interview.

Most applications follow a similar format and include the same categories of information. Let's examine the typical application form and suggest some useful guidelines for completing it. Chances are you will walk into a personnel office, request job vacancy information, and be asked to complete the application form immediately. If this happens, you need to have all the necessary information with you. Therefore, be sure you have a copy of your resume with you as well as the necessary biodata to complete the applications. Better still, take the application form with you so you have adequate time to thoroughly answer the questions. To do it properly, you may need to spend three to four hours completing the application form.

The standard application categories include many which should already appear on your resume. Most applications request the following:

1. Contact information (name, address, telephone numbers)
2. Position(s) sought
3. Social security number
4. Citizenship
5. Military status/service/preference
6. Examinations taken
7. Education and training completed
8. Work experience
9. Special skills and qualifications
10. Disabilities
11. Criminal record
12. Salary sought

The first thing you should do is ask for two copies of the application form or make a photocopy on which to draft a completed application. Then read the application thoroughly, and develop a strategy for making this application an outstanding document of your experience, qualifications, skills, and accomplishments which are directly focused on the stated qualifications. Assume the stated qualifications will also become the evaluation criteria. The more you write directly to those qualifications, the better your evaluation.

The most important sections on applications are education and training, work experience, and special skills and qualifications. Unfortunately, most application forms are designed for the ease of the evaluator and the convenience of the filing system and thus do not give you much room to detail your accomplishments—at best, one to two inches. Customize these sections of the application form by stressing your skills and accomplishments. Avoid discussing only formal duties and responsibilities as normally found in position descriptions. Assuming you have conducted research on the job, your discussion of education, training, work experience, and special skills and qualifications should focus on the skills required for the particular job. These requirements are normally outlined in personnel manuals and position descriptions. Try to eliminate extraneous information which may distract an evaluator or appear as a weakness. You should choose those things that will enhance your application in direct relationship to the requirements of the job.

When addressing the salary questions, state "open" or write in the civil service classification or rating code. In so doing, the reader will assume you will accept the salary specified for the particular position.

Be sure you answer all questions and fill in all the blanks. If something does not apply, write in "N/A" (Not Applicable). Otherwise, evaluators may assume you did not follow instructions and left the application incomplete. Avoid giving them a reason to be negative toward your application and thus screen you out from eligibility.

Type the application form neatly, sign and date it, and attach the necessary customized add-on sheets which detail your qualifications in direct reference to the position specifications. Also, attach a copy of your resume if it is designed to further reinforce the application. A little redundancy at this point may be helpful. Your resume will probably be easier to read and better focused than the application form you were forced to complete. The resume allows you to present yourself in the best light possible. While it may not help your application, it can't hurt, and it just may give you an "extra edge" over your competition!

TAKE EXAMINATIONS

Once you have completed and submitted the application, the next step will be for someone to evaluate it to determine if you (1) meet the minimum qualifications to take an entrance examination, (2) should be placed on an eligibility list, or (3) notified for an interview. In many cases, the application is, in effect, the test. It is reviewed, evaluated, scored, and ranked with other applications. Points are given for all those items you stressed in the customized sections of your application.

In other cases, one must pass a test or a series of tests in order to get on an eligibility list. Different types of tests are designed to measure general aptitude, specific skill levels, physical abilities, and health status.

You can and should prepare for government tests similarly to college entrance exams. Your local library or bookstore may have copies of practice tests or they can refer you to the proper sources. Almost all tests governments administer to applicants are in some practice form. Arco Publishing, for example, publishes numerous self-directed practice test books for a variety of positions with federal, state, and local governments. Many of these books are good investments.

At the same time, try to gather as much information as possible about the particular test to be administered. Many governmental units will issue a booklet or handouts which describe the test, present sample questions, and outline the rules for scoring the examination. For example, some scoring rules are designed to discourage guessing and thus severely penalize you for wrong answers. You need to know this before taking the examination.

On the day of the test, be sure you are rested, arrive at the testing site early, read the instructions carefully, and move along as rapidly as possible. Many people do not do well on tests because they fail to manage their test-taking time well. Should you not do well on the test, all is not lost. Many agencies permit you to re-take the test at some later date.

BECOME ELIGIBLE

After submitting your application and completing the necessary testing, expect at least six weeks before you hear whether you have been placed on an eligibility list or register. City governments normally take longer to respond than state and county governments. In many cases this will be a long, drawn-out process of waiting, waiting, and waiting. Make sure you continue job search activities in the meantime.

Types of eligibility lists will vary from government to government. The standard eligibility process consists of the personnel office ranking all applicants and selecting three or more best qualified candidates, as measured by the evaluation of their applications and examination scores, to submit to the operating unit or officials responsible for completing the hiring process. These individuals, in turn, select those individuals they wish to interview.

At this stage the formal and informal hiring processes converge. What often happens is that a program supervisor has already identified someone she is interested in, even prior to initiation of the formal recruiting procedures. After helping the candidate move through the formal hiring procedures—by providing tips on how to enhance the application form and take the test—this same individual is called for an interview and often hired. In some cases the formal hiring process may result in identifying candidates who are better qualified than the one being sponsored. In this case, the hiring officials may choose the unknown candidate because he or she would better meet the needs of the office.

ATTEND INTERVIEWS

If you are selected and scheduled for an interview, follow the interviewing tips we outlined in Chapter 9. This is the most important step in the employment process. Everything you did prior to this step has been focused on getting the interview. How well you conduct yourself in the interview will largely determine if the job will be offered to you.

Government hiring officials are no different from other employers when it comes to interviewing candidates. They want *value*. They seek individuals who are competent, intelligent, honest, and likeable. You need to communicate your value to the interviewer(s). Above all, you must communicate who you are, what you *can* and *will* do, and where you are going.

APPEAR KNOWLEDGEABLE BUT ACKNOWLEDGE THE UNIQUE

Make sure you also communicate that you are *knowledgeable* about the organization and operations. But be very careful how you communicate your knowledge and competence. Many public employees still feel their particular agency, office, and operations are really *unique*. They believe knowledge and experience acquired on some other problem or in another organization may not transfer well to their situations. This bias toward being different or unique is probably more a function of the extreme insulation government employees experience within the bureaucracy, as well as their need to feel important, than an objective measure of reality. Few government operations, in fact, are unique, and many government employees could learn a great deal by talking to others in different offices and agencies. But since they still believe they are unique, make sure you respond to their need to know that you know something about them, but not that you know more than they do.

Be very careful how you communicate your knowledge and competence. Many public employees still feel their particular agency, office, and operations are really unique.

By no means should you indicate during an interview that you have some general textbook knowledge or experience from elsewhere which you will apply to this program or office to deal with a specific problem. If you demonstrate your knowledge and competence in this manner, the interviewers may view you as naive and stupid. After all, they have a unique operation outsiders do not and cannot understand. In such a situation it is best to be a good listener who demonstrates a willingness to learn and contribute to the organization. Somewhere during the interview you should clearly state that you know they are unique; your approach would be adapted to their uniquenesses. For this statement you should receive a great deal of support. It could be the decisive factor separating you from other candidates interviewing for the job. In the end, such deference to power could get you hired!

13 GATHER INFORMATION FOR APPLICATION

*K*nowledge is always power when conducting a job search. This is especially true when seeking public employment. You will find a great deal of general information on government and periphery institutions, but you will need to do a considerable amount of research to uncover the detailed information necessary to locate the job you want. Through research you will learn to communicate effectively with hiring officials.

In this chapter we identify several important information sources you should consult prior to applying for a government position. These information sources give you both knowledge and power.

GOVERNMENTS FILL POSITIONS

As you conduct a job search on government, keep in mind that governments hire individuals to fill positions. The emphasis is on *positions*, not individuals. While employers in the private sector can often create a position around an individual, few government agencies can do so. Positions in government are difficult to create. Once created, they are difficult to abolish. As a result, government agencies frequently have positions they don't really need. Nonetheless, they keep these positions rather than abolish them, because such positions sometimes come in handy for other purposes—agencies can "park" their deadwood and incompetents in them or assign their political outcasts to this organizational equivalent of "Siberia".

Government personnel systems are highly structured and follow specific rules and regulations. Positions tend to be well-defined in terms of specific duties and responsibilities. Indeed, government has turned position descriptions and classifications into a science, and personnel systems are well-defined to specify qualifications, measure performance, conduct performance appraisals, and relate one position to another in a hierarchy of positions which defines the work of agencies. You must be well-prepared to encounter these relatively sophisticated personnel systems. You must understand position descriptions, position classifications, job requirements, and qualifications which tend to be spelled out in vacancy announcements issued by government personnel offices.

You will need more than just a slick resume, great personality, and terrific answers to interview questions to land a government job. After all, positions come first and individuals come second. The question you will constantly need to address in government is this:

> Do I have the specific qualifications, as detailed in the vacancy announcement, to qualify for this position?

If your application results in a "yes" answer, then you proceed to the next stage of being further screened for the position.

INFORMATION NEEDS

Your research should focus on answering five major questions for organizing your job search:

1. What are the jobs?
2. Where are the jobs?
3. Who has the power to hire?
4. How do organization X and program Y operate?
5. What do I need to do to get a job with organization X?

The first two questions can be answered by consulting various directories and books found in most libraries as well as the specialized job listing services and job banks identified in Chapter 12. The last three questions can only be answered by talking with knowledgeable people associated with the organization. You need to probe as much as possible for details in order to focus your job search on particular organizations, positions, and individuals.

WHAT ARE THE JOBS?

This question can be answered by consulting several books and directories in the reference and government sections of your local library. The Department of Labor publishes several useful resources for surveying various job titles. At a minimum you should examine:

- *The Dictionary of Occupational Titles*
- *The Occupational Outlook Handbook*

Your library might also carry the following books which examine government jobs:

- *The American Almanac of Government Jobs*, Ron and Caryl Krannich
- *The Book of U.S. Government Jobs*, Dennis Damp
- *Find a Federal Job Fast!*, Ron and Caryl Krannich
- *How to Get a Federal Job*, David Waelde
- *How to Get a Federal Job*, Krandall Kraus
- *Opportunities in State and Local Government*, Neal Baxter
- *Opportunities in Federal Government Careers*, Neal Baxter

National Textbook Company publishes several books relevant to specific career areas in government:

- *Opportunities in Fire Protection*
- *Opportunities in Government Service*
- *Opportunities in Health and Medical Careers*
- *Opportunities in Law Careers*
- *Opportunities in Law Enforcement and Criminal Justice*
- *Opportunities in Library and Information Science*
- *Opportunities in Paralegal Careers*
- *Opportunities in Public Health*
- *Opportunities in Recreation and Leisure*
- *Opportunities in Social Work*
- *Opportunities in Teaching*
- *Opportunities in Transportation*

These and other useful guides to government are listed in the resource section at the end of the book.

In addition to conducting library research on identifying different jobs, you can write or visit various government personnel offices for detailed information on different jobs. State personnel offices, for example, will send you information on job titles, descriptions of duties and responsibilities, entrance requirements, and salaries and benefits if you telephone or write directly to them requesting the information.

Many units of local government may have several personnel systems operating simultaneously.

At the local level you can write or visit the personnel departments of various units of government to acquire information on specific positions. This office may publish a brochure or handbook or provide looseleaf handouts on particular positions. Remember, many units of local government may have several personnel systems operating simultaneously. Police and fire departments may have separate personnel departments. While most school systems are set up as special districts, relatively independent of city and county governments, in five states they are part of city or county governments. In these cases, the city or county education department will maintain a personnel system separate from other departments.

At the federal level you should visit the Federal Job Information Centers (FJIC) which are located in 50 cities throughout the United States. These centers list position vacancies, including position descriptions. In addition, FJICs have a book which is the bible for getting information on particular positions: *Qualification Standards for White-Collar Positions Under the General Schedule*. It consists of two looseleaf binders and a volume on blue-collar positions. Position descriptions written in the language of personnel offices are included for white-collar jobs (the X-118 manual) and blue-collar jobs (the X-118A manual). You may have difficulty getting access to these volumes since FJIC personnel tend to guard them as internal documents. However, you should be able to see them by requesting to examine the books in their office. You cannot purchase these volumes.

A final source of information on identifying different types of public sector jobs is the most basic and important—talk to someone in a position that interests you. Ask them about:

1. What they do.
2. How they got there.
3. Advantages and disadvantages.

4. Duties and responsibilities.
5. A typical day on the job.
6. Advancement opportunities.
7. Salaries and benefits.
8. The future.

Most people will discuss their work with you and provide you with important tips on how to enter the public service.

WHERE ARE THE JOBS?

This question can be answered by consulting several directories as well as many of the resources identified in the previous and subsequent sections and in Chapter 12. Several directories identified in Chapter 7 provide addresses for locating various units of government and personnel offices. The most important ones include:

Counties: *The County Year Book*

Municipalities: *The Municipal Year Book*

States: *National Directory of State Agencies*
The Book of the States

Federal: *United States Government Manual*
The Federal Yellow Book
The Congressional Yellow Book
The Congressional Directory
Directory of Federal Executives
Guide to Federal Technical, Trade and Labor Jobs
Washington Information Directory

Overall: *Government Directory of Addresses and Telephone Numbers*
The Government Job Finder
Taylor's Encyclopedia of Government Officials

Most of these directories are found in the reference section of your local library.

One of the easiest sources of job listings to access is referenced in your telephone directory. Many county, city, and state personnel offices maintain on Employment Hotline or Employment Information Jobline. You dial the number and a recording describes a list of positions available for a particular week and provides the necessary application information. Check your telephone book under the particular government unit, and call the number. The recording should include all available positions, from city manager to clerk typist. Many of these same jobs are routinely listed with your local state employment office. Call this office to learn which government positions they list. Most professional and local organizations of government officials also maintain their own job hotline information. For detailed information on their hotlines and other job services for government employment, consult Daniel Lauber's *The Government Job Finder* (River Forest, IL: Planning/Communications).

Another source of information worth examining are case studies of various units of government and agencies. In almost every state some enterprising scholars, journalists, or concerned citizens have written books and articles on county and municipal governments as well as specific local and state agencies and programs. Several excellent books have been written on Federal agencies, the most popular being TVA, FBI, CIA, Justice, Energy, and Interior. Such works help specify some of the major issues facing these agencies as well as their internal structure and work cultures.

You might also try to acquire copies of telephone directories for various units of government. All government organizations will have an in-house telephone directory—the one document that seems to hold the organization together. This is an invaluable source of information on the internal structure of the organization as well as key contact points for making your telephone calls and visiting offices. Many of these telephone directories are organizational roadmaps. They may include a recent organizational chart, a functional breakdown of the agency by section, room number, and telephone number, and an alphabetical listing of employees with their room and telephone numbers. The federal government actually publishes and sells telephone directories for each department. You can get these publications by contacting:

Superintendent of Documents
U.S. Government Printing Office
Washington, DC 20402

Most telephone directories sell for $12-18.

Governmental units and agencies produce tons of information, much of which is relevant to your job search and which is available upon request. Most publish or print organizational charts, current listings of their personnel and office locations, and statistical breakdowns of who does what and where. Some of this information is in the form of published directories, whereas other information is in the form of brochures, or looseleaf stapled pages. For example, if you want the names and addresses of key foreign service personnel abroad, the Foreign Affairs Information Management Center of the U.S. Department of State maintains a Publishing Services Division. This unit publishes a small pocket-sized, but extremely useful, directory entitled *Key Officers of Foreign Service Posts: Guide for Business Representatives.* Regularly updated and including useful foreign mailing tips, this directory can be purchased directly from the U.S. Government Printing Office. A little probing on your part—either by telephone or personal visit—should uncover the information you need. However, you will need to get this type of information from offices other than personnel. Most government organizations have a public information office or ombudsman whose job is to respond to such requests for information. In some counties, towns, and cities, you may need to call the county executive's, commissioner's, mayor's, or city manager's office for this information.

Your final source of information on the "where" of government consists of the people you talk to by telephone and in person. Use your telephone extensively in gathering such information. Personal visits are the most useful for getting in-depth information, the telephone is by far the most efficient way of gathering information. If you are reluctant to make "cold calls" to strangers, we suggest you examine these books on how to overcome shyness and become more effective on the telephone:

Dynamite Tele-Search: 101 Techniques and Tips for Getting Job Leads and Interviews, Ron and Caryl Krannich (Manassas Park, VA: Impact Publications).

High Impact Telephone Networking for Job Hunters, Howard Armstrong (Holbrook, MA: Bob Adams, Inc.)

Cold Calling Techniques (That Really Work) Stephan Schiffman (Holbrook, MA: Bob Adams, Inc.)

Power Calling: A Fresh Approach to Cold Calls and Prospecting, Joan Guiducci (Mill Valley, CA: Tonino)

WHO HAS THE POWER TO HIRE?

This question also will take some research effort on your part. You already know three things important for answering this question:

1. Personnel offices are in charge of conducting part of the hiring, but usually not the most important parts.

2. The program supervisors in the operating units are normally the key hiring people.

3. Several directories list the names, addresses, and telephone numbers of key officials.

Yes, what is generally the case may not be true all of the time. For example, personnel offices in many units of government may play the central role in the hiring process. Indeed, some city managers have strengthened the role of their personnel departments in order to gain greater control over relatively autonomous city agencies. In most government organizations the personnel offices will be responsible for recruiting and selecting certain types of positions.

Therefore, you need to conduct research on the particular organization that interests you. You need to ask specific questions concerning *who* normally is responsible for various parts of the hiring process:

- describing positions
- announcing vacancies
- receiving applications
- administering tests
- selecting eligible candidates
- choosing whom to interview
- offering the job

If you ask these questions about a specific position, you will quickly identify who has what powers to hire. Chances are the power to hire is shared between the personnel office and the operating unit. You cannot neglect the personnel office, and in some cases it will play a powerful role in all aspects of the hiring. Your research will reveal to what degree the hiring function has been centralized, decentralized, or fragmented within a particular unit of government.

HOW DO ORGANIZATION X AND PROGRAM Y OPERATE?

Answers to this question will help you break through the stereotypes and images of performance packaged for public consumption. This question is answered by using three information gathering approaches:

1. Reading literature on the agency.
2. Attending meetings to observe, make contacts, and ask questions.
3. Interviewing informed individuals.

Most agencies and units of government have a great deal of printed matter about their operations. Most of this information is available to the public, although the ease of access will vary. A good starting point is the annual budget. Depending on what type of budget system operates—line item, performance, PPBS, or zero-base—the budget should both raise and answer numerous questions. Most budgets tell you who is getting how much, where, and for what anticipated results. In addition, many agencies have their programs periodically evaluated. Program review or evaluation reports should be available through the planning, program evaluation, or central administration office. These reports will give you a good feel for not only the agency's or unit's goals and what it is doing at present, but also its problems and whether it is growing or cutting back. Other useful printed materials include project documents, training manuals, and operations handbooks for individual offices. You should get access to many of these documents to learn what is really going on inside the organization.

A good starting point is the annual budget . . . the budget should both raise and answer numerous questions.

Another useful source of information is public meetings of officials. In addition to revealing a great deal of information on the agency or unit of government, these meetings offer an opportunity for you to identify key decision-makers as well as meet them in public. At the local level, these meetings include various board meetings and public hearings on schools, zoning variances, streets, transportation, health, revenue sharing—you name the activity; there's always a meeting somewhere, sometime. City council meetings, while often boring, do involve key city officials as well as representatives of interest groups and contractors. These are good places to observe the workings of government and make contact with several groups doing business with government.

At the state and federal levels, meetings of officials abound, from legislative and congressional committee hearings to public hearings on agency programs. In Washington, DC, for example, each day the *Washington Post* publishes the major upcoming meetings on Capitol Hill and in agencies. Thousands of meetings go on within each agency every week. You can contact the public affairs office to find out what meetings are being held when, and which ones are open to interested observers.

WHAT DO I NEED TO DO TO GET A JOB WITH ORGANIZATION X?

This question will be answered by following our advice on prospecting, networking, and informational interviewing we outlined in Chapter 9. This question can only be answered by talking to people who know both the formal and informal hiring practices. As noted earlier, in government the formal system is usually well defined in terms of applications, tests, eligibility lists, and interviews. You can get this information by calling or writing the personnel office.

There is no better information and advice than that given by the individual who will play a major role in the hiring process.

But in most cases you must go beyond the formal system and personnel office in order to learn how best to conduct your job search. This means talking to people in the operational unit. Our experience is that most people in the program offices are relatively easy to talk with. They are interested in learning about potential candidates prior to initiating the rather lengthy, time-consuming, and frustrating formal recruitment process. These busy people do not have a great deal of time to spend on the hiring process, since this is not one of their formal duties and responsibilities. Therefore, information that would help them ease the hiring burden may be welcome. Contrary to what many job seekers may think, if done properly, the informational interview is not an imposition on hiring personnel. You are helping them arrive at a decision while they are helping you gain important knowledge for improving your job search. If they like you, chances are they will give you useful tips on how to get a job in their organization. There is no better information and advice than that given by the individual who will play a major hiring role.

WHAT DO I DO WITH THIS INFORMATION?

Your information gathering tasks involve locating important information, analyzing it, and presenting it in a *usable* form. Gathering information for "understanding" is necessary. But you must move from understanding to *application* if you are to be effective in finding a job. After analyzing and synthesizing your research findings, you must incorporate the information into an effective strategy for improving your job search. The information needs to be:

1. Incorporated into an outstanding resume and application forms targeted toward specific positions.

2. Converted into effective prospecting, networking, and informational interviews.

3. Used for conducting excellent job interviews.

This means you must make incremental movements toward achieving your stated goals. More specifically, you must *discipline yourself* to pick up the telephone and make three to five telephone calls each day. You must get behind your typewriter or wordprocessor and knock out three letters each day. Above all, you must take to the street, pounding the pavement and "pressing the flesh", for job leads and interviews.

Information gathering is one important step in the job search process. More important, on a regular basis you must manage a set of discrete job search activities which are closely related to one another. Without taking action based on your research, you may "understand" a great deal, but you will go nowhere. Knowledge becomes power when it is converted to effective action.

14

ADAPT YOUR JOB SEARCH TECHNIQUES

*T*he job search techniques identified in Chapters 7, 8, and 9 work for most job situations in either the public or private sectors. However, you must adapt these techniques to the particular governmental units and agencies you encounter. Your research should be the basis for determining to what degree you should adjust your strategies and techniques.

HIDDEN VERSUS ADVERTISED JOB MARKETS

When dealing with government, you cannot make the assumption 80 percent of the jobs are found on the hidden job market. This simply is not true. Public service personnel systems are structured to ensure that no jobs are hidden from public view; nearly 100 percent must be advertised.

Therefore, the difference in strategy is that you want to both identify job vacancies before they are advertised and effectively target those that are advertised. This requires greater attention to the advertised job market.

The real challenge in a government job search is to both locate and work the advertised job market. Information and communication on government job vacancies is chaotic and inherently difficult to obtain given the decentralized nature of government agencies. As noted earlier, agencies may be required to publicize job vacancies, but they also may decide to limit the scope of advertising to a few selected bulletin boards in the personnel office and public library. Your task is to develop an effective strategy aimed at *coordinating information* within this formal advertised job market. The strategy involves monitoring publicized sources of government job listings. This may require a combination of subscribing to job listing services and job banks, visiting job centers, telephoning personnel offices and agencies for the latest job vacancy information, and periodically visiting key sites where job vacancy announcements are most likely posted.

WORKING THE FORMAL HIRING PROCESS

Once you locate a government job vacancy, you must follow formal procedures in order to become eligible for the job and be selected for an interview. This means properly completing application forms—complete all blanks, date and sign it, and submit it before the deadline—taking the proper tests, and monitoring your progress within the formal system. In some cases your application will be automatically forwarded to the office with the vacancy. In other cases, you may become eligible for a class of positions, but your application will not be automatically forwarded. Once a job vacancy occurs, you must take the initiative or "apply"—with your eligibility rating and application form. If this happens, you must continuously monitor the job vacancies—both through the formal listing sources and the informal system of personal contacts.

WRITING RIGHT WITH DEPTH

The language of government tends to be more technical and jargonistic than the language of private business. Try to identify the language being used in particular agencies and use some of the terminology on your application form and resume.

You should develop a resume even though most government positions only require completion of an application form. As we noted earlier, federal agencies soon will be permitted to accept resumes if they choose to do so. In some cases, especially for high-level positions, you will be required to submit a resume in lieu of an application form. In other cases, you should attach your resume to the completed application. You should do this for two reasons. First, most application forms are designed for the designed for the administrative convenience of personnel offices—they yield basic accounting data for merit system and affirmative action requirements or help this office quickly screen candidates. They are not structured to present your qualifications in direct relation to the requirements for a particular position. As such, your strengths often become buried in a great deal of extraneous information, such as your social security number, military status, and schools attended. When you attach the resume to the application form, you begin highlighting and communicating your most important information to the hiring officials. You control what information should be emphasized in direct relation to the position requirements. You lose this control when you are forced to complete an application form. If done properly, your resume can serve as a powerful "executive summary" for your application.

You should develop a resume even though most government positions only require completion of an application form.

You also should try to customize the application as much as possible, especially the "Experience" section, so that it stresses your skills, abilities, and accomplishments in relation to the position requirements. Most government application forms ask you to list your "duties and responsibilities". The problem with such instructions is that you are being asked to regurgitate formal position descriptions. These descriptions merely tell employers what you are *supposed* to do—not what you *actually* do or your accomplishments. Therefore, when responding to the "Duties and Responsibilities" section, stress your *accomplishments* rather than your assignments.

Your choice of language is important when completing applications and writing resumes for government audiences. Be careful in using the highly generalized and "soft" language of functional and transferable skills with government agencies. Try to be as specific as possible about your accomplishments or achievements in direct relation to specific jobs. You need to include the "where" and "when" along with the "what". The organization and language of an *improved chronological resume* are best suited for government audiences when developing a resume and completing an application form. Quite frankly, most functional resumes are weak resumes which tend to communicate little beyond some highly generalized skills. They do not distinguish you from millions of other individuals who basically say the same things about themselves. On the other hand, public employees are used to looking for "the details". They look for content and depth, which includes formal job titles, names of employers, and dates of employment.

NETWORKING ADJUSTMENTS

Networking works just as well—if not better—in the public sector as it does in the private sector. However, you will need to make some adjustments for particular agencies.

For example, since they are public organizations with public servants, most government agencies have formal information dissemination offices established to respond to all types of questions and requests. Most are relatively open. Since they have no competition, they have nothing to hide. Indeed, some offices are security problems because they give away too much information!

In addition to personnel offices, you should contact public information, public affairs, and/or ombudsman offices. These offices will give you a great deal of information, including printed materials and names and phone numbers of key individuals you should contact. Often it is much easier to call one of these offices for the information than play detective by using time-consuming prospecting and networking techniques which will probably yield the same referrals. Telephone one of these offices and ask whom you should speak to about a particular position or job field. Chances are they will give you the name and telephone number of the key person. This procedure eliminates a lot of wasted time networking for the same information.

Once you have located the right people to talk to, then it's time to network. Follow the same procedures we suggested in Chapter 9. At this stage your goals should be to:

1. **Identify positions which may become vacant before they are formally advertised.** If you can locate such positions, you will have more time to do the necessary research and make key contacts for preparing an outstanding application which should qualify you for eligibility in the formal hiring system. You will learn how to best "tailor" your application around the position requirements. In some cases you may even become "sponsored" ("wired") for the vacancy by the people you meet while networking.

2. **Gather information for making critical decisions about government jobs.** The basic problem you and others face in both the public and private sector job markets is information—you either lack job information or you get incomplete information on the what, where, when, and how of getting a job. Your

> networking activities become key information gathering and coordinating activities. You basically take to the telephone lines and streets to centralize a job information system which is extremely decentralized, fragmented, and incomplete.

Whatever you do, make sure you network for job information and referrals. While you may get a government job based solely on the quality of your formal application, you'll be even more successful in the government job market if you learn to network according to our advice in Chapter 9. Try it when looking for a government job. You'll be surprised how effective networking works for government jobs. It will help you quickly find the right government job for you.

PART IV

MOVING INTO GOVERNMENT

*Y*ou face numerous alternatives when seeking a government job. You must decide which level of government you prefer working with: federal, state, or local? While most government jobs are with the executive bureaucracies, numerous opportunities also are available with the legislative and judicial branches of government. And within each branch, bureaus and offices offer several job options.

The four chapters in Part IV examine several choices available to you as well as effective strategies for landing a job with various government employers at each level. Each chapter is designed to provide you with a basic understanding of various levels and branches of government and equip you with practical strategies for landing the job you want. Chapters 16, 17, and 18 focus on local, state, and federal government. Chapter 19 focuses on employment in the legislative and judicial branches of the federal government.

Previous editions of this book included a special chapter on the Standard Form 171 (SF 171), the application form required for most federal government positions. That chapter has been eliminated in this new edition, because the U.S. Office of Personnel Management (OPM) indicates it will officially retire the SF 171 as of December 31, 1994. As we go to press, our "inside" information is that agencies will be free to develop their own application forms as well as accept resumes—a further attempt on the part of OPM to decentralize personnel decisions to the agency level. If OPM proceeds according to this latest plan, which already has been delayed several times, we're in for some surprises. Expect to experience some unexpected consequences of another well-meaning but somewhat naive "reinventing government" initiative. Our best prediction is that many agencies will continue accepting the SF 171 along with resumes. Most agencies simply are unprepared to develop and process their own special application forms. We expect a great deal of chaos to result from this application change because most agencies are ill-equipped to handle resumes and other application forms. Ironically, the new applications are likely to be more difficult for individuals to complete: they will require completing separate applications for each agency and position rather than applying with a single application form, such as the SF 171. While this new application system ostensibly is easier for both applicants and agencies, don't bet on it. It has the potential of being very messy for all parties involved.

Indeed, we predict within two years OPM will return to a new version of the SF 171 after learning this form has more merit than most critics were willing to admit. However, it will probably be reintroduced in an electronic format as the federal government moves in the direction of paperless application forms. OPM is likely to develop and supply new application software necessary for agencies to accept electronic applications and resumes which will then be scanned by search and retrieval software now being used in the private sector. Government application and screening processes will finally enter the electronic age, as outlined in Peter Weddle's *Electronic Resumes for the New Job Market* (Impact Publications, 1995) and Joyce Lain Kennedy and Thomas J. Morrow's two books—the *Electronic Job Search Revolution* and the *Electronic Resume Revolution* (Wiley & Sons, 1994).

We believe OPM's new application change is fraught with numerous implementation problems. Stay tuned to what may be one of the most interesting application evolutions—if not revolutions—in the history of the federal government! And get ready to write resumes for federal agencies which should follow our writing and distribution principles as outlined in Chapter 8. Beginning in 1995, job seekers can expect to encounter new computerized applicant screening systems such as the Microcomputer Assisted Rating Schedule (MARS) and the Telephone Application Processing (TAP) now being developed within OPM.

In the meantime, we strongly recommend getting a copy of Russ Smith's *The Right SF 171 Writer* (Manassas Park, VA: Impact Publications). This book will take you a long way to completing an outstanding federal application, regardless of the future status of the SF 171 with agencies. Your application will shine if it follows the principles and advice outlined in Smith's book.

15

LOCAL GOVERNMENTS

*L*ocal governments in the United States are comprised of a variety of government institutions which make up the overall quilt-patch pattern of American government. These governments truly represent the type of governmental system the Founding Fathers explicitly designed: a safe (from tyranny) system where no one majority rules, one which checks and balances itself by dividing and overlapping powers and functions at different levels. Altogether this system employs 11 million individuals or one-twelfth of the total American work force. Given an annual turnover rate of 14 percent, coupled with an annual growth rate of nearly 1 percent, local government units offer numerous job opportunities for those who understand how and where to find them. Given the highly decentralized and fragmented nature of these governments, you must conduct research on the what, where, and who of particular local government units in order to best understand them.

DIVERSITY OF UNITS

Local governments come in numerous categories, types, shapes, and sizes. They are truly a diverse collection of local governing authorities divided into five categories:

1. **Counties:** These local units of government function in all parts of the country except Connecticut, Rhode Island, and the District of Columbia. Normally the largest governing unit in terms of area next to state governments, 3,043 counties employ 2,196,000 individuals who provide services to nearly 225 million people. Once primarily a rural form of government, today the majority of counties are urban. Some counties have taken over the functions of municipalities (Miami-Dade County). Counties are referred to as "parishes" in Louisiana and "boroughs" in Alaska.

2. **Municipalities:** Incorporated for urban areas, these 19,296 units of government employ 2,662,000 individuals. While most municipalities are political subdivisions of counties, in a few states where city-county consolidation has taken place, certain municipalities are independent of counties (cities in Virginia) or they have taken over the functions of counties (Baltimore, Baton Rouge, Indianapolis, Jacksonville, Nashville, Philadelphia, St. Louis, San Francisco). Depending on the state, municipalities are variously referred to as "cities", "towns", "villages", and "boroughs".

3. **Townships:** These political subdivisions of counties are found in 20 states, mainly in the New England, Mid-Atlantic, and Midwest states. Altogether 16,666 townships employ 415,000 people who provide special services to about 20 percent of the American population. Some states refer to these units of government as "towns" (Wisconsin, New York, and New England), "locations" (New Hampshire) and "plantations" (Maine). Townships are governed by elected boards of supervisors or trustees and share powers with county governments and other jurisdictions.

4. **School Districts:** Both independent and dependent school districts function throughout the United States. Independent school districts have their own elected boards, revenue base, and administrative organization. These function everywhere except in Virginia, Maryland, North Carolina, Hawaii, Alaska, the District of Columbia. Dependent school systems are partly under the control of state, county, and municipal

governments. Altogether 14,556 school districts employ 5,045,000 individuals.

5. **Special Districts:** These units of government function to provide special services not provided by other units of government. While nearly 2,000 of these units are multi-purpose districts, most specialize in performing a single function. The most frequently performed functions, in rank order, include: fire protection, water supply, soil conservation, drainage, cemeteries, sewerage, school buildings, irrigation and water conservation, parks and recreation, hospitals, flood control, highways, libraries, natural resources, and other functions. Depending on the state, special districts also are referred to as "authorities", "boards", or "commissions". These 33,131 units of government employ 612,000 individuals. Sometimes school districts also are included in this category since they are essentially single-purpose special districts.

Different governing systems are used for different types of local governing units. Most counties, for example, use the commission, council-administrator, or council-elected executive form of government. Municipalities are of four types: weak mayor-council, commission, strong mayor-council, or council-manager form.

The five types of local governing authorities are by no means structured in a logical and efficient manner. Most have developed over time in response to state legal requirements, local needs, and political convenience. In most states, one unit of government will overlap with another. For example, counties perform some functions within municipalities, and townships may encompass school districts, counties, and municipalities. Illinois, with the largest number of local government units of any state (6,627), has one of the most concentrated, diverse, overlapping, and confusing systems of local government. On the other hand, Virginia, with its 430 units of local government, has the most streamlined and logical system. However, even Virginia's much praised system of city-county consolidation gives rise to overlapping and shared functions. For example, Prince William County Government, serving one of the fastest growing counties in the state and nation, is composed of five types of agencies which are, to varying degrees, under the control of a County Board of Supervisors and County Executive:

1. Staff and the Board of County Supervisors
2. State/local cooperative agencies
3. Agencies with administrative boards
4. Offices reporting to the County Executive
5. Departments reporting to the County Executive

In addition, several other offices and agencies function as part of this county government: constitutional offices (Offices of the Clerk of the Circuit Court, Commonwealth's Attorney, Sheriff), agencies involved in the administration of justice, sanitation districts, and the School Board. The personnel office in this county government provides administrative support for recruiting individuals for many—but not all—county government positions. Typical of so many other local units of government, this county government exhibits a high degree of internal fragmentation along representational and functional lines.

Local governments are street-level governments that do the nitty-gritty work necessary to keep communities both democratic and decent.

COMMON FUNCTIONS

Local governments have one major characteristic in common which distinguishes them from state and federal governments. These are street-level governments that do the nitty-gritty work necessary to keep communities both democratic and decent. They maintain close contact with citizens, because they are basically service delivery units providing specific services in specific neighborhoods: sanitation, fire and police protection, education, health, street lighting, and maintenance. Their cadres of street-level bureaucrats are on the firing line with citizens, politicians, local media, and interest groups. This is the action-filled level of government. For many public employees, local government is where one finds the action and excitement of public service. These small to large communities provide opportunities for individuals to work closely with citizens and elected representatives, experiment with public policies, and see the results of their efforts.

The major local government function is education. Altogether 55 percent of local government officials are in education. Of the 6 million employees, nearly 2.5 million are classroom teachers. For 1991, this education bureaucracy required a $12 billion annual payroll. The table on page 239 summarizes the distribution of local government functions by employees and payrolls.

LOCAL GOVERNMENT EMPLOYMENT AND PAYROLLS, 1991

Function	*Employees*		*Payroll*	
	1000s	**Percent**	**1000s**	**Percent**
TOTAL	**10,930**		**$22,113**	
1. Education	6,074	55.5	12,132	54.8
2. Health & Hospitals	790	7.2	1,587	7.1
3. Police Protection	674	6.1	1,699	7.6
4. Judicial & legal	200	1.8	442	1.9
5. Highways	305	2.7	607	2.7
6. Public welfare	275	2.5	485	2.1
7. Financial administration	212	1.9	376	1.7
8. Fire protection	341	3.1	771	3.4
9. Parks & recreation	271	2.4	353	1.5
10. Sanitation & sewerage	238	2.1	570	2.5
11. National resources	39	0.3	70	0.3
12. All other	1,198	10.9	2,657	12.0

Source: U.S. Bureau of the Census, 1993

OPPORTUNITIES AND POSITIONS

The best local government opportunities will be found in the larger, more diverse, and financially well endowed units of government. These consist of the large urban county governments, municipalities of 200,000 population or more, and large school districts. Small counties, towns, townships, and special districts, while affording unique public service opportunities and a chance to be a "big fish in a small pond", usually do not provide much career advancement nor offer competitive salaries. If you work for one of these units of government and you wish to advance your career and salary, you will most likely have to resign and move to a larger unit of government. In many respects, the ideal unit of government encompasses an urban area of 200,000 to 500,000 people. Governments of this size have sufficient resources and opportunities to allow individuals to make local government a professional career.

The largest city governments offering numerous job opportunities include the following:

LARGEST CITY GOVERNMENTS BY EMPLOYEES AND SALARIES, 1991

City	Employees (1000s)	Change, 1980-91	Average Monthly Salary
New York, NY*	444	+21	$2,907
Washington, DC*	48	+6	3,046
Los Angeles, CA	44	+23	3,658
Chicago, IL	42	-10	3,002
Philadelphia, PA	31	-6	2,869
Baltimore, MD*	30	-31	2,538
San Francisco	26	+19	3,728
Memphis, TN*	23	+18	2,230
Boston, MA*	21	-25	2,528
Houston, TX	20	+11	2,214
Detroit, MI	20	-9	2,587
Nashville-Davidson, TN*	17	-5	2,523
Virginia Beach, VA*	15	+50	2,252
Dallas, TX	15	+7	1,945
San Antonio, TX	14	+40	2,345
Indianapolis, IN	13	0	2,147
Denver, CO	13	0	2,807
Buffalo, NY*	12	-14	2,502
Phoenix, AZ	12	+33	3,059
San Diego, CA	11	+37	3,017
Austin, TX	11	+37	2,550
Norfolk, VA*	11	0	2,295
Honolulu, HI	10	+10	2,797
New Orleans, LA	10	-23	1,623
Jacksonville, FL	11	0	2,688
Seattle, WA	11	+10	3,344
Austin, TX	11	+37	2,550

Source: U.S. Bureau of the Census. *Includes city operated schools.

Employment opportunities in local government generally follow population growth and decline trends. As a community's population grows, so do the number of local government employees and street-level services. Community growth means more schools and teachers, more police and fire protection, more health facilities, and more sanitation, welfare, and recreation services. Communities with declining population will tend to downsize their local government bureaucracies. Indeed, many city governments that grew during the early to mid-1980s experienced considerable population growth attendant with booming local economies. However, many of these cities experienced economic downturns at the end of the 1980s and may no longer continue to expand their city bureaucracies. Growth will shift to other cities in the 1990s, especially in Florida, Georgia, Ohio, Texas, Arizona, Utah, and Nevada. Expect to see considerable growth in the cities and county governments near Las

Vegas, Seattle, Orlando, Daytona Beach, West Palm Beach, Atlanta, Dallas, Minneapolis, Raleigh-Durham, Austin, and San Jose.

Some of the best opportunities in the public sector—both within government and among peripheral organizations—at the local level will be found in the growth communities of the 1990s. As population continues to increase and economies boom, so too will public services in these communities. During the next five years the following communities are expected to experience the most rapid growth in new jobs as well as declines in employment.

PROJECTED JOB WINNERS, 1993-1998

Metro Area	Total New Jobs
Washington, DC-MD-VA	206,767
Orange County, CA	177,898
Atlanta, GA	168,300
Phoenix-Mesa, AZ	148,703
Los Angeles-Long Beach, CA	139,108
San Diego, CA	134,863
Tampa-St. Petersburg-Clearwater, FL	123,672
Orlando, FL	119,336
Philadelphia, PA-NJ	116,815
Riverside-San Bernardino, CA	110,695
Dallas, TX	110,363
Houston, TX	95,545
Chicago, IL	95,324
Seattlc-Bellevue-Everett, WA	90,313
Detroit, MI	86,601
Minneapolis-St. Paul, MN-WI	80,045
Baltimore, MD	73,730
Charlotte-Gastonia-Rock Hill, NC-SC	72,598

PROJECTED JOB LOSERS, 1993-1998

Metro Area	Employment Decline
Lawton, OK	-2.67%
Great Falls, MT	-2.14
Houma, LA	-1.59
New York, NY	-0.91
Flint, MI	-0.68
Beaumont-Port Arthur, TX	-0.63
Enid, OK	-0.52
Jacksonville, NC	-0.44
Abilene, TX	-0.38
Grand Forks, ND-MN	-0.10
Amarillo, TX	-0.05

Source: Woods & Poole Economics, Inc., employment forecasts, 1993, as reported in *Places Rated Almanac,* p. 57.

You should uncover opportunities most closely in line with your interests and skills when you do research on various units of government. You may find a position which is ideal for you. If you seek career advancement, the small units of government will provide you with important local government experience which you can transfer to larger units of local government.

The largest number of positions and opportunities will be found in the most labor intensive units and departments of government. "Teacher" is still the largest single occupational category at all levels of government. In terms of departments and offices within local government, the largest offices tend to be police, fire and rescue, health, social services, finance, development, libraries, parks and recreation, and general services. However, many of the jobs in these offices are for low-level clerical and other support personnel. An example of a county government would include the following distribution of personnel by agency, office, and department:

Agency	Personnel	
	Full-Time	Part-Time
1. County Attorney	9	0
2. County Executive	15	0
3. Department of Extension and Continuing Education	13	0
4. Department of Health	72	0
5. Electoral Board and General Registrar	6	16
6. Community Mental Health, Mental Retardation and Substance Abuse Services Board	80	0
7. Park Authority	58	25
8. Library	71	0
9. Social Services	94	0
10. Community Corrections	3	0
11. Office of Consumer Affairs	8	0
12. Office of Economic Development and Tourism	6	0
13. Office of Emergency Services	0	0
14. Juvenile Detention Home	27	0
15. Office of Management Information and Audit	30	0
16. Office of Personnel	26	0
17. Office of Planning	34	0
18. Office of Project Management	4	0
19. Office of Telecommunications	9	0
20. Office of Youth	2	0
21. Development Administration Department	87	0
22. Finance Department	73	0
23. Fire and Rescue Services Department	116	400 (volunteers)
24. General Services Department	66	0
25. Police Department	272	87
26. Public Works Department	39	0

Distribution of positions will vary depending on the functions of each local government vis-a-vis other governmental units as well as to what extent part-time and volunteer personnel are used or services have been contracted-out to private firms. For example, several small and rural communities, as well as large cities such as Virginia Beach (population 393,000), maintain volunteer fire departments. In other communities refuse collection may be contracted-out to local collectors or performed only by private companies. In still other communities a local function normally performed by a municipal government may, instead, be performed by the county government, i.e., parks and recreation, libraries, corrections, mental health. In other cases the same functions may be shared between units of government or through a Council of Governments arrangement.

Since local governments perform numerous housekeeping and development functions, they offer a variety of white and blue-collar opportunities which are similarly found in large organizations in the private sector. These include white-collar and professional jobs for:

Accountants	Equal opportunity officers
Computer programmers	Draftsmen
Data processors	Program analysts
Doctors and nurses	Dietitians
Engineers	Medical technologists
Fire fighters	Housing counselors
Lawyers and attorneys	Budget analysts
Planners	Real estate specialists
Police officers	Librarians
Secretaries	Clerks
First-line supervisors	Social workers
Mid-level managers	Contracts and procurement officers
Extension agents	
Communications operators	Chemists
Systems analysts	Morgue attendants
Legislative clerks	Court reporters
Probation officers	Tax analysts
Tax assessors	Supply officers
Naturalists	Food processors
Traffic analysts	Employment specialists
Museum workers	Architects
Investigators	Horticulturalists
Recreation supervisors	Teachers and trainers

The following blue-collar positions also are well represented throughout local government units:

- Laborers
- Guards
- Signal shop foremen
- Carpenters
- Welders
- Stock workers
- Car wash operators
- Inspectors
- Park maintenance persons
- Brick masons
- Street maintenance persons
- Zoo keepers
- Sewer maintenance persons
- Bus drivers
- Mechanics
- Plumbers
- Water pump operators
- Custodians
- Painters
- Refuse collectors
- Electricians
- Pool managers
- Landscape architects
- Parking meter collectors
- Tree trimmers
- Heavy equipment operators

These and many other positions relevant to local government are described in *The Dictionary of Occupational Titles*.

Most units of government classify positions according to educational requirements, duties, responsibilities, and salary ranges. When conducting your research, you should examine the job classifications to identify the various options available. Each position will require a certain level of qualifications ranging from years of formal education, training, and certification to years of comparable experience. If you examine and analyze these job classifications and attendant descriptions, you should be able to identify formal entrance requirements, possible career advancement opportunities, and potential long-term earnings.

EFFECTIVE STRATEGIES

There is no single best strategy for getting a job in local government. Each of the 86,743 local jurisdictions has a different hiring system—both formal and informal—which you must identify through your research. These systems range from very informal and personal hiring practices in a small township or rural county to a highly professionalized merit system in the large urban counties and municipalities. In some cases, you can still pull political strings to get a job through local political machines, relatives, friends, and acquaintances. The local township supervisor, commissioner, city council member, or mayor may sponsor you for a position on either his or her staff or within a department.

There are no hard and fast rules for approaching local governments. It depends on several factors:

- How well developed is the formal hiring process?
- How political is the local bureaucracy?
- How professional are both elected representatives and government employees?

- How is the hiring process structured in relation to competitive, merit, and equal opportunity criteria?

In some cases, especially for blue-collar positions, you may be able to apply for a non-civil service position and be hired and placed on the payroll within two weeks. However, in most cases, you will find the application and selection processes to be lengthy, taking anywhere from six weeks to eight months. In some cases, especially for police and fire positions, recruitment takes place once a year. If you miss the examination date, you must wait another year before being considered for eligibility.

In any case, you should pursue both a formal and informal job search strategy. Your research and networking activities should reveal useful information about the local hiring culture, particularly on who appears to have the power to hire. For the sake of a simple example, let's assume the operating unit has the power to hire, and the personnel office provides standard information dissemination and application processing functions. In this typical case, all job vacancy announcements will originate in the operational unit, but they will be formally announced and processed through the personnel office. You can easily begin your job search with a telephone call. You call a special telephone number to get a tape recorded listing of vacancies for which the personnel office is accepting applications. Your next step is to visit the personnel office. However, if the local government does not maintain a tape recording or provide such information over the telephone, your first step then should be to visit the personnel office. This office will give you an application form as well as a listing of position descriptions and hiring criteria for the same positions outlined on the recorded telephone message.

Local government vacancy announcements issued by personnel offices typically include information on both salaried and hourly positions. Here are several examples of such announcements issued by one county government:

ASSISTANT TO THE COUNTY EXECUTIVE
G-28/Low-$40

Position # 800-85
Office of the County
County Executive

This position is responsible for providing support services and performing administrative activities for the County Executive; to undertake assignments in all areas of County government as directed by the County Executive; must have excellent communication skills. Requires Bachelor's degree or equivalent in public administration or related field with 3-5 years increasingly responsible local government experience; a minimum of two years supervisory experience at department director level or above or other comparable level is desired in addition to an MPA or MBA. Minimum beginning salary low-$40, depending on experience and education, plus excellent fringe benefits. Apply with cover level and resume to Personnel Director (include address and telephone number for personnel office).

CIVIL ENGINEER II
(Four Positions)
Negotiable $

Position #823-6R
DDA

County of 200,000 is a rapidly developing jurisdiction. Candidates will have the opportunity to contribute to the dynamics of that growth, and to make a positive impact on the quality of life in the jurisdiction. Successful candidates should have analytical and creative problem solving skills, and be willing to work with the community to assure quality development. Duties consist of working within a team setting, reviewing development plans for compliance with County policies and regulations, and working with other County and State agencies. Requirements for the position include: thorough knowledge of civil engineering principles and their modern application to the design and construction of land development projects; familiarity with new stormwater management design methods and operation of hydraulic computer models; and ability to express ideas clearly and concisely, both orally and in writing. Minimum qualifications: Bachelor's degree or equivalent in civil engineering, with eligibility for registration as a professional engineer; and 2-3 years in professional engineering work, including supervisory experience. Please state salary requirements. Salary negotiable depending upon personal qualifications.

CLERK TYPIST II
G-10-1/$17,897

Position #1115-3
Planning

Requires high school graduate or equivalent, supplemented by a course in typing; and 1-2 years clerical and typing experience. Must pass 55 wpm typing test before closing date. Duties include, but are not limited to the following; assisting the receptionist; typing; filing; coordinating zoning text amendments for public hearings; serving as the key clerk typist for zoning violations; revenue handling; some data entry/retrieval; and maintaining logs. Successful candidate should have word processing experience or interest in learning word processing. Some overtime required.

DATA CONTROL TECHNICIAN
G-15/$22,681-23,068

Position # 1108-1
Community Services Board

Temporary full-time position available for 7 months working with Director, Management Information Services Community Services Board. Requires high school graduate or equivalent including course work in data processing and 2 years experience in data control functions and computer operations. Duties include: reviewing input and output for accuracy, assisting data entry personnel, collecting data from contract agencies, coordinating flow of projects and assisting in preparation of technical reports. Experience in HP-3000 and HP-150 preferred; ability to work independently.

DEPUTY ANIMAL WARDEN
G-17-1/$22,234

Position # 000083-100
Animal Control Bureau

Requires high school graduate or equivalent with 1-2 years experience in the care of animals and/or dealing with the public. Polygraph, background investigation, physical examination, and valid driver's license required. Apply by: Eligibility List.

POLICE OFFICER I
G-16/$22,691

Position # 000087-92
Police Department

Applicants must be 21 years old, high school graduate or equivalent and possess a motor vehicle operator's license. Applicants must pass written, polygraph, psychological, and physical examination and a background investigation.

CHILD SUPERVISOR I
(Male)
G-15-1/$10.70 Hour

Position #400-85
Juvenile Detention Home

Temporary, part-time. Seeking qualified *male* relief worker to supervise male detainees. Requires two years of college, or high school graduate with three years experience working with children or teenage groups. Flexible schedule, no less than 4-5 days a month, shift includes 7am - 3pm; 3pm - 11pm; 11pm - 7am. Must pass pre-employment physical.

CROSS GUARDS
$313.73/Bi-weekly

Police Department

Part-time. Openings in the four areas of county. Valid driver's license, automobile, and telephone required. Must pass pre-employment physical. If interested, contract Lt. Smith for applications, between 9:30am and 2:30pm, Monday-Friday, at 333-2222.

CUSTODIAN I
G-7-1/$8.71/Hour

Position #201-85
General Services

Hours: 5pm - 10pm, Mon-Fri. Requires any combination of education and experience equivalent to completion of the 8th grade. Must pass pre-employment physical. Apply by: Eligibility List.

In order to learn about such vacancies, you must constantly monitor the listings issued by the personnel office. These offices normally compile all position vacancies and announce them as a group every week. If you call the personnel office on Monday morning, you may get the latest listing of job vacancies for the week. The positions outlined above were included in a six-page weekly handout for a suburban county of 250,000 residents.

Should you identify a position which both interests you and for which you are qualified, the next step is to complete the application. Follow the useful hints we outlined in Chapter 12 on how to complete an outstanding application. Next, take any tests required. While you wait for the results, continue your research with the hiring officials. Make sure you communicate to them that you are interested in and qualified for the position and that you have completed the formal application process. Should they like you in particular and you appear equally qualified compared to other candidates, your chances of being selected for the position will be excellent.

USEFUL RESOURCES

Your best resource for conducting research on particular units of local government will be the local governments themselves. Most local authorities publish a general information guide or organizational manual for public distribution. You can normally get a copy of this publication by calling or visiting the public affairs office or, depending on the particular unit of government, the superintendent of schools', county executive's, mayor's, or city manager's office. Your local public library also should have such information on file. If not, ask the librarian for assistance. The librarian should be able to direct you to the proper sources for detailed information on the inner workings of the local government, including organizational charts, functions of units, position descriptions, job classifications, personnel, and salary ranges.

Other sources of information on local governments include *The County Year Book*, which includes profiles on individual counties and names and phone numbers of over 12,000 county officials. Similar information is included on municipalities in *The Municipal Year Book*. We especially like the new *Government Directory of Addresses and Telephone Numbers*. This directory includes addresses and telephone numbers of county and municipal government offices throughout the United States as well as information on professional associations of county and local government officials at both the state and national levels. Most libraries have copies of these reference books; the new *Government Directory* also is available through Impact Publications.

Several professional associations of local government officials can provide information on employment opportunities in local governments. Each functional group of local government employees has its own professional association at the national level, normally headquartered in Washington, DC, New York City, Chicago, or Los Angeles; many have state branches. The major such associations which include local government employees are:

- Academy for State and Local Governments
- American Association of Port Authorities
- American Library Association
- American Institute of Architects
- American Institute of Certified Public Accountants
- American Institute of Planners
- American Planning Association
- American Public Gas Association
- American Public Power Association
- American Public Transit Association
- American Public Welfare Association
- American Public Works Association
- American Society for Public Administration
- American Water Works Association
- American Public-Safety Communications Officers, Inc.
- Building Officials and Code Administrators International
- Government Finance Officers Association
- Institute of Internal Auditors
- Institute of Transportation Engineers
- International Association of Assessing Officers
- International Association of Auditorium Managers
- International Association of Chiefs of Police
- International Association of Fire Chiefs
- International City/County Management Association
- International Institute of Municipal Clerks
- International Personnel Management Association
- Municipal Finance Officers Association
- National Association of Counties
- National Association of Housing and Redevelopment Officials
- National Association of Regional Councils
- National Association of Tax Administrators
- National Association of Towns and Townships
- National Civic League
- National Council for Urban Economic Development
- National Environmental Health Association
- National Fire Protection Association
- National Institute of Government Purchasing
- National Institute of Municipal Law Officers
- National League of Cities
- National Municipal League
- National Recreation and Park Association

- National School Boards Association
- Solid Waste Association of North America
- United States Conference of Mayors

Counties within each state also operate their own associations. For example, in Alabama it's call the Association of County Commission of Alabama; in Illinois, the Urban Counties Council of Illinois; and in Texas, the Texas Association of Counties. The National Association of Counties (NACo, 440 First St., NW, Washington, DC 20001, Tel. 202/393-6226) is an umbrella organization for 28 separate associations of county officials, such as county administrators, civil attorneys, engineers, health officers, human services administrators, park and recreation officers, planners, surveyors, treasurers and finance officers, and Hispanic and Black county officials. Municipalities and townships in many states also operate associations at the state level.

It's important to know about these associations, because many county and local governments routinely announce job vacancies with professional associations at the state and national levels. For information on placement services, job banks, employment databases, and job vacancy announcements through these and other professional government groups, we recommend Daniel Lauber's newest edition of the *Government Job Finder*. This book is filled with a wealth of contact information for finding local government job vacancies through such organizations.

Another useful source of information on local governments is public employee associations and unions which primarily engage in collective bargaining. These are some of the fastest growing and most militant public employee organizations in the United States:

- American Federation of Police
- American Federation of State, County, and Municipal Employees
- American Federation of Teachers
- Fraternal Order of Police
- The International Brotherhood of Teamsters, Chauffeurs, Warehousemen and Helpers of America
- The International Association of Fire Fighters
- National Teachers Association

Contact information for these and other associations of local employees is included in the *Encyclopedia of Associations*, *National Trade and Professional Associations in the United States*, and *The Municipal Yearbook*. These and other relevant directories should be available in the reference section of most libraries.

16

STATE GOVERNMENTS

*F*inding a job with state governments is similar to finding a job with federal and local governments. During the past three decades, state governments have become increasingly professionalized. In most cases, entrance into state government jobs follows well defined formal procedures which adhere to equal opportunity, affirmative action, and merit hiring criteria. Jobs tend to be very competitive, requiring written applications, testing, and lengthy screening processes and waiting periods. The jobs increasingly require higher levels of education and technical skills.

What exactly do state governments do? What types of jobs are available? How do you gain entrance to the job you want? This chapter addresses these questions by focusing on various opportunities available and effective strategies for getting a job with state governments.

FUNCTIONS

With the exception of foreign policy and national defense, state governments perform similar functions as federal and local governments combined. One step removed from the street-level nature of local government, state governments provide numerous services to populations within their jurisdictions. While local governments place primary emphasis on providing elementary and secondary education, health, and police and fire protection services, the 4,521,000 state employees place primary emphasis on providing higher education, health, highway, and correctional services. The following table summarizes the distribution of state government employees by states and average monthly earnings:

STATE EMPLOYMENT AND EARNINGS, 1991

State	Employees (1000s)	Average Monthly Earnings
California	325	$3,366
New York	269	3,032
Texas	228	2,355
Florida	163	2,272
Illinois	141	2,584
Ohio	141	2,569
Michigan	139	3,016
Pennsylvania	124	2,642
Virginia	114	2,298
New Jersey	113	3,139
Georgia	112	2,054
North Carolina	108	2,092
Washington	96	2,589
Indiana	90	2,466
Massachusetts	88	2,609
Maryland	87	2,648
South Carolina	81	2,017
Tennessee	76	2,149
Kentucky	76	2,268
Missouri	74	2,012
Wisconsin	69	2,988
Oklahoma	68	1,945
Minnesota	66	2,681
Connecticut	58	3,137
Iowa	56	2,681
Colorado	53	2,925
Oregon	55	2,457
Arizona	51	2,312
Hawaii	51	2,474
Kansas	49	2,152

New Mexico	41	2,255
Utah	39	2,179
West Virginia	34	1,955
Nebraska	29	2,135
Alaska	22	3,442
Maine	21	2,503
Rhode Island	20	2,611
Delaware	20	2,340
Nevada	19	2,635
Idaho	18	2,256
Montana	17	2,256
New Hampshire	16	2,319
North Dakota	15	2,196
Vermont	13	2,393
South Dakota	13	2,033
Wyoming	11	2,086

Source: U.S. Bureau of the Census, 1993

STATE EMPLOYMENT BY FUNCTIONAL AREA, 1991

Function	Total (1000s)
1. Education	1,999
2. Health & hospitals	724
3. Highways	259
4. Public welfare	217
5. Natural resources	162
6. Judicial & legal	112
7. Financial administration	149
8. Other government administration	53
9. Police protection	87
10. Parks & recreation	44
11. Sanitation & sewerage	3
12. All other	712

Source: U.S. Bureau of the Census, 1993

Approximately one of every 37 workers in the United States is employed by state governments. While education remains the largest function of state governments, the state role in education tends to be more support and administrative than direct service in nature. Higher education is primarily controlled and administered by state governments. However, only 30 percent of all individuals performing state educational functions are classroom teachers. The remaining 70 percent provide support for higher education and administer intergovernmental programs to assist education programs at the local level. By contrast, 36 percent of all officials—and 65 percent of all educators—at the local level are classroom teachers.

Health is another major function of state governments. While local governments concentrate 7 percent of their personnel (790,000 employees) on various health programs, state governments assign 16 percent of their personnel (724,000 employees) to these programs. The difference is in economies of scale. The health function is shared by state and local governments. Except in large urban areas, local governments concentrate on providing basic health services, such as family planning, dental, maternal and child health, general medical and emergency, food inspection, solid waste, sewage disposal and drinking water inspection, birth and death recordkeeping, pharmaceutical, and mental health and retardation services. On the other hand, state governments maintain most public hospitals (50 percent of all hospitals), laboratories, medical schools, long-term psychiatric hospitals, and related health facilities. In many states and locales, basic health care functions will actually be performed by state employees who work within a county or municipality. Partially funded by local governments, they are state employees providing health maintenance within the local government jurisdiction.

Highways are another major state government function. State governments have developed and maintain a large and costly infrastructure for road transportation. Highway departments absorb 6 percent of all state government personnel and 6 percent of the total state government payroll.

During the past fifteen years employment in state government overall has increased while some functions have declined. Employment in state highways, for example, declined from 302,000 employees in 1970 to 259,000 in 1991. On the other hand, employment in public welfare has grown considerably—from 92,000 in 1970 to 217,000 in 1991. During the 1980s state spending increased by more than 100 percent.

FRAGMENTED STRUCTURES

Traditionally state governments were extreme examples of weak, fragmented, and largely incapable governing institutions. Powers were divided among numerous constitutionally elected officers within the executive branch so that no one individual or office could centralize power. State governments became known as relatively powerless and inept institutions, major breeding grounds for corruption and incompetence. Access to a state government job was largely a function of whom you knew; especially useful were one's connections with elected officials.

The old days of state governments have changed dramatically. During the past 30 years most state governments have increased their institutional capabilities. Most state governments have rewritten their constitutions, reformed their governmental structures around a limited number of constitutional officers, and streamlined the courts and bureaucracy. Various reform movements—most emphasizing the values of efficiency, effectiveness, and a politically neutral bureaucracy, have left a profound imprint on the structure of state governments today. Governors have more power, bureaucrats are more professional, and civil services regulate the hiring and firing of personnel. Jobs in state government lead to significant public service careers.

Despite major reform efforts, state governments have not been completely reformed along the lines of a centralized, unified executive. Governors' powers are proscribed by legal restrictions on tenure in office, weak veto and appointive powers, and the presence of competing constitutional officers. Off-setting the weak executive is a relatively powerful and independent bureaucracy made up of a confusing array of offices, agencies, bureaus, commissions, and boards. The majority of this so-called state bureaucracy is not under the formal control of the executive. Instead, the majority of agencies are controlled by the legislature! This type of fragmentation affects the hiring process regardless of the presence of civil service regulations and merit criteria. In some cases, agencies and commissions operate as independent governments within government. Highway departments, for example, are difficult to control in many states. Other agencies are the political property of certain legislative committees. In the end, no one seems to govern in many state governments.

State governments are by no means the same in terms of structure, functions, and hiring practices. In the Midwest, for example, the states of Michigan, Wisconsin, and Minnesota have reputations for being more program-oriented, with relatively strong civil service systems limiting the role of party patronage in the hiring process. On the other hand, Illinois, Indiana, and Ohio are more political; interest groups and political parties are relatively strong, and they tend to be more job-oriented than in many other states. Given these differences, there are no hard and fast rules for best approaching the hiring process in state governments. Again, you must do your research on the particular state that interests you. Your research will determine to what degree the formal and informal hiring processes operate. You will learn what role "political pull" plays in landing certain jobs.

Approaching state government is unlike approaching any other government because of the fragmentation both between and within the various branches of government. Well developed legislative and judicial branches offer job opportunities relating to legislative and judicial affairs. Fragmented bureaucracies under the partial control of both the legislative and judicial branches offer a variety of opportunities normally associated with executive bureaucracies in government.

LEGISLATIVE OPPORTUNITIES

During the past 30 years, state legislatures have become more full-time and professional. Especially in large states, such as California, New York, Pennsylvania, Illinois, and Ohio, legislatures have developed information processing and administrative infrastructures to manage their affairs. Each state legislature has created legislative agencies. The most common ones include:

- **Legislative Reference Services:** These offices assist the legislature with research on legislative matters.
- **Bill Drafting Services:** These offices are established by state legislatures to draft bills for legislative action.
- **Legislative Councils:** These offices are staffed by professional researchers who provide timely information to the legislature (also include Legislative Reference Services and Bill Drafting Services in some states). These offices range in size from five employees in South Carolina to over 200 in Pennsylvania.
- **Budgeting and Audit Staffs:** Offices with these staffs provide the legislature with budget and audit services.

In addition, specialized staffs, focusing on particular policy issues of various Senate and House standing committees, also function in state legislatures.

Typical of the various legislative agencies and standing committees is the example of the Texas state legislature. Many of the following standing committees and agencies have assigned staffs:

Senate Officers and Staff Services

President
President Pro Tem
Secretary
Sergeant at Arms

House of Representatives Officers and Staff Services

Speaker
Speaker Pro Tem
Sergeant at Arms
House Research Organization

Senate Standing Committees

Administration
Criminal Justice
Economic Development
Education
Finance
Health and Health Services
Intergovernmental Relations
Jurisprudence
Natural Resources
Nominations
State Affairs

House Standing Committees

Agriculture and Wildlife Management
Appropriations
Business and Industry
Calendars
Corrections
Criminal Jurisprudence
Economic Development
Elections
Energy Resources
Environmental Affairs

County Affairs
General Investigating
Government Organization
Higher Education
House Administration
Human Services
Insurance
International and Cultural Relations
Investments and Banking
Judicial Affairs
Judiciary
Licensing and Administrative Procedures
Financial Institutions
Local and Consent Calendars
Natural Resources
Public Education
Public Health
Public Safety
Redistricting
Science and Technology
State Affairs
Transportation
Urban Affairs
Ways and Means

Legislative Agencies

Legislative Audit Committee
Legislative Budget Board
Legislative Library Board (includes Legislative Reference Library services)
Sunset Advisory Commission
Texas Legislative Council (includes Data Processing, Document Production, Legal, and Research Divisions)

While most of these staffs are developed to provide general information gathering, analysis, and policy proposals to state legislatures as a whole, individual legislators also maintain personal staffs. Similar to personal staff members of U.S. Congressmen, state level personnel staff members perform numerous functions ranging from highly personal services, such as babysitting for a legislator, to more professional services, such as responding to constituent inquiries and drafting a piece of legislation to be sponsored by the legislator.

Legislatures are one of the most exciting arenas of government. They are the most important centers of power at the state level. They make laws, control large segments of the bureaucracy, and serve as stepping stones to higher political and administrative offices.

State legislatures also are challenging arenas for job seekers. Personal and committee staff members have little control over their agendas. Work and workloads vary depending on what pops up from the legislative arena at any particular time. Legislative staffs are notoriously understaffed and overworked. Long hours, crisis management, and pressure to perform are indicators of the particular lifestyle associated with legislative jobs. Few people make legislative work a career. Two to five years normally affords enough experience and contacts to move on to other forms of public employment. The "other" employment may be in a good state government job secured through political connections; in a position with an interest group doing business with the legislature; or in a job at the federal level with the U.S. Congress or in an executive agency. State legislative experience often pays off in terms of future job opportunities in the public and/or private sector. It is a way of moving from one set of public sector institutions to another.

The state legislative experience often pays off in terms of future job opportunities in the public and/or private sector.

State legislatures do not have well developed systems for recruiting personnel for staff positions. Except in cases where specific scientific, technical, and policy expertise is required and such positions are advertised, political process is still the major route to securing most legislative jobs. Personal staff positions are acquired through word-of-mouth and by contacting a state legislator or his or her staff members. But there is little mystery in securing such positions. You do not necessarily need to know someone or get referred for these positions. When a vacancy occurs—which frequently happens due to the pressures of the job and the high turnover of young staff members wishing to continue their educations—if you are available and your skills appear appropriate, you may be hired immediately.

While some state legislatures will have a formal placement service for collecting resumes and dispensing job vacancy information, your best approach is to make direct and personal contact with individual legislators and their staffs. You want to plug into the word-of-mouth job networks which play a central role in the hiring process. Call them on the telephone, visit them in their offices, leave your resume, and follow-up on your contacts. Timing is critical. You can be sure most legislators will not advertise staff vacancy needs. They will first check their networks and the resumes they have on hand. If you make a good impression both on paper and in person, you should have a good chance at getting one of these jobs. Remember, all states except Nebraska have two-house legislatures. Be sure to conduct your job search in *both* houses.

However, keep two things in mind when looking for a legislative job. First, not all state legislatures have a wide range of job opportunities. Small states, such as New Hampshire and Vermont, have very few legislative job opportunities. Professional staff assistance is limited and personal staffs are extremely small—perhaps nonexistent. Second, these jobs do not pay well. While some jobs may appear glamorous, many are basic clerical jobs—answering telephones, sorting mail, and responding to inquiries. Boredom and burnout are frequent occurrences. The high road of legislative drama involved with tackling big policy issues is reserved for very few people. Nonetheless, legislative work is an excellent stepping stone for working in agencies and private organizations doing business with the state. The experience and personal contacts for future networking are invaluable benefits of such work. A two year investment in legislative work can pay off handsomely in the long run.

JUDICIAL ARENA

The judicial bureaucracy is the smallest of all. A highly fragmented system, the states attorney's office and the state court system comprise the basic entry points into the judiciary. Many positions in this system either require legal training as a lawyer or paralegal or are basically clerical and support staff positions.

The typical structure of a state judicial system includes four levels of courts:

1. **Supreme Court:** Stands at the apex of the state court system. Also known as the Supreme Judicial Court or Court of Appeals in some states.

2. **Intermediate Appellate Courts:** All but 15 states have these courts. Depending on the state, they are variously referred to as Court of Appeals, Superior Court, Appellate Division of Supreme Court, Court of Criminal or Civil Appeals, or District Court of Appeals. These courts primarily review the decisions of lower courts.

3. **Trial Courts of General Jurisdiction:** These courts try major criminal and civil cases. They are referred to in some states as Circuit Courts, District Courts, Court of Common Pleas, Chancery Courts, and Superior Courts.

4. **Trial Courts of Limited Jurisdiction:** These courts deal with minor cases, their judges have the least legal training, and the political process is important to staffing these courts. Trial courts vary widely in terms of names and types: Juvenile Courts, Justice Courts, Probate Courts, Small Claims Courts, Orphan's Courts, Courts of Oyer and Terminer, and City and Town Courts.

While most courts divide their work into civil and criminal cases, the Office of Circuit Court also performs numerous non-court legal functions: issues marriage licenses, registers wills and probate, records land titles, files suits, and maintains the criminal and civil court dockets.

States attorneys, elected at the county level, prosecute all criminal cases in the lower courts. A typical states attorney's office might consist of an elected states attorney, eight assistant attorneys, a secretary, and four clerical support staff. Hiring practices will vary by state and local jurisdiction. For example, the state attorney's office may use the county personnel office for announcing vacancies and screening candidates especially for the support staff positions. However, for the professional legal positions, the informal system is most important. Lawyers tend to use word-of-mouth to identify candidates. They "spread the word" among their colleagues and fellow alumni to locate qualified candidates. The most they formalize the hiring process is when they contact the local bar association. In the end, the informal networks will be decisive in determining who gets the job.

At the state level, a similar hiring pattern operates for the supreme, appellate, and lower courts. The State Supreme Court maintains a personnel office, but this office normally does not hire for positions outside its office. It provides administrative support and gives guidelines to hiring offices. The general district and juvenile courts, which may have staffs of 20 or more, will do their own hiring. However, they normally coordinate position vacancy announcements through county or city personnel offices.

Entry into these courts is best approached by monitoring the county personnel offices and contacting individual judges and court personnel who normally identify personnel needs and make the final hiring decisions. School ties and the ole boy/girl system will operate more in hiring for positions in the state judiciary than in the executive bureaucracy. Consequently, your best approach, again, is to research the organization, contact individuals through referrals and informational interviews, and leave copies of your resume. Be sure to regularly follow up to see if and when vacancies may occur.

Two resources on the state courts are *Want's Federal-State Court Directory* and the *Directory of State Court Clerks and County Courthouses*. Published annually, both directories are available from the publisher: Want Publishing Co., 1511 K St., NW, Washington, DC 20005, Tel. 202/783-1887, or may be found in some libraries.

EXECUTIVE BUREAUCRACY

The state executive bureaucracy hires for similar positions found at the local and federal levels. They employ general administrative and clerical personnel as well as white and blue-collar specialists ranging from scientists to prison guards. Thousands of jobs will fall into the following functional and service areas that the Council of State Governments uses to classify state administrative officers:

FUNCTIONAL JOB AREAS IN STATE GOVERNMENT

Adjutant General
Administration
Aeronautics
Aging
Agriculture
Air Quality
Alcohol and Drug Abuse
Archives
Arts Council
Attorney General
Banking
Budget
Chief Justice
Child Labor
Children and Youth Services
Civil Rights
Coastal Zone Management
Commerce
Community Affairs
Comptroller
Consumer Affairs
Corrections
Court Administration
Crime Victims Compensation
Criminal Justice Data
Criminal Justice Planning
Debt Management
Data Processing
Development Disabled
Drinking Water
Economic Development
Education
Emergency Management
Emergency Medical Services
Elections Administration
Employee Relations
Employment Services
Energy
Environmental Protection
Equal Employment Opportunity
Facilities Management
Federal Liaison
Finance
Fire Marshal
Fish and Wildlife
Fleet Management
Food Protection
Forestry
Gaming Officials
General Services
Geographic Information Services
Geological Survey
Governor
Hazardous Waste Management
Health
Higher Education
Highway Safety
Highways
Historical Preservation
Horse Racing
Housing Finance
Human Resources
Information Systems
Inspector General
Insurance
International Trade
Job Training
Juvenile Rehabilitation
Labor-Arbitration and Mediation
Latino Affairs
Law Enforcement
Licensing
Lieutenant Governor
Lobby Law Administration
Lottery
Mass Transportation
Medicaid
Mental Health and Retardation
Mined Land Reclamation
Mining Safety
Motor Vehicle Administration
Native American Affairs
Natural Resources
Occupational Safety
Oil and Gas Regulation
Ombudsman
Parks and Recreation
Parole and Probation (Adult)
Personnel
Planning
Post Audit
Pre-Audit
Press Secretary (Governor's)
Printing
Public Broadcasting
Public Defender
Public Lands
Public Utility Regulation
Public Works
Purchasing
Railroads
Records Management
Recycling
Retirement (teacher)

Social Services	Veterans Affairs
Soil Conservation	Veterinarian
Solid Waste	Vital Statistics
State Fair	Vocational Education
State Library	Vocational Rehabilitation
State Police	Water Quality
Telecommunications	Water Resources
Textbook Approval	Weights and Measures
Tourism	Welfare
Transportation	Wellness (State Employee)
Treasurer	Women
Unemployment Compensation	Workers Compensation

Most state bureaucracies have a central personnel department, or merit system, which performs the normal hiring functions of announcing vacancies, accepting applications, administering tests, screening candidates, and forwarding eligibility lists and applications to hiring officials. Most of these offices are charged with the responsibility of seeing that the hiring process follows equal opportunity, affirmative action, and merit selection criteria.

Your best strategy for getting a job with a state agency is to use both the formal and informal systems. The *formal system* requires you to:

1. **Regularly monitor the job listings issued by the personnel department.** You can do this by telephone, or personal visit to various public locations where announcements are posted. Personnel departments issue position vacancy announcements for those found with local governments. They may be issued every week, 10-days, or two weeks in the form of an "Equal Opportunities Bulletin".

2. **Complete all required application forms.** These will vary depending on the particular agency and position. The state personnel offices should be able to give you information on what application forms are required by particular agencies and positions.

3. **Take all required tests.** These may be a combination of written, oral, physical, and polygraph tests, depending on the requirements of different agency's positions.

At the same time, the *informal system* at the state level operates similarly to the information system at the local and federal levels. Consequently, you should:

4. **Research state agencies.** You do this by consulting numerous published sources and informed individuals.

5. **Contact individuals in the agencies for information and referrals.** You do this by conducting informational interviews with agency employees with whom you discuss your interests and skills, and seek advice and referrals.

With enough persistence in the informal system, as well as attention to the details of the formal system, you should be successful in locating a job appropriate for your interests and skills.

Political pull still plays a role in state government . . . But you must be careful when to use it.

We do not advise you to pull political strings to get a state government job. At the same time, we do not advise you against doing so. Political pull still plays a role in state government, as it does in all levels of government. But you must be careful when to use it. Most agencies will respond to the use of "professional connections" to gain information on your skills and abilities. Most will resist political pressures to hire a particular individual.

On the other hand, many positions in state government are appointive positions. They go with the spoils of elective office. Individuals in these positions will have discretion to hire staff members. Political connections will probably work for these positions.

However, the general rule is to know your state organization. There is no substitute for conducting research on the hiring process. If you are thorough in your research, you will learn which positions with which agencies should be approached through the political system.

COMPENSATION

State government salaries compare favorably to local and federal government salaries. They are usually better than local government salaries, but not as generous as federal government compensation. In general, the larger the unit of government, the better the compensation. Large cities tend to pay their officials at comparable rates to state officials. However, a considerable amount of diversity is apparent between and within state governments. In Texas, for example, elected and appointed officials are paid very respectable salaries, but public employees are poorly paid. States in the Northeast ($2,888) and West ($2,862) pay the highest average monthly salaries whereas those in the South ($2,224) and Midwest ($2,589) pay the lowest.

Average full-time pay varies considerably from state to state. In 1991, for example, the monthly earnings of state employees in Alaska averaged $3,442 whereas employees in Mississippi averaged $1,887. The average monthly salary for all state employees was $2,565. This figure represents about 8 percent less than the average earnings of federal employees ($2,778) but 5 percent higher than the average earnings of local government employees ($2,445). Average monthly salaries for state government employees in each state for October 1991 were as follows:

State	Salary	State	Salary
Alaska	3,442	Delaware	2,340
California	3,366	New Hampshire	2,319
New Jersey	3,139	Arizona	2,312
Connecticut	3,137	Virginia	2,298
New York	3,032	Florida	2,272
Michigan	3,016	Kentucky	2,268
Minnesota	3,001	Montana	2,256
Wisconsin	2,988	Idaho	2,256
Colorado	2,925	New Mexico	2,255
Iowa	2,681	Alabama	2,216
Maryland	2,648	North Dakota	2,196
Pennsylvania	2,642	Utah	2,179
Nevada	2,635	Kansas	2,152
Rhode Island	2,611	Tennessee	2,149
Massachusetts	2,609	Nebraska	2,135
Washington	2,589	Louisiana	2,123
Illinois	2,584	Wyoming	2,086
Ohio	2,569	Georgia	2,054
Maine	2,503	South Dakota	2,033
Hawaii	2,474	South Carolina	2,017
Indiana	2,466	Missouri	2,012
Oregon	2,457	Arkansas	2,007
Vermont	2,393	West Virginia	1,955
North Carolina	2,386	Oklahoma	1,945
Texas	2,355	Mississippi	1,887

KEY RESOURCES

Several excellent resources are available to take the mystery out of state governments. One of the most useful resources is *The Book of the States*. Published by the Council of State Governments (Iron Works Pike, P.O. Box 11910, Lexington, KY 40578, Tel. 606/231-1939 or 800/800-1910 for orders only), the book provides timely articles and statistical summaries on the legislative, judicial, and executive branches of state governments as well as the intergovernmental system which relates state governments to the federal and local governments. The Council of State Governments also publishes four other volumes which are essential reading for anyone interested in state employment:

- *National Organizations of State Government Officials*
- *State Administrative Officials Classified By Function*
- *State Elected Officials and the Legislatures*
- *State Legislative Leadership, Committees, and Staff*

Each volume lists the names and addresses of key individuals. For example, if you are interested in seeking a job on a state legislator's staff you should consult the volume entitled *State Elected Officials and the Legislatures* for the names and addresses of each legislator in each house of each state. If you are interested in working for a legislative agency or standing committee of the state House or Senate, consult the volume entitled *State Legislative Leadership, Committees, and Staff* for the names and addresses of the key people you should contact. Consult Daniel Lauber's *Government Job Finder* for sources of state job listings.

The Council of State Governments also publishes several other materials which should be useful in your research:

- *State Government News* (monthly magazine)
- *State Government* (quarterly journal)
- *State Government Research Checklist*
- *The Conference Calendar* (lists monthly meetings between the Council and state officials)
- *Backgrounder Series* (brief reports on state government) Research Reports Suggested State Legislation

Some of the best sources of information on particular career fields in state government are the numerous professional associations of state employees. Among these are:

- Academy of State and Local Government
- American Association of State Highway and Transportation Officials
- Association of State and Interstate Water Pollution Control Administrators
- Association of State and Territorial Health Officials
- Association of State and Territorial Solid Waste Management Officials
- Association of State Correctional Administrators
- Chief Officers of State Library Agencies
- Conference of Chief Justices
- Conference of State Court Administrators
- Council of Chief State School Officers
- Council of State Community Affairs Agencies
- Council of State Governments
- Council of State Housing Agencies
- Council of State Planning Agencies

- Education Commission of the States
- National Assembly of State Arts Agencies
- National Association for State Information Systems
- National Association of Historic Preservation Officers
- National Association of Secretaries of State
- National Association of State Alcohol and Drug-Abuse Directors
- National Association of State Auditors, Comptrollers, and Treasurers
- National Association of State Aviation Officials
- National Association of State Boards of Education
- National Association of State Budget Officers
- National Association of State Comptrollers
- National Association of State Credit Union Supervisors
- National Association of State Departments of Agriculture
- National Association of State Mental Health Program Directors
- National Association of State Park Directors
- National Association of State Personnel Executives
- National Association of State Purchasing Officials
- National Association of State Retirement Administrators
- National Association of State Treasurers
- National Association of Tax Administrators
- National Center for State Courts
- National Conference of Commissioner on Uniform State Laws
- National Conference of Lieutenant Governors
- National Conference of State General Service Officers
- National Conference of State Legislatures
- National Conference of State Liquor Administrators
- National Council of State Housing Agencies
- National Council of State Legislatures
- National Council of State Travel Directors
- National Governors' Association
- National State Auditors Association
- State and Territorial Air Pollution Program Administrators
- State Auditor Coordinating Council

Contact information on these and other associations of state and local officials is found in *The Encyclopedia of Associations*, *National Trade and Professional Associations in the United States*, and *The Government Directory of Addresses and Telephone Numbers.*

In the end, your single best source of information will be the people you meet who answer your questions and volunteer useful tips on how the system works in a particular state, branch of government, agency, or office. If you ask a great number of questions about the employment process and specific jobs, you will be rewarded for your efforts with information you can use in getting the job you want.

17

THE FEDERAL GOVERNMENT

For many job seekers, the federal government is where the action is. Pay is good; benefits are excellent; in spite of occasional reductions-in-force (RIF), security is virtually guaranteed; many jobs are exciting; and more status, prestige, and financial compensation is afforded federal employees than state and local officials.

But getting a job with the federal government is another matter. This level of government appears complex, confusing, and difficult to enter. Competition is fierce, applications are complex, and the hiring process can take time. Hiring procedures are not uniform. The legislative, judicial, and executive branches each have their own hiring systems. Within the executive branch, the U.S. Postal Service, CIA, FBI, and Foreign Service hire differently from many other agencies. And certain agencies and positions are exempted from standard personnel regulations.

This chapter is designed to simplify the federal job finding process relevant to the executive bureaucracy. Chapter 18 examines employment opportunities in the legislative and judicial branches, including Capitol Hill, the congressional bureaucracy, and Supreme Court.

STRUCTURE

The federal government employs nearly 3 million civilians and 2 million military personnel who move more than $1.5 trillion each year into more than 83,000 state and local governments, 150 countries, and an enormous private sector of vendors, contractors, and nongovernmental organizations. The business of this government is incredible. It staffs and manages whole communities, such as the Pentagon and military bases at home and abroad. It is literally a cradle to the grave government: delivering babies; providing day care services; extracting taxes; educating, hiring, and retiring individuals; providing social security and health care; and burying the dead.

The business of government is incredible. It is literally a cradle to the grave government.

Federal employees work for over 100 different agencies in the three branches of government. The executive branch is divided into three major types of agencies:

- The Executive Office of the President
- The Departments
- Independent Agencies

The federal government also consists of numerous corporations, government-sponsored enterprises, boards, committees, commissions, and quasi-official agencies which employ thousands of individuals.

While each agency has its own personnel office, the Office of Personnel Management (OPM), an independent executive agency, stands at the apex of the federal personnel system. Until the late 1980s, OPM played an important role in directly recruiting and screening applicants for many types of positions and for certain agencies. However, as key personnel functions, such as issuing vacancy announcements, rating applicants, and training, were increasingly decentralized to individual agencies in the 1980s, today OPM plays a more supportive role in helping agencies meet their personnel needs. This office is responsible for issuing government-wide personnel regulations; providing support services to agencies; managing some application, testing, and screening processes; providing limited training services; assisting agencies in meeting their personnel needs; and extending benefits to employees and government retirees.

The following table summarizes employment distribution by government branches, major agencies, and geographic dispersion of agency personnel:

FEDERAL CIVILIAN EMPLOYMENT BY AGENCY, 1994

AGENCY	Total Employees	Percent in Washington Metro area
TOTAL	**2,984,597**	**11.9**
Legislative Branch	**36,949**	**94.1**
–Congress	20,404	100.0
▪ U.S. Senate	7,581	100.0
▪ U.S. House of Representatives	12,807	100.0
–Architect of the Capitol	2,229	100.0
–Congressional Budget Office	223	100.0
–General Accounting Office	4,546	65.4
–Government Printing Office	4,352	88.4
–Library of Congress	4,605	99.4
–Office of Technology Assessment	206	100.0
–U.S. Tax Court	304	98.4
Judicial Branch	**27,945**	**7.2**
–United States Courts Supreme Court	362	100.0
–U.S. Courts	27,500	5.7
–U.S. Court of Vets Appeals	83	100.0
Executive Branch	**2,919,703**	**11.5**
–Executive Office of the President	**1,595**	**99.4**
▪ White House Office	396	100.0
▪ Office of Management & Budget	531	100.0
▪ Office of Administration	188	100.0
▪ Council of Economic Advisors	31	100.0
▪ Executive Residence at White House	87	100.0
▪ Office of U.S. Trade Representative	183	95.5
–Executive Departments	**1,928,651**	**13.1**
▪ Agriculture	115,542	11.5
▪ Commerce	37,333	53.9
▪ Defense	898,154	9.5
▪ Education	4,687	69.2
▪ Energy	20,056	38.3
▪ Health & Human Services	129,374	23.7
▪ Housing & Urban Development	13,019	26.0
▪ Interior	80,058	12.6
▪ Justice	97,712	21.9
▪ Labor	17,072	37.9

▪ State	25,819	34.0
▪ Transportation	65,293	15.3
▪ Treasury	162,058	15.7
▪ Veterans Affairs	262,474	2.9
–Independent Agencies	**989,457**	**8.2**
▪ Environmental Protection Agency	18,250	32.9
▪ Equal Employment Opportunity Commission	2,917	25.5
▪ Federal Deposit Insurance Corporation	19,596	18.5
▪ Federal Emergency Management Agency	6,006	26.3
▪ General Services Administration	19,677	32.8
▪ National Aeronautics and Space Administration	23,437	22.8
▪ National Archives and Records Administration	3,160	41.2
▪ Nuclear Regulatory Commission	3,386	66.8
▪ Office of Personnel Management	5,866	42.8
▪ Panama Canal Commission	8,478	00.1
▪ Securities and Exchange Commission	2,698	67.1
▪ Small Business Administration	7,515	18.4
▪ Smithsonian Institution	5,506	90.3
▪ Tennessee Valley Authority	18,990	00.1
▪ U.S. Information Agency	8,085	49.5
▪ U.S. International Development Cooperation Agency	4,183	53.6
▪ U.S. Postal Service	809,369	2.7

Source: U.S. Office of Personnel Management, Office of Workforce Information, Statistical Analysis and Services Division, May 1994.

The total federal government workforce represents 18 percent of all public employees. Eighty-eight percent of federal employees work outside the Washington, DC Metro area, including 112,033 who work abroad. The three largest civilian employers are Defense, Postal Service, and Veterans Affairs, which employ 30.0, 27.1, and 8.7 percent of the total federal workforce respectively.

Federal employment has been relatively stable over the past 25 years. Between 1960 and 1980 federal employment increased by 22.9 percent, for an average annual increase of 1.1 percent. In 1981 federal employment actually decreased by 67,000 and by another 39,000 in 1982. As indicated in the statistical table on page 27 of Chapter 2, agencies experiencing major cutbacks in the 1980s were the Tennessee Valley Authority, General Services Administration, Interstate Commerce Commission, Office of Personnel Management, U.S. International Development Cooperation Agency, Government Printing Office, Small Business Administration, and the Departments of Education, Commerce, Housing and Urban Development, Labor, Energy, Health and Human Services, Transportation, and Agriculture. On the other hand, several agencies experienced major increases in personnel throughout the 1980s: Federal Deposit Insurance Corporation, U.S. Postal Service, Smithsonian Institution, U.S. Information, and the Departments of Justice, Treasury, Defense, Veterans Affairs, and State. Despite major cutbacks in some agencies, federal government employment actually increased by 8.8 percent between 1980 and 1990, representing an average annual increase of just under 1 percent.

THE FEDERAL EMPLOYEE

Federal employees are often stereotyped in terms of characteristics. Excluding employees with the U.S. Postal Service, Congress, Tennessee Valley Authority, Central Intelligence Agency, Defense Intelligence Agency, and the National Security Agency, and foreign nationals employed overseas, the "typical federal civilian employee" on September 30, 1993 (2,120,116 employees profiled by the U.S. Office of Personnel Administration) approximated the following aggregate statistics:

Demographic Characteristics

Age:	43.8 years
Length of Service:	14.9 years
Education Level:	37% have Bachelor's Degree or higher
Gender:	56% men and 44% women
Race/National Origin:	28.2% minority group members: 16.7% Black, 5.6% Hispanic, 3.9% Asian/Pacific Islander, 2.0% Native American
Handicapped Status:	7% have handicaps
Veterans Preference:	27.5% have veterans preference (16.5% are Vietnam Era veterans)
Retired Military:	4.3% of total; 0.5% officers and 3.8% enlisted personnel

Job Characteristics

Annual Base Salary:	$36,875 worldwide; $46,096 in Washington, DC-MD-VA-WV Area
Special Rates:	11% paid higher rates for retention in shortage occupations
Pay System:	74% General Schedule, 16% wage systems, and 10% other
Work Schedule:	93% full-time, 4% part-time and 3% intermittent
Tenure:	90% permanent appointments; 87% full-time permanent appointments
Occupation:	84% White-Collar (23% Professional, 26% Administrative, 19% Technical, 14% Clerical, 2% Other), 16% Blue-Collar
Supervisory Status:	10.6% Supervisors and 2.1% Managers
Union Representation:	73% eligible and 59% represented
Service (Position):	80.1% Competitive, 19.5% Excepted, and 0.4% Senior Executive Service

COMPETITIVE AND EXEMPTED SERVICES

The federal civil service classifies positions into competitive or exempted services. The majority of federal government positions are in the *competitive service.* These positions fall under the civil service regulations, codified in the Civil Service Reform Act of 1978, which are administered by the Office of Personnel Management. Such positions must adhere to the "merit principles" of openness, fairness, and nondiscrimination. These position come under Presidential authority, are subject to periodic reduction-in-force regulations and hiring freezes, and follow internal seniority rules.

At the same time, Congress, the judiciary, and several agency positions are exempted from these regulations. These positions lie outside the authority of OPM and are subject to individual agency personnel regulations. Individuals in these positions do not accumulate civil service seniority which would apply to other positions in the competitive service. Executive agencies classified in the *exempted services* include:

- Central Intelligence Agency
- Defense Intelligence Agency
- Executive Protective Service (Secret Service—Uniformed Branch)
- Federal Bureau of Investigation
- Federal Reserve System, Board of Governors
- Library of Congress
- Federal Courts
- General Accounting Office
- U.S. International Development Cooperation Agency
- National Science Foundation (only scientific, engineering, and a few high-level managerial positions are exempted)
- National Security Agency
- U.S. Nuclear Regulatory Commission
- Postal Rate Commission
- U.S. Postal Service
- U.S. Department of State (Skilled specialists and experienced secretaries only; all others take the foreign service exam.)
- Tennessee Valley Authority
- U. S. Mission to the United Nations
- Veterans Affairs, Department of Medicine and Surgery

These agencies have their own set of personnel procedures for hiring and managing personnel. Therefore, individuals apply directly to these agencies.

Exempted positions are positions which are not subject to OPM standards. Such positions are exempted because they are difficult to fill through normal recruitment channels. These positions include:

- Professional & Administrative Careers (PAC)—GS-5 thru GS-7
- Teachers in Department of Defense overseas dependent schools
- Attorneys
- Doctors, dentists, and nurses with the Department of Veterans Affairs
- Scientists and engineers with the National Science Foundation
- Chaplains with the Veterans Administration and Justice Department
- Drug enforcement agents

CLASSIFICATIONS, COMPENSATION, SEX, AND RACE

The total federal workforce is divided into two major classification systems. White-collar professional, administrative, scientific, clerical, and technical employees are paid according to the *General Schedule* (GS), which is graded from GS-1 to GS-15 and uniformly applied throughout the federal government. The following table summarizes the pay rates on the General Schedule.

GENERAL SCHEDULE OF FEDERAL SALARY RATES BY GRADE, 1994

	Within-Grade Step Increases									
Grade Levels	ONE	TWO	THREE	FOUR	FIVE	SIX	SEVEN	EIGHT	NINE	TEN
GS-1	11,903	12,300	12,695	13,090	13,487	13,720	14,109	14,503	14,521	14,891
GS-2	13,382	13,701	14,145	14,521	14,683	15,115	15,547	15,979	16,411	16,643
GS-3	14,603	15,090	15,577	16,064	16,551	17,038	17,525	18,012	18,499	18,986
GS-4	16,393	16,939	17,485	18,031	18,577	19,123	19,669	20,215	20,761	21,307
GS-5	18,340	18,951	19,562	20,173	20,784	21,395	22,006	22,617	23,228	23,839
GS-6	20,443	21,124	21,805	22,486	23,167	23,848	24,529	25,210	25,891	26,572
GS-7	22,717	23,474	24,231	24,988	25,745	26,502	27,259	28,016	28,773	29,530
GS-8	25,159	25,998	26,837	27,676	28,515	29,354	30,193	31,032	31,871	32,710
GS-9	27,789	28,715	29,641	30,567	31,493	32,419	33,345	34,271	35,197	36,123
GS-10	30,603	31,623	32,643	33,663	34,683	35,703	36,723	37,743	38,763	39,783
GS-11	33,623	34,744	35,865	36,986	38,107	39,228	40,349	41,470	42,591	43,712
GS-12	40,298	41,641	42,984	44,327	45,670	47,013	48,356	49,699	51,042	52,385
GS-13	47,920	49,517	51,114	52,711	54,308	55,905	57,502	59,099	60,696	62,293
GS-14	56,627	58,515	60,403	62,291	64,179	66,067	67,955	69,843	71,731	63,619
GS-15	66,609	68,829	71,049	73,269	75,489	77,709	79,929	82,149	84,369	86,589

Pay rates for Senior Level (SL) and Scientific & Professional (ST) positions range from $79,931 to $115,700. Senior Executive Service (SES) pay rates range from $92,900 to $115,700.

These salary rates encompass most white-collar positions in the competitive service. Exceptions include higher salary rates for employees in 27 major metropolitan areas. These employees receive percentage salary adjustments due to the higher costs of living in these areas.

Trade, labor, and other blue-collar workers—70 percent of whom are employed by the Departments of Army, Navy, and Air Force—are paid on the *Federal Wage System* (WG). Grades range from WG-1 to WG-15 and the pay in each grade varies for each of 137 geographical areas. Over

400,000 employees are classified as WG. Other pay systems operate for the Senior Executive Service—management and executive positions that used to classified as GS-16 to GS-18 positions—the U.S. Postal Service, the Foreign Service, law enforcement officials, and a few other positions.

The total federal workforce is relatively representative of the distribution of males and females in the general population: 56.7 percent of all federal employees are female. However, a disproportionate number of males occupy the senior levels (GS 13-15 and SES) of the civil service —74 percent.

Contrary to what many people may believe, minorities are extremely well represented at all levels in the federal government. Indeed, the federal workforce employs a disproportionate number of minorities in comparison to their general distribution in the population. Blacks in particular are over-represented in the U.S. Postal Service (20.8 percent of postal work force versus 10.3 percent in national labor force), raising serious questions about possible reverse discrimination. Blacks, Hispanics, and other minorities occupy 26 percent of all positions in the federal government, including 12 percent of all GS 13-15 and SES positions. They are disproportionately represented at the GS 1-4 Levels (38.5 percent) and within the blue-collar Wage Grade system (33 percent). For many minorities—especially Blacks—the federal government is an attractive and exceedingly open employment arena.

JOB TYPES AND ALTERNATIVES

The federal government hires individuals in five categories of jobs (PATCO). In 1994 these consisted of the following:

- **Professional Occupations (23%):** These require knowledge of science or specialized education and training at a level equal to a bachelor's degree or higher. Examples include engineers, accountants, biologists, and chemists. Engineers (95,000) and nurses (40,000) are the largest professional groups with the federal government.

- **Administrative Occupations (26%):** Require increasingly responsible experience or a general college education. Examples include personnel specialists and administrative officers.

- **Technical Occupations (19%):** These are associated with a professional or administrative field, but they are nonroutine in nature. Examples include computer and electronic technicians.

- **Clerical Occupations (14%):** These involve work which supports office, business, or fiscal operations. Examples include clerk-typist, mail and file clerk.

- **Other Occupations (2%):** All other occupations not classified as professional, administrative, technical, or clerical. Includes many blue-collar and trade occupations, such as painters, carpenters, and laborers.

The federal government has as many different types of positions as the private sector. A complete list of positions would take up the remainder of this book. Therefore, we will examine the major classifications as well as identify those positions which employ the largest number of individuals.

The Office of Personnel Management, using a numerical code, classifies all General Schedule positions into 22 occupational groups and families. These include:

GS-000	Miscellaneous Occupations
GS-100	Social Science, Psychology, and Welfare
GS-200	Personnel Management and Industrial Relations
GS-300	Administrative, Clerical, and Office Services
GS-400	Biological Sciences
GS-500	Accounting and Budget
GS-600	Medical, Hospital, Dental, and Public Health
GS-700	Veterinary Medical Science
GS-800	Engineering and Architecture
GS-900	Legal and Kindred
GS-1000	Information and Arts
GS-1100	Business and Industry
GS-1200	Copyright, Patent, and Trade-Mark
GS-1300	Physical Sciences
GS-1400	Library and Archives
GS-1500	Mathematics and Statistics
GS-1600	Equipment, Facilities, and Service
GS-1700	Education
GS-1800	Investigation
GS-1900	Quality Assurance, Inspection, and Grading
GS-2000	Supply
GS-2100	Transportation

Wage System occupations are also classified into groups and families. These consist of 36 WG categories:

WG-2500	Wire Communications Equipment Installation and Maintenance Family
WG-2600	Electronic Equipment Installation and Maintenance Family
WG-2800	Electrical Installation and Maintenance Family
WG-3100	Fabric and Leather Work Family
WG-3300	Instrument Work Family
WG-3400	Machine Tool Work Family
WG-3500	General Services and Support Work Family
WG-3600	Structural and Finishing Work Family

WG-3700	Metal Processing Family
WG-3800	Metal Work Family
WG-3900	Motion Picture, Radio, Television, and Sound Equipment Operation Family
WG-4000	Lens and Crystal Work Family
WG-4100	Painting and Paper Hanging Family
WG-4200	Plumbing and Pipefitting Family
WG-4300	Pliable Materials Work Family
WG-4400	Printing Family
WG-4600	Wood Work Family
WG-4700	General Maintenance and Operations Work Family
WG-4800	General Equipment Maintenance Family
WG-5000	Plant and Animal Work Family
WG-5200	Miscellaneous Occupations Family
WG-5300	Industrial Equipment Maintenance Family
WG-5400	Industrial Equipment Operating Family
WG-5700	Transportation/Mobile Equipment Operation Family
WG-5800	Transportation/Mobile Equipment Maintenance Family
WG-6500	Ammunition, Explosives, and Toxic Materials Work Family
WG-6600	Armament Work Family
WG-6900	Warehousing and Stock Handling Family
WG-7000	Packing and Processing Family
WG-7300	Laundry, Dry Cleaning, and Pressing Family
WG-7400	Food Preparation and Serving Family
WG-7600	Personal Services Family
WG-8200	Fluid Systems Maintenance Family
WG-8600	Engine Overhaul Family
WG-8800	Aircraft Overhaul Family
WG-9000	Film Processing Family

White-collar GS positions employing the largest number of individuals consist of:

- Accountants and auditors (GS-510)
- Administrative assistants and officers (GS-341)
- Air traffic control specialists (GS-2152)
- Budget analysts or officers (GS-560)
- Civil rights analysts (GS-160)
- Computer specialists (GS-334)
- Contract representatives (GS-962)
- Contract and procurement specialists (GS-1102)
- Criminal investigators (GS-1810 and GS-1811)
- Economists (GS-110)
- Engineers (GS-800 series)
- Equipment specialists (GS-1670)
- Financial institution examiners (GS-570)
- Foresters (GS-460)
- Internal revenue officers (GS-1169)
- Lawyers (GS-905)

- Loan specialists (GS-1165)
- Management analysts (GS-343)
- Nurses (GS-610)
- Personnel management specialists (GS-201)
- Physicians (GS-602)
- Physicists (GS-1310)
- Production controllers (GS-1152)
- Program analysts (GS-345)
- Quality assurance specialists (GS-1910)
- Social insurance representatives and administrators (GS-105)
- Social insurance claims examiners (GS-993)
- Supply management specialists (GS-2003) and inventory management specialists (GS-2010)
- Teachers (GS-1710)
- Training instructors (GS-1712)

Blue-collar occupations, both under the GS and WG systems, which employ the largest number of individuals include:

- Accounting technicians (GS-525)
- Aircraft mechanics (WG-8852)
- Claims clerks (GS-998)
- Clerks (GS-300 and GS-500 series)
- Clerk-typists (GS-322)
- Computer operators (GS-332)
- Data transcribers (GS-356)
- Electricians (WG-2805)
- Electronics mechanics (WG-2604)
- Engineering aides and technicians (GS-802)
- Financial administration workers (GS-503)
- Firefighters and other fire protection workers (GS-081)
- Food service workers (GS-7408)
- Forestry technicians and smoke jumpers (GS-462)
- Heavy mobile equipment mechanics (WG-5803)
- Janitors or porters (GS-3566)
- Laborers (WG-3502)
- Machinists (WG-3414)
- Mail and file clerks (GS-305)
- Maintenance mechanics (WG-4749)
- Medical technicians (GS-600)
- Nursing assistants (GS-621)
- Personnel clerks and assistants (GS-203)
- Pipefitters (WG-4205)
- Reporting stenographers, shorthand reporters, and clerk stenographers (GS-312)
- Secretaries (GS-318)
- Sheet metal mechanics (WG-3806)
- Supply clerks and technicians (GS-2005)
- Tax accountants and examiners (GS-592)

For more information on these positions, see Russ Smith's *The Right SF 171 Writer*, Neale Baxter's *Opportunities in Federal Government Careers*, the Department of Labor's *The Dictionary of Occupational Titles* and *The Occupational Outlook Handbook*, and publications and handouts issued by the Office of Personnel Management and personnel offices of individual agencies.

JOB LISTINGS

Federal job seekers need to know where to find job listings for agency vacancies. All federal agencies are required to send information on nonstatus job vacancies to the Office of Personnel Management. OPM, in turn, publishes a weekly bulletin—the *Federal Job Opportunity Listing* (FJOL)—which lists the vacancies. Each Federal Job Information Center has a copy of the FJOL which you can review for your information.

Vacancies listed in the FJOL include information on the position title, series, grade level, opening and closing dates for accepting applications, location of job, and how to acquire application information.

When you get ready to apply for a position, make sure you do so within the designated opening dates. Some positions may be open for applications for only 10 days whereas others are open for 30 days. Some are open indefinitely, indicating the federal government is continuously hiring individuals for those positions ("open continuous positions"). In most cases you must contact the agency hiring authority for complete information on application procedures. They should provide you with a complete vacancy announcement that outlines the requirements for the position. It will tell you if you need to take any tests, outline the duties and responsibilities, and specify which documents you must submit to be considered for the position. In most cases the FJOL will give you a name and telephone number to call to request this information. Once you receive the application information, you are well advised to carefully read the vacancy announcement and complete your application form in direct response to the requirements of the position.

If you are looking for a complete listing of all vacancies available throughout the federal government, including both status and nonstatus positions, it's best to subscribe to a private listing service. The most comprehensive such listings are the *Federal Career Opportunities* published by the Federal Research Service, and the *Federal Jobs Digest,* published by Breakthrough Publications.

TESTS

Contrary to what many people believe, the federal government no longer administers a Civil Service Examination. This does not mean you do not need to take some type of examination. In some cases, especially for positions that require demonstrated skill proficiency, a test may be required. Indeed, you can be assured most clerical positions involve such a proficiency test. Other positions, such as Foreign Service Officer with the State Department, require a written and oral Foreign Service Examination which is given once a year. Many jobs with the U.S. Postal Service also require written examinations. If you are interested in the U.S. Postal Service, you should acquire two books written by Veltisezar Bautista on this subject: *The Book of U.S. Postal Exams* and *The Book of $16,000-$60,000 Post Office Jobs*.

Whether or not a test is required depends on the particular position. Each vacancy announcement will indicate whether or not a specific examination is required. In most cases, applicants will not need to take an examination. They only submit their Standard Form 171 (SF 171—the federal government's standard application form which is now being discontinued), an agency application form, or a resume in response to a vacancy. The vacancy announcement specifies application requirements.

ADMINISTRATIVE CAREERS WITH AMERICA (ACWA)

A relatively new class of positions—the Administrative Careers With America (ACWA) program—does require a written entrance examination in most cases. These entry-level GS-5 to GS-7 positions are most relevant to recent college graduates with little or no professional experience. Begun in 1990 as the successor to the old PACE program, ACWA is now one of the federal government's major testing programs for individual's wishing to advance into professional and administrative positions.

While favoring college graduates, the ACWA program is by no means limited to those with college educations. Under this program, requirements for entry into GS-5 positions include passing the relevant written test and one of the following:

- Four-year college degree (bachelor's); or
- Three years of responsible experience; or
- An equivalent combination of education and experience.

Entry into GS-7 positions includes passing the relevant written test and meeting one of the following requirements:

- A bachelor's degree and one of these Superior Academic Achievements:
  - –A G.P.A. of 3.0 or higher for all undergraduate courses completed in the last two years of study.
  - –A G.P.A. of 3.5 or higher in a major or during the last two years of undergraduate study in major.
  - –Rank in the upper third of college or university class (or major subdivision).

–Member of a national honorary scholastic society (beyond freshman year) recognized by Association of College Honor Societies; or

- One year of graduate education, law school, or a graduate degree; or
- One year of work experience in a related field, equivalent to a GS-5 or higher position in the federal government.
- An equivalent combination of education and experience.

The Administrative Careers With America program covers nearly 100 different entry-level administrative and professional occupations which are filled through one of two application methods—a written examination or an application based on scholastic achievement as reflected by an applicant's grade point average (3.5 to 4.0). This program is especially appropriate for recent college graduates and other qualified entry-level job seekers. Positions in this category start at the GS-5 and GS-7 levels. Individuals can apply for jobs under this program within nine months of graduation, or upon completion of qualifying academic courses or three years work experience.

Written examinations under the ACWA program are given in six different occupational groups which encompass nearly 100 different entry-level occupations:

1. Health, Safety and Environmental Occupations
2. Writing and Public Information Occupations
3. Business, Finance, and Management Occupations
4. Personnel, Administration, and Computer Occupations
5. Benefits Review, Tax, and Legal Occupations
6. Law Enforcement and Investigation Occupations

A seventh group of occupations does not require a written examination —only "positive education requirements" which means a grade point average of 3.5 or above on a 4.0 scale; a 3.45 grade point average is rounded up to 3.5. Individuals with such a grade point average qualify under the Outstanding Scholar Program. Individuals meeting these requirements apply directly to the Personnel Director of the federal agency they are interested in working with. Examples of positions in this group requiring positive educational requirements include: archeology, archivist, community planning, economist, education program, foreign affairs, general anthropology, general education and training, geography, history, international relations, manpower research and analysis, museum curator, psychology, social science, and sociology.

The written ACWA examination primarily stresses reasoning and analytic skills rather than knowledge of job-specific subject matters. Since the examination attempts to measure your overall capabilities, you cannot easily prepare for it overnight. If you plan to take the ACWA examination, you may want to sensitize yourself to the types of questions asked by examining a test preparation book on the subject: *ACWA: Administrative Careers in America* (New York: Arco, 1991). Keep in mind the ACWA tests focus on reasoning abilities—not content knowledge—a skill you cannot quickly acquire from a test preparation book.

APPLICATIONS

Since the federal hiring process is oriented toward filling specific **positions**, you must become familiar with positions and agencies rather than a general rating process. Once you learn about a vacancy, contact the individual and office in charge of issuing the vacancy announcement for complete information on application procedures and deadlines. In most cases the vacancy announcement requires completion of a formal application, which until December 1994 is the SF 171. This one to two-page announcement will outline the duties and responsibilities of the position, indicate the level of experience sought, and specify all documents required to be submitted with your application package. It will also specify a particular deadline for receipt of applications, unless it is an "open continuous position". Read the vacancy announcement very carefully for key words relating to the knowledge, skills, abilities, and other requirements (KSAOs) for the job. You must demonstrate these KSAOs in the "Experience" descriptions of your SF 171. Failure to do so will eliminate you from consideration or result in a low rating.

The key to getting a federal job is a powerful Standard Form 171 (SF 171). You must write it right if you want your application to stand out from many other SF 171s being submitted for the same position. With an expertly crafted SF 171, your chances of getting a federal job will be greatly enhanced. We strongly recommend getting a copy of Russ Smith's *The Right SF 171 Writer* for guidance on how to best prepare this critical application form. After December 30, 1994, however, check with each agency to see if they still accept SF 171s. Many agencies may issue their own application forms as well as accept resumes.

STRATEGIES

Successful federal job applicants know how to cut through the confusing and frustrating hiring process. What separates them from unsuccessful candidates is their:

- Knowledge of individual agencies, personnel processes, and job openings.

- Skill in developing and marketing a good application, especially a well-crafted SF 171, which clearly communicates their experience, qualifications, and strengths to agencies.

- Patience, persistence, and drive in seeing the process through.

You should begin your job search with a thorough understanding of both the formal and informal hiring processes in the federal government. While you can get a job by only following the formal system of responding to vacancy announcements, taking tests, and completing application forms, your odds will improve considerably if you also pursue jobs in the informal system of prospecting, networking, informational interviews, and referrals. In the end, your success will depend on how well you *relate* the formal and informal systems to one another.

The structure of the federal hiring process is similar to the structure of American governments in general—exhibits an incredible amount of decentralization, fragmentation, overlap, redundancy, and chaos. The hiring system is anything but logical, efficient, and effective. For example, if you want a research intelligence position, the CIA is only one of many agencies performing these functions. The Defense Intelligence Agency in the Department of Defense, Intelligence and Research Bureau in the State Department, and the National Security Council in the Executive Office of the President, and the Federal Bureau of Investigation (FBI) essentially do the same type of work. Almost every department has its own police and/or investigative force—not just the FBI. Indeed, personnel at the CIA will tell you to talk to their friends at the Defense Intelligence Agency or the Intelligence and Research Bureau in the State Department—agencies they may have worked for prior to moving to the CIA. The congressional bureaucracy, through the Federal Research Division of the Library of Congress, also engages in similar functions. These agencies duplicate each other and contribute to the overall redundancy of the federal government.

Other occupations also are represented in numerous agencies which overlap and duplicate each other. Take the case of personnel training opportunities. Most large agencies have their own training sections which conduct in-house training—not just the Office of Personnel Management. Trainers at OPM will direct you to fellow professionals in the various Departments and Independent Agencies who also conduct training. Such redundancy is uncovered when you conduct your information interviews. And, as we will see in Part IV, such networking leads to similar positions in the private sector with contracting and consulting firms as well as with associations that do business with various government agencies.

While redundancy may seem to be a waste of taxpayers' money, it may also contribute to the overall effectiveness of government by providing important internal checks and balances on policy. Whatever its costs and benefits, in a job search you need to recognize and use redundancy to your advantage. You do this by contacting several agencies for information and referrals on job opportunities in the same functional area. Remember, no single agency of government performs a unique function. Counterpart functions will be found in several agencies. Your job is to do the necessary research to uncover the counterparts.

Decentralization also should be used to your advantage. You should develop contacts with key personnel in the operating units or program offices—where the hiring decisions are finally made. Since units tend to be isolated from one another because of decentralization, you should conduct several informational interviews within and between agencies. In fact, it is not unusual to discover that one office does not know what another office is doing, even though it is in the same agency, housed in the same building, and even located next door!

The formal structure of hiring in the federal government presents a deceptive picture of a centralized, organized, coordinated, and efficient government personnel system.

The formal structure of hiring in the federal government overlays a great deal of decentralization, fragmentation, and chaos. It presents a deceptive picture of a centralized, organized, coordinated, and efficient government personnel system. This image initially encourages people to apply but then intimidates them sufficiently enough to dissuade many from following through. Do not be intimidated or dissuaded from achieving your objective. The key to success is in understanding the system and using this understanding to your benefit.

The Office of Personnel Management, formerly known as the Civil Service Commission, is an independent executive agency. It stands at the center of the federal government's merit personnel system. Many people —including some OPM employees—believe you must apply for federal jobs through this agency. This is true in nearly 20 percent of the cases, but it is not true for over 2 million federal positions. All federal agencies hire their own personnel. In so doing, they may receive direct assistance from OPM in the form of announcing vacancies, scrutinizing applications, and screening candidates. The degree of involvement with agencies depends on several factors, such as classification as exempted positions or the degree of organizational capabilities the agency has to conduct their own hiring. Nonetheless, for some federal positions, you will have to deal directly with the Office of Personnel Management.

Since the federal personnel reforms of January 1980, OPM has been decentralizing several personnel functions to individual agencies. But decentralization has not been uniform. Some agencies are capable of hiring whereas others are still more dependent upon OPM for assistance. In other cases, OPM's role increasingly is marginal to the hiring process. Overall, OPM performs general support function for agencies, such as providing information and assisting them in the selection and training processes.

OPM does perform one essential function for your job search campaign: dispenses information on procedures and opportunities. In addition to its 10 regional headquarters, OPM's Federal Job Information Centers (FJICs) are located in 50 cities, including Guam and Puerto Rico, which are considered subregional centers or key geographical locations for dispensing federal employment information. These offices maintain a list of job vacancies (the FJOL) available in their region and local area. However, you should approach these FJICs with some degree of caution and healthy skepticism. The major functions of FJICs are to provide information on job opportunities in particular agencies, hand out application forms, and conduct testing for specific entry positions. OPM representatives at the FJICs will tell you to follow the formal procedures; most deny the existence of an informal system or, at best, they will not endorse it. This is understandable, because their job is to promote the formal system rather than help you learn the most effective methods for penetrating the bureaucracy. They are the promoters, managers, and keepers of long employment lines.

OPM outlines the formal hiring system by advising candidates to follow these steps:

1. **Acquire position vacancy announcements and application forms:** Go to the FJIC for listings of job openings (FJOL) and information on procedures for getting a federal job. This results in a pile of literature and forms. Alternatively, OPM may advise you that the particular position you desire does not fall within the scope of OPM procedures, such as exempted positions and agencies.

2. **Follow instructions in announcements:** Each announcement will give specific instructions on application deadlines, position description, qualifications, content of application package, tests required, and application procedures. Follow these instructions very carefully. Failure to adhere to any instruction, however minor such as dating or signing your application, will automatically disqualify you.

3. **Complete your application:** At least through December 1994, this is the SF 171—the federal government's version of an obituary resume or application form. Send it directly to the hiring agency. After December 1994, this may include a resume and some other type of application form. It's best to inquire

with specific agencies concerning their application requirements. You usually send your application to the office that issued the vacancy announcement—the agency personnel office.

4. **Take any required tests:** If any are required, they will be listed on the vacancy announcement. You usually need to complete the test and receive a qualifying score before submitting your application.

5. **Wait for agency to evaluate your qualifications and call you for an interview:** Once you complete your application and submit it to the agency, evaluators will examine it and give you a rating based on the information supplied in the application. While OPM used to give all such ratings, it now only does so in some cases; much of this authority has been decentralized to agencies. Agencies normally select the top three rated candidates to interview.

6. **Wait to be selected:** If you are interviewed, you will need to wait some time before the agency makes its final decision.

The one common theme running throughout this formal hiring process is that you must *wait.* Indeed, you must have a great deal of patience and perseverance from the moment you review a vacancy announcement to the time you are selected for a position.

Passive waiting is not a good job search strategy.

While this is a very logical, and seemingly efficient, hiring process, it is not particularly effective for the individual. Passive waiting is not a good job search strategy. If you follow OPM's advice, your chances of getting a job are about as good as responding to newspaper want ads or standing in line at an employment firm—very limited. There is a great deal of mystery to this process which OPM does not reveal to the public. Remember, the federal government hires approximately 1,000 people each day. But the FJICs only list a few of these positions and usually only those positions available in their particular region or city as well as all positions classified as Senior-Level (certain GS-13 through GS-15 positions) and a few Senior Executive Service positions. In other words, your local FJIC may not provide you with useful information on the availability of jobs in particular agencies at your level of qualifications nor in other regions or cities.

There is a good reason for this information situation. OPM does not know what positions are available beyond the limited number reported to OPM. In fact, no one in the federal government knows all the positions vacant on a particular day, week, or month. The federal government simply does not keep such information on itself.

Since OPM's information on job openings is limited to nonstatus positions appearing in the *Federal Job Opportunity Listing* (FJOL), you must directly contact the personnel offices of each agency for a complete listing of vacancies. Alternatively, two private firms—the Federal Research Service and Breakthrough Publications—every two weeks compile and publish catalogs of approximately 3,000 vacancies (both status and nonstatus) at the GS-5 levels and above. While these publications are relatively comprehensive, they miss many positions which are listed only on the bulletin boards of agency personnel offices, circulated to a limited number of government offices, or posted outside agency cafeterias and snack bars.

Your alternatives to spending $39 for a six issue subscription to *Federal Career Opportunities Report* (Federal Research Service) or $34 for a six issue subscription to *Federal Jobs Digest* are most unattractive. The federal job information structure definitely favors individuals who physically are located in the Washington, DC Metropolitan area or in regional cities and have the time and patience to telephone or walk from one agency personnel office or cafeteria bulletin board to another. If you live outside Washington or the regional cities, you encounter serious problems. You can visit your FJIC every week or telephone every agency every week for information on vacant positions. After spending $200 a week on long-distance telephone calls, the $34 and $39 for the job listing services will seem cheap and convenient. Moreover, you will avoid traveling to an FJIC and standing in line for limited information. The FJIC is mainly designed to help people apply for the GS-1 through GS-5 entry-level positions or for blue-collar positions. Visit the FJICs, but beyond learning about formal application procedures and acquiring some literature, including application forms, don't rely exclusively on the FJICs in your job search. Again, the federal government is highly decentralized and fragmented within and between agencies. Your job will be to centralize and coordinate those aspects of the federal government job market that interest you. No one—including private employment and executive search firms—can do this for you. If they claim they can, don't believe them. Only **you** can get a federal job.

TAKING EFFECTIVE ACTION

The informal federal hiring system is similar to the informal systems found at the state and local government levels. Since agencies continually face personnel problems because of normal turnover, they must recruit periodically. A personnel need is first identified in the operating unit and then communicated to the agency personnel office where it is formally announced in accordance with merit, affirmative action, and equal opportunity considerations. During the lengthy formal process of announcing the position, gathering applications, and selecting candidates, agency personnel often try to hedge against uncertainty by looking for qualified personnel in the informal system. This means giving information on the vacancy to friends and acquaintances in their networks in the hope of attracting qualified candidates. Fearing the unknown, officials often welcome an opportunity to meet informally with a candidate, especially in the format of an informational interview.

If your timing is right, you may uncover a pending vacancy in an operating unit. Again, the personnel office will be the last to learn about the vacancy in the agency. Furthermore, the position description may be written around your resume and application or the agency may assist you in customizing your application in line with the position description. If agency personnel send you to their personnel office to rework your application, this is a good signal that you are under serious consideration for a position. Although we have no accurate figures on the phenomenon of "wiring" positions, it probably occurs in many GS-13 and above positions. Some observers, such as Richard Irish (*Go Hire Yourself Employer*) estimate that 95 percent of these positions are filled through agency "promotion". While we doubt the figure is that high, nonetheless, the practice is widespread. Such practices arise from personnel fears of agencies. Many agency heads wish to avoid leaving critical personnel problems to chance decisions of low-level officials in personnel offices.

The informal system consists of following the same general job search steps we outlined earlier as well as adapting them to the federal personnel setting:

1. **Research federal agencies:** The more information you can gather on agency work and personnel procedures, the better your chances of getting a job with an agency. Your research may even result in deciding not to apply for certain agencies and positions—you may discover agencies undergoing major cutbacks, experiencing significant morale problems, exhibiting dreadful work environments, or offering deadend positions.

2. **Focus on a few agencies for intensive research:** Specific jobs are found in specific agencies. The more details you gather at the level of the hiring officials, the better the probability of getting a job.

3. **Conduct informational interviews with agency personnel:** Make contacts with officials in the hiring units. Seek informa-

tion, advice, and referrals. Take copies of your resume *and* complete application with you to these interviews and leave copies for future reference.

4. **Apply for agency vacancies with a customized application:** Develop a customized application according to the advice found in Russ Smith's *The Right SF 171 Writer.* Use this version of the SF 171 or any other relevant application form when applying for agency vacancies.

5. **Prepare to interview with the hiring supervisor:** If you pass the formal screening process with your customized application and other documents, and hiring personnel in the operating units like you, you should be called for an interview and, hopefully, offered the job.

The formal and informal systems of federal employment for GS-9 to GS-15 level positions are outlined on page 289.

The informal system continues to yield more reliable and trustworthy information than the formal system.

We do not recommend mobilizing partisan political "pull" with agencies. Bureaucrats in general do not like to respond to blatant political pressures from elected officials. Such strategies may work wonders at some state and local units of government where the "good ole boys" are still powerful—but be careful with the Feds. There are exceptions, however. Perhaps you know a congressman who is on a powerful budget or appropriations committee affecting a particular agency. The congressman and his or her legislative assistants may know key people in the agency, and they will write you a standard letter of introduction. But do not expect miracles to happen with such a letter or by dropping names of big shots. In fact, the President of the United States only directly controls 2,000 of 3 million civilian government positions. Even the President may not be able to help you with the relatively autonomous and resistant bureaucracy!

Federal bureaucrats understand and thrive on the informal system, but political patronage and political pull are considered tacky, if not illegal, these days. In this respect, government bureaucrats are no different from

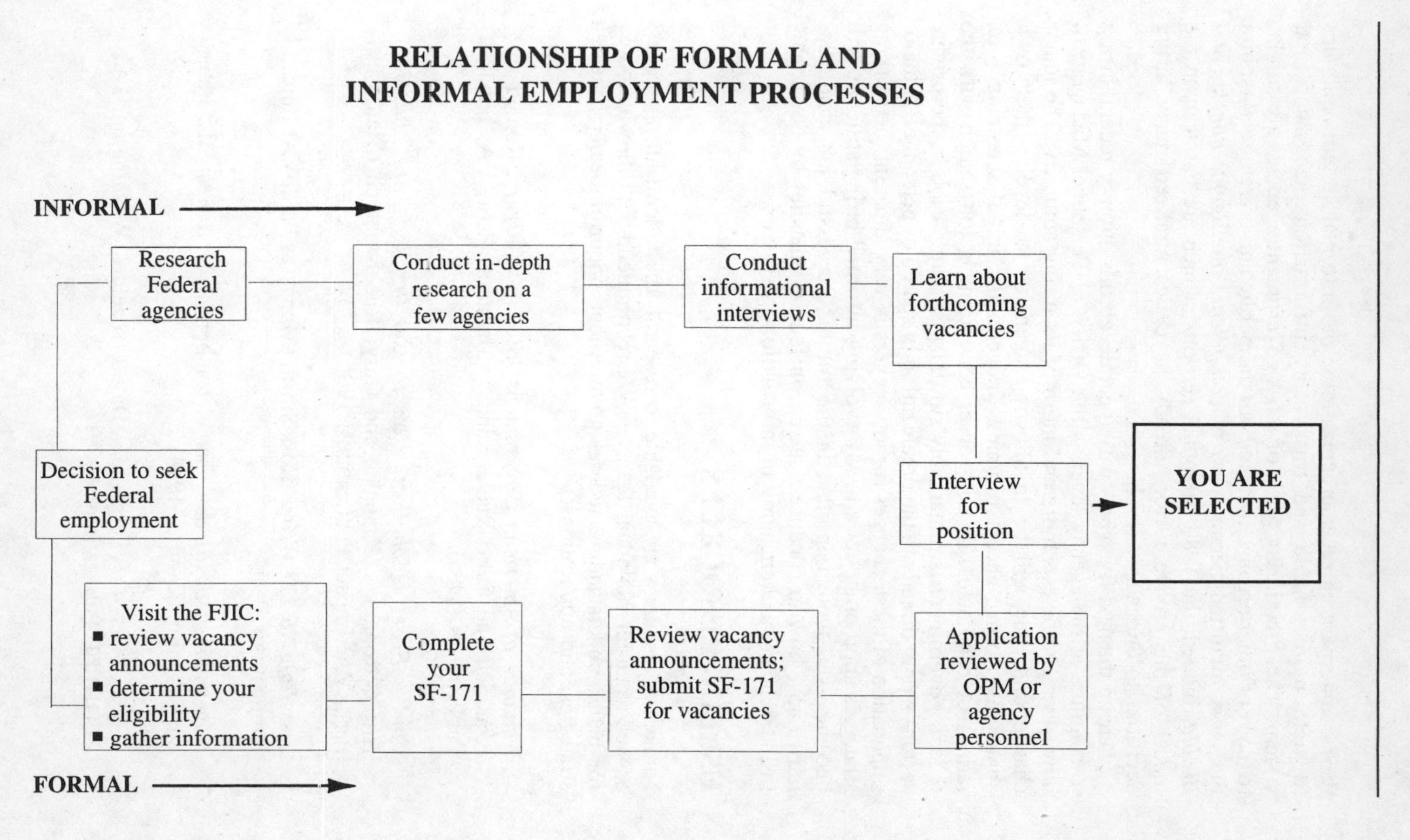
RELATIONSHIP OF FORMAL AND
INFORMAL EMPLOYMENT PROCESSES
INFORMAL
Research Federal agencies
Conduct in-depth research on a few agencies
Conduct informational interviews
Learn about forthcoming vacancies
Decision to seek Federal employment
Interview for position
YOU ARE SELECTED
Visit the FJIC:
■ review vacancy announcements
■ determine your eligibility
■ gather information
Complete your SF-171
Review vacancy announcements; submit SF-171 for vacancies
Application reviewed by OPM or agency personnel
FORMAL

their counterparts in other organizations: the informal system continues to yield more reliable and trustworthy information than the formal system. Thus, the hiring goals of most government agencies are similar to those of other organizations in both the public and private sectors: hire the most qualified person who is *competent, intelligent, honest, and likable*. Indeed, the 1980 personnel reforms, which are based upon the model of the private sector, already have decentralized many hiring decisions to the agency level.

During the next five years we expect decentralization of federal hiring to continue at the agency level as the Office of Personnel Management downsizes and divests more and more of its hiring authority. The major change this time will be in allowing agencies to develop their own application forms, accept resumes, and conduct initial screening (i.e., rating) of candidates. In this sense, conducting a job search with the federal government is remarkably similar to finding a job in the private sector—apply directly to the organization in search of personnel. A major implication of these changes for job seekers is very apparent: networking strategies appropriate for a newly evolving informal hiring structure will become even more important in the future. Successful job candidates must know how to conduct research on federal agencies by developing inside contacts and engaging in information interviews.

USEFUL RESOURCES

Numerous resources are available to research the federal hiring process as well as target individual agencies. We recommend the following books for better understanding federal government opportunities, job search strategies, and applications:

Almanac of American Government Jobs and Careers, Ronald L. Krannich and Caryl Rae Krannich (Manassas Park, VA: Impact Publications, 1995).

Find a Federal Job Fast! How to Cut the Red Tape and Get Hired, Ronald L. Krannich and Caryl Rae Krannich (Manassas Park, VA: Impact Publications, 1995).

The Right SF 171 Writer, Russ Smith (Manassas Park, VA: Impact Publications, 1994).

Government Job Finder, Daniel Lauber (River Forest, IL: Planning/Communications, 1994).

How to Get a Federal Job, David Waelde (Washington, DC: FEDHELP Publications, 1989).

How to Get a Federal Job, Krandall Kraus (New York: Facts on File, 1986).

Opportunities in Federal Government Careers, Neale Baxter (Northbrook, IL: National Textbook, 1992).

ACWA: Administrative Careers With America, Eve P. Steinberg (New York: Arco, 1991).

Book of U.S. Government Jobs, Dennis V. Damp (Moon Township, PA: D-Amp Publications, 1994).

Federal Jobs for College Graduates, Robert Goldenkoff and Dana Morgan (New York: Arco, 1991)

If you are particularly interested in federal law enforcement careers with agencies such as the FBI, CIA, NSA, DIA, the Drug Enforcement Agency, and related agencies, a good resource is John W. Warner, Jr. *Federal Jobs in Law Enforcement* (New York: Arco, 1992). For your convenience, all of these resources are available through Impact Publications.

Two excellent publications provide a wealth of information on the federal personnel system, particularly on employee benefits, labor-management relations, health and retirement systems, and promotions and transfers. Each of these volumes is updated annually:

Federal Employees' Almanac, Joseph Young (ed.). Send $9.95 (or $12.95 for first class) to: Federal Employee's Almanac, P.O. Box 7528, Falls Church, VA 22040.

Federal Personnel Guide. Send $9.95 ($12.95 for first class) to: Federal Personnel Guide, Key Communications Group, Inc., P.O. Box 42578, Washington, DC 20015. You can order by phone by calling 301/656-0450 or 301/656-2923.

Both organizations publishing these books also publish useful newsletters. Joseph Young's weekly *Federal Employees' News Digest* costs $49 for one year. Another weekly newsletter, the *Federal Personnel Weekly News Update*, is available on a subscription basis at $59 for one year. For further information and subscriptions to these two newsletters, write to:

Federal Employees' News Digest Inc.
P.O. Box 7528
Falls Church, VA 22040

FPG Weekly News Update
4350 East-West Highway
Bethesda, MD 20814

As noted previously, the federal government does not maintain a current listing of all jobs available in the federal government. Instead, two private firms—the Federal Research Service and Breakthrough Publications—track federal job vacancies and publish bi-weekly catalogs of job vacancies available throughout the government. These job listing services provide the most comprehensive collection of vacancies available anywhere. *Federal Career Opportunities* costs $7.95 per copy or $39 for 6 issues, $77 for 12 issues, or $175 for 26 issues. Most issues run about 64 pages and list 3400+ jobs at the GS-5 through Senior Executive Service, jobs abroad, application process and contact information, part-time and temporary positions, and "how to" articles on job hunting techniques. For information on this publication, write or call:

Federal Research Service, Inc.
P.O. Box 1059
Vienna, VA 22180
Tel. 703/281-0200

Another private firm publishes a similar bi-weekly listing of federal jobs as well as a *Federal Jobs Kit*. Each issue contains about 3,000 jobs for all professions and occupations, including blue-collar jobs. Subscription rates are $34 for six issues, $59 for 12 issues, and $125 for 25 issues. For further information, you can write or call their toll-free number:

Federal Jobs Digest
325 Pennsylvania Avenue, SE
Washington, DC 20003
Tel. 800/824-5000

You can also subscribe to both the *Federal Career Opportunities* and *Federal Jobs Digest* through Impact Publications by completing the subscription information in the resource section at the end of this book.

A weekly newspaper, *The Federal Times*, also lists federal job vacancies. Contact them at: The Federal Times, ATTN: Subscription, Springfield, VA 22159-0260, Tel. 703/750-9000. Other federal jobs will be listed in the classified and/or business sections of local newspapers.

Individuals seeking legal opportunities with federal agencies can subscribe to a special job listing service. The Federal Reports, Inc. publishes a monthly listing of attorney and law-related job opportunities in the federal government as well as with other public and private employers in Washington, DC throughout the United States and abroad.

Subscription rates for this publication are $34 for three months, $58 for six months, and $104 for one year. Write or call them at:

Federal Reports Inc.
1010 Vermont Ave., NW, Suite 408
Washington, DC 20005
Tel. 202/393-3311

You can also contact agency personnel offices directly to get information on vacancies. Many of these offices will send you copies of vacancy announcements. Several personnel offices also maintain a job hotline with a recorded message of vacancies.

Many federal government positions require passing a written examination for eligibility. Arco Publishing (Prentice-Hall) produces several self-study guides to help individuals prepare for various civil service examinations at all levels of government. Among the many titles relevant to federal employment are:

- *Air Traffic Controller Qualifying Test*
- *Bookkeeper-Account Clerk*
- *Civil Service Administrative Tests*
- *Civil Service Arithmetic and Vocabulary*
- *Civil Service Handbook*
- *Civil Service Psychological and Psychiatric Tests*
- *Civil Service Reading Comprehension Tests*
- *Civil Service Tests for Basic Skills Jobs*
- *Correction Officer*
- *Federal Clerk-Steno-typist*
- *General Test Practice of 101 U.S. Jobs*
- *How to Get a Clerical Job in Government*
- *Postal Exams Handbook*
- *Post Office Clerk-Carrier*
- *Rural Carrier—U.S. Postal Service*
- *Special Agent: Treasury Enforcement Agent*

Several useful publications are available in the reference section of your local library. These are primarily directories which provide an overview of the structure of the federal government as well as provide the names and addresses of key individuals within each agency. Among the most important directories are:

- *U.S. Government Manual*
- *Federal Staff Directory*
- *Federal Yellow Book*
- *Government Directory of Addresses and Telephone Numbers*
- *Taylor's Encyclopedia of Government Officials*

- *Washington Information Directory*
- *Directory of Federal Executives*
- *Washington 94: A Comprehensive Directory of the Key Institutions and Leaders of the National Capital Area*

The Office of Personnel Management and the U.S. Government Printing Office publish several informative brochures and books on federal personnel which you may wish to examine. You can purchase them directly from the Superintendent of Documents, U.S. Government Printing Office, Washington, DC 20402. If you write to them, also ask for their catalog of publications on government jobs and personnel. You may, for example, want to purchase a telephone directory for a particular agency that interests you. Remember, the U.S. Government Printing Office is the largest publisher, printer, and bookstore in the country. It produces a wealth of reports and useful guides on the various functions and agencies of government. And they are eager to sell their publications!

You should also write or call the personnel offices of the agency that interests you. Many of these offices have publications describing various jobs and careers. For example, the U.S. Immigration and Naturalization Service of the Department of Justice publishes a question and answer brochure on becoming a Border Patrol Agent. The brochure addresses the major concerns of most applicants: duties, qualifications, conditions of employment, written and medical examinations, appointments, training, uniforms, career advancement, benefits, and special retirement.

Another useful source of information on federal jobs are the numerous federal and postal employee unions and organizations. Names, addresses, and telephone numbers of these groups are found in the *Encyclopedia of Associations* and the *National Trade and Professional Associations*.

JOB FAIRS

During the past few years several federal agencies have joined together in sponsoring job fairs. Organized by private contractors, most of the fairs are designed to quickly recruit individuals for high turnover and hard-to-fill positions, such as clerical and high-tech positions. Since many federal agencies need to quickly recruit personnel in these areas, the job fair becomes a useful mechanism for bringing numerous candidates to their agencies for interviews and job offers.

Job fairs usually consist of 20 or more agencies that come together for one or two days to provide information on career opportunities and interview potential candidates for specific positions. Each agency usually has a booth where it provides literature on the agency as well as has personnel to meet with interested candidates to discuss career opportunities within the agency.

When conducting research with agencies, be sure to check to see if they are planning to participate in an upcoming job fair that relates to your particular interests and skills. Since most job fairs with federal agencies are for either clerical or scientific and technical positions, don't expect to find job fairs for other types of positions. If your skills match those of the job fairs, this is a good way to get an overview of several federal agencies that are recruiting for similar positions as well as to interview for specific positions. Indeed, it's the fastest way to get hired with the federal government. In some cases, you can literally be hired the same day you interview for a position at the job fair!

A NEW "REINVENTED" FEDERAL GOVERNMENT?

As we go to press, several ambitious federal government changes are either on the drawing board or being initiated by the Clinton Administration through the "reinventing government" efforts outlined in Vice President Al Gores highly publicized National Performance Review (NPR) of September 7, 1993. The laudable goal is to create a government that works better and costs less. In other words, this is another—some would say perennial—attempt to cut red tape in order to get a bigger bang for the buck. Many people are rightfully cynical about such efforts, since these reforms appear to be old wine in new bottles. At least the language for government appears new—"empowerment", "customer service", "market dynamics", and "reengineering". Reconstituted for government, this decade-old management jargon has been extensively used by large corporations in the private sector to "reinvent" themselves. When adapted to the public sector, this language is added to old tried-and-true bureaucratic reform concepts of decentralization, productivity, leadership, efficiency, effectiveness, and cutback management.

Like most such reports, the National Performance Review received a great deal of press coverage as key politicians stepped forward for photo opps and credits, shared red tape anecdotes amongst admiring listeners, and declared a new day for a "reinvented" federal government. While the NPR sounds good on paper, similar to most such highly publicized reform efforts, this one faces numerous implementation problems.

But let's assume for the moment that many of the 384 proposed recommendations for reinventing the federal government get through the mine field of special interests, Congress, and agencies, and several proposals do indeed get implemented. What implications these changes will have for future federal employment remains speculative. The newly revised goal for streamlining the federal bureaucracy over the next five years (by 1999) is to now downsize the workforce by at least 272,900—up from an initial goal of 252,000. Most of this shrinkage is aimed at middle management and personnel, procurement, and administrative staffs. Agencies have buyout authority to reduce their personnel; they can offer up to $25,000 to federal employees who decide to resign or retire early. Some departments, such as Defense, Agriculture, and Housing and

Urban Development, have already been on the chopping block and thus will continue to downsize and reorganize. While these three departments will not be hotbeds of hiring, the departments of Justice, Labor, Education, and Health and Human Services, should experience steady growth in personnel over the next five years.

In the meantime—and in the aggregate—the federal government will probably continue hiring about 1,000 new employees each day and thereby increase in size by an annual rate of less than 1 percent, despite any new reinventing and downsizing efforts. Federal budget increases will continue to out-pace personnel increases, which raises a curious question—Where have all the personnel gone? Probably gone to consulting firms both inside and outside the Washington Beltway. The highly publicized reinventing government initiatives do not encompass our consultants in Chapter 20—an interesting fact public employee unions have an irritating habit of reminding the NPR group and the press when it comes time to layoff federal employees. Focusing only on "reinventing government"—and thereby neglecting to incorporate such peripheral public players as contractors/consultants and nonprofit organizations in the reinventing equation—raises serious questions about the "vision" of this new group of government reformers. Are they, in reality, playing another shell game of downsizing some agencies, increasing personnel in other agencies, and contributing to the overall growth of contractors/consultants and nonprofit organizations that are major beneficiaries of federal largess?

Perhaps one unintended consequence of this new reinventing government movement is to actually accelerate the revolving door between government and the private sector. Downsizing federal agencies without downsizing federal spending doesn't make much mathematical sense. If history is any lesson, this reform, too, will pass.

But what is new relates to the federal application and hiring system. The decentralization of federal hiring continues as the Office of Personnel Management relinquishes more and more of its direct involvement in agency hiring. And a potential mine field awaits this new change.

GET READY FOR THE NEW FEDERAL APPLICATION AND HIRING SYSTEM

We hesitate to provide detailed information on federal employment applications, especially the Standard Form 171 (SF 171), since this uniform application will be changing after December 31, 1994. Rather than revise the form, the Office of Personnel Management is permitting it to expire altogether. In a continuing effort of the Office of Personnel Management to further decentralize hiring decisions to the agency level, OPM will permit agencies to develop their own application forms, accept resumes, and continue to accept the SF 171. The push is on to move toward simplified application forms and questionnaires that can be electronically scanned. In many respects, this is a radical departure for most federal agencies which have become accustomed to screening applicants via the more detailed and laborious SF 171.

While these new changes are ostensibly designed to make the application process easily for both applicants and agencies, in reality it will probably result in just the opposite. For individuals such changes mean they must complete a separate application form for each position rather than submit a standardized application form, such as the SF 171, to each agency. For agencies, the number of applicants for each position will likely increase dramatically but the quality of information provided for screening purposes will probably decrease.

To what degree individual agencies will develop their own application forms or accept resumes as a substitute for the SF 171 is anyone's guess as we go to press. Our best guess is that many agency personnel offices, current federal employees, and job applicants will be initially shocked to discover the SF 171 will no longer be required.

As the dust settles and the realities of screening candidates in a post-SF 171 era set in, we believe many agencies will continue accepting SF 171s and also permit the submission of resumes. But agencies most likely will place greater emphasis on a well-prepared SF 171 than on a highly generalized one- or two-page resume. After all, agency hiring authorities have become accustomed to thinking in SF 171 terms.

After December 31, 1994, please check with each agency to learn what application forms are required and if you are permitted to submit a resume in lieu of, or in addition to, the SF 171. This information should be spelled out in detail on each vacancy announcement. We suspect many agencies will tell you they will accept an SF 171 as well as a one or two-page resume. Such a resume will serve you well if you develop it as an "Executive Summary" for your SF 171. Agencies will still look favorably on a well-written SF 171 that incorporates much of the language and terminology as identified in Russ Smith's *The Right SF 171 Writer.*

We will outline in our third edition of *Find a Federal Job Fast!* the newly evolving application system and what new application forms are permitted after December 1994. Stay tuned for what could very well become a decentralized, free-for-all application and hiring system!

18

CAPITOL HILL AND THE JUDICIARY

While the number of employees in the legislative and judicial branches is relatively small compared to executive agencies, rewarding employment opportunities abound nonetheless. Many of the jobs lead to long-term careers within their respective branches of government. They also serve as important stepping stones for jobs in the executive branch as well as amongst numerous peripheral public institutions.

EMPLOYMENT LEVELS AND PROCEDURES

The federal legislative branch employs nearly 40,000 individuals; the federal judiciary employs nearly 26,000. While the largest number of individuals work for Congress (22,000), nearly 20,000 individuals work

HOUSE OF REPRESENTATIVES

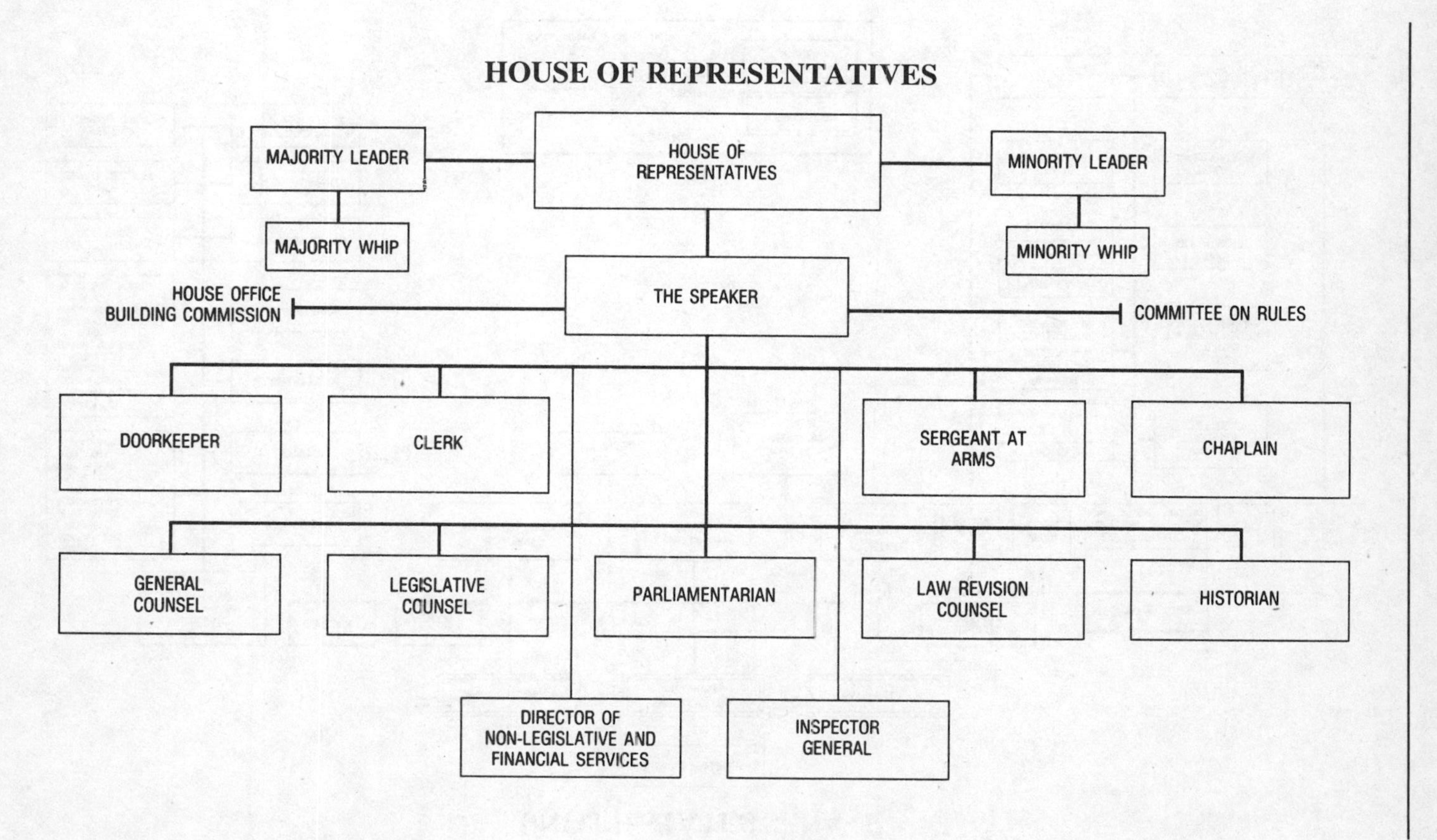

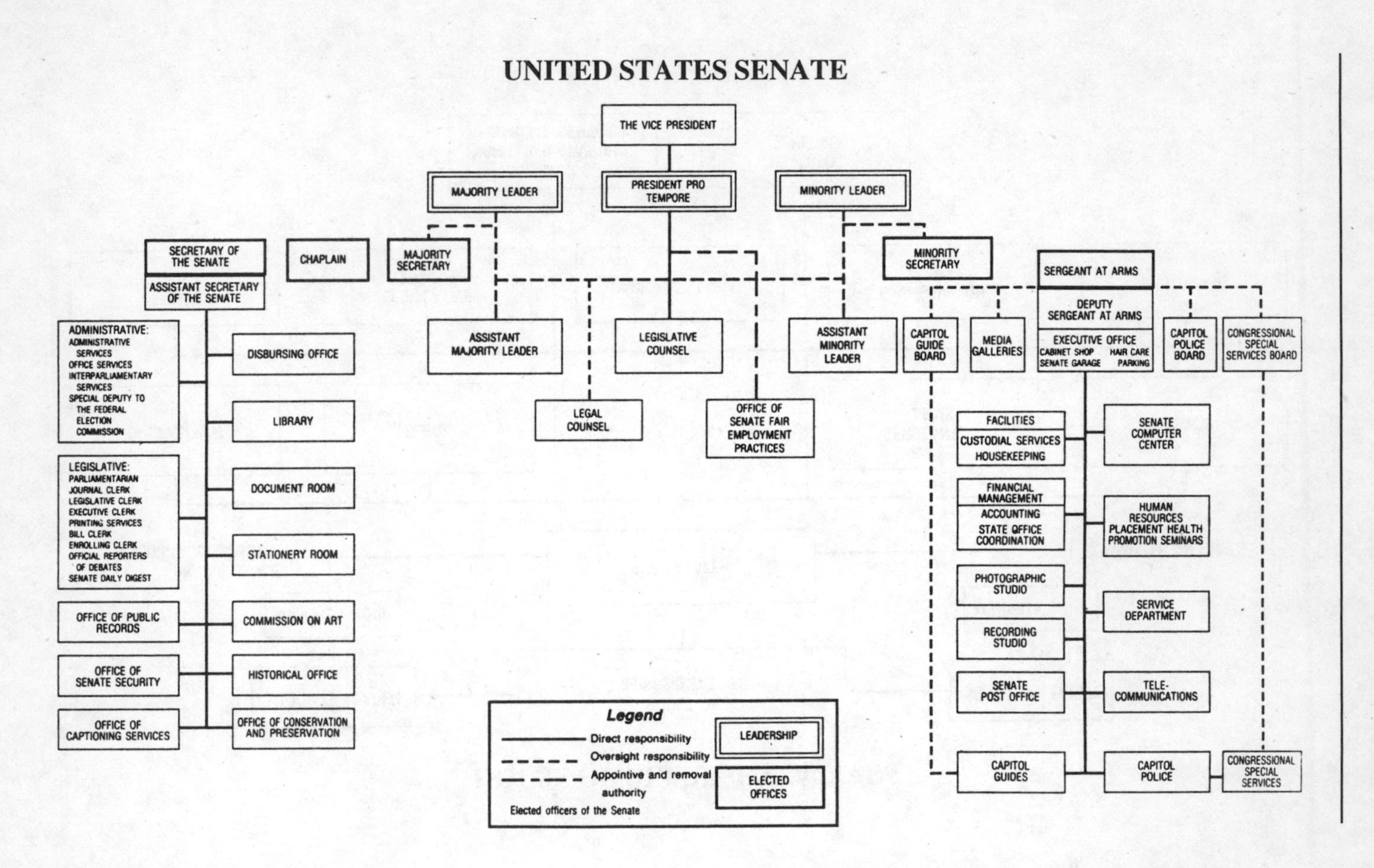
UNITED STATES SENATE
THE VICE PRESIDENT
MAJORITY LEADER
PRESIDENT PRO TEMPORE
MINORITY LEADER
SECRETARY OF THE SENATE
ASSISTANT SECRETARY OF THE SENATE
CHAPLAIN
MAJORITY SECRETARY
MINORITY SECRETARY
SERGEANT AT ARMS
DEPUTY SERGEANT AT ARMS
EXECUTIVE OFFICE
CABINET SHOP
HAIR CARE
SENATE GARAGE
PARKING
ASSISTANT MAJORITY LEADER
LEGISLATIVE COUNSEL
ASSISTANT MINORITY LEADER
CAPITOL GUIDE BOARD
MEDIA GALLERIES
CAPITOL POLICE BOARD
CONGRESSIONAL SPECIAL SERVICES BOARD
LEGAL COUNSEL
OFFICE OF SENATE FAIR EMPLOYMENT PRACTICES
ADMINISTRATIVE:
ADMINISTRATIVE SERVICES
OFFICE SERVICES
INTERPARLIAMENTARY SERVICES
SPECIAL DEPUTY TO THE FEDERAL ELECTION COMMISSION
LEGISLATIVE:
PARLIAMENTARIAN
JOURNAL CLERK
LEGISLATIVE CLERK
EXECUTIVE CLERK
PRINTING SERVICES
BILL CLERK
ENROLLING CLERK
OFFICIAL REPORTERS OF DEBATES
SENATE DAILY DIGEST
OFFICE OF PUBLIC RECORDS
OFFICE OF SENATE SECURITY
OFFICE OF CAPTIONING SERVICES
DISBURSING OFFICE
LIBRARY
DOCUMENT ROOM
STATIONERY ROOM
COMMISSION ON ART
HISTORICAL OFFICE
OFFICE OF CONSERVATION AND PRESERVATION
FACILITIES
CUSTODIAL SERVICES
HOUSEKEEPING
FINANCIAL MANAGEMENT
ACCOUNTING
STATE OFFICE COORDINATION
PHOTOGRAPHIC STUDIO
RECORDING STUDIO
SENATE POST OFFICE
CAPITOL GUIDES
SENATE COMPUTER CENTER
HUMAN RESOURCES
PLACEMENT HEALTH
PROMOTION SEMINARS
SERVICE DEPARTMENT
TELE-COMMUNICATIONS
CAPITOL POLICE
CONGRESSIONAL SPECIAL SERVICES
Legend
Direct responsibility
Oversight responsibility
Appointive and removal authority
Elected officers of the Senate
LEADERSHIP
ELECTED OFFICES

for four legislative agencies: Architect of the Capitol (2,316), General Accounting Office (5,391), Government Printing Office (5,058), and the Library of Congress (4,880). Other legislative agencies include the Congressional Budget Office (219), Office of Technology Assessment (193), U.S. Botanic Gardens (58), and the Copyright Royalty Tribunal (7). The Supreme Court employs 343, but the remaining federal courts employ 25,392 individuals. In fact, the federal court system is one of the fastest growing areas of government, increasing by 76.2 percent since 1980 (from 14,404 to 25,392 employees).

Legislative agencies generally follow similar formal recruitment procedures as executive agencies: position announcements, application forms, testing, eligibility lists, and interviews. However, being constitutionally separate from the executive branch, the legislative branch sets its own rules and regulations for recruitment and selection. While most executive agencies classify their positions according to the General Schedule and use OPM for determining eligibility and screening candidates, each legislative agency develops its own recruitment procedures separate from the GS Schedule and OPM operations. Furthermore, Congress uses its own recruitment procedures which are less structured and more personal in nature than recruitment in either executive or legislative agencies. The federal judiciary, however, is less structured; its hiring practices tend to follow a more personal approach commonly associated with jobs and careers in the legal profession.

This chapter outlines the basic principles for acquiring a job in two of the most overlooked areas of the federal government—the legislative and judicial branches. It examines legislative agencies, congressional organizations, the Supreme Court, U.S. Courts, and supporting organizations.

LEGISLATIVE AGENCIES

The legislative branch maintains its own bureaucracy to perform general housekeeping functions (Architect of the Capitol), provide information for decision-making and dissemination purposes (Library of Congress and Government Printing Office), and check the financial operations of executive agencies (General Accounting Office). Legislative agencies are relatively small in terms of personnel and budgets, but they offer numerous opportunities for enterprising job seekers.

Functions

The **General Accounting Office** (5,391 employees) performs important congressional oversight functions. It conducts audits of federal agencies and issues reports on how to improve the efficiency and effectiveness of government. It checks to what degree agencies have spent funds allocated by Congress. In so doing, it employs hundreds of individuals with specialties in accounting, economics, and operations research.

The **Library of Congress** (4,880 employees) is Congresses' information arm as well as the nation's largest and most comprehensive library. It employs hundreds of librarians and subject matter specialists. The Congressional Research Service, for example, is organized to provide congressional committees with information as well as conduct specialized studies. The Federal Research Division is Congresses' equivalent to the CIA and the Defense Intelligence Agency.

The **Government Printing Office** (5,058 employees) is the government's central printer and bookstore. It daily prints all major documents, such as the *Congressional Record* and the *Federal Register*, as well as pamphlets, magazines, reports, directories, and books commissioned by individual agencies.

The **Congressional Budget Office** (219 employees) provides Congress with budgetary data, analyzes fiscal alternatives, conducts budgetary studies, and forecasts government spending. This office provides an important congressional check to similar functions performed by the Office of Management and Budget in the Executive Office of the President.

The **Architect of the Capitol** (2,303 employees) is responsible for the maintenance of all congressional buildings and grounds.

The **United States Botanic Garden** (58 employees) collects, cultivates, and grows a large variety of plants for public exhibitions. It provides facilities for educational groups interested in the botanic garden.

The **Office of Technology Assessment** (193 employees) is one of the newest legislative agencies, founded in 1974. Its major role is to help Congress respond to the use of new technologies in society.

The **Copyright Royalty Tribunal** is the newest and smallest of the legislative agencies. Formed in 1976, its seven members determine the adjustment of copyright royalty rates for records, jukeboxes, and certain cable television transmissions.

Recruitment

Each legislative agency recruits its own personnel. Consequently, you will need to contact each agency to learn their particular procedures for announcing vacancies and selecting personnel. For example, the **General Accounting Office** issues vacancy announcements through its Office of Recruitment (202/275-6092). In addition, this office maintains a daily recorded message of job vacancies (202/275-6017).

The **Library of Congress** issues position vacancy announcements. If you want information on specific position vacancies, you can call the Recruitment and Placement Office at 202/707-5633 or 202/707-5620. This is also the Human Resources Office. You can also walk into this office between the hours of 8:30am and 4:30pm, Monday through Friday, to get copies of current vacancy announcements (Room LM-108, 101 Independence Avenue, SE, Washington, DC). The Employment Office also has information on job vacancies and conducts testing for clerical and typing positions. They will send you copies of their blue vacancy announcements upon request (Tel. 202/707-5627). This office maintains a recorded message explaining the general information on the application and testing procedures for the Library of Congress. You can access this message by calling 202/707-5295. The **Congressional Research Service** also has information on employment opportunities. You can either visit their Administration Office in Room 208 of the James Madison Building to review job vacancy announcements with the CRS or call them for information at 202/707-8823. We have had problems getting correct telephone numbers with the Library of Congress. If you do, call their operator at 202/707-5000 or report your problem to their Phone Repair Service at 202/707-7727.

The **Government Printing Office** has experienced an 11 percent cut in personnel since 1980 and often operates under hiring freezes. While they used to have a recording of daily vacancies, this service has been discontinued. Contact the Employment Branch (202/275-2951) for information on vacancies. You can also visit their office to review vacancy announcements: Government Printing Office, Room C106, North Capital and H Streets, Washington, DC).

The **Congressional Budget Office** provides job vacancy information by telephone (202/226-2621) or by visiting their Personnel and Security Office (House Annex 2, Room H2-493, Second and D Streets, SW, Washington, DC).

The **U.S. Botanic Garden** recruits its personnel through the Personnel Office of the Architect of the Capitol. Contact this office for vacancy announcements for both offices by calling 202/225-1231. You can also visit their office in Washington, DC to survey job vacancy announcements and ask questions about the employment process: Rooms 290-294, Second and D Streets SW.

The **Office of Technology Assessment** normally collects resumes for individuals who are interested in working in this office. You can call their Personnel Office at 202/224-8713 for job vacancy information. However, they do not encourage walk-ins since they don't maintain job vacancy announcements like many larger agencies. Better still, they encourage you to send them a resume and cover letter at any time. This office normally circulates resumes among staff members and keeps them on file for one year.

The **Copyright Royalty Tribunal** is so small and specialized that it virtually has no job vacancies. While it is supposed to have five appointed commissioners, five confidential assistants, and one General Council, at present it only has three commissioners, three assistants, and a General Council. The only opportunities available are with the Volunteer Law Clerk Program—nonpaid internships for law students—in the Washington, DC Metro area.

Your best job search strategy with these legislative agencies will be to contact the personnel offices for job vacancy information, complete any application forms required, submit your resume, and make informal contacts with key agency personnel. Follow the same procedures we outlined for the informal job search process in executive agencies.

The relatively unstructured and highly personal nature of the congressional hiring process requires knocking on doors, making personal contacts, and networking for jobs.

CAPITOL HILL

Finding a job with Congress requires an intimate knowledge of the congressional hiring process. Both the House and Senate maintain placement offices to primarily collect resumes. But the relatively unstructured and highly personal nature of the congressional hiring process requires knocking on doors, making personal contacts, and networking for jobs. This can involve anything from roaming the halls of the Dirksen and Hart Senate Office Buildings and the Cannon and Longworth House Office Buildings; contacting the Administrative Assistant and asking up front if he or she has any staff openings at present for someone with your qualifications; or networking for information, advice, and job leads by getting to know staffers who hang out at the local eating and drinking establishments, such as Hawk n' Dove, Bullfeathers, Tune Inn, Tortilla Coast, Irish Times, and Dublin as well as many bars and restaurants in Union Station and along Massachusetts Avenue.

However, before launching into such cold-calling and networking campaigns for penetrating the employment scene on Capitol Hill, you must understand the structure of Congress and the various opportunities available. For, in the end, job hunting with Congress involves 535 personal staffs and over 300 committees and subcommittees which have their own hiring practices and salary structures. In this sense, Congress consists of over 835 separate hiring systems!

Congressional work is not for everyone. Each year approximately 40 percent of all congressional employees leave for other work. While much of the work is interesting and challenging, for many people it is stressful and financially unrewarding. Few people make congressional work a career. For many, it is an important *stepping stone* to other types of public service work. Yet, this high turnover rate provides numerous opportunities for enterprising job seekers who wish to get some "Hill" experience before moving on to greener employment pastures.

Personal Staffs

Most congressional job opportunities are with personal staffs or committee staffs. There are 535 personal staffs—one for each member of Congress (100 in the Senate and 435 in the House of Representatives). Each of these staffs are divided into Washington-based staffs and home-district staffs. The normal Washington staff consists of 18 full-time and four part-time employees cramped into four to six small offices in the Russell Senate, Dirkson Senate, Rayburn House, Longworth House, or Cannon House Buildings as well as in Senate and House Annex buildings. The home-district offices are relatively small. They are usually staffed by political loyalists who are primarily oriented toward maintaining a positive image and promoting the re-election of their bosses. In the process of doing this, they respond to a great deal of constituent and interest group pressures.

The Washington-based personal staffs are organized to perform several functions for representatives. Research and subject matter specialists work closely with the Representative in the legislative arena. They follow legislation, conduct research, and draft bills. Other members of the staff function as ombudsmen, responding primarily to constituent inquiries and interest groups. And still others specialize in promoting the present image and future reelection of their boss and performing general housekeeping functions. An experienced Administrative Assistant, or AA, heads this staff.

Many personal staffs operate similar to boiler-room operations. Office space is extremely limited, work loads are unrealistic, most jobs are understaffed, and much of the work is reactive in nature. Little time is available for long-term planning and thoughtful analysis. A management study of congressional staffs conducted by the Congressional Management Foundation, for example, found congressional staffs in the following situation:

- Congressional workloads have grown dramatically during the past two decades:

- A 2000% increase in constituent mail between 1970 and 1980; volume of mail from constituents increased from 14.6 million to 300 million letters.

- An increase in bills introduced from 7,611 in the 84th Congress to 14,594 in the 96th.

- An increase in roll-call votes from 147 in the 84th Congress to 1,834 in the 96th.
- A 100% increase in both constituent casework and congressional hearings in this period—members' casework for constituents doubled to 10,000 cases per year.
- 60% of staff time is devoted to answering mail.
- The average congressional staffer is limited to 30 square feet of working space—compared to 64 square feet in the private sector.
- Congressional offices are extremely noisy, crowded with paper and files, and subject to occasional electrical failures.
- Average staff salaries are less than those with Federal executive agencies and in the private sector.

Given the nature of the work, working conditions, and salaries, no wonder there is a 40 percent turnover rate each year! Indeed, in the same study, 24 percent of congressional offices said they had difficulty in recruiting qualified staff members with Hill experience.

The Washington personal staffs are comprised of different types of individuals who perform various legislative and administrative-management functions. The figure on page 307 outlines the typical hierarchical structure of these personal staffs. The exact titles of staff members will vary from office to office. For example, a "Secretary" may sometimes be called a "Personal Aide" or a "Legislative Assistant" is called "Personal Staff".

The Congressional Management Foundation regularly monitors congressional staff positions, issues position descriptions, and conducts biannual salary studies. Major congressional staff positions and salary information for 1992 in the House of Representatives and for 1993 in the Senate include the following:

- **Administrative Assistant/Executive Assistant (AA):** The key staff person who is responsible for overall office functions, supervision of projects, district and Hill politics and personnel. Salary ranges: $55,000-$125,000. Average salaries: $98,316, Senate; $76,349, House.
- **Legislative Director (LD):** Directs legislative program or manages the Member's committee work, including committee prep work for hearings, witnesses, testimony, and legislative proposals, as well as general issues, oversights, and initiatives, floor work, and much more. Salary range: $30,000-$95,000.

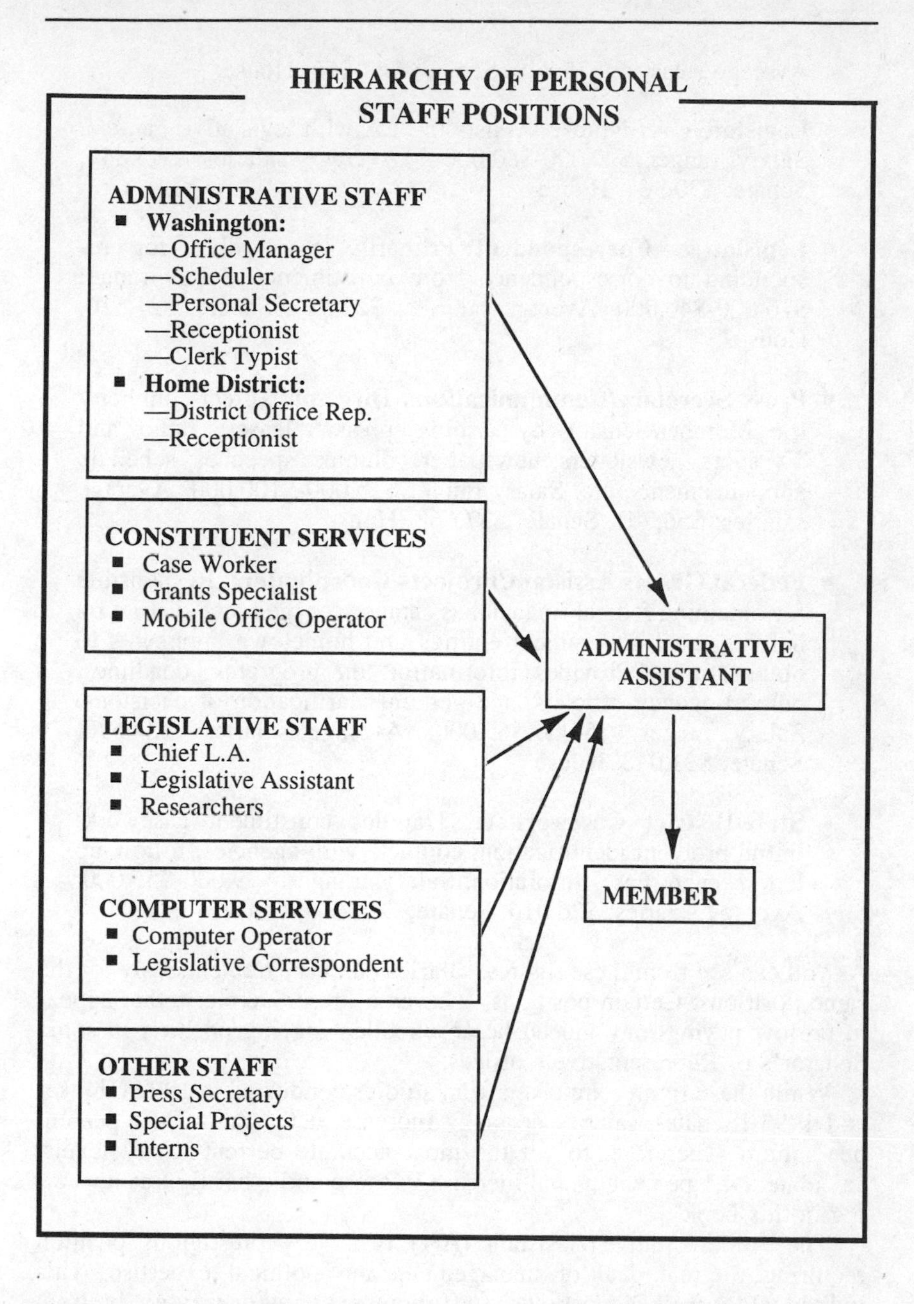

SOURCE: Kerry Dumbaugh and Gary Serota, *Capitol Jobs* (Washington, D.C; Tilden Press, 1982), p. 47.

Average salaries: $75,848, Senate; $47,866, House.

- **Legislative Assistant:** Assists the LA with legislative matters. Salary range: $20,000-$80,000+. Average salaries: $75,848, Senate; $30,364, House.

- **Legislative Correspondent:** Primarily responsible for responding to correspondence from constituents. Salary range: $10,000-$40,000. Average salaries: $22,511, Senate; $21,516, House.

- **Press Secretary/Communications Director:** Directs publicity for Member/Senator by issuing press releases, radio and TV spots, newsletters, newspaper columns, speeches, schedule announcements, etc. Salary range: $15,000-$100,000. Average salaries: $56,701, Senate; $37,668, House.

- **Federal Grants Assistant/Projects Coordinator:** Responsible for obtaining federal financial assistance for the home district by helping local government entities and hometown applicants to obtain funds. Provides information on programs, deadlines, helpful agency officials, and general clarification of decisions. Salary ranges: $5,000-$65,000. Average salaries: $34,570, Senate; $31,048, House.

- **State/District Caseworker:** Handles constituent casework: initial problem identification, contacts with agencies, follow-up letters, and case resolution. Salary ranges: $9,000-$55,000. Average salaries: $26,016, Senate; $24,416, House.

As you can see from these figures, salaries can vary tremendously for the same positions. Certain positions, such as a Press Secretary, that appear to be low paying may indeed be an excellent paying position in some Senator's or Representative's offices.

While these figures are taken from studies conducted in 1992 (House) and 1993 (Senate), salaries normally increase at the rate of 4.1 percent per annum. Therefore, to get the most accurate current salary levels, calculate a 4.1 percent annual increase in these and other figures appearing in this book.

The Administrative Assistant (AA) is a very prestigious position requiring a great deal of management and political expertise. This individual, as well as most other staff members, may or may not be from the Representative's district or Senator's state. Rather, staff members tend to be hired on the basis of their legislative expertise and political skills in Washington rather than on their loyalty to the district back home. The most important expertise involves the ability to conduct research, analyze, write, communicate, organize, meet deadlines, and work under extreme pressure. Writing is one of the most highly valued skills. You can quickly acquire subject matter expertise if you already possess these communication skills.

Salaries for full-time Senate and House employees range from $5,000 to $80,000 a year. According to 1992 House and 1993 Senate salary surveys conducted by the Congressional Management Foundation, the average Senate salary was $36,844—just below (2.4 percent) the average white-collar employee in federal agencies at $37,718. However, this salary gap widens when comparing Senate salaries to salaries of white-collar federal employees in Washington—Senate salaries are 20 percent below the average Washington salaries ($46,783). The average House salary for 1992 was $33,388. If you can believe the President's Commission on Federal Pay, these House salaries lagged 37 percent below comparable white-collar positions in the private sector.

However, such salary comparisons can lead to false conclusions since they leave out important information on tenure and seniority—key factors affecting salary averages. While the average federal employee has over 14 years of federal government experience, over 60 percent of House and Senate staffers have been in their positions for two years or less. Except for the Administrative Assistants, Legislative Directors, and Office Managers, as a whole this is a relatively young, inexperienced group essentially occupying entry-level positions. Considering their experience levels, they are probably well compensated.

The following table summarizes thc normal ranges and average salaries for various congressional staff positions:

SALARY AVERAGES FOR CONGRESSIONAL STAFF POSITIONS, 1992-93

POSITION	HOUSE	SENATE
■ Administrative Assistant	$76,349	$98,316
■ District Director	$48,642	N/A
■ Legislative Director	$47,866	$75,848
■ General/Counsel	N/A	$67,852
■ Washington Caseworker	N/A	$39,587
■ Press Secretary/ Communications Director	$37,668	$56,701
■ Office Manager/ Administrative Director	$35,825	$45,239
■ Executive Assistant/ Personal Secretary/Scheduler	$34,155	$48,502
■ Federal Grants/Projects Director Projects Coordinator	$31,048	$34,570
■ Systems Administrator	N/A	$33,870
■ Legislative Assistant	$30,364	$45,057
■ Appointments Secretary/ Scheduler	$26,358	$35,237

▪ Computer Operator/ CMS Specialist	$25,716	$25,244
▪ Systems/Mail Manager/ Correspondence Director	$25,716	$28,834
▪ Washington Office Assistant	N/A	$23,318
▪ Legislative Correspondent	$21,516	$22,411
▪ Office Secretary/Clerk	$20,965	N/A
▪ Receptionist	$20,813	$20,107
▪ Correspondence Assistance/ Mail Room Staffer	$19,640	N/A

State/District Positions

▪ District Aide/Field Rep.	$29,609	N/A
▪ District Caseworker	$24,416	N/A
▪ State Director	N/A	$65,913
▪ Regional Director	N/A	$39,243
▪ Field Representative	N/A	$30,600
▪ State Caseworker	N/A	$26,016

The Congressional Management Foundation study also found that congressional staff benefits vary considerably from office to office as well as compared to federal executive agencies and companies in the private sector. Nine out of ten Senate offices but less than 50 percent of House offices give their employees automatic Cost of Living Adjustments (COLA's). Merit raise systems operate in only 41 percent of Senate offices but in 77 percent of House offices. Most employees receive at least 2-3 weeks vacation, and 54 percent of these offices provide additional vacation time for staff members who have worked in their offices for three years or more. Only 45 percent of these offices have a sick-leave policy, but 60 percent of the offices allow at least six weeks of paid maternity leave. Written staff policies are found in 64 percent of the congressional offices.

Getting a job on a Senator's or Representative's personal staff requires a great deal of persistence, perseverance, and luck. While there is a high turnover rate, there also is high competition for these staff positions. Some offices will receive 1,000 resumes for a single vacancy. They regularly receive unsolicited resumes from job seekers who "shotgun" Capitol Hill with their paper qualifications. Many individuals wish to work for a particular Representative and thus they continually monitor staff vacancies in one office. Others are eager to work anywhere on the "Hill" so they can get experience to strengthen their resume and make important contacts.

While there are several congressional placement services available to help job seekers circulate their resumes, your best job search strategy will be to make personal contacts with key people on the Hill. You must plug into the word-of-mouth networks. The key person you need to know—the one who normally has the power to hire—is the Administrative

Assistant. Above all, research individual staff offices to identify impending vacancies and to determine who has the power to hire. The high turnover rate on Capitol Hill virtually assures that hiring will be done on ad hoc, emergency bases. The more you can get into the networks to let people know about your interests, skills, abilities, and availability, the better your chances of getting a job.

If you don't know someone to start networking on Capitol Hill, at least call your Representative. His or her staff should, as a courtesy to a constituent, get you started by providing you with useful advice on how to initiate a "Capitol Hill" search. They may give you names of people to talk to and review your resume for future reference. At the same time, you can use the "cold turkey" approach: call a Representative's office and pointblank ask "Who makes the hiring decisions in this office?" Once you get this information, try to get an appointment to see this person. If you can't get an appointment, try someone else on the staff who will at least give you information and job leads.

The high turnover rate on Capitol Hill virtually assures that hiring will be done on ad hoc, emergency bases.

Since you do not have to be from a Representative's district to get a personal staff job, 535 personal staffs offer similar job opportunities for you. Given the lack of a central personnel office for these staff positions, your most effective job search strategy will involve networking. You must contact individual offices to identify job vacancies and advertise your qualifications. The Washington-based positions are biased toward individuals who are physically present in Washington and who can make the necessary networking telephone calls and personal visits.

Your job search will go much easier if you know someone who knows a Representative. This person, in turn, can give you an introduction and recommendation. Using this contact, you can call a Representative's office and ask to speak to the AA or his or her assistant. You want to conduct several informational and referral interviews. Mention that Mr. or Ms. Smith "recommended that I contact you concerning possible staff vacancies on Capitol Hill". Ask for an appointment to discuss your interests. Be sure to make this a general request for information rather than ask for a job on the AA's staff. Chances are there are no vacancies at present, but the AA and other staff members often know about vacancies on others' staffs. When a vacancy does arise, it is frequently filled through word-of-mouth referrals. If you happen to be in the right place at the right time, you may be considered for the position.

Since the job search on Capitol Hill primarily involves networking, it will take time, and you can expect numerous deadends and rejections. However, you must continue networking until your timing is right in relation to unexpected vacancies. Remember, competition for Capitol Hill positions is very keen. When you land a job, most likely it will occur unexpectedly because the whole hiring process is somewhat chaotic and unpredictable.

Committee Staff

The bulk of Congresses' work is done through various committees: standing, select, joint, and ad hoc. Standing committees are permanent committees with full time professional staffs. These staff members conduct research, write reports, and draft legislation for committee members. The committees also are subdivided into subcommittees which have their own staffs. Altogether, there are more than 300 committees and subcommittees in both the House and Senate. Some of the major committees and subcommittees operating in the House for the 103rd Congress (1993-1994) include:

AGRICULTURE
- Department Operations and Nutrition
- Environment, Credit, and Rural Development
- Foreign Agriculture and Hunger
- General Farm Commodities
- Livestock
- Specialty Crops and Natural Resources

APPROPRIATIONS
- Agriculture, Rural Development, Food and Drug Administration
- Commerce, Justice, State, and Judiciary
- Defense
- District of Columbia
- Energy and Water Development
- Foreign Operations, Export Financing, and Related Programs
- Interior
- Labor, Health and Human Services, and Education
- Legislation
- Military Construction
- Transportation
- Treasury, Postal Service, and General Government
- VA, HUD, and Independent Agencies

ARMED SERVICES
- Military Acquisition
- Military Forces and Personnel
- Military Installations and Facilities

- Oversight and Investigations
- Readiness
- Research and Technology

BANKING, FINANCE, AND URBAN AfFAIRS
- Consumer Credit and Insurance
- Economic Growth and Credit Formation
- Financial Institutions Supervision, Regulations and Deposit Insurance
- General Oversight, Investigations, and the Resolution of Failed Financial Institutions
- Housing and Community Development
- International Development, Finance, Trade, and Monetary Policy

BUDGET (Task Forces rather than Subcommittees)
- Budget Process
- Community and Natural Resources
- Defense and International Affairs
- Economic Policy
- Health
- Human Services
- Income Security
- State and Local Government

DISTRICT OF COLUMBIA
- Fiscal Affairs and Health
- Government Operations and Metropolitan Affairs
- Judiciary and Education

EDUCATION AND LABOR
- Elementary, Secondary, and Vocational Education
- Human Resources
- Labor-Management Relations
- Labor Standards, Occupational Health, and Safety
- Postsecondary Education and Training
- Select Education and Civil Rights

ENERGY AND COMMERCE
- Commerce, Consumer Protection, and Competitiveness
- Energy and Power
- Health and the Environment
- Oversight and Investigations
- Telecommunications and Finance
- Transportation and Hazardous Materials

FOREIGN AFFAIRS
- Africa
- Asia and the Pacific
- Economic Policy, Trade, and Environment
- Europe and the Middle East
- International Operations
- International Security, International Organizations, and Human Rights

- Western Hemisphere Affairs

GOVERNMENT OPERATIONS
- Commerce, Consumer, and Monetary Affairs
- Employment, Housing, and Aviation
- Environment, Energy, and Natural Resources
- Human Resources and Intergovernmental Relations
- Legislation and National Security

HOUSE ADMINISTRATION
- Accounts
- Administrative Oversight
- Elections
- Libraries and Memorials
- Office Systems
- Personnel and Police

JUDICIARY
- International Law and Governmental Relations
- Civil and Constitutional Rights
- Crime and Criminal Justice
- Economic and Commercial Law
- International Law, Immigration, and Refugees

MERCHANT MARINE AND FISHERIES
- Coast Guard and Navigation
- Environment and Natural Resources
- Fisheries Management
- Merchant Marine
- Oceanography, Gulf of Mexico, and the Outer Continental Shelf

NATURAL RESOURCES
- Energy and Mineral Resources
- Insular and International Affairs
- National Parks, Forests, and Public Lands
- Native American Affairs
- Oversight and Investigations

POST OFFICE AND CIVIL SERVICE
- Census, Statistics, and Postal Personnel
- Civil Service
- Compensation and Employee Benefits
- Oversight and Investigations
- Postal Operations and Services

PUBLIC WORKS AND TRANSPORTATION
- Aviation
- Economic Development
- Investigations and Oversight
- Public Buildings and Grounds
- Surface Transportation
- Water Resources and Environment

RULES
- Rules of the House
- The Legislative Process

SCIENCE, SPACE, AND TECHNOLOGY
- Energy
- Investigations and Oversight
- Technology, Environment, and Aviation
- Science

SMALL BUSINESS
- Minority Enterprise, Finance, and Urban Development
- Procurement, Taxation, and Tourism
- Regulation, Business Opportunities, and Technology
- Rural Enterprises, Exports, and the Environment
- SBA Legislation and the General Economy

STANDARDS OF OFFICIAL CONDUCT (no subcommittees)

VETERANS' AFFAIRS
- Compensation, Pension, and Insurance
- Education, Training and Employment
- Hospitals and Health Care
- Housing and Memorial Affairs
- Oversight and Investigations

WAYS AND MEANS
- Health
- Oversight
- Select Revenue Measures
- Social Security
- Trade

The Senate has similar committees, subcommittees, and task forces. Most are counterparts to the House organizations.

The House and Senate also operate several Select and Special committees, Joint Committees with the Senate, and a variety of Boards, Commissions, and Advisory Organizations; many have their own staffs as well as functioning subcommittees:

House Select and Special Committees

- Democratic Congressional Campaign Committee
- Democratic Steering and Policy Committee
- National Republican Congressional Committee
- Permanent Select Committee on Intelligence
- Republican Policy Committee

Joint Committees

- Joint Committee of Congress on the Library
- Joint Committee on Printing

- Joint Committee on Taxation
- Joint Committee on the Organization of Congress
- Joint Economic Committee

Boards

- Board for International Broadcasting
- Board of Visitors to the Air Force Academy
- Board of Visitors to the Coast Guard Academy
- Board of Visitors to the Merchant Marine Academy
- Board of Visitors to the Military Academy
- Board of Visitors to the Naval Academy
- Congressional Award
- House of Representatives Page Board

Commissions

- Canada-United States Interparliamentary Group
- Commission on Security and Cooperation in Europe
- Commission on the Bicentennial of the Senate
- Commission on the West Central Front of the United States Capitol
- European Parliament-U.S. Congress Meeting Group
- Franklin Delano Roosevelt Memorial Commission
- House Commission on Congressional Mailing Standards
- House Office Building Commission
- Japan-United States Friendship Commission
- Martin Luther King, Jr., Federal Holiday Commission
- Mexico-United States Interparliamentary Group
- Migratory Bird Conservation Commission
- National Commission for Employment Policy
- North Atlantic Assembly
- Permanent Committee for the Oliver Wendell Holmes Devise Fund
- Senate Arms Control Observer Group
- Senate Central American Negotiations Observer Group
- Senate Office Building Commission
- The Interparliamentary Union
- U.S. Capitol Preservation Commission
- U.S. Senate Commission on Art

Advisory Organizations

- Arms Control and Foreign Policy Caucus
- California Democratic Congressional Delegation
- Congressional Arts Caucus
- Congressional Automotive Caucus
- Congressional Black Caucus
- Congressional Border Caucus
- Congressional Caucus for Women's Issues
- Congressional Clearinghouse on the Future
- Congressional Club
- Congressional Hispanic Caucus
- Congressional Human Rights Caucus
- Congressional Populist Caucus

- Congressional Rural Caucus
- Congressional Space Caucus
- Congressional Steel Caucus
- Congressional Sunbelt Caucus
- Congressional Textile Caucus
- Democratic Study Group
- Environmental and Energy Study Conference
- Export Task Force
- Federal Government Service Task Force
- House Wednesday Group
- New York State Congressional Delegation
- Northeast-Midwest Congressional Coalition
- Pennsylvania Congressional Delegation
- President's Committee on Mental Retardation
- President's Export Council
- Republican Study Committee
- Senate Caucus on International Narcotics Control
- U.S. Association of Former Members of Congress
- U.S. Capitol Historical Society
- U.S. Congressional Travel and Tourism Caucus
- U.S. House of Representatives Find Arts Board

Committee and subcommittee work is both interesting and hectic. Many staff members receive a great deal of job satisfaction because they help formulate important legislation. At the same time, these jobs involve long hours attendant with unrealistic work loads and deadlines.

Since each committee and subcommittee focuses on a particular policy area, many of these professional positions require highly qualified subject matter specialists. While many members of personal staffs are young and inexperienced generalists, in contrast, committee and subcommittee staff members tend to be older and experienced specialists. Committee and subcommittee staff positions also tend to pay better than personal staff positions.

Similar to finding a job on a personal staff, getting a job on a committee or subcommittee staff requires a great deal of networking, persistence, and perseverance. There are no formal hiring procedures, and hiring practices will differ from one committee to another. Therefore, you need to do a great deal of research on each committee and subcommittee in determining the best job search strategies.

Professionalism, along with politics, play key roles in getting committee and subcommittee positions. The most important hiring individual is the Chair of the committee or subcommittee. If the Chair is a Democrat, the committee and subcommittee staff members will most likely be Democrats. If the chair shifts from a Democrat to a Republican, the staff too will change. Therefore, entry into these positions begins with the Chair of the committee or subcommittee.

When conducting a job search with these committees and subcommittees, it is best to start with the committee or subcommittee chairperson's AA. This individual usually will be responsible for staffing his or her bosses' committee or subcommittee. Use a similar networking approach as you would use in landing a personal staff position. Research the committee or subcommittee, try to get a contact to the Chair, contact the AA for an informational interview, and request information, advice, and referrals to this Senator's or Representative's committees or subcommittees. If you have sufficient subject matter expertise, are persistent, and indicate a political preference, you will be in a strong position for landing one of these jobs.

Professionalism, along with politics, play key roles in getting committee and subcommittee positions.

Changing the Guard

One of the best times to conduct a "Capitol Hill" job search is immediately following a congressional election. Indeed, given the relatively high turnover rates of House and Senate members these days, job opportunities on Capitol Hill are numerous. Newly elected members need to quickly form a staff in Washington. Should House and Senate majority control shift from one political party to another, numerous job vacancies will arise in the various committee and subcommittees. If you closely monitor congressional elections and identify newly elected members, you will locate individuals who have immediate staffing needs. Although they will bring a few of their district-level campaign workers and loyalists to Washington for key staff positions, they must recruit other staffers from among the pool of applicants based in Washington.

Your best strategy is to call the newly elected Senator's or Representative's office as soon as you learn he or she has been elected. Your goal should be to arrange an interview rather than send a resume. After all, the Senator or Representative may receive hundreds of unsolicited resumes from past and present Capitol Hill staffers who are either losing their jobs because of election defeat or are looking for greener, and less stressful, pastures.

USEFUL RESOURCES

Several useful resources are available to guide you through the congressional maze. You should begin by reading a wonderful insider's guide to finding a job on Capitol Hill:

Capitol Hill: An Insider's Guide to Finding a Job in Congress, Kerry Dumbaugh and Gary Serota (1984)

Although now out of print and somewhat dated, you may be able to find a copy of this book in a few libraries. This book is both a primer on the internal structure of Congress and a how-to guide to pulling the right strings. It includes a wealth of useful information, including tips on "Hill speak", networking strategies, and names and addresses of bars and restaurants most frequented by congressional staffers.

After orienting yourself with *Capitol Jobs*, you should begin targeting your job search on various personal, committee, or subcommittee staffs. Our companion volume—*The Almanac of American Government Jobs and Careers* (Manassas Park, VA: Impact Publications)—includes the names, addresses, and phone numbers of key contacts in Congress. In addition to this book, you may want to consult the latest editions of following directories for the names, addresses, and telephone numbers of key representatives, staff people, and committees and subcommittees:

- *The American Almanac of Politics*
- *Congressional Yellow Book*
- *Congressional Staff Directory*
- *Congressional Directory*

The House and Senate also publish telephone directories which you should consult: *United States Senate Telephone Directory* and *Telephone Directory: United States House of Representatives.* Costing between $10 and $15, both directories can be purchased directly from the U.S. Government Printing Office, Washington, DC 20402. The following telephone number will also give you current information on Senate and House members, committees, and subcommittees: 202/224-3121.

You may wish to leave a copy of your resume with the non-partisan **congressional placement offices**. These offices provide job application, interview, and referral services for both personal staff and committee positions. The House Placement Office is located in House Annex #2, Room H2-219 (3rd and D Streets, SW, Washington, DC 20515). This office encourages individuals to walk in for information. While it primarily recruits individuals for clerical and secretarial positions, administers typing, shorthand, and computer proficiency tests, and conducts impromptu interviews, it also functions as a referral office for other types of congressional positions. For example, if a House member or Committee Staff needs a particular type of employee, it may contact this office for information on applicants. The office, in turn, will refer candidates to the appropriate staff. It does not hire for such positions since hiring decisions are made within the Representative's or Staff's office. Before being interviewed, the House Placement Office will ask you to complete an application form and talk to staff members. Its interviewing hours are from 10:30am to 4pm, Monday through Friday. You will need to fill out an application before being interviewed. The interview primarily focuses on explaining how the House Placement Office operates. For more information, call 202/226-6731.

The Senate Placement Office is located in the Hart Senate Office Building, Room 142, Washington, DC 20510. Similar to the House Placement Office, this office operates on a walk-in basis. Interviewing hours are 10am to 12noon and 1pm to 3pm, Monday through Thursday. On Friday this office is open 10am to 12noon and from 1pm to 2pm. The personnel in this office primarily interview individuals to identify interests and then refer them to the proper hiring officials with the Senators' and Staff's offices. For more information, call this office at 202/224-9167.

Please keep in mind that these offices are not designed to find you a job. Providing assistance only in the form of testing and referrals, these placement offices primarily collect resumes and forward them upon request to various offices which already have numerous unsolicited resumes. They can give you useful tips on the recruitment process on Capitol Hill. Therefore, it does not hurt to cover all bases by contacting these offices and getting your resume in their files.

Two other offices also provide assistance to job hunters on Capitol Hill: the Democratic Study Group (Tel. 202/225-5858—places its job listings with the House Placement Office) and the Republican Study Committee (433 Cannon House Office Building, Tel. 202/225-0587).

The Congressional Management Foundation (CMF) monitors personnel developments on Capitol Hill. Every two years it publishes a survey of job descriptions and salaries with congressional offices as well as conducts numerous seminars for Hill staffs. They also publish a useful manual for Capitol Hill interns: *A Congressional Intern Handbook.* You can contact them at:

Congressional Management Foundation
513 Capitol Court, NE, Suite 100
Washington, DC 20002
Tel. 202/546-0100

Two other resources provide useful financial information on various staff positions. *The Report of the Clerk of the House*, published quarterly, provides details on the financial structure of each Representative's office. This document will give you all the information you need for researching House salaries. You can get a free copy from the House Document Room which is located in Room H226 of the Capitol Building (Tel. 202/225-3456). A similar document, *The Report of the Secretary of the Senate*, is available on Senate staff salaries. It is free for the asking through the Senate Documents Room (Room B04) in the Hart Senate Office Building (Tel. 202/332-7860).

A variety of other publications are available on various aspects of Congress. Before venturing into this arena, you should have a thorough understanding of the structure and functions of the House and Senate. Your local library should have such basic reference works as the *Congressional Directory*, *Congressional Staff Directory*, and the *Congressional Yellow Book*. They also should have the *Congressional Quarterly*, *The Almanac of American Politics*, and several books on how Congress works and how to lobby Congress. The lobbying books are especially useful, because they are written in a how-to format. They reveal the internal structure of congressional organizations and outline useful strategies for influencing each organization—strategies which can be directly adapted to your job search. You, in effect, want to "lobby" Congressional organizations with your resume, experience, skills, and personality.

THE JUDICIARY

The judicial branch, the fastest growing branch of government, consists of the Supreme Court, a variety of U.S. Courts, and supporting organizations. Altogether, these organizations employed 28,015 individuals in November, 1993, which represents an 85 percent increase in personnel since September, 1980. While employment with the Supreme Court only increased by 4.7 percent during this same period—from 336 to 352—most of the increase took place outside Washington, DC in the U.S. Courts. These courts went from 14,847 employees in September 1980 to 27,581 in November 1993.

Finding employment within the judiciary is similar to finding employment in the legislative branch—networking and direct application.

The Supreme Court is a relatively small organization with only 352 employees. Court employees consist of the Clerk of the Court, Marshall, Reporter of Decisions, Press Officer, Librarian and their staffs as well as messengers and security officers. These individuals are appointed by the Court. Law clerks, on the other hand, are appointed by the Justices.

The Clerk of the Court has the largest staff, consisting of more than 30 individuals. The Marshall of the Court is responsible for seating arrangements, paying the Justices' salaries, and dispersing court funds. The Reporter of Decisions has general editing, printing, and publication responsibilities relevant to court opinions. The Press Officer provides public information. The Librarian is responsible for maintaining a 250,000 volume library. Messengers are selected by the Marshall of the Court; they replaced the former page system and work directly with the Justices. Approximately four law clerks provide staff assistance to each Justice.

Several other individuals and groups work directly with the court, but they are not court employees. These consist of:

- **Office of Solicitor General:** The third highest ranking Department of Justice official who is responsible for representing the federal government before the Court.

- **Supreme Court Bar:** Admits 6,000 individuals to the Supreme Court Bar each year.

- **U.S. Judicial Conference:** The "Board of Trustees" for the federal judicial system. Receives staff assistance from the Administrative Office of the U. S. Courts.

- **Administrative Office of the U.S. Courts:** Supervises the administration, salaries, and benefits of federal court support personnel—except the Supreme Court. Prepares and submits budgets of all U.S. district courts as well as the 11 circuit courts of appeal. The Washington, DC staff consists of over 650 employees. Contact the Human Resources Division at 202/273-1270 for information concerning their Washington, DC staff positions. Since hiring is decentralized to individual field staffs, you will need to contact each court in the field for information on employment opportunities. This central office only hires for its own immediate needs.

- **Federal Judicial Center:** The research, training, and development arm of the federal judiciary. It has a staff of 117. While they normally advertise vacancies in the *Washington Post* rather than take phone calls, you can contact them as follows for personnel information: Federal Judicial Center, Thurgood Marshall Federal Judiciary Building, One Columbus Circle, NE, Washington, DC 20002, Tel. 202/273-4165.

- **Supreme Court Historical Association:** Nonprofit group organized to educate the public about the federal judiciary. It has a staff of 10. You can contact them at 202/543-0400.

- **U.S. Sentencing Commission:** Develops sentencing policies and practices for the federal criminal justice system, including guidelines prescribing the appropriate form and severity of punishment for offenders convicted of federal crimes. You can contact them at the United States Sentencing Commission, Suite 2-500 South Lobby, One Columbus circle, NE, Washington, DC 20002-8002, Tel. 202/273-4500.

ADMINISTRATIVE OFFICE OF THE U.S. COURTS

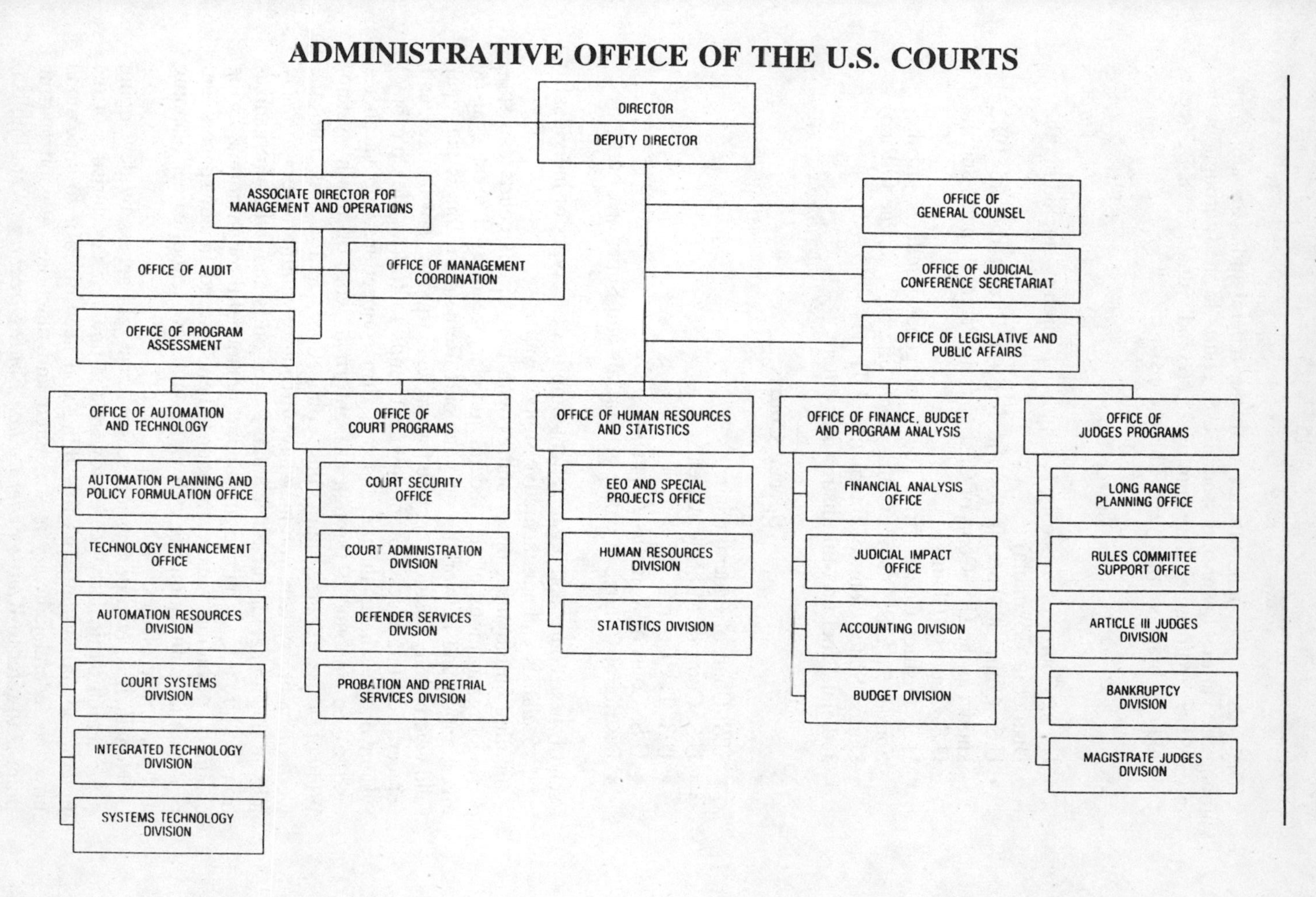

The bulk of job opportunities with the federal judiciary are found among the various lower and special U.S. courts located throughout the United States. Altogether, they employ 27,663 individuals or 98.7 percent of all judicial branch employees. These consist of:

Lower Courts

- U. S. Courts of Appeals (12 judicial circuits, including the District of Columbia)
- U.S. Court of Appeals for the Federal Circuit (before 1982 known as the U.S. Court of Customs and Patent Appeals and the U.S. Court of Claims)
- U.S. District Courts (trial courts of general federal jurisdictions— 91 U.S. District Courts, including DC and Puerto Rico)
- United States Court of International Trade
- Judicial Panel on Multidistrict Litigation

Special Courts

- U.S. Court of Federal Claims
- U.S. Court of Military Appeals
- U.S. Tax Court
- U.S. Court of Veterans Appeals
- District of Columbia: Court of Appeals and Superior Court

Each of these courts and organizations employs two types of individuals: legal specialists and administrative support staff.

Finding employment opportunities with the various courts and supporting organizations of the federal judiciary requires a great deal of investigation and networking on your part. Remember, this is the legal field where many positions require formal legal training, law degrees, and bar certification; access to employment tends to follow the "ole boy" system of classmate, alumni, and law firm connections. Job vacancies tend to be announced through the informal word-of-mouth system. Without a law degree, numerous connections, and a link into the word-of-mouth system, you may have difficulty gaining access to many jobs in this arena. On the other hand, these courts and judicial organizations do hire a large number of support personnel through normal hiring channels, including vacancy announcements placed in newspapers and professional publications as well as through law school career planning and placement offices.

Nonetheless, enterprising job seekers can gain access by developing a job search particularly geared toward the unique characteristics of the federal judicial system. The first thing you need to do is to understand how the federal judiciary is structured and functions. A good starting point is to refer to *Want's Federal-State Court Directory* (Want Publishing Co., 1511 K St., NW, Washington, DC 20005, Tel. 202/783-1887, $35.00 plus $4.50 shipping). This directory provides an overview of the structure of the court system. If you are interested in state and county court systems, you should get Want's other directory: *Directory of State Court Clerks and County Courthouses* ($65.00 plus $4.50 shipping).

You also may want to call the Supreme Court Public Information Office, United States Supreme Court Building, 1 First Street, NE, Washington, DC 20543, Tel. 202/479-3211, for information on the various judicial organizations. They can refer you to the necessary sources. From there, you should directly contact each judicial organization—both court and support groups—for information and advice. In the case of federal courts outside Washington, DC, contact the court directly as well as the local bar association or law school for information and advice. The Administrative Office of the United States Courts (Washington, DC 20544, Tel. 202/273-1530) will also provide information on the lower courts. Many law schools maintain placement offices which can provide advice on how to best approach the federal circuit and district courts within their geographic area.

PART V

WORKING ON THE PERIPHERY

While government is usually equated with the public sector, numerous nongovernmental organizations also define the public sector. These organizations are involved directly or indirectly in "public" business. Better still, they offer numerous job and career opportunities for government employees as well as others interested in public sector work.

Take, for example, government employees. Many of them have little knowledge of worklife outside their agencies. Indeed, looking for employment outside government can be a frightening experience replete with possible rejections and failure. Lacking appropriate job search skills and information on nongovernmental job opportunities, many people fail to make career transitions to rewarding jobs outside government. However, this need not happen if they understand their skills, use effective job search techniques, and locate job vacancies among appropriate public organizations.

Each year thousands of individuals make successful transitions from government to the private sector. How they do it is no big secret. For many, the first step is to identify organizations that seek the skills of government employees. The most logical groups are those doing business with government agencies. Many of these "organizations on the periphery" maintain close relations with agencies, hire former government employees, and are major beneficiaries of government spending. The classic examples are former employees of the departments of Defense, Energy, and Commerce who now work for private contractors who do business with their former agencies. Other public organizations receive financial support from sources outside government for the purpose of affecting how government conducts its business.

Numerous public service opportunities are available with organizations outside government. These organizations range from nonprofit foundations and charitable organizations to lobbyists, professional associations, and consulting firms. They all have one thing in common: they operate in a public arena. Some directly initiate policies for improving the welfare of communities. Others influence both the content and implementation of governmental policies.

The five chapters in this section outline public employment opportunities with various organizations functioning on the periphery of government. Many of these organizations provide exciting and rewarding job opportunities for individuals primarily oriented toward public sector work. The chapters outline a basic orientation for gaining access to the networks which provide entry to the organizations.

19

THE NEW PUBLIC SECTOR

*M*ost people think the public sector is government consisting of various executive, legislative, and judicial organizations. However, numerous nongovernmental organizations are important players in the public arena. They influence the content of policy at both the decision-making and implementation stages. For many government agencies, these nongovernmental groups provide essential services for ensuring the success of government operations and programs. Taken together, these "public sector" organizations constitute a network of employment opportunities for individuals interested in public sector jobs and careers.

TYPES OF ORGANIZATIONS

The new public sector consists of literally thousands of organizations engaged in some form of public activity. The activities include:

- Representing and supporting trade, professional, social, and political groups.
- Providing contractual services to government agencies.
- Promoting social programs and political causes.
- Influencing the content of public policy.
- Performing public functions.
- Financing and promoting the political candidacies of elected officials.

Most nongovernmental organizations engaged in public activities have permanent, full-time staffs. Many are headquartered or maintain offices or representatives in the Washington, DC Metro area where they have ready access to legislators and bureaucrats as well as a pool of experienced and talented personnel to run their organizations. A disproportionate number of such organizations are found across the Potomac River in suburban Alexandria, Virginia.

The major types of nongovernmental organizations operating on the periphery of government consist of:

- Contracting and consulting firms
- Trade and professional associations
- Non-profit organizations
- Foundations and research organizations
- Political support groups and lobbyists

While these are private organizations, all deal with government or each other in some manner. For example, consulting firms, research organizations, and foundations partly depend on government funding for their livelihoods. Trade and professional associations, lobbyists, and law firms represent the interests of their members and clients among legislators and agencies. Nonprofit organizations are often partly funded by government, and they too attempt to influence the shape and implementation of public policy. Political Action Committees (PACs) and political parties mobilize resources from trade and professional associations to advance the candidacies of elected officials.

NETWORKS OF OPPORTUNITY

The various nongovernmental organizations also constitute a network of employment opportunities for enterprising job seekers. Since most organizations perform similar functions in different specialty areas, job seekers can readily move within and among nonprofit organizations, trade and professional associations, contracting and consulting firms, and government organizations. A public career path for an individual in Washington, DC, for example, might consist of the following job moves:

- Research analyst with a nonprofit organization—2 years
- Legislative assistant on Capitol Hill—2 years
- Policy analyst with a federal agency—5 years
- Legislative liaison with a trade association—3 years
- Fund raiser with a Political Action Committee—2 years
- Senior associate with a consulting firm—present job

While such job changes may appear to be evidence of job hopping, each new job is most likely a logical move up the public sector career ladder. After all, jobs on Capitol Hill tend to be transient; they do not lend themselves to congressional careers. Because federal careers tend to quickly plateau, long-term employment within federal agencies does not result in major career advancement nor exceptional financial rewards. Since many associations are small, they provide limited career advancement. Nonprofit organizations often pay poorly. And consulting firms may be small and family-owned and thus offer limited promotions. In such a public employment environment, individual career advancement is achieved by making several job moves among different types of public organizations.

Each new job is most likely a logical move up the public sector career ladder. Job-hopping is the best way to advance your career.

The end result, or final career pattern, for the public career-minded job changer may be 20 years of "public service" experience with six different organizations followed by establishing one's own contracting, consulting, or lobbying firm. Such an individual will have valuable public experience and important contacts for launching what will hopefully become an exciting and rewarding career in their own business.

JOB-HOPPING THROUGH THE REVOLVING DOOR

Many observers refer to such a career pattern as "job-hopping" and the public job networking and change phenomena as "the revolving door". Used in the pejorative, these terms nonetheless accurately describe the phenomena. However, there is nothing inherently wrong with job hopping through the revolving door. These are facts of worklife for career advancement in the public sector. For many people, staying with one organization for many years is a career death sentence. Especially if you work for small organizations, job-hopping is the best way to advance your career. While on occasion the revolving door results in obvious conflicts of interest, on the whole it is probably functional for government. Many of the functions required by government must be contracted-out to organizations with specific government skills and experience. The only way these organizations can acquire the necessary skills and experience is to hire individuals who know the details of government. And who knows government better than former government employees?

THE SUCCESSFUL PUBLIC JOB SEEKER

Successful public job seekers understand and use the networks within and between public sector organizations. They know the what, where, and how of finding jobs in what appears to be a maze of different types of organizations. In making the transition from government to the private sector, they learn how to write excellent resumes and network for job openings according to the principles outlined in Part II for conducting an effective job search.

If you seek employment with these nongovernmental organizations, you should first visit your local library and consult five excellent directories:

- *Encyclopedia of Associations*
- *The Consultants and Consulting Organization Directory*
- *The Foundation Directory*
- *National Directory of Nonprofit Organizations*
- *Research Center Directory*

These directories provide a good overview of public organizations employing millions of public-oriented individuals. Each directory provides invaluable information on thousands of organizations, including names, addresses, telephone numbers, contact persons, functions, activities, and size of organization. If you spend a day or two in the library surveying these key volumes, you will quickly identify numerous organizations providing alternative job opportunities for someone with your interests and skills.

Several other directories provide useful information on job opportunities in this public arena. Some, but not all, libraries will have these books:

- *Career Guide to Professional Associations*
- *Directory of Professional and Trade Organizations*
- *National Trade and Professional Associations in the United States*

- *Non-Profits' Job Finder*
- *Washington Information Directory*
- *Washington Representatives*

Each of the following chapters further discusses the use and content of these and other resources.

Once you have completed your library research, you should be prepared to begin contacting organizations by telephone, letter, or in person. The following chapters will assist you in developing an approach most appropriate for each type of organization.

20 CONTRACTORS AND CONSULTANTS

*M*uch of what gets done in government is actually done through contractors and consultants. During the past 30 years more and more government services and programs have been contracted-out to private firms. The extreme case is the U.S. Department of Energy. While it only has 20,226 full-time employees, this department also supports over 100,000 contractors and consultants!

As governments enter another decade of downsizing, limited personnel growth, and cutbacks in agency personnel, the trend for the remainder of the 1990s appears to be in the direction of even greater use of consultants and contractors to get the business of government done. We expect one unintended consequence of recent reform efforts to "reinvent" the federal government will be the increased use of consultants and contractors. Similar to the proverbial shell game, reinventing government means shrinking employment within government but enlarging the consultant/contractor employment arena.

ROLES

Consultants and contractors play important roles in providing services to government. All branches of government use these services to varying degrees for several reasons:

- They require specialized information not available through their present staffs.
- They need special services and products only available from the private sector.
- It is often more cost-effective to contract-out services than to increase the number of agency personnel to provide the services in-house.
- Many services are short-term and thus can be most quickly and effectively performed by outside consultants and contractors.

Much of the work of government involves obligating funds and administering contracts to private firms rather than providing direct government services.

At the state and local levels, contractors may provide sanitation services, road construction, health care, and building construction and maintenance. Innovative efforts to "privatize" many traditional state and local government functions has resulted in some cases where prison management and educational programs have been contracted-out to private firms. At the federal level these firms run a variety of federal programs, staff offices, conduct numerous studies, and regularly supply agencies with every conceivable type of durable and nondurable goods from pencil sharpeners to submarines.

Almost every job in the private sector will be performed in government. Ironically, these government jobs are performed by private firms on contract with government agencies. Therefore, much of the work of government employees involves obligating funds and administering contracts to private firms rather than providing direct government services. Government procurement, the business of acquiring goods and services from the private sector, is big business within government.

Contractor services are performed at the contractor's or agency's site. In many cases, an agency will provide office space for a contractor's staff which then performs services in offices adjacent to agency personnel. In many government agencies, such as the Department of Labor in Washington, DC, it is difficult to identify who is a government employee or a contractor occupying agency offices. In other agencies, such as the Department of Energy's Long Island nuclear site, contractors are housed in a building separate from agency personnel.

UNDERSTANDING THE PROCUREMENT PROCESS

Local governments are the major direct service units in American government. Local officials provide services to citizens in specific neighborhoods. Being labor intensive units of government, local governments employ millions of individuals as teachers, police officers, and public works and sanitation officials. Outside local government, public services are less direct, involving fewer face-to-face contacts between citizens and public employees. At the federal level, employees are the most removed from direct contact with citizens. Federal employees tend to disproportionately engage in the process of developing programs, obligating funds, and monitoring programs implemented by state and local officials and private contractors.

The work of consultants centers around the **procurement process**. Procurement is the process by which government acquires goods and services. Well defined rules and regulations govern the process by which agencies can contract-out various services. In many state and local jurisdictions this process is poorly structured, weakly regulated, and subject to a great deal of mismanagement, conflicts of interest, and corruption. It is not uncommon, for example, to find elected officials and public employees steering contracts to friends and relatives and receiving kickbacks from the "ole boy" networks. Consequently, competition for government contracts is most limited at the state and local levels. Private firms tend to "colonize" agencies by maintaining long-term relations with key individuals in agencies who prefer their services to any other outside competitors. In communities where universities have a major presence, professors from the local institution often develop special relations with local government agencies, especially with their former students who are in positions to award contracts to their mentors.

Procurement at the federal level is a different matter altogether. While local and state governments tend to provide a large number of street-level services through their public safety, public works, and highway departments, federal employees do not. Direct services tend to be contracted-out to private consulting and contracting firms. The federal government strictly regulates the procurement process through a well defined set of general regulations:

- Federal Acquisition Regulations (FAR)
- Competition in Contracting Act of 1985 (CICA)

In addition, each agency develops more detailed regulations based upon the FAR and in line with the CICA. Altogether, over $350 billion a year flows from federal agencies to the private sector through this process.

One major result of the federal procurement process has been to create competition among consulting and contracting firms. For example, all goods and services amounting to $10,000 or more ($25,000 in the case of the Department of Defense) must be procured through competitive bidding or negotiation processes (new pending reform regulations should raise this amount to $100,000). This normally takes the form of sealed bids for equipment or negotiations with agency personnel for services. Once a procurement need is identified and defined by agency personnel, contractors are identified and the procurement process follows specific rules and procedures. If a service is for less than $10,000, contracting officials must contact at least three firms for competitive bids. If the amount is more than $10,000, then the officials must issue a Request for Proposal (RFP). An announcement must be published in the *Commerce Business Daily (CBD)* for at least 30 days. During that time firms request copies of the solicitation which outlines the Statement of Work and evaluation criteria for judging proposals. Firms normally have 30 days to develop and submit detailed proposals. Once proposals are received and reviewed by contracting officers and technical personnel, the firm receiving the highest evaluation on both technical and cost criteria receives the award. This may take anywhere from one to three months after the closing date for submitting proposals.

While all federal agencies are supposed to follow these rules for ensuring competition, informal systems also operate to limit competition. Many agencies prefer working with a single contractor and thus they "wire" RFPs to favor one particular contractor. This is done by specifying in both the Statement of Work and the evaluation criteria various requirements which only one firm is likely to meet. An example of this practice is an RFP we received from a military base. The solicitation requested proposals to provide career planning services to military spouses located near a specified city in a remote area of the United States. While the RFP had to be advertised in the *CBD* and proposals received over a 30-day period, an interesting amendment was issued which severely limited competition. Among ten new evaluation criteria for judging offerors' resumes, it included the following minimum criteria:

> A list of all (City X) employers with whom the bidder has an established working relationship. The ability to prepare a variety of resume styles and appropriate selective marketing brochures. This should be demonstrated with an attachment showing a minimum of 12 resumes or marketing brochures which the service provider has personally prepared.

Obviously only a few firms—perhaps only one—could meet such specific evaluation criteria. Not surprisingly, the firm to win the contract would probably be based in the specified city and previously did work with the individuals responsible for developing the RFP. They may have written the Statement of Work and evaluation criteria for the program officials!

Similar to "wiring" positions around the qualifications of a specific individual, "wiring" contracts for specific firms by specifying narrow evaluation criteria and developing unique Statements of Work is a notorious practice found throughout the federal government. Certain agencies have reputations for engaging in such practices more than other agencies. Officials continue to play these games as long as no one protests. After all, contractors do not want to get the reputation for being "difficult" and thus quickly become *persona non grata* among contracting officials who prefer doing "business as usual". However, occasionally protests are lodged and solicitations are invalidated. Indeed, the authors protested a procurement training solicitation issued by one federal agency in August, 1985. The solicitation was published in the *CBD* but the closing date was 12 days after it appeared—an obvious violation of the FAR and CICA which require a minimum of 30 days. Certain officials in the agency were trying to obligate funds for Fiscal 1985 and had wired the RFP for a particular firm. When we protested this violation, we learned there were obvious competing political factions among the contracting officials and technical personnel. They both knew they were in violation of the rules, but one had forced the other to attempt this improper procurement. Had we not protested, the funds would have been obligated and the favorite contractor of certain agency personnel would have received a nice end-of-the-year- spending windfall. Our protest was upheld and the funds were not obligated. Needless to say, we are probably *persona non grata* with certain individuals in this agency.

But compared to state and local governments, competition in contracting is more prevalent at the federal level. Indeed, the FAR and CICA rules of 1985 should have far reaching implications in undermining many of the informal "wiring" practices which have gone on for years in some federal agencies.

FLUIDITY IN HIRING

It is extremely important to understand this procurement process if you are interested in working for consulting and contracting firms. The process creates a job market situation which is very fluid, unstable, and unpredictable. A typical organizational structure for a small to middle-sized firm is outlined on page 339.

Many firms keep a small *core staff* which is employed full-time to respond to RFPs and manage a lean organizational infrastructure. As contracts are won, they hire two types of additional personnel—often on a consulting basis—for implementing the contract. *Associates* normally

TYPICAL STRUCTURE OF SMALL AND FLEXIBLE CONSULTING FIRM

Consultants

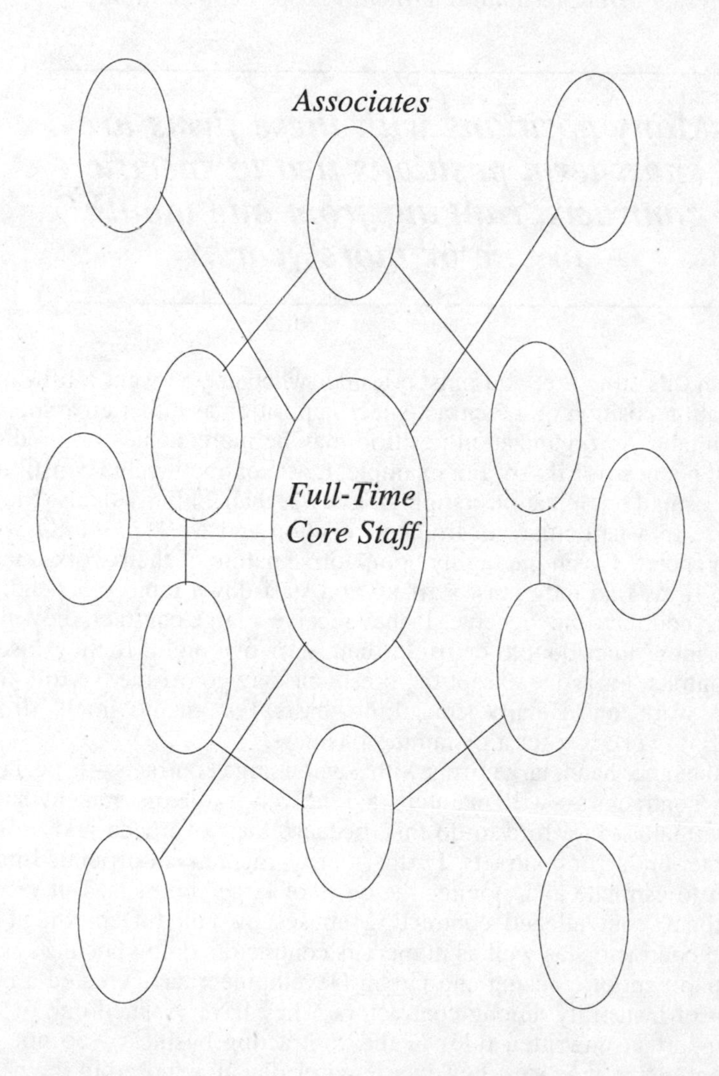

work closely with the core staff on several projects; these individuals are relatively loyal to the firm and are given a disproportionate amount of contract work as individuals or subcontractors. *Consultants* are less closely linked to the firm; they have specific skills not found with the core staff or associates, and they tend to freelance with several such firms. Therefore, many positions with these firms are short-term positions tied to specific contracts, ranging from one month to one or more years. Most contracts are for one year with options to renew contracts up to two to three years before resubmitting them for open competition.

Many positions with these firms are short-term positions tied to specific contracts, ranging from one month to one or more years.

Given this structure, you must consider whether you want a full-time organization position or a contract-specific position as either an associate or consultant. An organization position may be more stable and predictable, but not necessarily so. For example, most contracting and consulting firms are small organizations employing fewer than 25 individuals. Many specialize in a particular government function and work primarily with a few agencies. Given the highly competitive nature of their work, many of these firms find they must staff-up and staff-down rapidly depending on which contracts they receive. If they receive a large contract, they may need to more than double or triple their staff overnight. If they lose a large contract, everyone except the president may go off the payroll and, instead, work on a daily consulting basis. For many small firms, contracting work is a feast or famine business.

On the other hand, large firms with several large contracts—especially defense contractors—will maintain a relatively large permanent staff. They normally can afford to do this, because their overhead and profits are greater on larger contracts. Furthermore, procurement officials find it difficult to estimate and monitor the costs of large contracts. But recent revelations about alleged contracting abuses by noted Department of Defense contractors as well as numerous contractors doing business with the Department of Housing and Urban Development have created a new element of instability among contractors. They have violated one of the most important unwritten rules of the contracting business—do not get your contracting practices, however legal or illegal, exposed in the news media and thus endanger the careers of agency personnel. Many firms involved in the scandal-ridden Housing and Urban Development (HUD) contracting practices of the late 1980s also took several politicians with them.

THE FIRMS

Consulting and contracting firms working with the federal government are frequently referred to as the "Beltway Bandits", a reference to both their physical location near the suburban Beltway (Interstate 495) and occasional revelations of contracting abuses. Over 3,000 contracting and consulting firms operate in the Washington, DC Metro area. They provide a vast array of services to government agencies. Most, however, specialize in one or two government functions, such as training government personnel, operating service programs, and developing new weapons systems. The size of these firms will range from one individual operating from a basement or study to 1,000 or more employees occupying 250,000 square feet of office space at $30 per square foot. While many of the firms are located in the Washington, DC Metro area, they also are found in major cities throughout the country. In contracts involving research and development activities, more than 100 universities compete for contracts. The University of California, Los Angeles, for example, plays a key role in the development and operation of America's nuclear weapons systems at the Los Alamos "campus" in Alamagordo, New Mexico. A large number of defense contractors and specialized research and management organizations are located around Seattle, San Francisco, Los Angeles, Dallas, Houston, Chicago, Minneapolis, Boston, and New York.

The largest, most visible, and recently the most vulnerable contractors are associated with the military-industrial complex. They receive over $130 billion each year in defense contracts. If one were to characterize the federal government in terms of its allocation of human and financial resources, it would be safe to conclude this government has an extraordinary preoccupation with nurturing its military establishment. Indeed, 30.5 percent of all civilian government employees work for the Department of Defense. Add to this number another 266,000 employees with the Department of Veterans Affairs, thousands of employees with the CIA, DIA, and other intelligence agencies, and 1.5 million service personnel and you have a government with over 60 percent of its total personnel devoted to military and international security matters. Then examine budgetary realities—the federal government spends over 20 percent ($300 billion) of its total budget on national defense.

Numerous private contracting and consulting firms are beneficiaries of military spending. In 1992 the Department of Defense awarded over $136 billion in contracts. The 25 major contractors included:

- Martin Marietta Corporation ($1,600,769,000)
- Lockheed Aeronautical Systems, Co. ($1,270,638,000)

- General Electric Company ($917,807,000)
- Hughes Aircraft Company ($880,112,000)
- McDonnell Douglas Corporation ($829,426,000)
- Foundation Health Corporation ($761,262,000)
- Grumman Aerospace Corporation ($599,473,000)
- TRW, Inc. ($554,776,000)
- Loral Vought Systems ($533,495,000)
- General Dynamics Corporation ($470,057,000)
- Boeing Skorsky Lhx. Program Off. ($457,412,000)
- United Technologies Corp. ($420,853,000)
- Rockwell International Corp. ($399,264,000)
- Westinghouse Electric Corp. ($380,619,000)
- Raytheon Company ($354,230,000)
- McDonald Douglas Space Systems Co. ($340,073,000)
- American Telephone and Telegraph Co. ($244,573,000)
- International Business Machines Corp. ($241,521,000)
- Teledyne Industries, Inc. ($239,576,000)
- Science Applications International Corp. ($228,862,000)
- Lockheed Missiles & Space Co. ($204,118,000)

These military contractors are large corporations employing thousands of individuals. Martin Marietta, the world's largest defense contractor, employs over 100,000 people. For information on defense contractors, see the following Department of Defense (Directorate for Information Operations and Reports) publications: *Prime Contract Awards by Region and State Fiscal Years 1992, 1991, and 1990*; *500 Contractors Receiving the Largest Dollar Volume of Prime Contract Awards for RDT&E, 1992*; and *Companies Participating in the Department of Defense Subcontracting Program First Three Quarters Fiscal Year 1993*. These publications are available through the U.S. Government Printing Office, Washington, DC 20402 (these three publications are referenced by the following numbers: DIOR/P06-92, DIOR/P02-92, and DIOR/P14-93/03).

Contractors involved with other government agencies can be identified by contacting the procurement or public relations offices of agencies. For example, the U.S. Agency for International Development (USAID) awards millions of dollars in contracts to hundreds of contracting/consulting firms. The following international development firms are major recipients of USAID contracts. They specialize in everything from accounting and agriculture to education, energy, environment, and small business enterprise:

- Abt Associates
- Academy for Educational Development
- American AG International, Inc.
- Black and Veatch International
- Camp, Dresser and McKee International, Inc.

- Chemonics International
- Coopers and Lybrand
- Development Alternatives, Inc.
- Development Associates, Inc.
- Executive Resource Associates
- Futures Group
- John Snow Public Health Group, Inc.
- Louis Berger International
- Management Sciences for Health
- Robert Nathan Associates
- Pragma Corporation
- Price Waterhouse
- Scientex Corporation
- Winrock International

A complete listing of USAID contractors is found in the annual *Current Technical Services Contracts and Grants* directory which is available through USAID's Office of Procurement (Procurement Support Division, Agency for International Development, 1100 Wilson Blvd., 14th Floor, Rosslyn, VA 20523, Tel. 703/875-1270). Other federal procurement offices should provide you with a listing a contractors that work with their agencies.

Given recent downsizing of the military, defense contractors have fallen on hard times as they attempt to adjust to the new post-Cold War budgetary realities. Many are consolidating, diversifying, and going out of business. The largest and most aggressive firm is Martin Marietta which is in the process of becoming a mega-defense contractor as it merges with several other major defense contractors.

LOCATING OPPORTUNITIES

Several useful information sources are available for locating opportunities with various contracting and consulting firms. The single most comprehensive source of names, addresses, phone numbers, and annotated descriptions of firms is found in *The Consultants and Consulting Organizations Directory* and *Who's Who in Consulting* (Detroit: Gale Research Company). Most libraries have current editions of the three-volume *Directory*. It lists over 3,000 consulting firms according to the following categories:

1. Agriculture, Forestry, and Landscaping
2. Architecture, Construction, and Interior Design
3. Art, Graphics, and Communications Media
4. Business and Finance
5. Computer Technology, Telecommunications, and Information Services

6. Education and Personal Development
7. Engineering, Science, and Technology
8. Environment, Geology, and Land Use
9. Health, Medicine, and Safety
10. Human Resource Development
11. Management
12. Manufacturing and Transportation
13. Marketing and Sales
14. Politics and Social Issues

Since these volumes include all types of consulting firms, regardless of their public or private orientation, you will need to read through the various annotated descriptions to find which firms are primarily involved in government contract work. An example of a typical entry under the "Human Resource Development" section is:

> **BERGSTRALH-SHAW-NEWMAN, INC.**
> 236 Montezuma Ave. Phone: (505) 984-1650
> Santa Fe, NM 87501 Founded: 1978
>
> **Staff:** 18. **Principal Executives:** Kermit L. Bergstralh, Chairman; M. Ed Shaw, President; Robert B. Newman, Senior Vice President; **Consulting Activities:** Designs, develops and implements management improvements and in-house training programs for highway, transportation and public works agencies in the United States, Canada and other countries. Services include department-wide performance and organizational reviews, management system designs, manpower and personnel management improvements, personnel classification plans, employee performance appraisals, salary plans and training materials production. Training production includes videotapes, slidetapes, other audiovisual materials, instructors' guides and trainee workbooks.

Although this is the best directory of such firms, keep in mind it does not include all contracting and consulting firms—only those willing to reveal information on their operations to Gale Research Company. Many firms do not want to publicize their operations through this or other public information resource directories. Consequently, you will have to locate these firms through other resources and investigative efforts. Your best source of information will be government procurement offices that actually award contracts to specific organizations.

If you are interested in working for firms which primarily focus on state and local government, you should contact the appropriate contracting office to get a list of the firms doing business with particular governmental units and agencies. In fact, this will be your most important source of information. You will learn who has what contract, for how long, and for how much. This information should be public information in most jurisdictions. In addition, you should look at the contractor's work—be it a report or other type of product—to gain information on the work being performed by the firm. Such information will give you something concrete to talk about with representatives of the firm once you decide to conduct an informational interview.

At the federal level your information sources on contracts are numerous. One of your best sources is the *Commerce Business Daily (CBD)*, which is available in most libraries. Issued five days a week, this Department of Commerce publication lists information on all upcoming competitive contracts for $10,000 or more as well as contracts awarded to particular firms for the amounts of $25,000 or more. You should pay particular attention to the "Contract Awards" section. This section identifies which firms received contracts for what amounts. A good job search strategy is to continuously monitor who receives contracts and contact the firm when you see an award made in your area of expertise or interest. But you must do this immediately upon seeing the announcement since there is a lag time between when a contract is awarded and when it is announced in the *CBD*.

We suggest this *CBD* job search strategy because typically firms operate in the following manner. The firm submits a proposal complete with a management structure, job descriptions, and resumes. But once they receive the award, the proposed staff changes due to the unavailability of some individuals proposed. At this time, the contractor must find new personnel and get them approved for the contract. In other words, the contractor now has a personnel problem or vacancy which must be filled immediately. If your qualifications and timing are right, you may find a job very quickly with such a firm. At the same time, you will make an important contact which could lead to having your resume included in other proposals. Most contractors are happy to receive resumes since they are continuously in need of personnel to propose for as well as staff new projects. Indeed, many contractors maintain in-house resume or talent banks which they continuously refer to when dealing with their personnel needs. Staffing-up is always a problem employers prefer to solve before it becomes a major project implementation issue with clients.

You should also monitor the section of the *CBD* dealing with impending contracts. Once you become familiar with various specialty areas within the consulting business, you can nearly predict which firms will submit proposals for which projects. Knowing this, you can call a firm and mention your interest and availability in being included in their proposal. They may even offer you a short-term contract to help write the proposal should you have such interests and skills. In some cases, individuals manage to get included in two or more proposals for the same contract, thus better ensuring they will get the work once the contract is awarded. Some firms have no problems with your inclusion in competitors' proposals while others frown on such opportunism. But in the contracting game, where competition is heavy, the basic goal is to get the contract and cash flowing.

Another source of information on contractors is the contracts procurement, or acquisitions office in each agency. Some offices, such as the U.S. Agency for International Development (USAID), provide a listing of firms doing contract work with their agency. Others are less organized and willing to provide such information. Also, ask the officials *which* contractors are doing *what* and *whom* you might contact. Sometimes these individuals are very open with such information and will make several useful suggestions. On the other hand, agency officials may guard this information as private and confidential, even though it is public information. For example, USAID used to make copies of its quarterly *Functional Report: Current Indefinite Quantity Contracts* available upon request. This is a key document revealing which USAID contractors have a "special" relationship with USAID. The Indefinite Quantity Contract (IQC) is a unique contracting mechanism which enables USAID to acquire short-term technical services—normally for 120 days or less—by issuing a "work order" to firms which qualify as eligible for IQCs. In other words, the IQC limits competition to a few USAID-approved firms. This special contracting mechanism and agency-contractor relationship ostensibly saves USAID time and avoids lengthy and sometimes difficult negotiation procedures. At the same time, the IQC is highly valued by many firms. These are bread-and-better contracts which regularly pay salaries and overhead and keep full-time staffs and associates employed especially during periods between large contracts. IQCs can be important to enterprising job seekers focusing on consulting firms. For example, if you contact firms with IQC status, you may find they have work in your skill and interest area. However, USAID recently restricted distribution of this IQC document to only a few contractors; others must be screened through the USAID's Public Relations Office. Most individuals and organizations outside the USAID contracting family must submit a Freedom of Information Act request in order to see this document. Other federal agencies also may restrict information on their contractors and thus you may need to formally request the information through the Freedom of Information Act.

You will find that some firms largely specialize in one function in a single agency whereas other firms do contract work in one or many functional areas with several agencies. For example, if you are interested in working for a firm in the field of energy or environmental protection, you should contact the Contracts Office at the Department of Energy or Environmental Protection Agency for a list of contractors. Once you have this information, you will know whom to contact. The firms working with these agencies also may be doing similar work in other agencies and in private industry. Call the firms and let them know you are interested in working for them. Try to set up an appointment for an interview. Make sure you get your resume in their file. Indeed, many firms refer to this file, or resume bank, when they need personnel for new projects. While they may not have a vacancy at the time you contact them, they very well may submit a proposal which results in a position for you.

Many consulting firms also periodically place employment ads in the newspaper in either the classified or business sections. In the case of the federal government, most consulting firms will place job listings in the *Washington Post*, especially the Sunday edition. You should monitor these sections of the newspaper. However, don't expect to get a job by responding to these ads. Many firms periodically place such ads in order to increase the number of resumes for their files. Sometimes they are in the process of bidding on a project, so they advertise for resumes to put in a particular proposal. If you manage to get your resume in the proposal and the firm wins the contract, you have a job. But more often than not, such ads are "fishing expeditions" with no particular vacancy available at the time of the ad. They want to build their stock of resumes for certain skill areas in the event they need to quickly respond to an RFP. Individuals interested in international development consulting—especially accountants, agriculturists, medical personnel, teachers, engineers, and project managers—should submit their resume to Talent Bank, TransCentury Corporation, 1901 N. Fort Myer Drive, Suite 1017, Arlington, VA 22209, Tel. 703/351-5500 (call for information and a registration form which should accompany your resume). This organization maintains a resume bank (free of charge) for short-term international consulting.

PROFESSIONAL POSITIONS

Most contracting firms hire individuals with strong analytical, communication, and technical skills. Given the nature of consulting work, consultants are hired as problem-solvers. They must quickly analyze situations, devise plans of action, and often implement projects. Such activities require a great deal of analytical skill and the ability to communicate to clients both orally and in writing. Projects continuously require flows of paper—workplans, monthly reports, memos, evaluations, studies—between the consultants and clients. If you are both a good and fast writer, stress these facts to potential employers. They especially need smart, quick thinking, fast writers.

While most firms hire general support staff positions for word processors, receptionists, secretaries, and accountants, most continuously seek technical specialists. Defense contractors hire a disproportionate number of engineers, systems analysts, and computer specialists. Research firms hire policy analysts with skills unique to specific programs and agencies. Other firms need specialists in a variety of areas. If you survey the *Commerce Business Daily* notices, you will quickly get a sense of which technical specialties are in demand.

It is much easier to break into a consulting firm if you have previous government experience in a specialty area involving contractors. Your special knowledge and contacts with agency personnel will make you very marketable among firms working in your area. Indeed, much of the "revolving door" with government involves employees leaving an agency and working for the same contractor they previously worked with inside the agency. These individuals become key contact people and informants for the firm. Furthermore, since agency personnel usually think they are unique and thus outsiders cannot possibly understand their problems, situations, and needs, they prefer working with one of their own.

Educational qualifications also are important with consulting firms. They prefer individuals with MAs and PhDs because government places emphasis on educational qualifications of contractors' personnel when awarding contracts. After all, agency personnel working with contracts tend to be well educated—many have MAs and PhDs. When it comes to educational background, they prefer working with consultants who are at least their equal or have higher educations. At the very minimum, a BA degree is expected.

But how do you break into the consulting game if you don't have government experience, technical skills, or higher education? If you have strong analytical and writing skills, you should be able to land a position. These firms continuously need such skills. Often they find their technical personnel with government experience cannot write. Therefore, they must have on their staff individuals who can write and edit. If you get into a firm based on your analytical and writing skills, you may be able to quickly pick up the technical aspects of the work and in time be able to work directly with clients on projects. In the meantime, you will probably stay in the background providing support for technical personnel.

The best skill to have is an ability to to work with agency personnel who are suspicious of outsiders and who feel their agency is "unique".

This is a very basic and typical pattern of how individuals break into the government consulting business and become specialists in a short time even though they lack experience as a government employee. In the long run, the best skill to have is an ability to work with agency personnel who are suspicious of outsiders and who feel their agency is "unique". They respond best to firms they feel recognize their uniqueness, respond to their problems, and can be trusted. Responsiveness and trust are perhaps the most important elements in developing and maintaining a good consultant-client relationship. On-the-job experience in interacting with clients is the basic requirement for becoming an effective consultant. Education and previous government experience will not be enough.

INDEPENDENCE AND NETWORKS

If you are thinking of starting your own independent consulting business on either a part-time or full-time basis, you should talk to consultants who have taken this road. They can provide you with useful tips on avoiding the pitfalls of independence as well as suggest useful strategies for becoming successful. You might also read a few of the ever increasing number of how-to books on entering the consulting business. Among the best titles are:

- *The Consultant's Kit: Establishing and Operating Your Successful Consulting Business*
- *Consultants Handbook*
- *Cashing In On the Consulting Boom*
- *Consultant's Proposal, Fee, and Contract Problem-Solver*
- *Consulting: The Complete Guide to a Profitable Career*
- *How to Become a Successful Consultant*
- *How to Succeed As an Independent Consultant*
- *Marketing Your Consulting and Professional Services*

If you are especially interested in the federal contracting process, you should consult Richard Porterfield's *The Complete Guide to Winning Government Contracts* (New York: Wiley & Sons) as well as Barry McVay's two primers for getting started in federal contracting:

- *Getting Started in Federal Contracting: A Guide Through the Federal Procurement Maze*
- *Proposals That Win Federal Contracts*

Several of these titles can be ordered directly from Impact Publications.

If you wish to monitor federal contracts of more than $25,000, you may want to subscribe to the *Commerce Business Daily.* This daily publication is available on an annual subscription basis from the Superintendent of Documents, U.S. Government Printing Office, Washington, DC 20402 (costs between $200 and $270 a year, depending on shipping method).

Several professional networks can provide information on consulting job opportunities. Many consultants belong to professional organizations in their specialty areas. These organizations often list job vacancies with consulting firms. Within many of these associations, consultants form their own interest groups or sections to focus on various aspects of consulting work. For example, the American Psychological Association has a Division of Consulting Psychologists. Many local chapters of the

American Society of Training and Development have a Consultants' Section. These groups regularly meet to exchange ideas and promote their interests and themselves. Some associations specialize in consulting. For example, several professionals have formed their own professional organizations:

- Academy of Health Care Consultants (Chicago)
- American Association of Hospital Consultants (Arlington, VA)
- American Association of Political Consultants (Baltimore)
- American Consulting Engineers Council (Washington, DC)
- American Society of Agricultural Consultants (McLean, VA)
- Association of Management Consultants (Milwaukee)
- Institute of Management Consultants (New York City)
- National Association of Public Employer Negotiators and Administrators (Chicago)
- National Council of Professional Services Firms (Washington, DC)

Several other organizations publish directories of consultants and consulting organizations as well as newsletters in various specialized fields. If you are interested in management consulting, for example, you may want to contact Kennedy Publications/Consultant News, an organization which publishes two newsletters (*Consultant News* and *Executive Recruiter News*) and a useful annual directory, *The Directory of Executive Recruiters*: Kennedy Publications, Templeton Road, Fitzwilliam, NH 03447 or call 603/585-2200 or 603/585-6544. The directory also is available through Impact Publications.

21 TRADE AND PROFESSIONAL ASSOCIATIONS

America is truly an organizational society. While we place great value on individualism and reward it accordingly, we also place a deal great of trust in the power of organized group efforts. Indeed, 70 percent of all Americans belong to at least one association; 25 percent belong to four or more associations. Some people manage memberships in fifteen or more organizations.

A particularly unique characteristic of American organizations is the ease with which one can join, participate in, and leave them for other organizations. Most organizations, for example, require little involvement on the part of the individual other than writing a check for annual membership dues. The rewards of such check-writing membership are many—you receive a membership card, magazine, newsletter, and perhaps special offers for insurance and travel. In addition, your name and address are sold to other organizations which send mailings on how to become a member of their organization too. The number of memberships one can acquire is primarily limited by one's time and financial resources.

Trade and professional associations are particular types of organizations involved in pursuing goals through public means. Since most associations promote the interests of their members by influencing government policies, they become involved in the political process. In this sense, they are public organizations maintaining close relationships with elected representatives and government agencies.

This chapter examines associations involved with influencing government. While many Americans work for organizations which are members of these associations, thousands of other Americans work directly for the associations. They are responsible for seeing that the association serves the best interests of its members. How one goes about locating an association and finding a staff job with one of these organizations are the subjects of this chapter.

THE ORGANIZATIONS

National trade and professional organizations consist of various types of organizations such as trade associations, labor unions, and professional, scientific, and technical societies. While no exact statistics are compiled on the number of such organizations, best estimates put the number at over 50,000 associations in the United States. The largest number operate at the state and local levels—more than 100,000, many of these are local chapters of parent organizations—at the state level alone. Approximately 23,000 associations are national in scope, with many having affiliated regional groups and local chapters. More than 400 organizations function as association management firms involved in managing the affairs of over 500 national associations and nearly 1000 local and regional associations. Altogether, associations employ nearly 9 million people.

Associations differ according to their orientations. Trade associations, for example, provide assistance to businesses; they are mainly concerned with promoting members' products and services. These consist of representatives from retail (35 percent), service (20 percent), and manufacturing (15 percent) industries. Professional associations tend to be primarily oriented to advancing and applying knowledge and setting professional standards. Scientific societies are primarily organized to promote knowledge for knowledge's sake. Labor unions promote the economic and social well-being of their members.

The size of associations varies from a few members to millions. The powerful Motor Vehicle Manufacturers Association, for example, has only 10 corporate members whereas the American Association of Retired Persons has nearly 30 million individual members. Staff size also varies from one part-time employee to more than 1,200 full-time employees. Large associations have annual budgets of over $2.5 million and staffs of 50 or more people. Medium-sized associations have annual budgets between $500,000 and $2.5 million and staffs of between 11 and 50 employees. Small associations have annual budgets under $500,000 and staffs of fewer than 10 people. Nearly 500 associations have annual budgets exceeding $5 million. Another 400 associations have annual budgets between $2 million and $5 million.

The largest concentration of associations is in the Washington, DC Metro area. Just over 2,300 associations or 31 percent of all national associations are headquartered in Washington, DC; 17 percent are located in Chicago and another 14 percent are headquartered in New York City. The remaining 38 percent are located in other cities throughout the United States, especially in San Francisco, Los Angeles, Cleveland, and Philadelphia.

The percentage of associations moving to the Washington, DC area has increased dramatically during the past 20 years. In 1971, for example, only 19 percent of national associations were headquartered in Washington, DC; 26 percent were located in New York City; and 15 percent were found in Chicago. The movement to Washington, DC is in recognition and response to the significant role national legislation plays for members of trade and professional associations. Today, more than 3,200 associations are active in Washington, DC. The largest concentration is found along Connecticut and L Streets in downtown Washington. However, more associations are moving into suburban Washington communities. Alexandria, Virginia, for example, is now home to over 200 national associations. In fact, the number of associations in Alexandria increased from 40 in 1981 to 150 in 1986!

ASSOCIATION MANAGEMENT FIRMS

Job opportunities are by no means limited to the associations themselves. Over 400 association management firms provide a variety of management services to small associations on a contractual basis: government relations, legal counseling, membership recruitment, accounting, data processing, records management, research and intelligence, and publications. The granddaddy of these firms—Fernley and Fernley of Philadelphia—was established in 1886. The largest association management firm today is Smith, Bucklin and Associates with offices in Chicago and Washington, DC. In the association management business for nearly 35 years, this firm provides services to more than 125 clients.

If you are interested in working for association management firms, you should conduct research on how they are structured and function. For example, some of these firms represent only a single association. Other firms are considered multi-management firms since they handle several associations. These firms are found throughout the United States—not just in Washington, DC. The major multi-management firms—in charge of at least seven associations—are:

MAJOR ASSOCIATION MANAGEMENT FIRMS

Name	Phone Number	State
▪ Accent on Management	614/221-1900	OH
▪ Administrative Systems, Inc.	708/655-0112	IL
▪ The Administrators, Inc.	602/952-8116	AZ
▪ Association Headquarters	609/985-2878	NJ
▪ Association Management Center	708/965-2776	IL
▪ Association Management Systems	708/369-2406	IL
▪ Association Services International	913/262-4510	KS
▪ Association and Society Management, Inc.	512/454-8626	TX
▪ Banister and Associates, Inc.	614/895-1355	OH
▪ Clemons and Associates	410/931-8100	MD
▪ CM Services	708/858-7337	IL
▪ Davis/Replogle & Associates	213/937-5514	CA
▪ George K. Degnon Associates, Inc.	703/556-9222	VA
▪ Don Dillon Associates	214/233-9107	TX
▪ Drohan Management Group	703/525-1191	VA
▪ Executive Management Associates	818/986-8066	CA
▪ Fernley and Fernley, Inc.	215/564-3484	PA
▪ Martin Fromm and Associates	816/444-3500	MO
▪ The Guild Associates	617/426-7400	MA
▪ Haeger and Associates, Inc.	312/661-1700	IL
▪ Hauck and Associates, Inc.	202/452-8100	DC
▪ Headquarters Group, Inc.	212/481-3038	NY
▪ Humes and Associates	312/922-6222	IL
▪ IMG/The Association Development Group	703/438-3101	VA
▪ Anthony J. Janetti	609/256-2300	NJ
▪ The Kellen Company	404/252-3663	GA
▪ Kinder Association Managers	714/261-2591	CA
▪ Management Concepts, Inc.	919/779-5709	NC
▪ Marketshare, Inc.	301/656-9011	MD
▪ The Messersmith Group	916/443-9023	CA
▪ Olson Management Group	919/787-5181	NC
▪ Professional Relations and Research Institute, Inc.	508/526-8330	MA
▪ S & S Management	203/243-3977	CT
▪ The Joseph E. Shaner Company	410/752-3318	MD
▪ Slack, Inc.	609/848-1000	NJ
▪ Smith, Bucklin & Associates, Inc.	202/857-1100	DC
▪ Thomas Associates, Inc.	216/241-7333	OH
▪ A.P. Wherry & Associates, Inc.	216/899-0010	OH

LOBBYING AND PACs

If the major involvement of most individuals with associations is writing a check for annual membership dues, where does all the money go? The money goes toward renting office space and supporting staffs engaged in a variety of activities in addition to seeing that members receive their membership cards and certificates, magazines, and newsletters. For trade and professional associations, their activities center on promoting the common interests of members.

Most large associations are organized to lobby federal, state, and local governments. Full-time staffs engage in numerous activities aimed at congressional committees, executive departments, and regulatory agencies to both protect and promote their members' interests. These activities include:

- Providing information to officials on the organization's position on various issues; sometimes this includes drafting legislation for congressional committees and writing policy papers for agencies.

- Testifying before committees.

- Monitoring the day-to-day actions of Congress, agencies, and other lobbying groups.

- Mobilizing constituent support for or against government candidates with money and campaign workers. The National Rifle Association (NRA), for example, is reputed to have the capability to organize, virtually overnight, mass mailings to its more than 3 million members.

- Assisting favored congressional candidates with money, campaign workers, and votes.

- Developing networks, coalitions, and alliances with other associations in support of various policy positions.

Trade and professional associations, whether they operate at the federal, state, or local levels, are affected by the legislative process. Trade unions, for example, are very active at the state level to ensure that state legislatures avoid passing right-to-work legislation which would significantly undermine union membership. State bar associations lobby to fix legal fees and prevent members from advertising. Local Chambers of Commerce are active at City Hall to ensure that local ordinances are conducive to a positive business climate. The National Rifle Association (NRA) and the National Association of Manufacturers (NAM) continuously lobby for legislation in favor of their members.

Since the 1970s, a new form of association activity has developed in the form of Political Action Committees (PACs). First initiated by the American Medical Association in 1961, today approximately 3500 PACs funnel funds into the campaigns of favored congressional and presidential candidates as well as representatives at the state and local levels. PACs are normally associated with particular associations. They provide job opportunities in addition to the regular associational staff positions. We examine the case of PACs in Chapter 24.

WORK AND COMPENSATION

Most associations consist of members, a Board of Directors, numerous committees, and a professional staff. Committees, such as education and trade show, are especially important to day-to-day operations. Committees are used to mobilize members' expertise and involve members in promoting the activities of the association.

The work of associations requires a variety of skills from handling mass mailings to drafting legislation and conducting training programs. Public relations and writing skills are highly valued. Most associations need individuals who are talented in doing the following:

- **Maintain communication with members and government officials:** write newsletters, edit magazines, develop press releases, maintain mailing lists, issue special reports and publications.

- **Develop proposals and propose legislation:** issue information and position papers to members of congress and agency personnel, and draft legislation.

- **Expand contacts with influential groups and individuals:** network by telephone, letter, and personal visits to develop supportive relations between the association and important others.

- **Respond to inquiries:** answer questions, conduct research, and supply materials.

- **Organize meetings:** manage all logistics involved in organizing the annual membership meeting, executive board meetings, and special meetings.

- **Conduct training:** identify training needs, organize instructors and participants, develop brochures and training materials, and entertain.

Above all, staff members must have strong communication and organization skills as well as enjoy working with people. The nature of association work also requires one to be flexible in dealing with the day-to-day work of the association. Since these are membership-driven organizations, staff personnel must be responsive to members' needs.

Depending on the size of the association, the work environment stresses the importance of managing communication and networking.

Individuals who have strong written and oral communication skills, as well as good interpersonal and networking skills, are highly valued. Many individuals who work for associations have previously worked on Capitol Hill where they acquired such skills in the offices of Congress. At the same time, many Capitol Hill employees have previously worked for associations. Because of the complementary nature of associational and congressional work, employees tend to develop working relations with each other which result in a "revolving door" between personnel in associations and on Capitol Hill. If you have Capitol Hill experience, especially in drafting legislation and networking, you will be very marketable with associations.

Individuals who have strong written and oral communication skills, as well as good interpersonal and networking skills, are highly valued.

Salaries with associations vary. Large and well established associations tend to pay better than small associations. Recent salary surveys (1991) indicate that the average CEO salary is $121,368 in the Washington, DC area, $111,373 in New York City, and $109,253 in Chicago. The average salary for the top officer in all associations nationwide was $83,000. Salaries tend to increase at the rate of 4 percent each year.

Salaries with associations are modest by most standards. Entry-level positions are often in the $19,000 to $23,000 range, with most professional positions paying in the low 30s to low 40s.

While compensation is not great, the benefits are relatively good. Association work does provide an exciting work environment for many people and it can lead to other career opportunities. The jobs are relatively secure. Most people work for an association for about three years before moving on to another association. For others, association work is a necessary stepping stone to Capitol Hill and consulting work with government agencies. And for others, association work is an excellent stepping stone to working for member organizations of the association and consulting firms that primarily work in the private sector. Like so many other public sector jobs, the name of the game in working with associations is to get contacts for networking your way to better job and career opportunities.

LOCATING ASSOCIATIONS

Several useful information sources are available for identifying associations appropriate for your job and career interests. The single, most comprehensive source for surveying various types of associations is the four-volume *Encyclopedia of Associations*. Found in the reference section of most libraries, the *Encyclopedia of Associations* provides names, addresses, telephone numbers, and annotated descriptions for nearly 23,000 national associations. The *Encyclopedia of Associations* classifies all associations into the following categories:

1. Trade, Business, and Commercial Organizations
2. Environmental and Agricultural Organizations
3. Legal, Governmental, Public Administration, and Military Organizations
4. Engineering, Technological, and Natural and Social Sciences Organizations
5. Educational Organizations
6. Cultural Organizations
7. Social Welfare Organizations
8. Health and Medical Organizations
9. Public Affairs Organizations
10. Fraternal, Foreign Interest, Nationality, and Ethnic Organizations
11. Religious Organizations
12. Veterans', Hereditary, and Patriotic Organizations
13. Hobby and Avocational Organizations
14. Athletic and Sports Organizations
15. Labor Unions, Associations, and Federations
16. Chambers of Commerce and Trade and Tourism Organizations
17. Greek and Non-Greek Letter Societies, Associations, and Federations
18. Fan Clubs

The following examples—two of the largest and most powerful interest groups—outline the type of information found in most listings of the *Encyclopedia of Associations*:

NATIONAL ASSOCIATION OF MANUFACTURERS
(Manufacturing)(NAM)
1331 Pennsylvania Ave., NW
Suite 1500 N. Jerry J. Jasinowki, Pres.
Washington, DC 20004 Phone (202)637-3000
Founded: 1895. **Members:** 12,500. **Staff:** 180.
Budget: $14,000,000. Manufacturers and cooperating nonmanufacturers having a direct interest in or relationship to manufacturing. Represents industry's views on national and international problems to government.

dustry's views on national and international problems to government. Maintains public affairs and public relations program. Reviews current and proposed legislation, administrative rulings and interpretations, judicial decisions and legal matters affecting industry. Maintains numerous policy groups: Government Regulation and Competition; Industrial Relations; International Economic Affairs; Resources and Technology; Taxation and Fiscal Policy. Affiliated with 150 local and state trade associations of manufacturers through National Industrial Council and 110 manufacturing trade associations.
Publications: *Briefing*, periodic (weekly when Congress is in session). *Bulletin*, periodic. *Directory of Officers, Directors and Committees*, annual. *NAM's Small Manufacturer: Issues and Information That Affect Your Business*, 8/year. Newsletter covering issues and events affecting small manufacturing businesses, particularly public policy; includes news of association activities. **Price:** Free to members. **Circulation:** 9,000. Also publishes *Washington 100* and *Winning in Public Affairs.* Also publishes reports and legal studies.
Convention/Meeting: annual conference. Also holds periodic Congress of American Industry.

AMERICAN ASSOCIATION OF RETIRED PERSONS

(Retirement)(AARP)
601 E St., NW — Phone: (202)434-2277
Washington DC 20049 — Horace B. Deets, Exec. Dir.
Founded: 1958. **Members:** 32,000,000. **Staff:** 1,200. **Regional Groups:** 10. **Local Groups:** 3,600. Persons 50 years of age or older, working or retired. Seeks to improve every aspect of living for older people. Has targeted four areas of immediate concern: health care, women's initiative, worker equity, and minority affairs. Provides group health insurance program, discounts on auto rental and hotel rates, and a specially designed and priced motoring plan. Sponsors community service programs on crime prevention, defensive driving, and tax aid, and the AARP Andrus Foundation, which awards grants to universities for gerontology research. Provides preretirement planning program; offers special services to retired teachers through National Retired Teachers Association, Division of AARP. Sponsors mail order pharmacy services. Maintains 20,000 volume library. **Computerized Services:** AGELINE on-line bibliographic database. Absorbed: (1984) Action for Independent Maturity; (1987) Institute of Lifetime Learning (founded 1963).
Publications: *AARP News Bulletin*, 11/year. Membership activities newsletter. **Price:** Included in membership dues. **ISSN:** 0010-0200. **Circulation:** 22,100,000. Advertising: accepted. *Modern Maturity*, bimonthly. Magazine for persons age 50 and above; contains articles on careers including part-time employment, the workplace, science and health, investments, personal relationships, and consumer information. **Price:** Included in membership dues; $5/year for nonmembers. **Circulation:** 22,400,000 million. **Advertising:** accepted. *Working Age*, bimonthly. Newsletter; includes research reports, case studies, legislative updates, and calendar of events. **Price:** Free. **ISSN:** 0883-2714. **Circulation:** 9,000. Also publishes books on housing, health, exercise, retirement planning, money management, and travel and leisure.
Convention/Meeting: biennial.

You should also consult the latest edition of the *National Trade and Professional Associations of the United States* directory (Columbia Books, Inc., 1350 New York Avenue, NW, Suite 207, Washington, DC 20005, Tel. 202/898-0662). This is an excellent resource for locating 7,500 national trade associations, labor unions, professional, scientific, or technical societies. Each organization is annotated and listed alphabetically as well as by subject and geographical area. Let's look at two entries:

> **AMERICAN MANAGEMENT ASSOCIATIONS** (1923), 135 West 50th St., New York, NY 10020. Tel. (212) 586-8100, Fax (212) 903-8168. *President & CEO:* David Fagiano. *Members:* 66,437. *Staff:* 880. *Annual Budget:* over $5 million. *Tel:* (212) 586-8100. *Hist. Note:* Merger (1973) of the American Management Ass'n (1923), the American Foundation for Management Research (1960), the Internat'l Management Ass'n (1956), the Presidents Ass'n (1961) and the Soc. for Advancement of Management (1912), the oldest society in the U.S. devoted to all types of management education. Maintains offices in Atlanta, GA; Watertown, MA; Chicago, IL; Hamilton, NY; Leawood, KS; New York, NY; San Francisco, CA; Saranac Lake, NY; and Washington, DC. AMA provides educational forums worldwide where members and their colleagues learn practical business skills and explore the best practices of world-class organizations through interaction with each other and expert faculty practitioners.
> *Publications:*
> Comp. Flash. m.
> Compensation & Benefits Review. bi-m.
> Management Review. m.
> Organization Dynamics. q.
> The President. m.
> Supervisory Management. m.
> Supervisory Sense. m.
> Trainer's Workshop. bi-m.
> H R Focus. m.
> *Annual Meetings:* March-April
> 1994-San Francisco, CA (H.R. Conference & Expo)/April 9-13
> 1995-Chicago IL(Hilton)/April 8-12
>
> **AMERICAN MEDICAL ASSOCIATION (1847)**
> 515 N. State St., Chicago, IL 60610-4377
> *Tel.* (312) 464-5000 *Fax:* (312) 464-4184
> *Exec. V. President:* James S. Todd, M.D.
> *Members:* 287,388. *Staff:* 1,200. *Annual Budget:* over $5 million. *Hist. Note:* Established in Philadelphia in 1847 and incorporated in Illinois in 1897. Principal spokesman for the U.S. medical profession with about 2000 local and regional medical societies. Maintains a Washington office. AMA and its affiliates support numerous political action committees throughout the country. Has an annual budget of approximately $185.3 million. *Membership:* $400/year.
> *Publications:*
> American Medical News. w. adv.
> Journal of the American Medical Ass'n. w. adv.
> American Journal of Diseases of Children. m. adv.
> Archives of Dermatology. m. adv.

Archives of General Psychiatry. m. adv.
Archives of Internal Medicine. m. adv.
Archives of Neurology. m. adv.
Archives of Ophthalmology. m. adv.
Archives of Otolaryngology. m. adv.
Archives of Pathology and Laboratory Medicine. m. adv.
Archives of Surgery. m. adv.
Archives of Family Medicine.
Semi-annual meetings: June and December
1994—Chicago, IL(Hilton & Towers)/June 12-16
1994—Honolulu, HI (Hilton Hawaiian Village)/Dec. 4-7
1995—Chicago, IL (Hilton & Towers)/June 11-15
1995—Washington, DC (Sheraton)/Dec. 3-6

Under the Subject Index, all organizations specialized in a particular functional area are grouped together. If, for example, you are interested in all associations dealing with nuclear energy, you will find the following organizations listed under the "Nuclear Energy" subject category:

- American Association of Physicists in Medicine
- American College of Nuclear Medicine
- American Nuclear Energy Council
- American Nuclear Insurers
- American Nuclear Society
- Health Physics Society
- Institute of Nuclear Materials Management
- Institute of Nuclear Power Operations
- International Association for Hydrogen Energy
- National Council on Radiation Protection and Measurements
- National Lead Burning Association
- National Association of Test, Research, and Training Reactors
- Nuclear Information and Records Management Association
- Nuclear Management and Resources Council
- Nuclear Supplies Association
- Professional Reactor Operator Society
- Radiation Research Society
- Society of Nuclear Medicine
- United States Council for Energy Awareness
- Universities Research Association

Columbia Books also publishes several other directories—*National Directory of Corporate Public Affairs, Washington Representatives, Washington '94, Baltimore and Annapolis Directory,* and *State and Regional Associations of the U.S.*—which might be useful to your research on associations. Revised each year, for example, *Washington '94* lists 3,400 key public and private organizations and the 15,000 who lead them in the Washington area. The book's 17 chapters outline the governmental, business, labor, political, cultural, educational, religious, and social power structure of Washington, DC. An index also identifies individuals with multiple affiliations and responsibilities with the various organizations. This and other books published by Columbia Books are available through Impact Publications.

Another excellent resource is the *Washington Information Directory* published by the Congressional Quarterly Inc. All major libraries should carry this volume in their reference section. The *Directory* classifies various government-related functions into 18 categories:

1. Communications and the Media
2. Economics and Business
3. Education and Culture
4. Employment and Labor
5. Energy
6. Advocacy and Public Service
7. Government Personnel and Services
8. Health
9. Housing and Urban Affairs
10. Social Services and Veterans' Programs
11. International Affairs
12. Law and Justice
13. National Security
14. Agriculture
15. Environment and Natural Resources
16. Science and Space
17. Transportation
18. Congress and Politics

Each category is further subdivided into functional areas. Within each subdivision the *Directory* lists agency, congressional, and nongovernmental organizations most concerned with the government function and agency. Each listing includes the name, address, telephone number, and a short annotation. For example, under the "Tourism" subdivision of the "Economics and Business" category, the following governmental and non-governmental listings appear among seven others:

Agency

U.S. Travel and Tourism Administration (Commerce Department), Main Commerce Bldg. 20230; 482-0136. David Edgell, acting under secretary. Information, 482-0137. Fax, 482-4279. Seeks to increase U.S. export earnings by increasing tourism-related trade. Formulates domestic and international trade policy; supports removal of restrictive trade barriers; conducts economic and demographic research; provides medium and small travel companies with technical assistance. Works with states and cities to provide information to travel industry and consumers on destinations in the United States, including accommodations, transportation, recreational facilities, and sightseeing attractions.

Congress

House Energy and Commerce Committee, Subcommittee on Transportation and Hazardous Materials, 324 Ford Bldg. (2nd and D Sts. SW) 225-9304. Al Swift, D-Wash., chairman; Arthur Andres, staff director and chief counsel. Jurisdiction over legislation affecting tourism and the U.S. Travel and Tourism Administration.

Senate Commerce, Science, and Transportation Committee, Subcommittee on Foreign Commerce and Tourism, SH-428 (mailing address: SD-508, Washington, DC 20510); 224-9325. John Kerry, D-Mass., chairman; Vacant, senior counsel. Jurisdiction over legislation affecting tourism.

Nongovernmental

American Hotel and Motel Assn., 1201 New York Ave. NW., #600, 20005; 289-3100. Kenneth F. Hine, president. Fax, 289-3199. Provides operations, technical, educational, marketing, and communications services to members. Monitors legislation and regulations. Library open to public by appointment.

American Society of Travel Agents, 1101 King St., #200, Alexandria, VA 22314; (703)739-2782. Earlene Causey, president. Fax, (703)684-8319. Membership: representatives of the travel industry. Works to safeguard the traveling public against fraud, misrepresentation, and other unethical practices. Offers training programs for travel agents. Consumer affairs department offers help for anyone with a travel complaint or industry problem.

Hosteling International, 733 15th St., NW, #840 (mailing address: P.O. Box 37613, Washington, DC 20013); 783-6161. Richard Martyr, executive director. Fax, 783-6171. Provides opportunities for outdoor recreation and inexpensive travel through hosteling.

Other annotated entries relating to nongovernmental "tourism" organizations found in the *Washington Information Directory* include:

- **Travel and Tourism Government Affairs Council**
- **Travel Industry Association of America**
- **U.S. Travel Data Center**

Another useful reference source is *The Professional and Trade Association Job Finder*. While this book is now out of print, it may be available in some libraries. This book identifies career services offered by various types of associations:

1. Professional and Trade Associations
2. Women's Organizations
3. Labor Unions
4. Employment Clearinghouses, Skills Registries, and Job Banks
5. Community Agencies

6. Apprenticeships
7. State and Local Government Agencies

Under the "Professional and Trade Association" section, for example, you will find this type of information:

> **National Association of Housing and Redevelopment Officials** (NAHRO), 2600 Virginia Avenue, NW, Washington, DC 20037, 202/333-2020. Career information is available. Semi-monthly NAHRO Monitor newsletter publishes available positions.

By surveying this book you will quickly identify key contact points for gaining access to job listings, personnel offices, newsletters, job banks, and journals which are organized to provide career and job information on each organization. The real advantage of this resource is that it provides important contact information for finding employment with both the association and member organizations. Many trade and professional organizations will list positions through their association newsletter, placement office, or job bank. Thus, this publication can provide access to nearly 30 million jobs.

Another useful source of information are telephone directories in any city, but especially in state capitals and Washington, DC. Most associations have listed telephone numbers. Look under the alphabetical listing for these key words:

American	International
Association	National
Education	Society
Institute	United

At least 70 percent of all associations begin their names with these key words. Also, try the Yellow Pages. In some communities these organizations will be listed under "Associations". Once you get a telephone number, call the organization for information. Most will be happy to send you a packet of information, including a sample brochure, magazine, newsletter, and application form.

STRATEGIES

Finding employment with associations should follow the job search strategies we outlined in Part II. By consulting the information sources in the *Professional and Trade Association Job Finder* you will locate the major sources for job vacancy listings, ranging from newsletters to computerized job banks. Many associations will place ads in local newspapers in either the classified or business sections, depending on the professional level of the position. You should monitor these job listings and respond with letters, resumes, and telephone calls. But do not spend all your time with these formal job listing sources.

Your most effective job search strategy will be networking. Contact associations for information, advice, and referrals. You can do this by:

- Contacting the placement service of associations for job listings and counseling.
- Joining the association and attending their regularly scheduled meetings where you can meet and talk to association members about their needs, your skills, and future job vacancies with this and other associations.
- Introducing yourself to individuals who work for associations.
- Responding to classified ads for association positions.
- Sending a copy of your resume and a cover letter to the head of the association.

Associations operate similarly to other organizations. Once they have a vacancy, they want to fill it as soon as possible. If they have your resume on file and someone knows you personally, your chances of getting called for a job interview and offered a job will be good.

One useful source on job search strategies are special workshops and seminars designed to assist individuals in developing effective job hunting skills and job leads for associations. First Class (202/797-5102) in Washington, DC, an open university program, every two months offers a course entitled "How to Land an Association Job" ($25). A few other organizations will occasionally offer similar short courses.

George Washington University offers a concentration in Association Management in its graduate Public Administration (MPA) program (Tel. 202/994-6295). While most of the students in this program already work for associations, a few also study for this degree with the goal of breaking into the association management field. DePaul University in Chicago also offers a graduate program in association management. Such programs should be excellent ways to "network" among fellow professionals in this field. Seminars and programs are led by individuals who work for associations and thus they can provide you with the latest tips on who is hiring whom among associations.

LISTINGS, PLACEMENTS, AND NETWORKS

Individuals who work for associations can keep abreast of employment opportunities with various associations by consulting a few organizations and publications specializing in job listings and referrals. The American

Society of Association Executives (ASAE) is the largest professional association of association executives. It maintains a Washington staff of 125 individuals who assist 20,000 members. ASAE publishes the biweekly *Career Opportunities Bulletin* which is available to nonmembers: $47 for five issues, $97 for 12 issues, or $177 for 24 issues. Members receive one to four additional issues for the same price. It also provides executive search services for all types of positions. For more information on ASAE and its publications and services, contact:

American Society of Association Executives
1575 Eye St., NW
Washington, DC 20005-1168
Tel. 202/626-2723 (Referral Services)
202/626-2742 (Information)

This association also publishes a useful annual directory of its membership: *Who's Who in Association Management.* The directory comes free with your membership, which can cost anywhere from $122 to $221 a year, depending on your affiliate status. Nonmembers can also purchase the directory separately by sending $150 (add $5.25 to $20 for shipping, depending on desired method) to the above address. Members receive the directory for $60 plus shipping. Call for shipping and payment details.

The Greater Washington Society of Association Executives provides similar services. It publishes an annual association salary survey as well as a directory of their 3,100 members—*The GWSAE Directory*. Nonmembers can purchase the directory for $120 ($115 plus $5 postage); members receive it free. Annual membership dues range from $40 (students/educators) to $285 (full association member), depending on your affiliation. Contact them at:

Greater Washington Society of Association Executives
1426 21st St., NW, Suite 200
Washington, DC 20036-5901
Tel. 202/429-9370

The U.S. Chamber of Commerce provides job assistance for executive positions with associations. Included among its over 220,000 members are nearly 1,200 trade and professional associations that belong to this organization. One useful service of the Chamber is its Referral Service which is organized especially for trade and professional associations. Chamber members send job listings to the Chamber of Commerce Relations office which, in turn, publishes them in its monthly *Position Available Bulletin.* You can subscribe to this publication at the following rates: $20.00 for six months (6 issues) or $35.00 for a full year (12 issues). You should subscribe through the following office:

Office of Chamber of Commerce Relations
U.S. Chamber of Commerce
1615 H St., NW
Washington, DC 20062-2000
Tel. 202/463-5580

The U.S. Chamber of Commerce is also a potential source of employment. It presently has a staff of 1,350 and an annual operating budget of over $5 million.

Two organizations publish useful newspapers and maintain job services for associations. *Association Trends*, a weekly newspaper ($72 for 50 weekly issues), also maintains a job referral service. This publication goes to 7,000 associations throughout the United States with a readership of nearly 25,000. You want to pay particular attention to two sections in this newspaper: "Executive Changes" and "Moves and Changes". The newspaper reports on who leaves which association and thus identifies potential job vacancies. The "Moves and Changes" section identifies associations moving office locations from one city to another. Normally, these associations have immediate staffing needs since most of their employees will not move with the association. *Trends* also maintains a "Free Resume" service. For $52 and 10 copies of your resume, they will place a 30-word classified ad describing the job you want in their Washington, New York, or Chicago editions for three consecutive weekly issues. When associations respond to your ad, *Trends* sends them a copy of your resume. The association then contacts you directly for more information or schedules you for an interview. Your only cost for this service is the $52 and 10 resumes. *Trends* will keep your file active for three months. You can get information on this publication and service by writing or calling:

Association Trends
7910 Woodmont Ave., Suite 1150
Bethesda, MD 20814
Tel. 301/652-8666

The United States Association Executive also publishes a weekly newspaper which includes a classified section with association job listings. You will want to monitor various sections relevant to your job search, especially "Executive Changes", "Classifieds", and various calendars of meetings. A one-year subscription to this newspaper, which includes 60-68 issues, costs $95. For further information, contact:

United States Association Executive
4341 Montgomery Avenue
Bethesda, MD 20814
Tel. 301/951-1881

22

NONPROFIT ORGANIZATIONS

Nearly 1 million nonprofit organizations operate in the United States. While most are too small to offer job opportunities, many are large community-based, national, and international organizations with substantial staffs and opportunities for career advancement.

Numerous nonprofit organizations also provide job opportunities for those interested in public service careers. A truly diverse group of organizations, they come in various types, forms, sizes, and interest orientations. They range from public assistance and utilities organizations to single-issue consumer advocacy groups. Most are organized to perform a needed public service or promote a particular cause. While most of these groups operate within a particular community, state, or nationwide, many others have extensive operations abroad, especially in poor Third and Fourth World nations. These groups provide emergency relief, feed the hungry, and extend child and maternal care, medical, and population planning services.

TYPES OF ORGANIZATIONS

Nonprofit organizations are by no means easy to classify. As legal entities, many of the trade and professional associations discussed in Chapter 21 have nonprofit status. However, nonprofits are more than just organizations with a legal designation. In terms of organizational goals, trade and professional associations are not nonprofit organizations, because they are oriented toward monetary gain.

Nonprofit organizations generally are organizations with a clear public service mission. Primarily nongovernmental entities, they are incorporated under state laws, exempt from federal taxes, and legally structured to receive tax deductible gifts and contributions. The governance structure cannot receive private financial gain from the organization. While many such organizations make money, the money must be directed to promote a public purpose.

Several types of nongovernmental and quasi-governmental organizations are good examples of public nonprofit organizations:

- Consumer advocacy groups focused on influencing the content of public policy
- Public assistance organizations with programs designed to assist various community groups
- Religious and charitable groups
- Medical and hospital groups
- Civil rights groups
- Public utilities groups
- Arts and museum groups
- Women's groups
- Public affairs groups

Many educational groups also are nonprofits, but groups such as the American Federation of Teachers (AFT), the National Education Association (NEA), and the American Association of University Professors (AAUP) are best viewed as professional associations; they combine membership, professional representation, lobbying, and political action functions.

Nonprofit organizations generally receive funding through public donations, corporate gifts, fund raising activities, government grants, and endowments. Foundations and local governments are major funding sources for these organizations. Given the public nature of such funding, staff members of many nonprofit organizations are paid relatively low salaries for their levels of responsibility. In many cases, staff positions with nonprofit organizations are primarily volunteer positions. This is especially true for nonprofit organizations that primarily operate at the local level.

SKILLS NEEDED

Nonprofit organizations hire all types of individuals. They especially need people with good communication, organization, public relations, program development, and fund raising skills. Because of the need to continuously find funding sources, individuals with fund raising skills are highly valued. Fund raising skills include writing grant proposals, soliciting donations, and expanding membership rolls.

Finding employment with nonprofit organizations is usually easier than getting a job with trade and professional organizations and consulting firms. This is due in part to the fact that nonprofit organizations tend to hire generalists and pay lower salaries than these other types of organizations.

Nonprofit organizations tend to hire generalists and pay lower salaries than other types of organizations.

RESOURCES AND CONTACTS

Your search for nonprofit organizations should begin in the library. A few books are available on jobs and careers with nonprofit organizations:

- *Careers in the Nonprofit Sector*
- *Doing Well by Doing Good*
- *Finding a Job in the Nonprofit Sector*
- *Good Works: A Guide to Social Change Careers*
- *Jobs and Careers With Nonprofit Organizations*
- *National Directory of Nonprofit Organizations*
- *Non-Profits' Job Finder*
- *Profitable Careers in Nonprofits*

Some of your most important resources will be found in the reference section of your local library. Here, you will find several books on various aspects of nonprofit organizations, from directories of nonprofit organizations at the national and local levels to how-to guides for improving the internal management and resources of these organizations. Some books outline job search strategies appropriate for nonprofit organizations as well as annotate the largest nonprofit organizations. Other resources, such as our *Almanac of International Jobs and Careers,* include extensive sections on nonprofit organizations operating in the international arena. Dan Lauber's unique *Non-Profits' Job Finder* primarily focuses on job listing services and databases appropriate for finding job vacancies with nonprofit organizations.

The most comprehensive listing of nonprofit organizations is a publication issued by the Internal Revenue Service: *Cumulative List of Organizations* (IRS: Publication 78). Updated and reissued annually, this directory lists over 250,000 charitable, fraternal, and private foundation organizations which qualify for tax deductible contributions. Although the IRS claims this list is not all inclusive, after you examine more than 1200 pages of these organizations, you quickly lose interest in looking for additional nonprofits not listed in this resource! Organizations are listed alphabetically and include the organization's name and its city and state location. You will need to do additional research to get the street address and telephone number for individual organizations as well as identify the mission, size, and staff of these organizations.

You also should examine the *Encyclopedia of Associations*. It includes contact and descriptive information on most nonprofit organizations with regional and national offices. The sections on Educational, Cultural, Social Welfare, Health and Medical, and Public Affairs Organizations will yield numerous names and addresses on several such organizations. For example, the following consumer organization appears in the "Public Affairs Organizations" section:

NATIONAL ORGANIZATION FOR WOMEN
(Feminism)(NOW)
1000 16th St. NW, Ste. 700 Phone: (202)331-0060
Washington, DC 20036 Patricia Ireland, Pres.
Founded: 1966. **Members:** 280,000. **Staff:** 30. **Regional Groups:** 9. **State Groups:** 50. **Local Groups:** 800. Men and women who support "full equality for women in truly equal partnership with men." Seeks to end prejudice and discrimination against women in government, industry, the professions, churches, political parties, the judiciary, labor unions, education, science, medicine, law, religions, "and every other field of importance in American society." Promotes passage of the Equal Rights Amendment and enforcement of federal legislation prohibiting discrimination on the basis of sex. Engages in lobbying and litigation. Works to increase the number of women elected to local, county, and state offices, the House of Representatives, and the Senate. Sponsors student essay contests. First president of NOW was Betty Friedan, author of the bestseller, *The Feminine Mystique.* **Telecommunications Services:** Fax, (202)785-8576. **Committees:** NOW/Equality/PAC; NOW/PAC
Publications: *NOW Times,* bimonthly. Newspaper. Local groups publish monthly newspapers.
Convention/Meeting: annual conference (with exhibits)—usually June or July

Several professional organizations provide assistance for individuals seeking employment with nonprofit organizations. The Society for Nonprofit Organizations is the only national society organized to promote nonprofit organizations. Its more than 5,000 member organizations constitute an important professional network of nonprofit executives and directors. The Society publishes a bimonthly journal (*The Nonprofit World*, $79 annual subscription for nonmembers) and regularly conducts workshops, provides technical assistance, and publishes resources for strengthening nonprofit organizations. The Society also distributes a resource center catalog that includes some books on careers in nonprofit organizations. You can contact this organization at the following address and phone number:

Society for Nonprofit Organizations
6314 Odana Rd., Suite 1
Madison, WI 53719
Tel. 608/274-9777

However, do not call this organization for information on jobs or for acquiring a directory of its members. They have neither. What they will do is refer you to their catalog as well as a job network organized for nonprofit organizations—Access.

Access maintains the largest and most comprehensive database on job opportunities with nonprofit organizations. They publish a monthly newspaper, *Community Jobs*, which includes numerous job vacancies with nonprofit organizations in the United States and abroad. They also operate a computerized resume database for employers and job seekers. For further information, you can contact this organization as follows:

Access: Networking in the Public Interest
30 Irving Place, 9th Floor
New York, NY 10003
Tel. 212/475-1001

The Taft Group, one of the nation's leading information and professional service firms for nonprofit organizations, provides numerous resources and services for individuals seeking employment with these organizations. The Taft Group provides executive search services for individuals seeking positions in development marketing and public relations. If you are interested in executive level positions, you may want to subscribe to their newsletter, *The Nonprofit Executive*, which provides the latest information on executive level developments. You can contact this organization by writing or calling:

The Taft Group
12300 Twinbrook Pkwy., Suite 520
Rockville, MD 20852-9830
Tel. 301/816-0210

INTERNATIONAL NONPROFIT ORGANIZATIONS

Numerous nonprofit organizations, both sectarian and religious, are also involved in international work. Primarily headquartered in and around New York City and Washington, DC, most of these nonprofits provide child and health care services, operate family planning programs, respond to natural disasters, feed the hungry, and resettle refugees in some of the poorest areas of Africa, Asia, and Latin America. The major nonprofit organizations include the following:

- Africare
- Agricultural Cooperative Development International
- American Friends Service Committee
- American Institute for Free Labor Development
- American Jewish Joint Distribution Committee
- Association for Voluntary Sterilization
- Cooperative for American Relief Everywhere, Inc. (CARE)
- Catholic Medical Mission Board
- Catholic Relief Services
- Christian Children's Fund, Inc.
- Church World Service
- Direct Relief International
- Family Planning International Assistance
- Food for the Hungry
- Foster Parents Plan International
- Heifer Project International
- Holt International Children's Services
- The Institute of Cultural Affairs
- Interchurch Medical Assistance, Inc.
- International Eye Foundation
- International Executive Service Corps
- International Human Assistance Programs, Inc.
- International Planning Parenthood Federation
- International Rescue Committee
- Lutheran World Relief
- MAP International
- Mennonite Economic Development Associates, Inc.
- Overseas Education Fund
- Partnership for Productivity International
- Pathfinder Fund
- People to People Health Foundation, Inc.
- Population Council
- Salvation Army
- Save the Children Federation, Inc.
- United Methodist Committee on Relief
- Volunteers in Technical Assistance (VITA)

- World Concern
- World Relief
- World Vision International

These organizations offer numerous and exciting opportunities for enterprising job seekers who are interested in working abroad. Information on these and many other international nonprofit organizations is found in our *Almanac of International Jobs and Careers* (Manassas Park, VA: Impact Publications, 1994).

LOCAL LEVEL NONPROFITS

Nonprofit organizations are most prevalent at the local level. In every city you will find numerous community service organizations. Frequently referred to as community-based organizations, these nonprofit groups provide a variety of social services in the areas of health, education, culture, recreation, rehabilitation, youth, senior citizen services, and local economic development. One of the largest such groups is the United Way which raises funds to provide general, programmatic, and emergency grants to other community service groups.

Local nonprofit organizations come in many types. In most large communities you should be able to locate a directory of community service organizations through your local government, United Way, or other community organization. Check the reference section of your local library for such a directory. These directories usually include three types of nonprofit organizations which comprise the local public service network: governmental, quasi-governmental, and nongovernmental. The United Black Fund Inc. of Greater Washington, DC, for example, publishes a *Directory of Community Service Organizations in the Washington Metropolitan Area*. The index lists nearly 1,000 community-based nonprofit organizations for the Washington, DC Metropolitan area in the following generic categories also relevant to other communities:

Abortion
Adoption
Advocacy
Adult Education
Alcoholics, Service to
Ambulance Services
Animal Care
Bail Bond
Birth Certificates
Child Abuse
Children Services
Clothing Distribution
Community Planning and Development
Consumer Information Protection
Correctional Services
Counseling Services
Credit Unions
Culture and Arts, Media Arts
Culture and Arts, Performing Arts
Culture and Arts, Services to the Field
Culture and Arts, Training and Education
Culture and Arts, Visual Arts
Day Care
Deaf, Services to

Death Certificates
Disease Control
Discrimination Complaints
Drug Abuse Prevention
Economic Development
Education, Alternative
Education, Basic
Education, Remedial
Emergency Assistance
Food Distribution
Foreign Born, Service to
Fund Raising and Charitable Organizations
Furniture Storage and Distribution
Group Homes, Adult
Group Homes, Children
Handicapped, Services to
Health Organizations
Hearing and Speech Impaired
Hospitals and Clinics
Household Goods, Storage, and Distribution
Legal Assistance
Libraries and Museums
Maternity Homes
Mental Health
Parks and Recreation Services
Pre-Natal Care
Public Assistance
Reading Assistance Referral Services
Regional Agencies Research
Senior Citizens, Services to
Social Security Assistance
Spanish Speaking, Services to
Thrift Shops
Transportation for the Elderly
Transportation for the Handicapped
Transportation, Public
Veterans, Services to
Visually Impaired
Vocational Services to
Volunteer Services
Women, Services to
Youth Organizations

If you are interested in working with a drug rehabilitation program, you will find 15 organizations with programs and services under the "Drug Abuse Prevention" category:

- Alcohol and Drug Abuse Control Coordinating Office
- Alexandria Methadone Treatment Center
- Bureau of Rehabilitation of the National Capitol Area
- Drug Intervention Counseling Action Program
- Family Service Counseling for the Deaf
- Family Services of Prince George's County
- Last Renaissance
- Latin American Youth Center
- Narcotics Treatment Administration (NTA)
- Palmer Park Counseling Center
- Rap, Inc.
- Shiloh Baptist Church Human Service Center
- Southeast Enrichment Center
- Surrattsville Community Counseling Center
- Washington Area Council on Alcoholism and Drug Abuse

Within this category, you will find brief annotated descriptions of each program.

STRATEGIES

Once you identify a nonprofit organization appropriate for your interests and skills, contact the organization by letter or telephone. Keep in mind that most nonprofit organizations have two tiers of decision-making: Board of Directors and staff. Hiring decisions may be made by one or the other or both levels, depending on the organization. Let the people at both levels know you are interested in working for them. For small nonprofits, schedule an appointment with the head of the organization or a member of the Board. For large nonprofits, you need to contact both the personnel office and individual hiring personnel within the various organizational units. Chances are you will have no problem being hired for a volunteer position as long as you are willing to help raise funds and organize activities. A full-time paid staff position will be more difficult to find. Nonetheless, make your contacts, conduct informational interviews, leave your resume with key people, and follow-up on referrals and interviews. If you engage in enough of these job search activities, you should be able to find the job you want.

You will find it is much easier to break into public sector work through these organizations.

REALISTIC EXPECTATIONS

Except with the largest nonprofit organizations headquartered in Washington, DC and New York City, career opportunities with nonprofit organizations are the least financially rewarding public service careers. For example, while the head of an association may earn $120,000 a year, the head of a similar sized nonprofit organization may only earn $60,000 a year. Furthermore, these organizations often lack good management practices, because their staff members lack managerial expertise and have limited funds to acquire the necessary management training and consulting services; some are organizational nightmares run by well-meaning but administratively inept individuals. Governing boards are often weak, and the organizations are frequently involved in difficult political situations.

While these characteristics of nonprofit organizations may be negatives for many job seekers, they are positives for others who seek unique and personally rewarding challenges. Since many of these groups are poor—

surviving by a hand-to-mouth existence through a combination of public donations, foundation grants, and government funding—many staff positions may be volunteer positions. Nonetheless, the work of these organizations is personally very rewarding for many people who are oriented to making a difference in the lives of others. Because nonprofit organizations pay staff members much less than other public organizations, you will find it is much easier to break into public sector work through these organizations.

Requiring fewer skills and limited experience, work in nonprofit organizations is open to people who are willing to devote their time and effort to the cause. Thus, they are excellent organizations in which to acquire public service experience as well as for networking with government agencies, associations, foundations, and local elites. Indeed, most nonprofit organizations are governed by a volunteer Board of Directors consisting of community leaders. As a staff member, you are responsible for day-to-day operations to these individuals. You will meet with these individuals and develop contacts with other community elites who provide funding for the organization. In the long run, these individuals may be helpful in advancing your career with other organizations.

23 FOUNDATIONS AND RESEARCH ORGANIZATIONS

Foundations and research organizations provide job opportunities for individuals with specialized organizational and subject-matter skills. They tend to seek well educated and experienced professionals. The work of these organizations supports the service activities of both governmental and nongovernmental organizations. Most are nonprofit organizations.

FOUNDATIONS

Foundations primarily provide funding for nonprofit organizations pursuing particular social, economic, and cultural programs. Nearly 22,000 foundations operate at both the national and local levels throughout the 50 States. While most of the large foundations (5,000+ with assets of $1 million or more or give at least $100,000 a year) have national and international orientations, a large number of smaller foundations operate primarily at the local level. These latter groups are often too small to support a full-time staff and thus look toward community foundations to administer their programs and funds. Indeed, during the past decade there has been a major growth in community foundations which provide funding for community-based nonprofit organizations.

Every large city has several local foundations engaged in providing grants to educational institutions and social service programs. In Washington, DC, for example, the largest foundation is the Public Welfare Foundation (2600 Virginia Avenue, N.W., Room 505, Washington, DC 20037, Tel. 202/965-1800) with assets of $290,842,400 (1992). In 1992 this foundation provided $17,469,850 in grants.This included grants to Friends of the Earth, DC ($250,000), Natural Resources Defense Counsel, NY ($250,000), Warren Wilson College, NC ($250,000), Food Research and Action Center, DC ($150,000), and For the Love of Children, DC ($150,000). This community foundation maintains a full-time staff of seventeen—twelve professionals and five support. Other large foundations also require full-time staffs to administer the grant process.

Foundations provide job opportunities for individuals with specialized skills. Like other nonprofit organizations, foundations have a two-tiered decision-making structure consisting of a Board of Trustees and an administrative staff. The staff positions primarily involve managing foundation funds, reviewing proposals, awarding grants, and administering programs. These activities require skilled professionals who can work well with grantees and board members. They require strong communication, analytical, and management skills.

Since most foundations are small, they have a limited number of staff positions. Therefore, your best job search strategy is to conduct research on these organizations and make personal contacts with either the staff or trustees. A good starting point for conducting research is *The Foundation Directory* published by The Foundation Center in New York City. Found in most library reference sections, this book lists information on 6,785 foundations with assets of more than $162 billion. While this represents less than 20 percent of all foundations, these foundations account for 91 percent of all foundation assets and 90 percent ($9 billion) of all grant dollars awarded each year by all foundations. *The Foundation Directory* is organized in the most detail for your purposes. Each foundation is listed alphabetically as well as by State and Subject. For example, the following information is included for two of the largest foundations:

LILLY ENDOWMENT, INC.
2801 North Meridian Street
P.O. Box 88068
Indianapolis, IN 46208 (317) 924-5471
Incorporated in 1937 in Indiana

Donor(s): J. K. Lilly, Sr., Eli Lilly, J. K. Lilly, Jr.
Financial data (yr. ended 12/31/92)**:** Assets, $2,607,538,024 (M); gifts received, $137,780; expenditures $131,737,051; qualifying distributions, $129,744,669, including $117,424,863 for 1,856 grants (high: $8,575,778; low: $2,500; average: $2,500-$8,575,778, $725,206 for 91 grants to individuals (high: $50,000; low: $4,500; average: $4,500-$40,000), $757,883 for 624 employee matching gifts and $750,000 for 3 program-related investments.
Purpose and Activities: Support of religion, education, and community development with special concentration on programs that benefit youth, develop leadership, and help develop state of the art fundraising to make non-profit organizations become more self-sustaining. Giving emphasizes projects that depend on private support, with a limited number of grants to government institutions, and tax-supported programs. Also supports limited grant program in economic education and public policy research.
Fields of interest: Elementary education, secondary education, economics, education, education—minorities, educational research, higher education, theological education, leadership development, community development, cultural programs, arts, historic preservation, minorities, community funds, disadvantaged, social services, youth, public policy, religion.
Officers: Thomas M. Lofton, Chair and President; William Bonifield, V.P., Education; Craig R. Dykstra, V.P., Religion; N. Clay Robbins, V.P., Community Development; Charles A. Johnson, V.P., Development; William M. Goodwin, Secy.-Tres.; Otis R. Bowen, M.D., Rev. William G. Enright, Earl B. Herr, Jr., Byron P. Hollett, Eli Lilly II, Eugene F. Ratliff, Herman B. Wells, Richard D. Wood.
Number of staff: 35 full-time professional; 32 full-time support.

THE ROCKEFELLER FOUNDATION
1133 Avenue of the Americas
New York, NY 10036 (212) 869-8500
Incorporated in 1913 in New York.
Donor(s): John D. Rockefeller, Sr.
Financial data (yr. ended 12/31/92)**:** Assets, $2,138,585,815 (M); expenditures, $114,621,476, qualifying distributions, $118,095,572, including $78,754,297 for 1,115 grants (high: $1,400,000; low: $316; $8,090,348 for 463 grants to individuals (high: $86,776; low: $39), $114,087 for 289 employee matching gifts, $6,111,670 for 102 foundation-administered programs and $5,167,000 for 4 program-related investments.
Purpose and Activities: The foundation offers grants and fellowships in three principal areas: international science-based development, the arts and humanities, and equal opportunities. Within science-based development, the focus is on the developing world and emphases are on the global environment; on the agricultural, health and population sciences; and on a very limited number of special African initiatives. The foundation also has smaller grant programs in international security and U.S. school reform. In addition, the foundation maintains the Bellagio Study and Conference Center in northern Italy for conferences of international scope and for residencies for artists and scholars.
Types of support: Fellowships, research, publications, conferences and seminars, special projects, grants to individuals, program-related investments, employee matching gifts, seed money, technical assistance.
Officers and Trustees: John R. Evans, Chair.; Peter C. Goldmark, Jr.,

Pres.; Kenneth Prewitt, Sr. V.P.; Danielle Parris, Acting V.P. for Communications; Hugh B. Price, V.P.; Lynda Mullen, Secy.; David A. White, Tres.; Sally Ferris, Dir. for Administration; Alan Alda, Ela R. Bhatt, Johnnetta Cole, Peggy Dulany, Frances FitzGerald, Daniel P. Garcia, Ronald E. Goldsberry, W. David Hopper, Karen N. Horn, Alice Stone Ilchman, Richard H. Jenrette, Robert C. Maynard, Alvaro Umana, Frank G. Wells, Harry Woolf.
Number of staff: 73 full-time professional; 1 part-time professional; 65 full-time support; 3 part-time support.

The Subject Index of the *Directory* classifies each foundation by purpose and activity:

Accounting
Adult Education
Africa
Aged
Agriculture
AIDS
Alcoholism
Animal Welfare
Anthropology
Archaeology
Architecture
Arms Control
Arts
Asia
Australia
Belgium
Biochemistry
Biological Sciences
Biology
Business
Canada
Cancer
Caribbean
Catholic Giving
Chemistry
Child Development
Child Welfare
Citizenship
Civic Affairs
Civil Rights
Communications
Community Development
Community Funds
Conservation
Crime and Law Enforcement
Cultural Programs
Dance
Delinquency
Dentistry
Dermatology
Disadvantaged
Drug Abuse
Education
Educational Associations
Educational Research
Elementary Education
Employment
Energy
Engineering
Environment
Europe
Family Planning
Family Services
Film
Fine Arts
Foreign Policy
France
Freedom
Gays and Lesbians
Government
Greece
Handicapped
Health
Heart Disease
Heroism
Higher Education
Historic Preservation
History
Homeless
Hospices
Hospitals
Hotel Administration
Housing
Human Rights
Humanities
Hunger
Immigration
Insurance Education
Intercultural Relations
International Affairs

International Development
International Relief
International Law
Israel
Italy
Japan
Journalism
Labor
Language and Literature
Latin America
Law and Justice
Leadership Development
Legal Education
Legal Services
Libraries
Literacy
Marine Sciences
Mathematics
Media & Communications
Medical
Mental Health
Mexico
Middle East
Military Personnel
Minorities
Museums
Music
Native Americans
Nursing
Nutrition
Ophthalmology
Palestinians
Parapsychology
Peace
Performing Arts
Pharmacy
Philippines
Physical Sciences
Physics
Poland
Political Science
Population Studies
Portugal
Psychiatry
Psychology
Public Administration
Public Affairs
Public Policy
Race Relations
Recreation
Rehabilitation
Religion
Rural Development
Safety
Schistosomiasis
Science and Technology
Scotland
Seaman
Secondary Education
Social Sciences
Social Services
Sociology
South Pacific
Southeast Asia
Southern Africa
Spain
Speech Pathology
Theater
Theological Education
Transportation
Turkey
United Kingdom
Urban Affairs
Urban Development
Venezuela
Vocational Education
Volunteerism
Welfare
Women
Youth

The Foundation Center also supports several foundation depositories or libraries throughout the United States. Each depository maintains comprehensive collections of information on foundation activities. If you are seriously interested in working for a foundation, you should visit one of these depositories to familiarize yourself with foundation operations.

RESEARCH FIRMS AND THINK TANKS

Over 12,500 research organizations provide job opportunities for individuals with specialized research skills. Most of these organizations conduct public related research. Many of them function as public think tanks, generating public policy options based upon research findings. While the largest number of research organizations are university research centers, thousands of other groups are primarily nonprofit research organizations. They receive their funding through a variety of public sources: government contracts, foundation grants, corporate philanthropy, individual donations, parent institutions, local revenue, membership fees, and sales of books, reports, journals, and other products. Salaries with research organizations tend to be better than those with most nonprofit organizations. They are most comparable to university faculty salaries, which are similar to association and government salaries.

The major sources for developing job leads on research organizations is the two volume *Research Center Directory*, published by Gale Research Company in Detroit. Found in most library reference sections, this comprehensive volume classifies over 12,500 research organizations into the following categories:

1. Agriculture, Food, and Veterinary Sciences
2. Biological and Environmental Sciences
3. Medical and Health Science
4. Astronomy and Space Sciences
5. Computers and Mathematics
6. Engineering and Technology
7. Physical and Earth Sciences
8. Business and Economics
9. Government and Public Affairs
10. Labor and Industrial Relations
11. Law
12. Behavioral and Social Sciences
13. Education
14. Humanities and Religion
15. Regional and Area Studies
16. Multidisciplinary Programs
17. Research Coordinating Offices and Research Parks

Typical entries provide useful contact information and annotated descriptions of activities engaged in by these organizations. The following examples are for three of the largest and most important public affairs-related research organizations:

AMERICAN ENTERPRISE INSTITUTE (AEI)
1150 Seventeenth St. NW Phone: (202) 862-5800
Washington, DC 20036
Christopher C. DeMuth, President
Organizational Notes: Independent nonprofit, nonpartisan research and educational organization, with its programs and studies monitored by panels of distinguished scholars, an academic advisory board, and a program

of distinguished scholars, an academic advisory board, and a program priorities advisory committee. *Founded:* 1943. *Sources of Support:* Contributions from foundations, corporations, and individuals. *Staff:* 100 persons.
Research Activities and Fields: Government regulation, economics, health, energy, foreign affairs, and political science.
Publications and Services: Research results in published books, periodicals, and a series of evaluative, foreign and defense, domestic affairs, and Institute studies. *Publications:* Economist (monthly); Public Opinion (bimonthly). *Meetings/Educational Activities:* Annual Public Policy week in December; sponsors televised debates and meetings featuring discussions among experts on major political issues. *Library:* 11,000 volumes and 300 periodicals.

BROOKINGS INSTITUTION
1775 Massachusetts Ave. NW
Washington, DC 20036 Phone: (202) 797-6000
Bruce K. MacLaury, President
Organizational Notes: Independent, nonprofit research, education and publication organization. *Founded:* 1916. *Sources of Support:* Endowment, industry, philanthropic foundations, individuals, and contracts with U.S. Government. *Annual Volume of Research:* $17,660,000. *Staff:* 85 research professionals, 160 others. *Affiliated Centers:* Maintains the Social Science Computation Center, providing computing and related services to the Institution. Also operates the Center for Public Policy Education, an educational division of the Institution.
Research Activities and Fields: Economics, including studies on what economic policies are most conducive to sustained growth of the U.S. economy, how social programs can be made more effective in an era of constrained resources, and how international economic relations can be improved; government, including studies on political institutions, regulation and economic policy, and social policy; and foreign policy, including defense analysis and international economics and trade studies, and U.S. relations with, and regional studies on, the Soviet Union, East Asia, and the Middle East. *Computers:* DECsystem 1090, VAX-11/785, VAX 8650.
Publications and Services: Research results published in books, professional journals, and phamplets. *Publications:* Monographs; Annual Report; Brookings Papers on Economic Activity (semiannually); The Brookings Review (quarterly); and Reprint Series (irregularly). *Meetings/Education Activities:* Sponsors conferences, and other educational programs for leaders in government, business, and the professions, including National Issues Forum and Executive Leadership Seminars on Critical Public Policy Issues. Programs for government officials include Seminar on Executive Leadership in Changing Policy Environment and conferences on issues in science and technology policy, new directions in national policy making, public management, and technology. Programs for corporate executives include conferences on federal government operations, federal policy making for science and technology, and seminars in Europe, Japan, the Soviet Union, and Korea. *Library:* Restricted collection of 80,000 volumes; Laura Walker, librarian.

2100 M Street, NW Phone: (202) 833-7200
Washington, DC 20037
William Gorham, President
Organizational Notes: Independent, nonprofit research organization. *Founded:* 1968. *Sources of Support:* Federal, state, and local governments, foundations, individuals, and corporate philanthropy. *Staff:* 105 research professionals, 47 supporting professionals, 41 others.
Research Activities and Fields: Domestic, social, and economic affairs, including multidisciplinary studies and government program evaluations in the areas of tax and budget reform, health policy, housing and community development, human resources, income security and pension, international activities, public finance, productivity and economic development, social services, and immigration. Also conducts research programs on employment and training, children's issues and family policy, minorities and social policy, poverty, state and local governments, transportation and community impact and demography. *Databases:* Coordinates and houses United States Renal Data System.
Publications and Services: Research results published in books, booklets, and project reports. *Publications:* Policy and Research Report (three times yearly); Annual Report; Policy Bites (bimonthly); supplements and summaries of reports, papers, reprints, and other communications of the Institute. *Meetings/Education Activities:* Conducts press briefings, policy seminars, and interdisciplinary conferences. *Other Services:* Offers technical assistance to state and local governments and to developing countries. Current projects include the development of national housing strategies in Eastern Europe, urban redevelopment in Jamaica, and an examination of health care financing in developing countries. *Library:* 32,000 volumes, 650 journals, and 5,000 reels of microfilm on social and economic issues; Camille Motta, librarian.

The major public interest think tanks offer numerous job opportunities for professionals interested in public policy issues. Most of these think tanks conduct research, issue policy proposals, and publish reports and books. Their professional and support staffs range in size from 10 to over 150. Most of these groups are located in Washington, DC. They include such conservative think tanks as the Cato Institute, The Heritage Foundation, and the Ethics and Public Policy Center as well as such liberal groups as the Center for National Policy and the Institute for Policy Studies:

Think Tank	**Estimated Annual Budget** (1995)	**Phone**
American Enterprise Institute	$12,000,000	202/862-5800 (DC)
The Brookings Institution	$20,000,000	202/797-6000 (DC)
Capital Research Center	$500,000	202/822-8666 (DC)
Cato Institute	$4,000,000	202/546-0200 (DC)
Center for National Policy	$1,200,000	202/546-9300 (DC)
Center for Policy Alternatives	$1,700,000	202/387-6030 (DC)
Economic Policy Institute	$1,800,000	202/775-8810 (DC)
Ethics and Public Policy Center	$1,400,000	202/682-1200 (DC)

Free Congress Foundation, Inc.	$4,300,000	202/546-4400 (DC)
The Heritage Foundation	$20,000,000	202/546-4400 (DC)
Hoover Institution	$20,000,000	415/723-0603 (CA)
Hudson Institute	$5,400,000	317/545-1000 (IN)
The Independent Institute	$1,000,000	415/632-1366 (CA)
Institute for Contemporary Studies	$3,800,000	415/981-5353 (CA)
Institute for Policy Studies	$2,700,000	202/234-9382 (DC)
Investor Responsibility Research Center	$4,500,000	202/234-7500 (DC)
Joint Center for Political and Economic Studies	$5,000,000	202/626-3500 (DC)
Manhattan Institute for Policy Research	$3,200,000	202/626-3500 (DC)
Pacific Research Institute for Public Policy	$1,000,000	415/989-0833 (CA)
Reason Foundation	$2,400,000	213/392-0443 (CA)
The Rockford Institute	$1,600,000	815/964-5053 (IL)
The Urban Institute	$20,000,000	202/833-7200 (DC)
Worldwatch Institute	$4,000,000	202/452-1999 (DC)

For more information on these and other think tanks, refer to the listings in the *Encyclopedia of Associations, Research Center Directory,* and *Public Interest Profiles* (Washington, DC: Foundation for Public Affairs, Congressional Quarterly, Inc.).

Many of the larger research organizations and think tanks will advertise for personnel through their personnel offices or professional associations. You should monitor job listings in newspapers, especially the *Washington Post* and *The Chronicle of Higher Education*, as well as contact both the personnel offices and key individuals within the organizations. The personal contact will be your best strategy. Since these organizations tend to hire subject matter specialists, you should contact individuals in the organizations who share your research expertise. Fellow professionals normally will be happy to provide you with job-related information and referrals. Also, be sure to contact your professional association for job leads. They may maintain a placement service which regularly includes job listings for such organizations.

24 POLITICAL SUPPORT, INFLUENCE, AND MANAGEMENT GROUPS

Our final set of peripheral organizations consists of an assortment of political support, influence, and management groups primarily centered in and around Washington, DC and state capitals. Consisting of Political Action Committees, political parties, lobbyists, lawyers, and political consultants, these groups primarily focus their activities on legislative and executive organizations in government. In contrast to most other peripheral groups, individuals working with these organizations are deeply involved in the political process of elections, campaign finance, legislative power, and executive influence.

The groups discussed in this chapter constitute a network of related organizations offering numerous job opportunities for individuals interested in nonelected political careers. Furthermore, they provide alternative career paths for individuals on Capitol Hill, in regulatory agencies, and with law firms. While many of the jobs we discussed earlier in government and among peripheral organizations are relatively apolitical, the jobs examined in this chapter lie at the heart of the American political process. These jobs follow the ebb and flow of politics, can be extremely rewarding both financially and personally, and are the glamour, glitter, and glory of the high road of politics and power. Most of these jobs require many years of experience on Capitol Hill, in the legal profession, and among influential political networks. They go to a uniquely talented group of individuals—many of whom are political junkies. However, administrative support positions with these organizations may require very little experience and thus are good entry points for acquiring experience in these fascinating professions.

These jobs follow the ebb and flow of politics, can be extremely rewarding both financially and personally, and are the glamour, glitter, and glory of the high road of politics and power.

POLITICAL ACTION COMMITTEES

Political Action Committees (PACs) are a relatively new phenomenon on the American political scene. The first PAC was established in 1961 by the American Medical Association: the American Medical Political Action Committee (AMPAC). In 1963 the National Association of Manufacturers provided seed money to establish the Business-Industry Political Action Committee (BIPAC). Today, approximately 8,250 PACs ostensibly raise money and contribute to the election campaigns of officials at the state and national levels. PACs registered with the Federal Election Commission now number 4,178—up from 608 in 1974. The pacesetting AMPAC and BIPAC remain two of the most influential PACs.

Most major corporations, labor unions, and lobbying groups have their own PACs. Others contribute to PACs which represent the interests of numerous groups. All PACs are either sponsored by or connected to corporations, labor organizations, membership groups, or trade associations. The Public Affairs divisions of these organizations are usually in charge of maintaining PAC activities.

The purpose of PACs is clear: raise and spend money on elected officials. They are organized as campaign finance arms of particular trade and professional associations or industries, such as AMPAC. Other PACs are organized as collective campaign finance organizations for several trade and professional associations and interest groups, such as BIPAC. The majority of PACs "invest" in incumbent candidates who are expected to look favorably on the interests of contributors. At times they target incumbents for defeat in expectation a newly elected official they helped fund will favor their interests. In the 1991-1992 election cycle PACs raised $385 million and spent $394 million; they spent $188.7 million on federal candidates. While fund raising was up 4 percent and spending grew more then 10 percent compared to the 1989-90 election cycle, PAC contributions to federal candidates in 1991-1992 increased by 19 percent. Very little of this money—less than $800,000—went to presidential candidates, the least amount contributed since 1976. Over 65 percent of PAC contributions went to House candidates; 34 percent went to Senate candidates; and 1 percent went to presidential candidates. Nearly 72 percent of the contributions went to incumbent candidates. Democratic candidates, who received 64 percent of all PAC contributions in 1992, remain the major beneficiaries of PAC contributions.

A new type of PAC is one associated with a particular political candidate but is classified and legally functions as a multi-candidate PAC. The rise of this hybrid type of PAC was most closely associated with former Vice-President George Bush's PAC: The Fund For America's Future. In 1986 this became the largest PAC of any potential 1988 presidential candidate—$3.9 million in resources, 24 staffers, and 9 consultants. Functioning similar to a miniature presidential campaign organization, The Fund For America's Future in early 1986 was headed by the deputy campaign manager of the Reagan-Bush '84 committee; the political director was the former head of Reagan-Bush voter registration; four regional political directors were hired; full-time staff were hired in Iowa and Michigan and were planned for New Hampshire; and the staff was rounded out with three researchers, consultants, professional fund raisers, and direct-mail specialists. Ostensibly an unaffiliated PAC, The Fund For America's Future allocated less than 4 percent of its funds to other candidates. For all intents and purposes, this PAC was Vice-President Bush's financial and organizational launching pad for the 1988 presidential campaign. This new type of PAC most likely will become a pacesetter for PACs in the 1990s. Closely affiliated with particular candidates, it opens a new element in the ever expanding revolving door of PACs, Capitol Hill staffs, political parties, lobbyists, political consultants, and trade associations.

Most PACs are multi-candidate organizations. Funded primarily by associations and industries, they funnel funds into the campaigns of particular individuals rather than into political parties. In so doing, these organizations require staff members who are talented in raising contributions, networking among the powerful, and targeting funds into particular campaigns. In addition, PACs such as BIPAC maintain two divisions. A political action division raises and targets funds. A political education division engages in public education programs favorable to the activities of PACs and business associations. This second division requires individuals with strong research and public relations skills.

U.S. Senate candidates receiving the largest contributions in 1993-1994 included the following:

Candidate	State	Party	Net Receipts
1. Hutchison, Kay Bailey	TX	Rep.	$7,004,006
2. Krueger, Robert	TX	Dem.	$4,585,255
3. Kennedy, Edward M.	MA	Dem.	$3,702,463
4. Feinstein, Dianne	CA	Dem.	$3,119,597
5. Fisher, Richard Welton	TX	Dem.	$2,856,205
6. Moynihan, Daniel Patrick	NY	Dem.	$2,582,065
7. Mack, Connie	FL	Rep.	$2,394,059
8. Lautenberg, Frank R.	NJ	Dem.	$2,299,937
9. Fields, Jack M., Jr.	TX	Rep.	$2,219,681
10. Wofford, Harris L.	PA	Dem.	$2,180,312
11. Lieberman, Joseph I.	CT	Dem.	$2,103,823
12. Mitchell, George J.	ME	Dem.	$1,923,250
13. Cooper, Jim	TN	Dem.	$1,791,270
14. Kerrey, J. Robert	NE	Dem.	$1,754,757
15. Sasser, James Ralph	TN	Dem.	$1,629,363
16. Hutchison, Kay Bailey	TX	Rep.	$1,617,039
17. North, Oliver Laurence	VA	Rep.	$1,569,197
18. Hatch, Orrin G.	UT	Rep.	$1,484,846
19. Kyl, Jon L.	AZ	Rep.	$1,456,917
20. Luger, Richard G.	IN	Rep.	$1,456,802
21. Robb, Charles Spittal	VA	Dem.	$1,342,073
22. Gorton, Slade	WA	Rep.	$1,336,917
23. Bryan, Richard H.	NV	Dem.	$1,271,680
24. Healy, Bernadine P.	OH	Rep.	$1,150,249
25. Barton, Joe L.	TX	Rep.	$1,086,862

PACs vary in how they hire personnel. Since they require experienced political fund raising skills, many work exclusively with a particular employment agency or executive search firm to locate key personnel. Others rely on word-of-mouth for recruiting key people from associations and Capitol Hill. Many PACs advertise in newspapers but only for part-time administrative support positions.

The world of PACs is a fascinating yet relatively uncharted employment arena. If you have the necessary skills and motivation, you will need to do a great deal of research on individual PACs as well as network into the proper informal channels which yield employment opportunities with these groups. If you know very little about PACs, read

Larry J. Sabato's excellent, well-researched book on this subject: *PAC Power: Inside the World of Political Action Committees* (New York: W. W. Norton) and Dan Clawson's *Money Talks: Corporate PACS and Political Influence* (New York: Basic Books). Edward Zuckerman's *Almanac of Federal PACs* (Amward Publications, 2030 Clarendon Blvd., Arlington, VA 22201, Tel. 703/525-7227, $97.50 plus $4.00 shipping) is the "bible" for identifying over 600 PACs that contribute at least $50,000 or more to congressional candidates. The public Records section of the Federal Election Commission (FEC) has a great deal of data on PACs. Contact them at:

Federal Election Commission
999 E Street, N.W.
Washington, DC 20463
Tel. 202/376-3140
Toll free: 800/424-9530

The Commission oversees the activities of PACs to make sure they conform with Federal laws. Consequently, the FEC compiles a great deal of information on the location and size of PACs. In particular, you should purchase the FEC's latest edition of the *933 Index* which is also entitled the "Gross Receipts and Expenditure Totals" ($4.00). This document rank orders all PACs according their total receipts and expenditures. The FEC also publishes a four-volume FEC *Reports on Financial Activity, 1991-92: Party and Non-Party Political Committees, Final Report* which is available for $10 from its Office of Public Records.

If you are interested in monitoring PACs, consider subscribing to Edward Zuckerman's semi-monthly newsletter, *The Political Finance and Lobby Reporter* (Tel. 703/525-7227, $287 for annual subscription).

A few PACs listed in the FEC documents also appear with descriptive information in the *Encyclopedia of Associations*. The BIPAC entry, for example, is annotated in the following manner:

BUSINESS-INDUSTRY POLITICAL ACTION COMMITTEE (BIPAC)
1747 Pennsylvania Ave., NW — Phone: (202) 833-1880
Washington, DC 20006 — Charles S. Mack, Pres. & CEO
Founded: 1963. **Budget:** $1,100,000. Businesspeople and other individuals who are concerned with "the steadily increasing trend toward centralization of our government and domination of the economy and the individual." Describes itself as the political arm of the business community. Not affiliated with any political party, it provides direct campaign support to U.S. congressional candidates who favor limited government, sound fiscal policies and the American system of free competitive enterprise. Conducts political education briefings and seminars for the business community.
Publications: *Election Insight* • Newsletter, quarterly • *Politics,* quarterly • Reports • Also publishes research studies.
Conventions/Meetings: periodic conference.

The two FEC documents will provide you with basic comparative data for targeting a job search on particular PACs. During 1991-1992, the 25 largest PACs were:

	Committee	Receipts
1.	Democratic Republican Independent Voter Education Committee	$9,393,542
2.	NRA Political Victory Fund	$5,971,253
3.	American Medical Association PAC (AMPAC)	$5,398,323
4.	American Federation of State, County, and Municipal Employees	$4,726,826
5.	Association of Trial Lawyers of America PAC	$4,492,163
6.	Realtors PAC	$4,479,564
7.	UAW Voluntary Community Action Program	$4,428,743
8.	National Education Association PAC	$4,427,266
9.	Emily's List	$4,139,346
10.	National Abortion Rights Action League	$3,922,154
11.	National Congressional Club	$3,854,577
12.	Machinists Non-Partisan Political League	$3,585,577
13.	American Telephone & Telegraph Company PAC	$2,757,250
14.	Transportation Political Education League	$2,454,490
15.	Dealers Election Action Committee of the National Automobile Dealers Association	$2,435,182
16.	American Federation of Teachers Committee on Political Education	$2,336,214
17.	United Parcel Service PAC	$2,255,707
18.	Active Ballot Club, A Department of United Food and Commercial Workers International Union	$2,195,220
19.	Presidential Victory Committee	$2,183,813
20.	International Brotherhood of Electrical Workers Committee on Political Education	$2,179,219
21.	National Right to Life PAC	$2,153,435
22.	CWA-COPE Political Contributions Committee	$2,144,817
23.	National PAC	$2,143,466
24.	Voice of Teachers for Education/Committee on Political Education of New York State United Teachers	$2,110,621
25.	American Citizens for Political Action	$2,071,629

During the past four years, the newest and fastest growing PACs have been single issue organizations, such as the National Abortion Rights Action League and the National Right to Life Political Action Committee, and womens' groups, such as Emily's List and Women's Campaign Fund, Inc., organizations devoted to increasing the participation of women in the political process.

The fastest growing PACs during the past four years, in terms of total receipts, have been:

- NRA Political Victory Fund
- Democratic Republican Independent Voter Education Committee
- American Federation of State, County, and Municipal Employees

- Association of Trial Lawyers of America PAC
- UAW Voluntary Community Action Program
- Emily's List
- National Abortion Rights Action League

The financial size and rankings of PACs will change during election years. PACs with the largest staffs also tend to be the ones with the largest amount of receipts and expenditures. AMPAC, for example, has a full-time staff of 48. Other PACs function as part of the Public Affairs divisions of corporations. Depending on the corporation, this division may have few job opportunities related to the PAC function. In many cases the PAC activity only involves writing a check. Indeed, 95 percent of the PACs are very small in terms of both contributions and staff involvement. A large number of PACs registered with the FEC make annual campaign contributions totalling less than $1,000. Consequently, it's important that you research the individual PACs to uncover how the organization and personnel are structured. You need not concentrate on more than the top 50 PACs.

Most PACs are attached to professional associations, labor groups, political parties, special and single interest groups, or corporations. If you are interested in working in the political arena of major corporations, you may want to contact the following corporate PACs which were the largest corporate PACs in 1992, raising between $550,000 and $2.8 million each:

1. American Telephone and Telegraph Company
2. United Parcel Service PAC
3. Federal Express Corporation PAC
4. NationsBank Corporation PAC
5. Union Pacific Fund for Effective Government
6. RJR Political Action Committee RJR Nabisco Inc.
7. Waste Management Inc. Employees' Better Government Fund
8. Philip Morris Companies Inc. PAC
9. General Electric Company PAC
10. Morgan Stanley & Co. Incorporated Better Government Fund
11. GTE Corporation Political Action Club
12. U.S. West Inc. Political Action Committee
13. Coastal Corp. Employee Action Fund
14. Bellsouth Telecommunications Inc. Federal PAC
15. Barnett People for Better Government Inc.
16. General Dynamics Corporation Voluntary Political Contribution Plan
17. Morgan Companies Political Action Committee
18. Central Bancshares of the South, Inc. PAC
19. Banc One PAC
20. Ford Motor Company Civic Action Committee
21. AFLAC Incorporated Political Action Committee
22. Fluor Corporation Public Affairs Committee
23. U.S. Tobacco Executives, Administrators, and Managers PAC
24. Atlantic Richfield Company, ARCO PAC
25. Merrill Lynch & Co. Inc. Political Action Committee

POLITICAL PARTIES

Political parties offer job opportunities for individuals interested in working at the heart of the political arena. The Democratic and Republican parties alone consist of thousands of relatively independent party organizations at the national, state, and local levels. While many of them are staffed by volunteers, many also have part-time and full-time paid positions.

Both the Republican and Democratic parties maintain full-time staffs at the national and state levels to provide assistance to local party organizations and individual candidates. The size of these staffs will vary depending on the electoral process. In 1986, for example, the Republican National Committee had a staff of approximately 400; the Democratic National Committee had a staff of 100. During presidential election years, the parties will enlarge their staffs considerably with temporary and part-time employees, many of whom are hired to staff phone banks. Altogether, political parties do not generate a large number of full-time paid positions.

While we normally think in terms of a two-party system, in actual practice hundreds of political parties operate in the United States at the national, state, and local levels. However, only a few are large enough to raise sufficient funds to support a staff, disseminate information, field candidates, and operate viable campaigns. Several political parties hire individuals for a variety of paid staff positions. Political parties with some staff presence include:

Party	Staff Size	Phone
▪ Citizens	2	202/659-8878
▪ Coalition for a Democratic Majority	4	202/466-4700
▪ College Republican National Committee	15	202/662-1330
▪ Conservative Party	5	212/689-8400
▪ Democratic Congressional Campaign Committee	25	202/789-2920
▪ Democratic Governors Association	2	202/797-6644
▪ Democratic National Committee	100	202/797-5900
▪ Fund for a Democratic Majority	6	202/546-2282
▪ Libertarian Party	5	713/686-1776
▪ National Black Republican Council	2	212/863-8628
▪ National Federation of Democratic Women	3	202/797-5900
▪ National Federation of Republican Women	8	202/863-8770
▪ National New Democratic Coalition	6	202/483-4805
▪ National Republican Congressional Committee	88	202/479-7000
▪ National Republican Heritage Groups Council	3	202/662-1345
▪ Republican Governors Association	8	202/863-8620

▪ Republican National Committee	400	202/863-8500
▪ Republican National Hispanic Assembly of the United States	4	202/662-1355
▪ Republicans Abroad	2	202/484-6652
▪ Republicans Abroad International	3	202/662-1390
▪ Socialist Labor Party of America	11	415/494-1532
▪ Young Democrats of America	2	202/797-5900
▪ Young Republican National Federation	6	202/484-6680

Of all the political parties, the Republican Party has the largest number of organizations and staff positions. This is in part due to the fact that the Republican Party is more centralized and disciplined than the Democratic Party.

Since the political process tends to be highly decentralized and centered around individual candidates for political office, state and national party organizations primarily provide support and assistance to thousands of party members and organizations at the local level. They do this through public education, consulting, technical assistance, and training activities. The funding of individual political campaigns, however, is centered around PACs and the fund raising activities of individual candidates. Given the decentralized nature of political parties, national and state political party jobs vary from fund raising to organizing meetings and conducting training. The Democratic and Republican National Committees each have a personnel office which can provide information on job vacancies. However, the hiring process with these and other political parties is very much an informal networking and word-of-mouth process. You can submit your resume to the personnel office, but your best strategy will be to make contacts with key individuals within the organizations.

The networking strategies outlined in Chapter 9 are most appropriate for gaining entry into these organizations. Whom you know becomes important to your networking approach. The more names you collect and drop as well as referrals you receive will strengthen your job search campaign with these organizations.

LOBBYISTS AND LAWYERS

While most large associations maintain full-time lobbyists and legal counsels on their staffs, other organizations function as lobbyists for various groups, including foreign governments. Variously termed political consultants, government relations firms, public relations and public affairs consulting firms, these are professional lobbying firms. They gather information, provide legal counsel, and lobby legislators and executive agencies for their clients. In short, they pedal information, advice, and influence to and for those willing to pay the price.

Given the multiple roles of lobbyists, the largest group consists of lawyers. Many have previous Capitol Hill experience as congressional staff or committee members. A significant number have been former Administrative Assistants, Legislative Assistants, and Press Secretaries for members of Congress. After all, much of their lobbying work involves legislators and the legislative process. Their intimate Capitol Hill knowledge and contacts prove invaluable in this profession. They monitor impending laws and regulations for their clients as well as push for or against laws and regulations which would affect them. They are the protectors and catalysts for the billions of dollars in government subsidies that go to their clients. Therefore, legal skills and the personal connections the legal field affords these individuals are central to this process.

Lobbyists are associated with law firms, professional lobbying organizations, or freelance as independent consultants. Many former Representatives leave the legislature to join such firms or develop their own clientele. Their major skill is their ability to gain access to key decision-makers. In Washington, DC alone, there are approximately 40,000 lawyers; 25,000 of them actively practice their profession. Of these, approximately one-fourth are in the lobbying business. Many of them are associated with law firms which hire paralegals and other support staff to conduct research and writing.

If you are interested in lobbying, keep in mind this is primarily an area dominated by lawyers who are well connected in both the corporate and government worlds. Their organizations do hire nonlawyers for support staff positions. However, this is strictly an informal, word-of-mouth hiring culture. A great deal of secrecy surrounds their organizations and activities. Therefore, you must know the right people, and the more influential people are the ones who can provide you with the necessary connections and access.

If you don't know the right people, try conducting library and networking research which will help develop your connections. Congressional lobbyists are required by law to register with Congress. Representatives of foreign governments must register with the Department of Justice. Consequently, a great deal of data is available on who does what for whom in the lobbying business. One of the easiest ways to locate information on these firms is to consult the latest annual edition of *Washington Representatives* (Washington, DC: Columbia Books). This directory lists all registered lobbyists and law firms representing interest groups. It also includes a Foreign Interests Index which lists lobbyists registered as agents of individual foreign governments. For example, two of the largest and most influential professional lobbying firms today are Thomas Hales Boggs, Jr. and Black, Manafort, Stone, & Kelly. The *Washington Representatives* directory provides inside information on firms as described in the following examples:

BOGGS, Thomas Hale, Jr.
Partner, Patton, Boggs and Blow
2550 M St., NW, Suite 800, Washington, DC 20037
Tel: (202) 457-6000 Fax: (202) 457-6315

Registered as lobbyist at U.S. Congress and as a Foreign Agent.
Clients: Ad Hoc Coalition for Intermarket Coordination, American Bankers Association, American Institute of Merchant Shipping, American Society of Association Executives, Association of Trial Lawyers of America, Bluebonnet Savings Bank, Chicago Board Options Exchange, Climate Council, CUC International, Dairy Institute of California, Dole Food Co., Doyon, Ltd., FAG Bearings Corp., Falconwood Corporation, Federation Against Inequitable and Regressive Taxation, FlexiVan Leasing, GE Capital Services, General Electric Co., Genstar Container Corp., International Swaps Dealers Association, International Union of Police Associations, Itel Containers International Corp., Leadership Council on Advertising, Louisiana Office of Conservation, Loyola University, Major League Baseball Players Association, Manhole Adjusting Contractors, MCI Communications Corp., National Association of Retail Druggists, National Automatic Merchandising Association, National Cable Television Association, New York Life Insurance Co., Newspaper Association of America, Options Clearing Corp., OSG Bulk Ships, Pacific Lumber Co., Peabody Coal Co., Project ACTA, Reefer Express Lines, Reliance Group Holdings, Schoenke & Associates, Sedgwick James, Charles E. Smith Companies, Thomson Publishing, Thomas US, Trans Ocean, Transamerica Natural Gas Corp., Travelers Inc., Triton Container Co., United Welfare Fund, USAir Group, Westinghouse Electric Corp., Woodlands Corp.

BLACK, MANAFORT, STONE, & KELLY
211 N. Union St., Suite 300, Alexandria, VA 22314
Tel: (703) 683-6612 Fax: (703) 683-6128
Background: A public affairs and government relations consulting firm.
Members of firm representing client organizations: Mary Arnold; Charles R. Black; Anne Burns; Linda Dark; Richard Davis; David Fenig; Matthew Freedman; Dean Gloy; James Healey; Peter Kelly; Andre LeTendre; Riva Levinson; Michael Lewan; Paul J. Manafort; Nicholas A. Panuzio; R. Scott Pastrick; Robert Stevens; Roger Stone; Evan Tracy; Deborah Willhite.
Clients: AlliedSignal; American Airlines; American Behavioral Healthcase Association; American Managed Behavioral Healthcare Association; Atlantic City Casino Association; Bethlchem Steel Corp.; Chrysler Corp.; Consortium for Passenger Rail; Cooper Hospital/University Medical Center; First Hospital Corp.; Harris & Associations; J&J Management Co.; Johnson & Johnson; Kashmiri American Foundation; Magal Security Systems; MGM Grand; Morton International; NEC USA; Nigeria; Occidental Petroleum Corp.; Philip Morris; Phoenix Home Life Mutual Insurance; Revlon Group; Roger Williams University; Textron; Tobacco Institute; Togo; Tourism Development Properties; Trump Organization; Uniao Nacional Para Independencia Total de Angola; Union Pacific; United Parcel Service; Victoria Consultants.

While Thomas Boggs tends to be closely associated with the Democrats and Black, Manafort, Stone, and Kelly tends to be associated with the Republicans, these lobbying firms are organized to be in the lobbying business over the long-term regardless of who occupies the White House. Consequently, drawing their staffs from both political parties enables them to work well with any administration. Nonetheless, the Boggs firm appears to have an edge with the Clinton Administration. The firm of Black, Manafort, Stone, and Kelly was closely associated with the Reagan and Bush Administrations.

Washington has numerous examples of the rising and falling fortunes of lobbying and political consulting firms. One of the fastest growing firms in 1985, for example, was Michael K. Deaver and Associates. Mr. Deaver left the White House in 1985, according to some, to cash in on his numerous connections with the Republican Administration—while his connections were still in place. His new firm became an instant success with several million dollars in contracts flowing in from foreign and domestic clients. However, Deaver and Associates quickly became a "flash organization"—set up only for short-term financial gain based upon a unique set of connections with powerful Republicans. Its quick demise in the face of conflict of interest charges became an object lesson in how not to launch such a high profile political consulting firm. On the other hand, former Secretary of State Henry A. Kissinger left the Ford Administration in the late 1970s and established Kissinger Associates, a highly successful international political consulting firm which has attracted some of Washington's top talent and millions of dollars worth of major international clients.

Lobbyists also have their own professional association. The American League of lobbyists has 250 members with a single staff member. Contact them at:

The American League of Lobbyists
P.O. Box 20450
Alexandria, VA 22320
Tel. 703/960-3011

POLITICAL CONSULTANTS

Political consultants specialize in providing information and advice on how to best run political campaigns and organizations. They work with PACs, political parties, lobbyists, and special interest groups. Most have a great deal of experience and are extremely talented both politically and technically. Some of the best known groups have been Patrick Caddall's polling organization, Cambridge Survey Research, and Richard Viguerie's conservative direct-mail fund raising group, Richard A. Vigerie Company. These organizations have been associated with a particular political group and perform key political functions: fund raising, campaign strategy, media coverage, and political information. Most use the latest technology to improve the political positions of their clients.

If you are interested in working for such firms, you should begin by reading several books on political consulting. Although somewhat dated, one of the best books on this subject is another well written and researched book by Larry J. Sabato: *The Rise of Political Consultants* to improve the political positions of their clients.

If you are interested in working for such firms, you should begin by reading several books on political consulting. Although somewhat dated, one of the best books on this subject is another well written and researched book by Larry J. Sabato: *The Rise of Political Consultants* (New York: Basic Books). It includes an examination of the history, roles, and organization of these groups as well as a listing of the major political consulting firms classified into four types of consulting skills and services: general, polling, media, and direct-mail. Dr. Sabato also identifies firms by party affiliation, ideological leaning, scope, and specialty. Also, see David M. Ricci's *The Transformation of American Politics: The New Washington and the Rise of Washington Think Tanks* (New Haven, CT: Yale University Press).

Your best job search strategy with these firms again is networking. Few of these firms advertise for personnel. They locate personnel through word-of-mouth and through direct contacts with individuals who self-market themselves.

Like so many others who work the political arena, these individuals live work-driven life styles of the political junkie.

Except for administrative support positions, keep in mind that these firms hire individuals with a great deal of experience and skills. Like so many others who work the political arena, these individuals live work-driven lifestyles of the political junkie. Dr. Sabato best captures their skills and lifestyles in his revealing study of these political operatives:

> . . . consultants are hard-working professionals: very bright and capable, politically shrewd and calculating and impressively articulate. They travel tens of thousands of miles every year, work on campaigns in a dozen or more states simultaneously, and eat, breathe, and live politics. They are no less political junkies than the candidates they serve.

Political consultants also have their own association or belong to specialty associations which can provide you with information and advice on entering this field. The 650 members of the American Association of Political Consultants tend to be generalists and media professionals. Contact them at:

American Association of Political Consultants
900 2nd Street, NW, #110
Washington, DC 20002
Tel. 202/371-9585

Political consultants specializing in polling tend to join one of these associations:

American Association of Public Opinion Research
P.O. Box 1248
Ann Arbor, MI 48106
Tel. 313/764-1555

Council of American Survey Research Organizations
3 Upper Devon Belle Terre
Port Jefferson, NY 11777
Tel. 516/928-6954

National Council on Public Polls
205 E. 42nd St., Rm. 1708
New York, NY 10017
Tel. 212/986-8262

PART VI

TAKE EFFECTIVE ACTION

25

TAKE EFFECTIVE ACTION

Understanding without action is a waste of time. And buying a how-to book without implementing it is a waste of money. Many people read how-to books, attend how-to seminars, and do nothing other than read more books, attend more seminars, and engage in more wishful thinking. While these activities become forms of therapy for some individuals, they should lead to positive actions for you.

From the very beginning of this book we stressed the importance of both understanding how the public sector operates and developing appropriate job search strategies for getting the job you want. We make no assumptions nor claim any magic is contained in this book. Rather, we have attempted to assemble useful information to help you organize an effective job search appropriate for the public sector. Individual chapters examined specific job search skills, such as writing resumes and conducting informational interviews, as well as outlined specific structures and opportunities among federal, state, and local governments and the peripheral institutions of trade and professional associations, consulting firms, nonprofit organizations, foundations, research organizations, and political support groups. We have done our part in getting you to the implementation stage. What happens next is your responsibility.

The methods we outlined in previous chapters have worked for thousands of individuals who have paid $2,000 to $12,000 to get similar information from the highly-paid professionals. While you may want to see a professional for assistance at certain steps in your job search, if you are self-motivated you can do everything on your own with a minimum expenditure of money. The major cost will be your time and effort.

But you must make the effort and take the *risk of implementing* this book. Looking for a job is a risky business. You try something new and place your ego on the line. You subject yourself to the possibility of being rejected several times. And this is precisely the major barrier you will encounter to effective job search implementation. For many people are unwilling to take more than a few rejections.

Understanding without action is a waste of time. And buying a how-to book without implementing it is a waste of money.

WELCOME REJECTIONS AS LEARNING OPPORTUNITIES

Planning is the easiest part of any task. Turning plans into reality is the most difficult challenge. It's relatively simple to set goals and outline a course of action divorced from the reality of actually doing it. But if you don't take action, you will not get your expected results. You must implement if you want desired results.

Once you take action, be prepared for rejections. Employers will tell you "Thank you—we'll call you," but they never do. Other employers will tell you "We have no positions available at this time for someone with your qualifications" or "You don't have the qualifications necessary for this position." Whatever the story, you will face many disappointments on the road to success.

Rejections are a normal part of the process of finding employment as well as getting ahead in life. Rejections offer an important learning experience which should help you better understand yourself, employers, and the job finding process. More important, you must be rejected before you will be accepted. Expect ten rejections or "nos" for every acceptance or "yes" you receive. If you quit after five or eight rejections, you prematurely end your job search. If you persist in collecting two to five more "nos," you will likely receive a "yes." Most people quit prematurely because their ego is not prepared for more rejections. Therefore, you should welcome rejections as you seek more and more acceptances.

GET MOTIVATED AND WORK HARD

Assuming you have a firm understanding of each job search step and how to relate them to your goals and each public sector institution, what do you do next? The next steps involve *motivation and hard work.* Just how motivated are you to seek public sector employment or change your career within the public sector? Our experience is that individuals need to be sufficiently *motivated* to make the first move and do it properly. If you go about your job search half-heartedly—you just want to "test the waters" to see what's out there—don't expect to be successful. You must be committed to achieving specific goals. Make the decision to properly develop and implement your job search and be prepared to work hard in achieving your goals.

FIND TIME

Once you've convinced yourself to take the necessary steps to find a job or change and advance your career, you need to find the *time* to properly implement your job search. This requires setting aside specific blocks of time for identifying your motivated abilities and skills, developing your resume, writing letters, making telephone calls, and conducting the necessary research and networking required for success. This whole process takes time. If you are a busy person, like most people, you simply must make the time. Practice your own versions of time management or cutback management. Get better organized, give some things up, or cut back on all your activities. If, for example, you can set aside one hour each day to devote to your job search, you will spend seven hours a week or 28 hours a month on your search. However, you should and can find more time than this for these activities.

Time and again we find successful job hunters are the ones who routinize a job search schedule and keep at it. They make contact after contact, conduct numerous informational interviews, submit many applications and resumes, and keep repeating these activities in spite of encountering rejections. They learn that success is just a few more "nos" and informational interviews away. They face each day with a positive attitude fit for someone desiring to change their life—I must collect my ten "nos" today because each "no" brings me closer to another "yes"!

Successful job hunters are ones who routinize a job search schedule and keep at it.

COMMIT YOURSELF IN WRITING

You may find it useful to commit yourself in writing to achieving job search success. This is a very useful way to get both motivated and directed for action. Start by completing the job search contract on page 408 and keep it near you—in your briefcase or on your desk.

In addition, you should complete weekly performance reports. These reports identify what you actually accomplished rather than what your good intentions tell you to do. Make copies of the performance and planning report form on page 409 and use one each week to track your actual progress and to plan your activities for the next week.

If you fail to meet these written commitments, issue yourself a revised and updated contract. But if you do this three or more times, we strongly suggest you stop kidding yourself about your motivation and commitment to find a job. Start over again, but this time consult a professional career counselor who can provide you with the necessary structure to make progress in finding a job.

A professional may not be cheap, but if paying for help gets you on the right track and results in the job you want, it's money well spent. Do not be "penny wise but pound foolish" with your future. If you must seek professional advice, be sure you are an informed consumer according to our "shopping" advice in Chapter 6.

RICHES DO INDEED AWAIT YOU

The public sector as outlined in this book is a fascinating arena for employment. You may not get rich monetarily by working in this arena, but many people are personally richer for having pursued public goals. If your primary goal is to pursue money, the public sector will frustrate you. But if your goals are to pursue an interest, practice a skill, or promote a worthwhile cause, the public sector offers unlimited opportunities.

Contrary to popular perceptions, this public sector is not stagnant nor declining. It remains dynamic and offers some of the most exciting employment opportunities found anywhere. You should open yourself to these opportunities by taking the necessary actions for achieving a successful job search in the public sector.

Jobs and careers should not become life sentences. You should feel free to change jobs and careers when you want to or need to. In fact, thousands of people make successful career transitions each year. Some are more successful than others in finding the right job. If you plan your public sector job search according to the methods outlined in previous chapters, you should be able to successfully land the job you want.

Treat yourself right. Take the time and effort to sail into today's public sector job market with a plan of action that links your qualifications to the needs of employers. You are first and foremost an individual with knowledge, abilities, and skills that many employers need and want. If you follow the advice of this book, you will put your best foot forward in communicating your qualifications to employers. You will find a job fit for you as well as pursue a satisfying lifestyle.

We have done our part to get you started. Now it's your turn to translate this book into successful action.

JOB SEARCH CONTRACT

1. I'm committed to finding a public sector job. Today's date is ___________.

2. I will manage my time so that I can successfully complete my job search and find a high quality job. I will begin changing my time management behavior on ___________.

3. I will begin my job search on _________.

4. I will involve ______________ with my job search.
   (individual/group)

5. I will spend at least one week conducting library research on different jobs, employers, and organizations. I will begin this research during the week of ___________.

6. I will complete my skills identification step by ________.

7. I will complete my objective statement by ________.

8. I will complete my resume by ________.

9. Each week I will:

   - make ___ new job contacts.
   - conduct ___ informational interviews.
   - follow-up on ___ referrals.

10. My first job interview will take place during the week of ______________.

11. I will begin my new job by ___________.

12. I will make a habit of learning one new skill each year.

Signature: ________________________

WEEKLY JOB SEARCH PERFORMANCE AND PLANNING REPORT

1. The week of: ____________.

2. This week I:
   - wrote ___ job search letters.
   - sent ___ resumes and ___ letters to potential employers.
   - completed ___ applications.
   - made ___ job search telephone calls.
   - completed ___ hours of job research.
   - set up ___ appointments for informational interviews.
   - conducted ___ informational interviews.
   - received ___ invitations to a job interview.
   - followed up on ___ contacts and ___ referrals.

3. Next week I will:
   - write ___ job search letters.
   - send ___ resumes and ___ letters to potential employers.
   - complete ___ applications.
   - make ___ job search telephone calls.
   - complete ___ hours of job research.
   - set up ___ appointments for informational interviews.
   - conduct ___ informational interviews.
   - follow up on ___ contacts and ___ referrals.

4. Summary of progress this week in reference to my Job Search Contract commitments:

   ____

   ____

   ____

   ____

   ____

THE AUTHORS

Ronald L. Krannich, Ph.D., and Caryl Rae Krannich, Ph.D., operate Development Concepts Inc., a training, consulting, and publishing firm. Ron received his Ph.D. in Political Science from Northern Illinois University where he also specialized in public administration, local government, comparative government, and Southeast Asian studies. Caryl received her Ph.D. in Speech Communication from Penn State University.

Ron and Caryl are former university professors, high school teachers, management trainers, and consultants. They have completed numerous projects on management, career development, local government, population planning, and rural development during the past twenty years. They have published several articles in major professional journals.

In addition to their extensive public sector work, the Krannichs are two of America's leading career and travel writers. They are authors of 25 career books and 11 travel books. Their career books focus on government jobs, international careers, nonprofit organizations, career transitions, and key job search skills. Their work represents one of today's most extensive and highly praised collections of career writing: *The Almanac of American Government Jobs and Careers, The Almanac of International Jobs and Careers, Best Jobs for the 1990s and Into the 21st Century, Change Your Job Change Your Life, The Complete Guide to International Jobs and Careers, Discover the Best Jobs for You, Dynamite Answers to Interview Questions, Dynamite Cover Letters, Dynamite Resumes, Dynamite Salary Negotiations, Dynamite Tele-Search, The Educator's Guide to Alternative Jobs and Careers, Find a Federal Job Fast, From Army Green to Corporate Gray, From Navy Blue to Corporate Gray, High Impact Resumes and Letters, Interview for Success, Job Search Letters That Get Results, Jobs and Careers With Nonprofit Organizations, Jobs for People Who Love Travel,* and *The New Network Your Way to Job and Career Success*. Their books are found in most major bookstores, libraries, and career centers. Many of their works are now available interactively on CD-ROM (*Job-Power Source*).

Ron and Caryl continue to pursue their international interests through their innovative *"Shopping in Exotic Places"* travel series. When they are not found at their home and business in Virginia, they are probably somewhere in Hong Kong, China, Thailand, Malaysia, Singapore, Indonesia, Papua New Guinea, Australia, New Zealand, Tahiti, Fiji, Burma, India, Nepal, Morocco, Turkey, Mexico, or the Caribbean pursuing their other passion—shopping and traveling for quality arts and antiques.

INDEX

C

D

E

CAREER RESOURCES

Contact Impact Publications to receive a free copy of their latest comprehensive and annotated catalog of over 1,000 career resources (books, subscriptions, training programs, videos, audiocassettes, computer software, and CD-ROM).

The following career resources, many of which are mentioned in previous chapters, are available directly from Impact Publications. Complete the following form or list the titles, include postage (see formula at the end), enclose payment, and send your order to:

IMPACT PUBLICATIONS
9104-N Manassas Drive
Manassas Park, VA 22111-5211
Tel. 703/361-7300 or Fax 703/335-9486

Orders from individuals must be prepaid by check, moneyorder, Visa or MasterCard number. We accept telephone and fax orders with a Visa or MasterCard number.

Qty.	TITLES	Price	TOTAL
	GOVERNMENT AND PUBLIC SERVICE JOBS		
___	ACWA: Administrative Careers With America	$13.00	______
___	Almanac of American Government Jobs and Careers	$19.95	______
___	Book of $16,000-$60,000 Post Office Jobs	$14.95	______
___	Book of U.S. Government Jobs	$15.95	______
___	Book of U.S. Postal Exams	$13.95	______
___	Civil Service Handbook	$9.95	______

___	Complete Guide to Public Employment	$19.95	______
___	Complete Guide to U.S. Civil Service Jobs	$9.95	______
___	Federal Jobs for College Graduates	$14.95	______
___	Federal Jobs in Law Enforcement	$15.95	______
___	Find a Federal Job Fast!	$12.95	______
___	General Test Practice for 101 U.S. Jobs	$9.95	______
___	Government Job Finder	$16.95	______
___	How to Get a Federal Job	$15.00	______
___	The Right SF 171 Writer	$19.95	______

CONSULTANTS AND GOVERNMENT CONTRACTING

___	Complete Guide to Winning Government Contracts	$19.95	______
___	Consultant's Proposal, Fee, and Contract Problem-Solver	$19.95	______
___	Getting Started in Federal Contracting	$21.95	______
___	Proposals That Win Federal Contracts	$24.95	______

NONPROFITS

___	Great Careers	$36.95	______
___	Finding a Job in the Nonprofit Sector	$95.00	______
___	Jobs and Careers With Nonprofit Organizations	$15.95	______
___	Non-Profit's Job Finder	$16.95	______
___	Profitable Careers in Nonprofits	$16.95	______

JOB LISTINGS & VACANCY ANNOUNCEMENTS

___	Community (Nonprofit) Jobs (1 year)	$69.00	______
___	Federal Career Opportunities (6 biweekly issues)	$39.00	______
___	Federal Jobs Digest (6 biweekly issues)	$34.00	______
___	International Employment Gazette (6 biweekly issues)	$35.00	______
___	The Search Bulletin (6 issues)	$97.00	______

KEY DIRECTORIES AND REFERENCE WORKS

___	American Salaries and Wages Survey	$94.95	______
___	Career Training Sourcebook	$24.95	______
___	Careers Encyclopedia	$39.95	______
___	Complete Guide for Occupational Exploration	$29.95	______
___	Consultants and Consulting Organizations Directory	$835.00	______
___	Dictionary of Occupational Titles	$39.95	______
___	Directory of Executive Recruiters (annual)	$39.95	______
___	Directory of Special Programs for Minority Group Members	$31.95	______
___	Encyclopedia of Associations	$949.00	______
___	Encyclopedia of Careers and Vocational Guidance	$129.95	______
___	Enhanced Guide for Occupational Exploration	$29.95	______
___	Government Directory of Addresses and Telephone Numbers	$129.95	______
___	Hoover's Business Directories: American Business, Emerging Companies, World Business	$99.95	______
___	Job Bank Guide to Employment Services (annual)	$149.95	______

___	Job Hunter's Sourcebook	$59.95	______
___	Job Seeker's Guide to Private and Public Companies	$359.95	______
___	National Directory of Addresses & Telephone Numbers	$99.95	______
___	National Directory of Nonprofit Organizations	$399.00	______
___	National Job Bank (annual)	$249.95	______
___	National Trade and Professional Associations	$79.95	______
___	Occupational Outlook Handbook	$22.95	______
___	Personnel Executives Contactbook	$149.00	______
___	Professional Careers Sourcebook	$79.95	______
___	Research Center Directory	$495.00	______
___	Washington Representatives	$95.00	______

MILITARY TO CIVILIAN TRANSITION

___	Beyond the Uniform	$12.95	______
___	Does Your Resume Wear Combat Boots?	$9.95	______
___	From Air Force Blue to Corporate Gray	$17.95	______
___	From Army Green to Corporate Gray	$15.95	______
___	From Navy Blue to Corporate Gray	$17.95	______
___	Job Search: Marketing Your Military Experience	$14.95	______
___	Re-Entry	$13.95	______
___	Retiring From the Military	$22.95	______
___	Veteran's Survival Guide to Good Jobs in Bad Times	$12.95	______

RELOCATION AND RETIREMENT

___	50 Fabulous Places to Retire in America	$17.95	______
___	100 Best Small Towns in America	$12.00	______
___	Complete Guide to Life in Florida	$14.95	______
___	Complete Relocation Kit	$17.95	______
___	Craighead's International Business, Travel, and Relocation Guide to 81 Countries	$485.00	______
___	Moving and Relocation Directory	$149.00	______
___	Places Rated Almanac	$21.95	______

CITY AND STATE JOB FINDERS

___	Finding a Job in Florida	$14.95	______
___	Jobs in Washington, DC	$11.95	______

How to Get a Job in . . .

___	Atlanta	$15.95	______
___	Boston	$15.95	______
___	Chicago	$15.95	______
___	Dallas/Fort Worth	$15.95	______
___	Houston	$15.95	______
___	New York	$15.95	______
___	San Francisco	$15.95	______
___	Seattle/Portland	$15.95	______
___	Southern California	$15.95	______
___	Washington, DC	$15.95	______

Bob Adams' JobBanks to:

___	Atlanta	$15.95	______
___	Boston	$15.95	______
___	Chicago	$15.95	______
___	Dallas/Fort Worth	$15.95	______
___	Denver	$15.95	______
___	Florida	$15.95	______
___	Houston	$15.95	______
___	Los Angeles	$15.95	______
___	Minneapolis	$15.95	______
___	New York	$15.95	______
___	Phoenix	$15.95	______
___	San Francisco	$15.95	______
___	Seattle	$15.95	______
___	Washington, DC	$15.95	______

Job Seekers Sourcebooks to:

___	Boston and New England	$14.95	______
___	Chicago and Illinois	$14.95	______
___	Los Angeles and Southern California	$14.95	______
___	Mid-Atlantic	$14.95	______
___	Mountain States	$14.95	______
___	New York and New Jersey	$14.95	______
___	Northern Great Lakes	$14.95	______
___	Pacific Northwest	$14.95	______
___	Southern States	$14.95	______
___	Southwest	$14.95	______

JOB SEARCH STRATEGIES AND TACTICS

___	40+ Job Hunting Guide	$23.95	______
___	110 Biggest Mistakes Job Hunters Make	$12.95	______
___	Change Your Job, Change Your Life	$14.95	______
___	Complete Job Finder's Guide to the '90s	$13.95	______
___	Complete Job Search Handbook	$12.95	______
___	Cracking the Over-50 Job Market	$11.95	______
___	Dynamite Tele-Search	$11.95	______
___	Electronic Job Search Revolution	$12.95	______
___	Five Secrets to Finding a Job	$12.95	______
___	How to Get Interviews From Classified Job Ads	$14.95	______
___	How to Succeed Without a Career Path	$13.95	______
___	Job Hunting After 50	$12.95	______
___	Joyce Lain Kennedy's Career Book	$29.95	______
___	Knock 'Em Dead	$19.95	______
___	Professional's Job Finder	$18.95	______
___	Right Place At the Right Time	$11.95	______
___	Rites of Passage At $100,000+	$29.95	______
___	Super Job Search	$22.95	______
___	Through the Brick Wall	$13.00	______
___	Who's Hiring Who	$9.95	______

BEST JOBS AND EMPLOYERS FOR THE 90s

___ 100 Best Companies to Work for in America $27.95 ________
___ 100 Best Jobs for the 1990s and Beyond $19.95 ________
___ 101 Careers $12.95 ________
___ American Almanac of Jobs and Salaries $17.00 ________
___ America's 50 Fastest Growing Jobs $9.95 ________
___ America's Fastest Growing Employers $14.95 ________
___ Best Jobs for the 1990s and Into the 21st Century $12.95 ________
___ How to Succeed Without a Career Path $13.95 ________
___ Job Seeker's Guide to 1000 Top Employers $22.95 ________
___ Jobs 1995 $15.95 ________
___ New Emerging Careers $14.95 ________
___ Top Professions $10.95 ________
___ Where the Jobs Are $15.95 ________

ALTERNATIVE JOBS AND CAREERS

___ Adventure Careers $9.95 ________
___ Advertising Career Directory $17.95 ________
___ Business and Finance Career Directory $17.95 ________
___ Career Opportunities in the Sports Industry $27.95 ________
___ Career Opportunities in TV, Cable, and Video $27.95 ________
___ Careers for Animal Lovers $12.95 ________
___ Careers for Foreign Language Speakers $12.95 ________
___ Careers for Sports Nuts $12.95 ________
___ Careers for Travel Buffs $12.95 ________
___ Careers in Computers $16.95 ________
___ Careers in Education $16.95 ________
___ Careers in Health Care $16.95 ________
___ Careers in High Tech $16.95 ________
___ Careers in Medicine $16.95 ________
___ Careers in the Outdoors $12.95 ________
___ Environmental Career Guide $14.95 ________
___ Environmental Jobs for Scientists and Engineers $14.95 ________
___ Health Care Job Explosion $14.95 ________
___ Marketing and Sales Career Directory $17.95 ________
___ Nurses and Physicians Career Directory $17.95 ________
___ Opportunities in Accounting $13.95 ________
___ Opportunities in Civil Engineering $13.95 ________
___ Opportunities in Computer Science $13.95 ________
___ Opportunities in Environmental Careers $13.95 ________
___ Opportunities in Financial Career $13.95 ________
___ Opportunities in Fitness $13.95 ________
___ Opportunities in Health & Medical Careers $13.95 ________
___ Opportunities in Law $13.95 ________
___ Opportunities in Medical Technology $13.95 ________
___ Opportunities in Microelectronics $13.95 ________
___ Opportunities in Paralegal Careers $13.95 ________
___ Opportunities in Teaching $13.95 ________
___ Opportunities in Telecommunications $13.95 ________
___ Opportunities in Television & Video $13.95 ________

___	Outdoor Careers	$14.95	______
___	Radio and Television Career Directory	$17.95	______
___	Travel and Hospitality Career Directory	$17.95	______
___	You Can't Play the Game If You Don't Know the Rules	$15.95	______

INTERNATIONAL, OVERSEAS, AND TRAVEL JOBS

___	Almanac of International Jobs and Careers	$19.95	______
___	Complete Guide to International Jobs & Careers	$13.95	______
___	Flying High in Travel	$18.95	______
___	Getting Your Job in the Middle East	$19.95	______
___	Guide to Careers in World Affairs	$14.95	______
___	How to Get a Job in Europe	$17.95	______
___	How to Get a Job in the Pacific Rim	$17.95	______
___	Jobs for People Who Love Travel	$12.95	______
___	Jobs in Russia and the Newly Independent States	$15.95	______
___	Jobs Worldwide	$15.95	______

SKILLS, TESTING, SELF-ASSESSMENT, EMPOWERMENT

___	7 Habits of Highly Effective People	$11.00	______
___	Discover the Best Jobs for You	$11.95	______
___	Do What You Are	$14.95	______
___	Do What You Love, the Money Will Follow	$10.95	______
___	Finding the Hat That Fits	$10.00	______
___	What Color Is Your Parachute?	$14.95	______
___	Where Do I Go From Here With My Life?	$10.95	______
___	Wishcraft	$10.95	______

RESUMES, LETTERS, & NETWORKING

___	200 Letters for Job Hunters	$17.95	______
___	Best Resumes for $70,000+ Executive Jobs	$14.95	______
___	Dynamite Cover Letters	$11.95	______
___	Dynamite Resumes	$11.95	______
___	Electronic Resume Revolution	$12.95	______
___	Electronic Resumes for the New Job Market	$11.95	______
___	Great Connections	$11.95	______
___	High Impact Resumes and Letters	$14.95	______
___	How to Work a Room	$9.95	______
___	Job Search Letters That Get Results	$15.95	______
___	New Network Your Way to Job and Career Success	$12.95	______
___	The Resume Catalog	$15.95	______
___	Resumes for Re-Entry: A Woman's Handbook	$10.95	______
___	The Secrets of Savvy Networking	$11.99	______

DRESS, APPEARANCE, IMAGE

___	110 Mistakes Working Women Make & How to Avoid Them	$9.95	______
___	John Molloy's New Dress for Success	$10.95	______
___	Red Socks Don't Work! Messages About Men's Clothing	$14.95	______
___	The Winning Image	$17.95	______

INTERVIEWS & SALARY NEGOTIATIONS

___ 60 Seconds and You're Hired!	$9.95	______
___ Dynamite Answers to Interview Questions	$11.95	______
___ Dynamite Salary Negotiation	$12.95	______
___ Interview for Success	$11.95	______
___ Sweaty Palms	$9.95	______

WOMEN AND SPOUSES

___ Doing It All Isn't Everything	$19.95	______
___ New Relocating Spouse's Guide to Employment	$14.95	______
___ Smart Woman's Guide to Resumes and Job Hunting	$9.95	______
___ Survival Guide for Women	$16.95	______
___ Women's Job Search Handbook	$12.95	______

MINORITIES AND PHYSICALLY CHALLENGED

___ Best Companies for Minorities	$12.00	______
___ Directory of Special Programs for Minority Group Members	$31.95	______
___ Job Strategies for People With Disabilities	$14.95	______
___ Minority Organizations	$49.95	______

COLLEGE STUDENTS AND GRADUATES

___ 150 Best Companies for Liberal Arts Grads	$12.95	______
___ Graduating to the 9-5 World	$11.95	______
___ How You Really Get Hired	$11.00	______

ENTREPRENEURSHIP AND SELF-EMPLOYMENT

___ 101 Best Businesses to Start	$15.00	______
___ Best Home-Based Businesses for the 90s	$10.95	______
___ Entrepreneur's Guide to Starting a Successful Business	$16.95	______
___ Have You Got What It Takes?	$12.95	______
___ How to Start, Run, and Stay in Business	$12.95	______

COMPUTER SOFTWARE

___ FOCIS: Federal Occupational and Career Information System	$59.95	______
___ JOBHUNT™ Quick and Easy Employer Contacts	$49.95	______
___ INSTANT™ Job Hunting Letters	$39.95	______
___ ResumeMaker	$49.95	______
___ Ultimate Job Finder	$59.95	______

CD-ROM

___ America's Top Jobs	$295.00	______
___ Companies International	$1995.00	______
___ Encyclopedia of Associations	$995.00	______
___ Job Power Source	$49.95	______

VIDEOS

___	Dialing for Jobs	$129.00	______
___	Find the Job You Want...and Get It! (4 videos)	$229.95	______
___	How to Present a Professional Image (2 videos)	$149.95	______
___	Inside Secrets of Interviewing	$39.95	______
___	Insider's Guide to Competitive Interviewing	$59.95	______
___	Networking Your Way to Success	$89.95	______
___	Very Quick Job Search	$129.00	______
___	Winning at Job Hunting in the 90s	$89.95	______

AUDIO PROGRAMS

___	Edge Rx For Success	$159.95	______
___	Find the Job You Want...And Get It!	$49.95	______
___	Five Secrets to Finding a Job	$29.95	______
___	Job Search: The Total System	$199.95	______

SUBTOTAL ______

Virginia residents add 4½% sales tax ______

POSTAGE/HANDLING ($4.00 for first title and $1.00 for each additional book) $4.00

Number of additional titles x $1.00 ----------- ______

TOTAL ENCLOSED ---------------- ______

SHIP TO:

NAME ____________________

ADDRESS ____________________

____

____

[ ] I enclose check/moneyorder for $ ______ made payable to IMPACT PUBLICATIONS.

[ ] Please charge $ ______ to my credit card:

Card # ____________________

Expiration date: ____/____

Signature ____________________

FIND A FEDERAL JOB FAST KIT

- **FIND A FEDERAL JOB FAST! How to Cut the Red Tape and Get Hired.** (3rd Edition). *Drs. Ron & Caryl Krannich.* The first book all federal job hunters need to read *prior to* targeting agencies and completing applications. Provides a sound overview of the federal hiring process. Reveals the inside story on locating job vacancies, completing a winning SF 171, marketing oneself among agencies, and getting quickly hired for many jobs. 197 pages. 1995. $12.95.

- **ALMANAC OF AMERICAN GOVERNMENT JOBS AND CAREERS.** (2nd Edition). *Drs. Ron & Caryl Krannich.* This directory provides the critical contact information on thousands of federal government agencies. Identifies job opportunities with executive, legislative, and judicial branches of government. Includes names, addresses, and phone numbers of personnel offices and job hotlines. Describes the work of specific agencies. 289 pages. 1995. $19.95.

- **THE RIGHT SF 171 WRITER.** *Dr. Russ Smith.* Finally, a comprehensive guide to completing the critical federal application form—The Standard form 171 (SF 171). Outlines what federal employers look for on the SF 171, major writing principles, the best language to use (KASO's), how to customize the form, and much more. Includes examples of completed SF 171's; special chapters on distribution and resources; and treatment of the SF 172 and veterans preferences. Useful appendices include sample forms, critical sections from the all-important *X-118 Handbook*, and addresses of the Federal Job Information Centers. A critical book every federal job seeker needs in order to produce the right application package. 180 pages. 1994. $19.95.

- **GOVERNMENT JOB FINDER.** *Daniel Lauber.* An indispensable directory to over 1,000 job sources. Includes periodicals with ads on government jobs; job hotlines; job matching services; and directories for all level of government in the U.S., Canada, and overseas. While this book primarily focuses on uncovering vacancies with state and local governments, it does include information on federal job sources. 340 pages. 1994. $16.95.

- **HIGH IMPACT RESUMES AND LETTERS: How to Communicate Your Qualifications to Employers** (6th edition). *Drs. Ron Krannich and William Banis.* The latest edition of this popular resume and letter writing book shows how to create powerful resumes that result in job interviews and offers. Filled with numerous examples. The perfect book for anyone needing to create a resume for a government job. 285 pages. 1995. $14.95.

- **QUICK AND EASY 171s.** *DataTech.* Here's the most advanced computerized SF 171 production program available today. If you plan to apply for a federal job, it's best to produce your SF 171 with this powerful software program. Turns blank paper into a completed SF 171 using most printers on the market. Direct support provides for over 50 dot matrix printers, the DeskJet 500, and laser printers that are compatible with the Hewlett Packard LaserJet II. Prints the form. Approved by the U.S. Office of Personnel Management. Available in 4 versions: **Personal** (single user only): $49.95; **Family** (2 users only): $59.95; **Office** (8 users only): $129.95; **Organization** (unlimited users): $399.95. For IBM or compatible systems only. Also available for Windows (please specify).

- **FOCIS: FEDERAL OCCUPATIONAL & CAREER INFORMATION SYSTEM.** *U.S. Office of Personnel Management.* This interactive program helps federal employees and job seekers obtain information about federal careers, occupations, agencies, current job openings, and training. Contains database on nearly 600 federal occupations and 300 federal organizations. Users with modems can dial into an OPM bulletin board, electronically transfer current job vacancy listings to their computer, and search for job openings using FOCIS. Federal employees can access in formation on more than 1,000 nationwide training courses. Software: three 3½" diskettes, 1.44 M high density. Documentation included. System: IBM-PC or compatible, PC-DOS 3.0 or higher operating system, 400K. Hard disk requires 2.5 to 12.7 Mb depending on the combination of modules installed. Language: dBase II plus compiled in Clipper. Drive should be a 286 or higher processor. An incredible buy at only $59.95!

- **FEDERAL CAREER OPPORTUNITIES.** The best and most comprehensive listing of current federal job vacancies. Includes 3,400 positions from grades GS5 thru SES. Organized by GS series within each agency. Published biweekly as a 64-90 page directory. Subscription rates: 6 issues, $39; 1 year (25 issues), $175.

SPECIAL SAVINGS ON TOTAL PACKAGE: Individuals can purchase the complete package (5 books, 6 issue subscription, and 2 software programs) for $224.95. Institutions requiring the organizational version (unlimited users) of *Quick and Easy 171s* can purchase this complete package for $699.95 (includes the 25 issue subscription to *Federal Career Opportunities*). Please add $7.00 shipping for complete package. If ordering individual titles, add $4.00 for first item and $1.00 for each additional item. Send your order to: IMPACT PUBLICATIONS, 9104-N Manassas Drive, Manassas Park, VA 22111 or Fax 703/335-9486 (Visa/MasterCard).

JOB SEARCH SKILLS KIT

- **CHANGE YOUR JOB, CHANGE YOUR LIFE: High Impact Strategies for Finding Great Jobs in the 90s**. *Dr. Ronald L. Krannich.* One of the most highly acclaimed career books ever written, the newest edition of this blockbuster outlines the key job and career issues facing millions of Americans. Comprehensive, up-to-date, specific, encouraging, and loaded with useful facts and advice, the book outlines how to develop the necessary skills and strategies for achieving success in the job markets of the 1990s. Covers everything from identifying the best jobs for the 90s to writing resumes, networking, interviewing, relocating to a new community, and starting a business. 363 pages. 1994. $14.95.

- **JOB SEARCH LETTERS THAT GET RESULTS: 201 Great Examples!** (2nd Edition). *Drs. Ron & Caryl Krannich.* Includes 201 examples of powerful letters that open the doors to job search success: letters to start your job search; letters that lay the ground work; letters for approaching employers; letters that respond to vacancy announcements; cover letters; resume letters, follow-up letters; thank you letters; letters to start your job in the right direction; and special and unusual letters. 264 pages. 1995. $15.95.

- **HIGH IMPACT RESUMES AND LETTERS** (6th Edition). *Ron Krannich & William Banis.* Four times excerpted in the *National Business Employment Weekly* of *The Wall Street Journal,* here's the book that shows how to understand today's job market, develop job search skills, select appropriate resume formats, write each resume section, and distribute resumes and letters into the most responsive channels. Debunks resume myths and includes the forms for producing and evaluating each resume section. 285 pages. 1995. $14.95.

- **THE *NEW* NETWORK YOUR WAY TO JOB AND CAREER SUCCESS** (2nd Edition). *Drs. Ron & Caryl Krannich.* Here's the first book to provide practical guidance on how to organize and mobilize effective job networks, prospect for new job leads, write effective networking letters, and conduct informational interviews. 188 pages. 1993. $12.95.

- **DYNAMITE TELE-SEARCH: 101 Techniques and Tips for Getting Job Leads and Interviews**. *Drs. Ron and Caryl Krannich.* Addresses one of the most important activities in finding a job—using the telephone for uncovering job leads, getting interviews, and following-up resumes, letters, referrals, informational interviews, and job interviews. Outlines major principles for effective telephone communication and presents numerous sample dialogues and handy checklists for organizing and conducting a powerful telephone job search. 1995. 180 pages. $11.95.

- **INTERVIEW FOR SUCCESS** (4th Edition). *Drs. Caryl & Ron Krannich.* Featured in the *National Business Employment Weekly* of *The Wall Street Journal,* here's one of today's most comprehensive interview books. Shows how to best prepare for different types of interviews, handle stress, observe etiquette, gather information, formulate key questions, rehearse tough questions, dress appropriately, communicate class, listen effectively, negotiate salary figure, and handle the critical post-interview period. 1993. $11.95.

- **DYNAMITE ANSWERS TO INTERVIEW QUESTIONS: No More Sweaty Palms!** (2nd Edition). *Drs. Caryl and Ron Krannich.* Outlines the best answers to key job interview questions. Includes sample answers to hundreds of questions interviewers ask in the critical job interview. Shows how to turn possible negative responses into positive answers that can mean the difference between being accepted or rejected for the job. 178 pages. 1994. $11.95.

- **HOW TO GET INTERVIEWS FROM CLASSIFIED JOB ADS** (2nd Edition). *Kenton W. Elderkin.* The only book devoted exclusively to showing how to get interview offers from newspaper and magazine advertisements and articles. Shows how to analyze them, whom to write, what to say, when to follow-up, where to find the best ads, why to pursue news articles, how to crack blind ads, and much more. 270 pages. 1993. $14.95.

- **DYNAMITE SALARY NEGOTIATIONS** (2nd Edition). *Drs. Ron & Caryl Krannich.* Outlines the major issues involved in determining salaries; secrecy, salary history, salary requirements, salary ranges, and negotiating tactics. Dispelling numerous myths and outlining many mistakes, this book reveals how to value positions; acquire salary information; calculate your worth; respond to ads and applications requesting salary history; handle tough interview questions; negotiate your salary and terms of employment; and finalize the job offer. 164 pages. 1994. $13.95.

SPECIAL OFFER ON COMPLETE SET: Purchase the complete set of nine books for $116.95. Please add $8.00 shipping for complete package. If ordering individual titles, add $4.00 for first item and $1.00 for each additional item. Send your order to: IMPACT PUBLICATIONS, 9104-N Manassas Drive, Manassas Park, VA 22111 or Fax 703/335-9486 (Visa/MasterCard).

JOBS WITH NONPROFITS KIT

JOBS AND CAREERS WITH NONPROFIT ORGANIZATIONS. *Drs. Ron and Caryl Krannich.* Identifies major nonprofit organizations providing attractive job alternatives: education, public affairs, medical, consumer advocacy, public assistance, charitable, religious, arts, museums, womens, public utilities, civil rights, and government. Describes major employers, summarizes job strategies, provides contact information. 232 pages. 1995. $15.95.

NON-PROFIT'S JOB FINDER. *Daniel Lauber.* Shows how to find thousands of jobs with nonprofits by using job hotlines, job matching services, and specialty periodicals with job listings. Includes tips on writing resumes and cover letters and interviewing. 325 pages. 1994. $16.95.

COMMUNITY JOBS. Subscribe to the leading publication on jobs with the nonprofit sector. Each monthly 40+ page issue includes informative articles, book reviews, resource lists, profiles of nonprofits, and over 200 job listings. Includes internships—from entry-level to executive director. Covers all types of organizations including environmental, international, arts, health, civil rights, and human services. $39 for 6 months; $69 for 1 year.

SPECIAL SAVINGS ON TOTAL PACKAGE: Individuals can purchase the complete package (2 books and 6 month subscription) for $69.95. Institutions requiring the 12 month subscription can purchase this package for $99.95. Please add $5.00 shipping for complete package. If ordering individual titles, add $4.00 for first item and $1.00 for each additional item. Send your order to: IMPACT PUBLICATIONS, 9104-N Manassas Drive, Manassas Park, VA 22111 or Fax 703/335-9486 (Visa/MasterCard).

INTERNATIONAL JOBS KIT

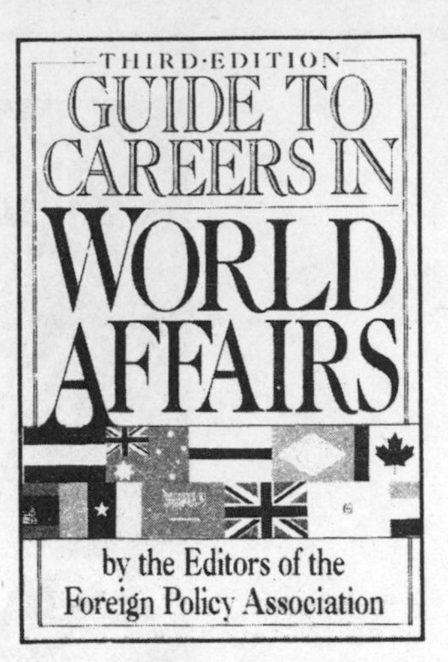

THE ALMANAC OF INTERNATIONAL JOBS & CAREERS: A Guide to Over 1001 Employers! (2nd edition). *Drs. Ron & Caryl Krannich.* Jam-packed with critical contact information on hundreds of organizations offering international job opportunities: government; businesses; consulting firms; nonprofit organizations; and universities. Includes special chapters on internships, teaching, and key resources. 350 pages. 1994. $19.95.

THE COMPLETE GUIDE TO INTERNATIONAL JOBS AND CAREERS (2nd edition). *Drs. Ron and Caryl Krannich.* Featured in the ***National Business Employment Weekly*** of *The Wall Street Journal,* this blockbuster dispels myths, assesses job outlook, outlines job opportunities, identifies effective strategies—from resume writing and networking to interviews—and reveals the major employers hiring international specialists. Includes special chapters on the travel industry and starting an international business. 318 pages. 1992. $13.95.

GUIDE TO CAREERS IN WORLD AFFAIRS (3rd edition). *Foreign Policy Association (ed.).* Completely revised for the 1990s, this outstanding guide describes hundreds of major employers in international business, consulting, finance, banking, journalism, law, translation/interpretation, nonprofit organizations, government, and the UN. Includes internships, graduate programs, job strategies, and contacts. 425 pages. 1993. $14.95.

JOBS IN RUSSIA AND THE NEWLY INDEPENDENT STATES, *Moira Forbes.* Great new book! Identifies numerous opportunities in Russia and the NIS—from business and government jobs to volunteer opportunities. Summarizes recent developments in each country, describes opportunities, and includes addresses of employers. 232 pages. 1994. $15.95.

HOW TO FIND AN OVERSEAS JOB WITH THE U.S. GOVERNMENT. *Will Cantrell and Francine Modderno.* The first book to focus solely on international job opportunities throughout the federal government. Profiles the major agencies offering international job opportunities. Describes agencies, qualifications required, and application procedures. 230 pages. 1992. $28.95.

SPECIAL OFFER ON COMPLETE SET: Purchase the complete set of five books for $89.95. Please add $7.00 shipping for complete package. If ordering individual titles, add $4.00 for first item and $1.00 for each additional item. Send your order to: IMPACT PUBLICATIONS, 9104-N Manassas Drive, Manassas Park, VA 22111 or Fax 703/335-9486 (Visa/MasterCard).
